T0386223

PAKISTAN'S NUCLEAR BOMB

HASSAN ABBAS

Pakistan's Nuclear Bomb

*A Story of Defiance, Deterrence,
and Deviance*

HURST & COMPANY, LONDON

First published in the United Kingdom in 2018 by
C. Hurst & Co. (Publishers) Ltd.,
41 Great Russell Street, London, WC1B 3PL
© Hassan Abbas, 2018
All rights reserved.
Printed in India

The right of Hassan Abbas to be identified as the author of
this publication is asserted by him in accordance with the
Copyright, Designs and Patents Act, 1988.

A Cataloguing-in-Publication data record for this book
is available from the British Library.

ISBN: 978-1-84904-715-9

This book is printed using paper from registered sustainable
and managed sources.

www.hurstpublishers.com

To Government College Lahore (Pakistan), my alma mater, whose motto 'Courage to Know' continues to inspire me;

To Nottingham University's School of Law (United Kingdom), where I studied international law, and whose motto 'A city is built on wisdom' nourished in me the unquenchable thirst for learning;

And to Tufts University's Fletcher School of Law & Diplomacy, from where I received my doctorate, and whose motto 'Peace and Light' engendered in me a passion to search for peace within and outside.

CONTENTS

ACKNOWLEDGEMENTS

This book primarily grew out of my Ph.D. work at the Fletcher School of Law and Diplomacy, Tufts University, where members of my dissertation committee—Professors Andrew Hess, Jessica Stern, and Robert L. Pfaltzgraff, Jr.—provided invaluable guidance, direction, and support. I am also very grateful to Professor Richard Shultz at the School who first gave me the idea to focus on this subject for my doctoral work and provided support throughout my process. It was a dream team to work with, and I can never pay back the intellectual debt I owe them.

I am also very thankful to the Project on Managing the Atom (MTA) and International Security Studies at the Belfer Center for Science and International Affairs, Kennedy School of Government, Harvard University for its support in the shape of a research fellowship during my work on this project (2005–9). Besides the research facilities at Harvard, the vibrant intellectual environment at Belfer was very inspiring. I am especially thankful to Dr Martin Malin, the executive director of MTA, Professor Matthew Bunn, and Dr Steven Miller for their support and scholarly guidance and encouragement during my years at Harvard. I am grateful also to Dr Jim Walsh of MIT and Professor John Holdren of Harvard for support during the early phase of my work. Patronage and guidance from Belfer Center's director and founding dean of the Kennedy School, Professor Graham Allison, in developing the framework of my work was also very precious. I have been extremely lucky to work with these towering scholars both at the Fletcher School and the Belfer Center. I am also grateful for the editing

ACKNOWLEDGEMENTS

support from Belfer Center's research assistant, Jonathan Janik. At the National Defense University in Washington DC (NDU), interns Aria Chehregani and Sheona Lalani helped me with updating the nuclear programme chronology and bibliography, and research assistants John Van Oudenaren and Brianna Harwart helped me in my search for various references. I am thankful to all of them for their support.

Thanks are also due to Michael Dwyer and Jon de Peyer of Hurst for their support in the publication process. I am also grateful to Mary Starkey for her valuable editing help. I am thankful to the leaders at NDU's College of International Security Affairs, Chancellor Michael Bell and Dean Charles B. Cushman, for their continued support for my research and writing endeavours. Conversations with my colleague the late Kenneth Baker, who earlier served in the US Department of Energy, helped me tremendously in understanding the US nuclear non-proliferation priorities. God bless his soul.

I am obliged as well to my NDU colleague Dr. Marco Di Capua, who earlier served as chief scientist at the U.S. department of Energy National Nuclear Security Administration, for going through the manuscript and providing valuable feedback and alerting me to use more appropriate technical terms at many places.

Interviews with Pakistani scientists, journalists, military officials, and scholars who followed Pakistan's nuclear programme over the years were very helpful in understanding the dynamics of Pakistan's nuclear policy and security context. I am thankful to Professors Ishtiaq Ahmed, Zafar Jaspal, and especially Mansoor Ahmed of Quaid-e-Azam University in Islamabad, who kindly shared his unpublished doctoral dissertation with me. Interviews with former army chief General Jahangir Karamat, former director general of the Inter Services Intelligence Lieutenant-General Asad Durrani, and Brigadier (retired) Naeem Salik were very valuable. The late Benazir Bhutto was also very kind to share her insights while I was working on my dissertation over a decade ago. Last but not the least, a research grant provided by the Smith Richardson Foundation via the Belfer Center helped the book project at a critical stage of its development.

Last but not the least, I must especially thank my wife, Benish, who remains my most important supporter. Her selflessness and enormous patience with me allowed me to finish this book.

1

INTRODUCTION

FRAMING THE QUESTIONS

I distinctly remember an interesting conversation with Pakistani nuclear scientist Abdul Qadeer Khan (A. Q. Khan) at an event celebrating his achievements as 'father of the Pakistani bomb' at the Marriott hotel in Islamabad in early 1994, during which he delivered a lecture on regional security challenges. Like most people in the country, I grew up venerating him as the nation's saviour for his role in Pakistan's nuclear programme and his contributions towards building Pakistan's nuclear bomb. Meeting him face to face, I was in total awe, but his charismatic personality and warm handshake further attracted me to him. A retired senior military officer introduced me to him, and perhaps that was the best way to catch Khan's attention. I was amazed by his keen interest in my educational background and career plans, and he was especially interested to know why I came to attend his event and what I had learnt from it. All of his main arguments revolved around the notion that Pakistan was now capable of dealing with the Indian threat given that Khan and his associates had made the country's security foolproof through the nuclear option. This assertion had been drilled into the Pakistani psyche through the media and state communications throughout the 1980s and 1990s.

In 2000, however, I faced a serious dilemma when I was tasked to evaluate evidence against Khan while I was serving as deputy director of investigations at Pakistan's National Accountability Bureau (NAB) in Islamabad. General Pervez Musharraf had constituted the NAB in October 1999 after he overthrew the country's democratic order and imposed military rule. The organization initially worked under his direct supervision. I had great admiration for Khan, but what I found in the official dossiers with which I was provided created serious doubts in my mind about the transparency of the nuclear programme's financial management and the integrity of those at the helm of affairs, including Khan. General Musharraf, as chief executive of the country, had instructed the NAB to consider pursuing a corruption case against Khan. I cannot here go into details of what was documented in the files, nor I can vouch for the authenticity of the charges against him. However, what can I share is what I recommended to the chairman of the organization. I argued that even if all the allegations were true, this case was too big for the NAB to handle. The nascent organization was assigned to probe and prosecute corrupt politicians, bureaucrats, and businessmen, and starting off with country's most popular person was not, in my view, a good idea. It could have proved to be the NAB's death knell, so perhaps institutional interests also prompted me to make such an assessment. In addition, with my law education and police training, I knew full well that intelligence reports and unverified statements by colleagues do not constitute legal evidence. My recommendation not to pursue the case through the NAB was accepted—and I have no regrets about it, as it was the right thing to do under the circumstances. I would guess that senior officials also weighed in with similar concerns. What was a total surprise to me, however, was the revelation that many senior military officials—both in the military hierarchy and within the nuclear programme—were very critical of Khan. Obviously they knew something that I had no clue about. To be fair, I must add that there were no direct nuclear proliferation charges in the said case. Interestingly, Khan was increasingly sidelined from his nuclear infrastructure management role after Musharraf's arrival in Islamabad.

The 2003 disclosures about the clandestine sale of Pakistan's nuclear technology to Iran, North Korea, and Libya forced Islamabad to move against Khan. On 4 February 2004 he addressed the Pakistani nation on television, confessing: 'The investigation has established that many of the reported activities did occur, and that these were invariably initiated at my behest.'[1] Serious suspicions lingered, however, as there was no way to conclude whether or not Khan made the statement under duress to bail out the powerful military, which under General Musharraf was running the state. Benazir Bhutto, who twice served as the prime minister of Pakistan (1988–90; 1993–6), unequivocally maintained that 'Dr Khan was asked to fall on the sword in the name of the national interest, which means a cover up for Musharraf'.[2] The director-general of the International Atomic Energy Agency (IAEA) at the time called Khan's activities only 'the tip of an iceberg' and claimed that 'Dr Khan was not working alone'.[3] This was a devastating blow to Pakistan's image as well as its morale. For Pakistan to have successfully developed nuclear weapons was nothing short of a miracle, and the nation took immense pride in it.

Irrespective of who was the prime culprit in Pakistan, in the eyes of the West (to borrow the words of MIT scholar Jim Walsh), 'Pakistan is absolutely the biggest and most important illicit exporter of nuclear technology in the history of the nuclear age.'[4] Bewildered and confused, most Pakistanis believed these charges to be exaggerated and manipulated. Others argued that, even if they are true, there is nothing wrong with sharing nuclear technology with friendly countries, as was done by many other states in possession of nuclear weapons (e.g. American and British support for the French nuclear programme).

This book critically examines how and why Pakistan acquired its nuclear weapons, and then delves deeper into the motivations and circumstances of the nuclear proliferation activities of Khan's network, with a special focus on Iran, Libya, and North Korea. For the first time in history all the elements of nuclear weapons development—the supplier networks, the material, the centrifuge technology and enrichment mechanism, and possibly the warhead designs—were outside direct state control at least for part of the time during this roughly sixteen-year proliferation crisis (1987–2003).[5]

It is important to probe the causes of Pakistan's nuclear proliferation. Was it a rogue operation orchestrated by one man, or was it a state-sanctioned operation? If the former, what were its motivational factors? Was it greed, a skewed nationalist agenda, religious beliefs, or an anti-Western/American operation, or possibly a combination of some or all of these? Interestingly, former Pakistan president Pervez

Musharraf in his memoirs forcefully argues that 'the show was completely and entirely A.Q.'s and he did it all for money'.[6] And if the state was indeed involved, then we must first understand how it operates in Pakistan, and who were the decision makers or wheeler-dealers behind such sensitive and potentially explosive policies and strategies. Another relevant issue to probe is the nature of the military and intelligence hierarchy during these times. Who led and managed the nuclear programme is also a crucial question. These interlinked and complicated queries demand scholarly attention. The need to comprehend the intricacies involved in this case is of the utmost importance, as the knowledge could serve as a basis to devise mechanisms that could potentially limit the chance of a repetition of such activities in Pakistan or anywhere else. As Peter R. Lavoy, a respected American scholar of South Asia, aptly argues, 'Debate over the strategic consequences of the spread of nuclear weapons is more than an academic exercise. It affects the price officials should be willing to pay for nonproliferation. This in turn influences the number and identity of states which might some day acquire nuclear weapons.'[7]

In this book I argue that scholars, analysts, and experts who have focused on this issue have so far ignored the larger picture—i.e. Pakistan's political and security arena and the impact of regional dynamics and international politics on it—and have also been too narrowly focused on the personality of Dr A. Q. Khan, which presents just one aspect of the proliferation crisis. Secondly, the research shows that this brand of nuclear proliferation could not have taken place without the political upheaval that Pakistan went through during those years. The civil–military tensions within Pakistan, weak and unstable state structures and institutions (political, security related, and judicial), flawed decision-making processes at the highest level (especially in the realm of the nuclear programme), the impact of the Afghan war on Pakistan's worldview, the lingering threat from India, and last but not the least the turbulent US–Pakistan relationship all facilitated, or in some cases enabled, nuclear proliferation. Within this convoluted political and security spectrum, the personal ambitions of some military and political leaders also had a significant role to play. The book also endeavours to show that the existing theories about what precipitated this sharing of nuclear secrets shed little light on the full gamut of circumstances that led to this dangerous situation. Giving away nuclear technology was the final step in an unholy game. It is necessary to try to unravel the thinking behind this operation and also to probe whether all of this was one big operation or a series of developments with different motivations and players. The shadowy workings of an illicit international nuclear smuggling network (with many Europeans playing a central role) serving many countries and clients cannot be ignored either. An important question is whether it was merely a demand and supply issue or whether something more intriguing was taking place. This book thus asks the question: Why did Pakistan acquire nuclear weapons technology, and what caused the nuclear proliferation from Pakistan to Iran, North Korea, and Libya?

The Context

Since the 2003 discovery and unravelling of Khan's network and his activities in the preceding years, a number of scholars have attempted to explain the causes and motivations behind this nuclear proliferation racket. The two most prominent theories on this question are worth introducing here to explain the contemporary context in which various issues in this book are framed.

The 'rogue factor' theory, according to Christopher Oren Clary, holds that 'Khan was largely a rogue actor outside of state oversight'.[8] Adherents of this theory contend that there is scant evidence to support the allegation of state authorization of Khan's nuclear dealings. They also argue that the benefits of these transactions to the Pakistani state are unclear, whereas the benefits to Khan as an individual are obvious.[9] Pakistani official investigations also came to the same conclusions: Khan was the mastermind, and he was primarily motivated by financial gain. Over two dozen scientists and senior military officials were questioned (and some remained in government custody for a while) including Mohammed Farooq, who supervised the Khan Research Laboratories' (KRL) contacts with foreign suppliers; Yasin Chohan, a metallurgist at KRL; Major Islam ul-Haq, Khan's personal staff officer; Nazeer Ahmed, a director at KRL; and Saeed Ahmed, the head of centrifuge design, as well as security managers at KRL and former army chiefs Generals Aslam Beg and Jahangir Karamat.[10]

Evidence was not lacking, but Musharraf decided to pardon Khan in recognition of his previous contributions to Pakistan's acquisition of a nuclear capability, and even allowed him to retain the illegal money he had made in the process, raising understandable suspicions.[11] Musharraf also cautioned that those trying to cast aspersions on the government and army's involvement in the nuclear proliferation were doing a disservice to Pakistan. He went on to say: 'Stop writing this. You don't know what would be the result of this reckless implication [for] every institution in the proliferation issue.'[12] The then US deputy secretary of state, Richard Armitage, also asserted that only individual Pakistanis were being investigated for nuclear proliferation, and that the government of Pakistan was not involved.[13] Pakistan's official investigations, as mentioned above, had also concluded that Khan committed these crimes in his personal and independent capacity, and various local and international media reports also provided details about his ill-gotten money from these activities.[14] David Albright and Corey Hinderstein, partially agreeing with this line of argument, also concluded that 'Khan was motivated by money, pan-Islamism, and hostility to Western controls'.[15] Key Pakistani investigators, according to the *New York Times*, have opined that Khan was motivated to defy the West, make himself a hero to the Islamic world, and gain wealth.[16]

However, as contended by a congressional research service report, even if Khan's aggressive marketing of nuclear materials and technology to Iran, North Korea, and Libya was designed to further his outsized ego and financial interests, 'he could not have functioned without some level of cooperation by Pakistani military personnel, who maintained tight security around the key nuclear facilities, and possibly civilian officials as well'.[17]

It is also argued that the A. Q. Khan network was a corrupted portion of a procurement system created by Pakistan in the 1970s and 1980s. Pakistan, according to this narrative, was compelled to give KRL greater autonomy and flexibility, but in the end, the flexibility essential for the success of Pakistan's acquisition efforts also enabled Khan's exports.[18]

Proponents of a different theory dismiss the claims of Khan's confession and the Musharraf pardon. Among these analysts is Seymour Hersh, who in an article in the *New Yorker* entitled 'The Deal' quotes a senior intelligence official:

One thing we do know is that this was not a rogue operation. How do you get missiles from North Korea to Pakistan? Do you think A. Q. shipped all the centrifuges by Federal Express? The military has to be involved, at high levels.[19]

Renowned Pakistani physicist and progressive activist Professor Pervez Hoodbhoy similarly argues:

These centrifuges weighed something like half a ton each. You can't put them in your coat pocket and walk away with them. ... If there were aircraft of the Pakistan air force that flew these centrifuges out—well, obviously there had to be somebody at the top who was also involved.[20]

Samina Ahmed, a Pakistani expert on nuclear issues and currently director of the International Crisis Group (ICG) covering South Asia, referring to the Pakistani investigations and Khan's pardon, maintains: 'It is state propaganda. ... The deal is that Khan doesn't tell what he knows. Everybody is lying.'[21]

Zahid Malik, Khan's official biographer, and many leading Pakistani columnists maintain a similar line of argument but for a different reason: to save him. This is a popular theory within Pakistan, given the reverence people have for Khan.

Other major investigative works, notably published in the *Atlantic Monthly*, *Los Angeles Times*, *Bulletin of the Atomic Scientists*, the *New York Times*, and the *Washington Post*, largely reached very similar conclusions, falling within the two broad theories explained above. For instance, in early 2004, as the Khan story was breaking in the international media, the *Washington Post* reported that Khan had told a friend and a senior Pakistani investigator that top Pakistani military officers, including General Musharraf, had known about Khan's assistance to North Korea's uranium enrichment efforts.[22] According to the same story, Khan also reportedly told investigators that General Mirza Aslam Beg, the former army chief (1988–91), was aware of similar assistance being provided to Iran, and that the 'two other Army chiefs, in addition to Musharraf, knew and approved of his efforts'.[23] One of the authors of this report is Kamran Khan, a renowned Pakistani investigative reporter known for his good contacts in military circles, which gives it added credibility. A detailed investigative piece in the *Atlantic Monthly* by William Langewiesche also makes a similar point: 'In 1991 ... General Aslam Beg returned from a trip to Tehran openly advocating the export of nuclear-weapons technology to Iran, and pointing to the several billion dollars' worth of state revenue that might be in the offing.'[24]

However, research on the subject falls short of fully explaining what led to this proliferation crisis. Part of the reason for this is the sensitive nature of the topic and a lack of credible evidence. Official proclamations of the government of Pakistan, a few Western media reports (apparently based on leaked official reports), and new statements by Khan (retracting his earlier confession) since his release from house arrest on the orders of Islamabad High Court in February 2009 provide useful but inconclusive evidence. At best we have half-truths, which can be deceptive. In general, the US officials have repeatedly expressed their confidence that Pakistan has shared valuable information on the subject even though the US ambassador to Pakistan, Ryan C. Crocker, had said in 2006 that the USA and the international community want to get more information about Khan's proliferation activities.[25] In response, Pakistan declared at the time that no more information should be expected and that the subject was closed.[26] The government of Pakistan argues that he is a national hero, and that national security concerns are also paramount in this case. Khan was released from house arrest after his lawyers successfully argued in the Islamabad High Court that there was no legal basis for his confinement, as the government of Pakistan never registered any case against him. Khan's lawyers became very active after President Musharraf's resignation in August 2008, and negotiated a deal with the government whereby he could move freely with full government security, and would avoid any comment on the nuclear proliferation issues.[27] The government attempted to minimize the risk of political fallout from Khan's continued house arrest through this arrangement, but experts consider it a dangerous gamble. For instance, David Albright maintains that Khan 'likely still has or can access sensitive nuclear technology' and hence 'remains a serious proliferation risk'.[28] After his release, Pakistan's Foreign Office again reiterated: 'The so-called A. Q. Khan affair is a closed chapter. It is counter-productive to speculate on the court's judgment.'[29] Since then Khan has regularly written columns for leading newspapers and has appeared in various Pakistani television talk shows as well. A thirteen-page revised confessional statement attributed to him was published by Fox News in September 2011, and in 2010 the *Washington Post* had also claimed to have access to some documents provided by Khan. Khan shifts proliferation blame on to various civilian and military officials, but there are serious questions about the authenticity of significant parts of these statements. These will be discussed thoroughly later in the book. Besides unearthing the mysteries of the story, the broader purpose here is to understand what facilitates nuclear proliferation.

A Glance at Theoretical Issues

The theoretical debate over how nuclear proliferation should be explained, and whether future nuclear proliferation can be predicted, has received fresh impetus since the unraveling of the Khan network in recent years.[30] The new international environment, in the aftermath of the 9/11 attacks, has brought new challenges to conventional wisdom about the spread of nuclear weapons. Several relevant major theories provide some valuable insights on the issue:

Deterrence Optimists and Proliferation Pessimists

Ever since nuclear weapons entered the scholarly discourse on strategic studies, starting perhaps with the publication of Bernard Brodie's much-acclaimed book *Absolute Weapon* in 1946,[31] scholars have been probing the subject from various perspectives, especially within the context of deterrence theory.[32] Largely, the discourse has been dominated by debates about whether nuclear weapons can promote stability or are a source of danger. For instance, Hans J. Morgenthau went to the extent of predicting that, 'if the nuclear armaments race cannot be brought under control before any number of nations will have nuclear weapons, only a miracle will save mankind'.[33] Kenneth Waltz, however, contends that 'possession of nuclear weapons may slow arms races down, rather than speed them up'.[34] Most of the literature on the subject can be broadly categorized into two contending camps: deterrence optimists and proliferation pessimists.

The scholars belonging to the first school broadly believe that nuclear deterrence works across different cultures, political systems, and state structures. They argue that the acquisition of nuclear weapons by more states does not necessarily destabilize the international order, and in fact possibly creates conditions for a more peaceful world. The scholars who subscribe to the second school, on the other hand, underscore the important differences in the technological conditions and political and organizational cultures of the states capable of acquiring nuclear weapons. These variations, they feel, could either impede or enhance deterrence stability. Given the volatile and unstable nature of international politics, inter-state and intra-state conflicts, and the rise of the influential non-state actors embracing extremist ideologies, it is a prudent policy to restrain, dissuade, and prevent acquisition of nuclear weapons by new states, the argument goes. Waltz, as indicated above, belongs to the first school, and Scott D. Sagan is the principal proponent of the second one. Their book *The Spread of Nuclear Weapons* is a classic exposition and discussion of these two views.[35]

The position of the deterrence optimists flows from the logic of rational deterrence theory.[36] This theory indicates that the possession of nuclear weapons by two states reduces the likelihood of war between them, primarily because the potential costs of war and its consequences are incalculable. Building his arguments within neo-realist structural theory, Waltz maintains that systemic pressures disable any two states possessing nuclear weapons from deviating from the point of logical decision making; that nuclear weapons are primarily an instrument of deterrence and their existence acts as a stabilizing factor in international politics. He strongly advocates the view that the acquisition of nuclear weapons by more states would actually lead to greater stability. Many prominent scholars, such as Bruce de Mesquita and John Mearsheimer, agree with this perspective.[37] Mearsheimer even predicted a more stable world if Germany, Ukraine, and Japan became nuclear powers,[38] whereas Peter R. Lavoy suggests that nuclear weapons could prevent future wars between India and Pakistan.[39]

The Kargil conflict, a limited military action in 1999 in the disputed Kashmir region between India and Pakistan (after both countries had conducted nuclear tests), on the face of it nullifies Lavoy's line of argument; but a deeper analysis of the issue (discussed in more detail in chapter 2) shows that both countries cautiously avoided escalation of the conflict and a full-fledged war. However, according to a RAND study, the role of nuclear capabilities in maintaining deterrence stability in South Asia is unclear, because in some sense deterrence stability is *over determined* by the weak conventional force capabilities of both states, the lack of political incentives to dramatically change the status quo, and the prohibitive costs of conventional warfare when viewed against both countries' economic weaknesses *as well as* their now overt nuclear capabilities.[40]

Ashley Tellis goes further than this by maintaining that the destabilizing effects of nuclear capabilities in South Asia are more obvious and observable, as nuclear weapons have permitted India and particularly Pakistan to initiate a range of unconventional conflicts at the lower end of the spectrum of violence.[41]

Reverting to the Sagan–Waltz debate, Sagan strongly believes that Waltz's optimistic view of nuclear weapons is dangerous for the world. Placing his arguments within the theoretical context of organizational theory, he maintains that military organizations in states with nuclear weapons suffer from certain common biases including inflexible routines and parochial interests. Such behavioural patterns, he argues, could lead to the breakdown of deterrence and trigger a major nuclear exchange. Differing with Sagan's stance and projecting a better future for nuclear deterrence, Ganguly and Hagerty[42] and Rajgopalan[43] support Waltz's position that nuclear weapons have acted as a deterrent in the India–Pakistan context. These scholars argue that the threatening language between Pakistan and India 'is nothing more than mere rhetoric to deter the other from considering the nuclear option'.[44] Sagan refutes this line of argument by claiming that states such as India and even more so Pakistan lack institutional mechanisms for civilian control over nuclear decision making, and their militaries are also 'inward looking', heavily influenced by domestic politics; therefore, decisions regarding nuclear weapons would potentially be taken based on issues of domestic stability rather than external threats. He also argues that the historical India–Pakistan rivalry and protracted ideological and territorial disputes may drive them up the nuclear ladder during a crisis. The on–off peace process between these two South Asia rivals since the jittery early post-nuclear test years (1999–2003), when military tensions increased, and in a similar challenging situation in the aftermath of the 2008 Mumbai terrorist attack, show that the debate remains highly relevant to the security dynamics of the region. The theory provides useful insights into Pakistan's pursuit of nuclear weapons and its nuclear behaviour over the years.

Organizational Politics and Bureaucratic Politics

Advocates of the organizational politics emphasize that nuclear policy making takes place within a set of institutional arrangements that govern decision making, and that these rules directly influence the nature and type of decisions. The organizational politics approach is often associated with Professor Graham Allison and his path-breaking book, *Essence of Decision*.[45] Allison created the organizational process model to explain the structure of government bureaucracies. According to this model, the government is a vast conglomerate of loosely allied organizations, each with a substantial life of its own. Government behaviour can be looked at as 'outputs' from large organizations operating in certain or specific patterns of behaviour. The organizational politics model suggests that decisions about nuclear weapons, like other government decisions, are the result of contests between powerful organizations with identifiable interests. Bureaucratic actors whose organizations are likely to benefit from the acquisition of nuclear weapons will actively pursue policy agendas to this effect.

The bureaucratic politics model,[46] another approach that Allison postulates in his book, makes some insightful conjectures. He argues that different governmental institutions compel and motivate bureaucratic players with different institutional agendas and priorities, implying that organizational interests drive bureaucrats. In other words, 'Where you stand depends on where you sit.' This dictum is often remembered as Miles' law, after the Truman-era official who coined it. Decisions, according to this model, are manipulated through bargaining processes and compromises defined by bureaucratic power-play dynamics.

In Allison's bureaucratic politics model, government officials are depicted as central players in a competitive game. These players focus on many issues, and, rather than being inspired by any strategic objectives, they make important decisions through politics or what Allison calls 'pulling and hauling'. This model is very useful in understanding Pakistan's acquisition of nuclear weapons technology, and the bureaucratic model provides some insights about A. Q. Khan's network's proliferation practices and his modus operandi within the institutions managing the nuclear programme. The theory explains how Khan, along with some other players in the military and civilian bureaucracy, was able to manipulate the system and transfer nuclear technology to

Iran, North Korea, and Libya, but it is less relevant for navigating the worldview and motivations of the proliferators.

Nuclear Myth-Makers

Peter R. Lavoy's theory of 'nuclear myth-makers'[47] explains how the views and opinions of influential individuals impact policy-making, especially in the realm of the nuclear policy of a state. Traditional accounts of nuclear proliferation often ignore the role played by individual actors and their motivations. Lavoy presents his formula to explain why and how the international spread of nuclear weapons occurs. He developed this concept primarily to understand why India pursued the acquisition of nuclear weapons. However, the formulation of this idea and the arguments he employed provides a valuable framework for my arguments explaining what caused the A. Q. Khan network to operate in the fashion that it did.

Lavoy starts off by giving a new meaning to the phrase 'nuclear myth-making'.[48] He contends that a state is likely to make the pursuit of nuclear weapons part of its national security strategy when national elites (nuclear myth-makers), who want their governments to adopt this strategy: (1) emphasize their country's insecurity or its poor international standing; (2) advance this strategy as the best corrective course for these problems; (3) articulate the political, economic, and technical feasibility of acquiring nuclear technology/weapons; (4) successfully associate these beliefs and arguments (nuclear myths) with existing cultural norms and political priorities; and finally (5) convince senior decision-makers to accept and act on these views.[49] There can be contending myths on offer at any given time, and in that scenario, according to Lavoy, the success of one myth over another depends on three factors:

1. the substantive content of the strategic myth and its compatibility with existing cultural norms and political priorities;
2. the ability of the myth maker to legitimize and popularize his or her beliefs among fellow elites and then to persuade national leaders to act on these beliefs; and
3. the process whereby institutional actors integrate the popularized strategic myths into their own organizational identities and missions.[50]

Whereas realist-inspired and security-oriented accounts of nuclear proliferation scenarios focus on the prior events or conditions that are said to trigger a certain strategic response, Lavoy's myth-making approach emphasizes the strategic beliefs and political manoeuvring that link these triggering conditions to the subsequent policy actions. As to how observers can identify the myth-maker and the agenda being pursued, public statements, policy debate, and myth-maker's movements can be insightful.[51] Khan and his close associates and collaborators in the influential state institutions were myth-makers in this sense, with a clearly defined agenda—as regards nuclear programme development, but especially so in the case of proliferation practices. Rather than convincing the top policy-makers of the state, they only needed to co-opt those individuals who mattered the most given that the whole operation, or series of operations, was meant to be clandestine.

For the purpose of understanding the A. Q. Khan network's activities, some aspects of Lavoy's theory require tweaking, as the focus of his study was different. In the case of Pakistan, 'existing cultural norms' and 'political priorities' were somewhat different from those in India. Khan and his supporters and provocateurs within the civil–military establishment were arguably influenced by nuclear nationalism, and their view of global politics was inspired by an anti-Western attitude.

Clash of Civilizations

The provocative thesis of the 'Clash of Civilizations' is based on the idea that the growing threat of violence arising from conflicts between cultures and countries springs from their religious traditions and dogmas. This expression was first used to describe the relationship between a supposedly Western civilization and the Islamic civilization in Bernard Lewis' 1990 article 'The Roots of Muslim Rage'.[52] However, the theory came to be associated with Samuel P. Huntington, a political scientist at Harvard University who developed this argument in an article entitled, 'The Clash of Civilizations?' published in *Foreign Affairs* in 1993.[53] He later expanded his thesis in a 1996 book, *The Clash of Civilizations and the Remaking of World Order*.[54] In this controversial theory of international relations, Huntington's central thesis is that major conflicts have always been marked by clashes between fundamentally different civilizations rather than between similar nations. He states that such conflicts occur on the boundaries between these civilizations. While identifying the extent and grounds of conflict, Huntington also studies the politics of post-colonialism and national identity and reviews many other possible sources of conflict awaiting the civilizations currently competing for resources and status within the world structure. He believes that clashes between civilizations are the greatest threat to world peace nowadays. In his words:

> Nation states will remain the most powerful actors in world affairs, but the principal conflicts of global politics will occur between nations and groups of different civilizations. The clash of civilizations will dominate global politics. The fault lines between civilizations will be the battle lines of the future.[55]

Huntington asserts that civilizations have no clear-cut boundaries, no definite beginnings and endings—but they develop and adapt. He argues that the hotspots are on the fault lines between civilizations: the Middle East, Chechnya, the Transcaucasia, Central Asia, Kashmir, Tibet, Sri Lanka, and Sudan. The West, he says, is the most powerful civilization, but its relative power is declining at the same time as Confucian and Islamic societies are rising to balance it. He further maintains: 'The late twentieth century has seen a global resurgence of religions around the world. That resurgence has involved the intensification of religious consciousness and the rise of fundamentalist movements. It has thus reinforced the differences among religions.'[56] This sounds prophetic at first.

Huntington further suggests that the importance of these conflicts is a part of the future; their frequency will increase because of the increased contacts and interaction between the different parts of the world.[57] His theory has been widely criticized for overgeneralization, disregarding local conflicts, and for inadequately predicting what has happened in the decade after its publication. Amartya Sen, for instance, argues that 'in partitioning the population of the world into those belonging to "the Islamic world," "the Western world," "the Hindu world," "the Buddhist world," the divisive power of classificatory priority is implicitly used to place people firmly inside a unique set of rigid boxes'.[58] Other divisions, such as between the rich and the poor, between members of different classes, nationalities, ethnicities, and occupations, he further argues, 'are all submerged by this allegedly primal way of seeing the differences between people'.[59]

Irrespective of the strengths and weaknesses of Huntington's arguments, the phrase 'clash of civilizations' has assumed a life of its own, and various writers and groups invest it with different meanings. In Pakistan, Huntington's 1996 book is widely available in bookstores and is often referred to in the media, mostly in critical terms.[60] However, among the fundamentalists in Pakistan it is a popular theme. For instance, Hafiz Saeed, leader of the banned militant group Lashkar-e-Taiba (Army of the Pure), while declaring the acquisition of atomic weapons a necessity for jihad in a public address in 2004, also praise Khan and said that he had not committed any crime by transferring nuclear technology to other Muslim countries.[61] He further said that Khan 'shared the technology for the supremacy of Islam. ... He is our hero, will remain our hero, and the government can't undermine his honor under American pressure.'[62] On another occasion he claimed: 'We believe in Samuel Huntington's Clash of Civilization and we will not rest until Islam becomes the dominant religion.'[63] Interestingly, Saeed launched a new political party called Milli Muslim League in August 2017.

When Benazir Bhutto was asked by a journalist about the possible motivations behind the nuclear proliferation activities of Pakistani nuclear scientists and their collaborators, she remarked:

> They think that the clash of civilizations, in which they believe, would be enhanced if the enemy—the West and most particularly the US—could be ringed by hostile countries with nuclear capability. They defeated one superpower, the Soviet Union, and now they want to defeat another. If they made some money on the side, fine.[64]

The potential relevance of this theory to the mindset of some scientists and officials involved in the A. Q. Khan nuclear proliferation network cannot therefore be ruled out. This may not equate to Lavoy's 'existing cultural norms' reference in the nuclear myth-making phenomenon, but it certainly provides a possible alternative worth probing further.

Nuclear Nationalism and 'Oppositionist Nationalists'

Nationalism has been one of the most influential forces shaping international politics. According to the *Penguin Dictionary of International*

Relations, this term is used in two related senses: 'In the first usage, nationalism seeks to identify a behavioral entity—the nation—and thereafter to pursue certain political and cultural goals on behalf of it. In the second usage, nationalism is a sentiment of loyalty toward the nation which is shared by people.'[65] In its essence it should be a benign force, which expresses itself in the shape of patriotism, but if it becomes too intense, as in the Second World War, then it can be devastating for peace and tranquility.[66] Michael Hechter in his book *Containing Nationalism* calls it the dark side of nationalism.[67] Nationalism-induced violence has indeed been a cause of various inter-state as well as intra-state conflicts in the post-Second World War era. However, it is a treatable problem in the opinion of Morgenthau as he argues that 'the greater the stability of society and the sense of security of its members, the smaller are the chances for collective emotions to seek an outlet in aggressive nationalism, and vice versa'.[68]

There are various types of nationalisms, ranging from ethnic- and expansionist-driven nationalisms to cultural-, religious- and diaspora-focused nationalisms, and the subject has been the focus of extensive academic and scholarly research.[69] The idea of nuclear nationalism is comparatively recent, however, and has not received much academic attention. M. V. Ramana, an Indian nuclear scientist, defines nuclear nationalism as a phenomenon 'which links national sovereignty with the possession of mass-destruction weapons and one's unhampered ability to amass them', and aptly calls it 'an unhealthy, even dangerous doctrine'.[70] Pervez Hoodbhoy, a Pakistani nuclear scientist, while commenting on Pakistan's nuclear tests in 1998, also used this concept in a similar fashion, when he said: 'Nuclear nationalism was the order of the day as governments vigorously promoted the bomb as the symbol of Pakistan's high scientific achievement, national determination and self-respect, and as the harbinger of a new Muslim era.'[71] Zia Mian, a Pakistani–American scholar, in an article titled 'Nuclear Nationalism', and David Ignatius, in his article 'The New Nationalism', also draw similar meanings from this phrase: popular nationalistic fervour in support of acquiring, retaining, or further developing a nuclear weapons programme.[72] Douglas Frantz, a leading journalist who has published on the issue of nuclear proliferation, maintains that 'what ever turned Khan into a rogue scientist, the consensus is that in the beginning, he was motivated by nationalism'.[73]

Another concept, framed by Jacques E. C. Hymans in his book *The Psychology of Nuclear Proliferation*, provides insights into the same phenomenon, but with a focus on individual leaders.[74] Based on the case studies of leaders of France, Australia, Argentina, and India, he coins the phrase 'oppositional nationalist' to describe leaders with definitive nuclear weapons ambitions. He says:

> Oppositional nationalists see their nation as both naturally at odds with an external enemy, and as naturally its equal if not its superior. Such a conception tends to generate the emotions of fear and pride—an explosive psychological cocktail. Driven by fear and pride, oppositional nationalists develop a desire for nuclear weapons that goes beyond calculation, to self-expression.[75]

Linking these concepts, the idea of nuclear nationalism can be expanded further. Nuclear myth-makers arguably also derive their inspiration from nuclear nationalism at an individual level (though they may not be in political leadership positions). This sense of nationalism in nuclear myth-makers can also potentially play a role in nuclear proliferation. In this study I argue that Khan and his Pakistani colleagues involved in nuclear sales were 'proliferation nationalists' who employed myth-making strategies to achieve their goals—for instance, supporting Iranian and Libyan nuclear programmes with a view to helping other Muslim countries in need of nuclear technology. According to Hoodbhoy, Khan espoused Islamic nationalism and believed that nuclear capability was 'essential to protect Islam against assault from those who hate Islam'.[76] The same motivation may have moved him and others to help save other Muslim countries from their perceived enemies. A study by French scholar Bruno Tertrais claims that the A. Q. Khan network tried to reach out to Syria, Egypt, and Saudi Arabia as well.[77] Details about such outreach programmes are sketchy, but this aspect needs further examination, especially in the post-2015 Iran nuclear deal scenario, as some Middle Eastern states as well as Turkey are contemplating nuclear programmes.

Clearly various factors were at play at different stages of the proliferation timeline, so the issue has to be looked at from a broader perspective. There are also questions about the extent of the sharing of nuclear secrets between Pakistan and the three cases under consideration. An in-depth analysis of each case—Pakistan–North Korea, Pakistan–Iran and Pakistan–Libya collaboration in the nuclear field—as case studies is hence deemed necessary for studying the subject. Besides the writings and assessments of experts on the subject, the writings and speeches of Khan are also very instructive for the purpose.[78] Pakistani journalist Zahid Malik's *Dr A. Q. Khan and the Islamic Bomb*[79] is widely believed to be the official biography of Khan given the close friendship between the two. The choice of title says a lot.

Among the book-length works on the subject, the following are especially noteworthy: *The Nuclear Jihadist* by Douglas Frantz and Catherine Collins; *The Genesis of South Asian Nuclear Deterrence* by Naeem Salik; *Deception* by Adrian Levy and Catherine Scott-Clark; *America and the Islamic Bomb* by David Armstrong and Joseph Trento; *Confronting the Bomb*, edited by Pervez Hoodbhoy; Gordon Corera's *Shopping for Bombs*; the 2007 Dossier on the A. Q. Khan network published by the International Institute of Strategic Studies (IISS), entitled *Nuclear Black Markets: Pakistan, A. Q. Khan and the Rise of Proliferation Networks*; and last, but by no means the least important, *Eating Grass: The Making of the Pakistani Bomb* by Feroz Khan. Pakistani scholar Mansoor Ahmed's unpublished Ph.D. dissertation, 'Pakistan's Nuclear Programme: Security, Politics and Technology' (2012), is also a valuable addition to this list.

The conclusions and findings of the study about the origins and consequences of the Pakistani nuclear programme have important policy implications. Various extremist religious organizations operating in South Asia and the Middle East are suspected of having designs on the nuclear assets of Pakistan. Recurrent political instability and a strengthening crime–terror nexus in Pakistan also raise critical questions about the safety and control of its nuclear weapons facilities. Major terrorist attacks targeting military and intelligence personnel and infrastructure in Pakistan since 2007 have increased the vulnerability of the state's security infrastructure. A handful of these attacks targeted critical installations close to Pakistan's nuclear facilities. This includes an attack on a nuclear missile storage facility at Sargodha on 1 November 2007 and the targeting of a bus carrying employees of the Pakistan Atomic Energy Commission (PAEC) on 4 September 2007.[80] However, there is no authentic report of a terrorist seizure of nuclear weapons or nuclear weapons-related materials in Pakistan, and that must be attributed to increased and improved security measures in and around all nuclear facilities in the country.

Pakistan's broader security orientation, including its nuclear policy, also has to be viewed from the point of view of US–Pakistan relations, which have witnessed haphazard ups and downs in recent decades. President Trump's apparent policy shift adopting a hard line toward Pakistan is a case in point. There is a long list of unmet expectations and frustrations on both sides. The warming of US–India relations, especially as regards civil nuclear energy collaboration; the unending Taliban insurgency in Afghanistan; strengthening Pakistan–China bonding; and US–Iran dynamics since the 2015 nuclear agreement are all critical factors at play when it comes to analysing Pakistan's nuclear policy. Many Pakistanis—including influential officials and analysts— believe that the United States will at some point attempt to rid Pakistan of its nuclear weapons. For the USA, security concerns about Pakistan's nuclear arsenal is one of the important drivers of its policy towards Pakistan. As the leading American scholar Graham Allison told me once, for America the scenario of 'loose nukes to terrorists, the transfer of weapons, and seizure of nuclear weapons by radical groups— powerfully motivate the US government's concerns about the security of Pakistan's nuclear arsenal. Moreover, the United States has an extremely important stake in ensuring that India and Pakistan avoid fighting the first major nuclear war, which could claim tens of millions of lives.'[81] Pakistan argues that its enhanced security measures and vastly improved nuclear command-and-control system deserve due recognition. Indeed, it cannot be denied that Pakistan has learnt some important lessons—the hard way, to be more specific—and it endeavours now to be accepted globally as a responsible nuclear weapons state. The concluding chapter of the book deliberates upon these aspects in more detail.

2

BACKGROUND

PAKISTAN–INDIA RIVALRY AND THE MAKING
OF A NATIONAL SECURITY STATE (1947–1972)[1]

This chapter delves deeper into the dynamics of the broader South Asian security environment, particularly the first twenty-five years of Pakistan's statehood (1947–72), which influenced the country's strategic culture. The term 'strategic culture' denotes integration of 'cultural considerations, cumulative historical memory and their influences in the analysis of states' security policies and international relations'.[2] A strategic cultural analysis offers important insights into the security policies pursued by Pakistan. While there is sufficient evidence to suggest that Pakistan's decision to acquire nuclear weapons was made in 1972, the security issues that confronted it in its formative years significantly influenced its regional as well as global outlook. The country's strategic culture therefore developed early on, and contributed to Pakistan's ambition to obtain nuclear capabilities. Jack Snyder describes strategic culture as 'the sum total of ideals, conditional emotional responses, and patterns of behavior that members of the national strategic community have acquired through instruction or imitation and share with each other with regard to nuclear strategy'.[3] This approach provides a useful aid to understanding Pakistan's security choices.

The neo-realist framework of the balance of power offers another lens through which many analysts attempt to study Pakistan's security perspectives. The historical roots of Pakistan's insecurity indicate that its motivations in its competitiveness towards India fall more in line with Stephen Walt's interpretation of the balance of power concept. Walt argues that states attempt to balance power not because of an unfavourable redistribution of international political, economic, or military capabilities, but rather in response to threats stemming from the identity, aggregate power, geographical proximity, offensive military might, and perceived intentions of adversaries.[4] Many South Asian scholars argue that Pakistan was born insecure,[5] while the declared purpose of its creation was to provide social, political, and constitutional security to the Muslims of South Asia. Security remained elusive, however, due to Pakistan's entrenched and often bloody rivalry with India, driving it to become a 'national security state'—a state where military institutions dominate decision-making processes in all major sectors of government. Pakistan's insecurity—perceived or otherwise—needs to be investigated for a fuller understanding of its dynamics.

Roots of Insecurity

Troubled Beginnings

It is argued by, among others, the renowned historian of South Asian studies Stanley Wolpert, that the creation of Pakistan was made possible by the extraordinary efforts of one man: 'Few individuals alter the course of history. Fewer still modify the map of the world. Hardly anyone can be credited with the creation of a nation state: Jinnah did all three.'[6] Muhammad Ali Jinnah led the All India Muslim League, the party that represented the interests of the Muslims of British India. Professor Ayesha Jalal calls him the 'sole spokesman' of the Muslims of the Indian subcontinent, and the Jinnah factor certainly had important consequences for the future of Pakistan.[7] Jinnah's brilliance overshadowed the weaknesses of the second-tier leaders of the Muslim League as he not only realized a window of opportunity to secure a state for his fellow Muslims, but also mobilized the movement, far quicker than the

BACKGROUND

Indian National Congress was able to. Indeed, Congress, the party that spearheaded the Indian freedom movement under Mohandas Karamchand Gandhi, had been in existence since the early twentieth century, while Jinnah's Muslim League picked up Dr Mohammad Iqbal's idea of a separate Muslim homeland (first projected in 1930) and then formulated it into a concrete demand in 1940, just seven years before eventual independence from the British. However, the Muslim League's fast-paced struggle from conception to demand also meant that the Pakistan movement and its stalwarts could devote very little time to the planning and preparation of the shape and nature of the new state called Pakistan. Nation building was hardly on their minds. In fact, they were not certain until the very end whether they would be able to achieve a separate state or not, as neither the British rulers nor the Hindu majority were willing to accept the division of India.[8] Some scholars are even of the view that the demand for Pakistan was actually meant to be Jinnah's bargaining chip to win more rights and privileges for the Muslim minority within India once the British left the region and India became an independent state.[9]

During most of the struggle for independence the Muslim feudal elites (especially in the Punjab province) did not commit to a separate Pakistan plan, and remained outside the fray. They did, however, join the struggle at the last moment, in 1946, realizing that the creation of Pakistan was inescapable. Also, they did so largely because it was in their economic interest, as their assets and agricultural land remained in the Muslim-dominated areas, which would become part of the new state. Chaudhry Muhammad Ali, a civil servant and a close associate of Jinnah, who rose to become prime minister of Pakistan in 1956, witnessed this remarkable transition and recorded it well:

> As public support for the idea of Pakistan gathered strength, Muslim politicians who were in training under the British in the art of contesting elections and in capturing such crumbs of power as the British allowed to fall, turned more and more toward the Muslim League. They were shrewd and hard headed men capable of being infected temporarily by mass enthusiasm but never forgetful of their own advantage.[10]

The institutional and administrative structure inherited by Pakistan resembled an imperial form of governance more suited to running a colony than an independent sovereign state. Due to low literacy levels and the scarcity of employment opportunities open to them, very few Muslims rose to high levels of bureaucracy in British India. Hence, on the eve of Partition Pakistan could obtain the services of very few experienced and highly skilled Muslim officials to run the new government. As a result, the new Pakistani leadership lacked the initial capacity to break out of the colonial shell left by the British. To remedy this serious shortcoming Pakistan followed the example of India by adapting and slightly modifying the British-codified Government of India Act of 1935 as its provisional constitution. The British needed this instrument to ensure predominance of the central authority.[11] This was meant to be a stopgap measure to unify the six ethnic groups that were to be blended into one nation, but was ill suited to manage the challenges faced by the country in the long run.

In terms of geography, Pakistan was awkwardly cut out from British India in two separate pieces, East and West Pakistan, separated by 800 miles, with part of India in between. Along with Partition came massive ethnic migration, accompanied by wholesale communal slaughter of Muslims by Hindus and Sikhs, and vice versa—seventeen million people shunted across frontiers of the two states created by Partition to reach their designated homelands—and millions vanished.[12] This tragedy haunted the beginning of the new state, and India became public enemy number one, out to destroy Pakistan.

Additionally, in a surprising move, the British viceroy, Lord Mountbatten, let it be known in the days leading up to Partition that he would like to be the head of state (governor-general) of both India and Pakistan. Jinnah refused to accommodate Mountbatten, and instead chose to become governor-general of Pakistan himself. This wounded Mountbatten's ego, and made Pakistan the target of his malevolence. Mountbatten left a record of his feelings on this issue:

> I asked him [Jinnah] "do you realize what this will cost you?" He said, "sadly it may cost me several crores [millions] of rupees in assets", to which I [Mountbatten] replied somewhat acidly, "it may well cost you the whole of your assets and the future of Pakistan." Mountbatten then got up and left the room.[13]

Thus, in addition to all the other ills inherited by the weak new state, came the added injured majesty of Lord Mountbatten, who, according to the renowned Indian writer H. M. Seervai, was determined neither to forget nor forgive this injury.[14] As a direct result, Pakistan greatly suffered in the division of assets.[15] As Mountbatten visibly befriended the Indian leadership, the Pakistani government interpreted his bias against it as an indication of Indian influence.

Those who believed that Pakistan would not be able to sustain itself had good reason to think so. It had neither infrastructure nor financial resources. Vast numbers of professionals who had run the essential services were Hindus and Sikhs, who emigrated from Pakistan to India, and there were no essential resources to fall back on. To make matters worse, there were millions of homeless Muslim refugees from India to be cared for, housed, clothed, and fed. Also, having witnessed slaughter and experienced chaos on their way to Pakistan, these migrants brought with them a negative and suspicious view of India. Such perceptions, influences, and experiences naturally shaped how Pakistan would view India in the times to come.

Pakistan ka matlab kya? La Illaha Illallah *(What does Pakistan stand for? There is no god but God)*

A divisive debate on the role of Islam in policy-making raised many challenges for the new state. During the Pakistan movement years (1940–7) a large number of religious parties and clerics opposed the very idea of Pakistan. Many of them believed that they had more potential for successful proselytizing in a united India. Since Pakistan was created in the name of Islam, however, the political leadership of the Muslim League, despite being secular, used religious sloganeering for political mobilization.[16] The idea gained broader public appeal slowly, but in the process transcended differences among Islamic sects and theoretically united all Muslims in British India under one umbrella. The grassroots issue of religious identity superseded the clerics and Islamic parties by empowering ordinary Muslims to organize rather than follow religious leaders. Also important to note was that Jinnah, the founding father of Pakistan, and many of the major financiers of the Pakistan movement belonged to the Shiite sect, and as a minority they were more committed to a secular state.[17] Jinnah demonstrated these inclinations in his first address to the Constituent Assembly of Pakistan on 11 August 1947 (three days before the country's official independence day):

You are free; you are free to go to your temples, you are free to go to your mosques or to any other place of worship in this State of Pakistan. You may belong to any religion or caste or creed; that has nothing to do with the business of the State.[18]

Jinnah's death thirteen months after the creation of Pakistan was a huge blow to the nation. Besides losing the 'sole spokesman' so early in the nation-building game, it shifted the balance of power away from secular ideologies in favour of non-democratic and conservative elements. Consequently, the new political leadership entangled itself in the debate surrounding the Islamic identity of Pakistan and resorted to Islam to create national unity and order. It didn't take very long for religious forces to claim to be the only group qualified to pronounce what Islam really meant. Religious political parties soon started denouncing the more secular political parties for encroaching on their domain. Within a few years, demands for Pakistan to be an Islamic state began to gain momentum. It is pertinent to mention here that when Pakistan emerged as a sovereign state it brought together disparate Muslim-majority provinces of the former British India, whose only unity lay in the insecurity engendered by the fear of Hindu domination. Additionally, the federal state was also looking to meld six different ethnic groups together.[19] Clearly, apart from rivalry with India, Islam was the only binding factor.

Although their efforts to turn Pakistan into an Islamic state did not initially succeed, the religious parties, realizing that they had plenty of room to manoeuvre given the ideological foundations of the state, went about pursuing their objective in a piecemeal fashion. They began by asking for constitutional provisions declaring Islam to be the state religion, and with the passage of time they raised the level and nature of their demands.[20] At about the same time, the anti-communist movements that had sprung up worldwide found support in Pakistan. Rumours began circulating to the effect that communists were gaining ground and expanding their influence in the country. Interestingly, the US National Security Council's 'top secret' 1951 report maintained that 'in Pakistan, the communists have acquired considerable influence in press circles among intellectuals and in certain labor unions', and argued that domination of Pakistan 'by unfriendly powers, either directly or through subservient indigenous regimes, would constitute a serious threat to the national security of the US'.[21] To counter communist infiltration, real or perceived, the religious parties, hitherto generally peaceful in outlook and character, started receiving support—both moral and monetary—from the government of Pakistan as well as the United States.

By 1953, however, the political environment had changed. The religious groups resorted to violent tactics and, in collaboration with some political forces, attacked the Ahmadiyya community, a minority sect, in the Punjab province. Abul Ala Maududi, the leader of Jamaat-e-Islami (JI, the Party of Islam), was among the main organizers of this 'activism'. Maududi, one of the most influential figures in contemporary Islamist politics in South Asia and elsewhere, benefited from the political confusion and turbulent disarray of the times. The Muslim League, the founding party of the country, had wasted six years in power without developing a constitution for the state and had delayed the holding of elections, generating disenchantment among the people. This gave political Islam a chance to raise its profile, and religious parties started making attempts to frame the issues from a religious perspective to attract public support.[22] Maududi opportunistically seized on this political shift quite effectively by expanding the base of his party over the years. Surprisingly, he was among those who had earlier vociferously opposed the idea of Pakistan. As Vali Nasr insightfully argues, the idea of Islamic revivalism projected by Maududi was not simply a cultural rejection of the West; rather, it was closely tied to questions of political power and its impact on identity formation, bringing religious discourse into the mainstream.[23]

The 1953 crisis was largely resolved when the Pakistani government called in the army to quell the violence and bring peace to the troubled areas. But this show of force only bolstered religious groups' confidence in their own strength. Maududi and many of his collaborators received death sentences for the role they played in this turmoil, later overturned by higher courts. Learning from the experience, religious parties started expanding their infrastructure and activities, and in the mid-1960s some of them, JI being the most prominent, were banned.[24] Changing their strategy, the religious parties then began developing contacts within the military establishment and intelligence organizations. Simultaneously, as Husain Haqqani maintains, 'Islamic Pakistan' in its formative years was also defining itself through the prism of resistance to 'Hindu India'.[25] Indians too were fostering jingoism, but luckily for them their clergy was not allowed to drive that trend.

The Kashmir Dispute

The Kashmir dispute has proved to be the most divisive and contentious issue between India and Pakistan. It has poisoned prospects of peace in South Asia since 1947. To explain the extent of the divergent viewpoints that led to confrontation and frustrations, a brief history of the dispute is pertinent here. This narrative largely reflects the Pakistani perspective, referring to sources routinely quoted in Pakistani textbooks, in order to show what ultimately pushed Pakistan into thinking about developing a credible deterrent in the form of nuclear weapons capability.

The crisis erupted when, on the eve of the partition of British India, Lord Listowel, Secretary of State for India, declared that the 565 princely states must join one of the two succeeding dominions, and that independence was not an option.[26] Princely states were in fact autocracies where the hereditary rulers exercised total power, and these were tied to the British Empire under different treaties and agreements. Thus, before the treaties were to lapse on 15 August 1947, each princely state was to accede to either India or Pakistan, taking into consideration its geography and the wishes of its people.

The state of Jammu and Kashmir, the largest of all the princely states, bordering Pakistan, India, China, and Afghanistan, occupied a particularly strategic position. There were about 4 million inhabitants of this territory and, according to the official 1941 census, overall 77 per cent of the people were Muslims; in Jammu, the traditional Hindu heartland, Muslims only had a slim majority (55 per cent), but in the Kashmir valley Muslims had an overwhelming majority (90 per cent).[27] Pakistan argued that, considering the religious, cultural, and geographical links between Pakistan and the state of Jammu and Kashmir, it should be awarded to Pakistan. India challenged this assertion on two points. First, Jammu and Kashmir naturally existed as a contiguous extension of India. Second, Sheikh Abdullah, the popular Muslim Kashmiri leader, supported the state's accession to India.

Meanwhile, the task of dividing the boundaries of the adjacent Punjab province between India and Pakistan, based on respective Hindu and Muslim majority populations, went to the Punjab Boundary Commission headed by a British lawyer, Sir Cyril Radcliffe. Pakistan took issue with Radcliffe and alleged that he, under the 'guidance' of Governor General Mountbatten, committed grave injustices against Muslim populations. In particular, Radcliffe was accused of complicity in the allocation of a Muslim-majority region named Gurdaspur to India with the specific purpose of maintaining a direct road from India to Kashmir. This kept open the possibility of Kashmir's accession to India, despite its Muslim-majority population. India, however, praised Radcliffe for his neutrality.[28]

Like all other aspects of the conflict, India and Pakistan had completely divergent viewpoints on the accession issue. India maintained that Maharaja Hari Singh, the Hindu ruler of the state of Jammu and Kashmir, signed the instrument of accession to join India on 26 October 1947. Singh's instrument of accession was final and irrevocable. But Pakistan argued that, due to an effective rebellion against him in the Kashmir valley and adjoining areas, he had lost his legal power to make such a decision, thus nullifying the instrument of accession. Pakistan also alleged that the accession document was signed under duress and was therefore illegal.[29]

The controversy led to violent conflict. Communal violence erupted in the region, and its spillover was expected to influence Kashmir, especially as it was adjacent to Punjab, which had experienced massive bloodshed. Soon the communal problems, which were already brewing in Jammu, had their impact on the Poonch and Gilgit sectors in Jammu and Kashmir. These had large, predominantly Muslim populations and maintained closer traditional and cultural ties to areas that became part of Pakistan. In response to the disturbances, the maharaja imposed martial law in Poonch, which resulted in many casualties.[30] In the Jammu district, according to British historian Alastair Lamb, about half a million Muslims were forcibly displaced by Hindus and Sikhs, and as many as 200,000 of them disappeared in August, September, and October 1947.[31] At this stage, rogue tribal bands from the Federally Administered Tribal Areas (FATA) of Pakistan moved in and fought their way up to Srinagar, the capital of Kashmir. The government of

Pakistan denied involvement with the violence, arguing that its humble military and administrative infrastructure was incapable of managing such an infiltration. A noted Indian scholar, Prem Shankar Jha, accurately reflecting the Indian position on the issue, stated: 'The raids into Kashmir by the Pathan tribesmen were not spontaneous retaliations aimed at saving their Muslim brethren from Dogra genocide, but were carefully planned and instigated at least … a whole month before any of the alleged atrocities … took place.'[32] Pakistan did indeed have a hand in it.

India's governor general Mountbatten, while provisionally accepting the maharaja's accession to India, stated that it was subject to the will of the people, to be ascertained through a plebiscite, and later suggested inviting the United Nations to send observers to 'ensure that the necessary atmosphere was created for a free and impartial plebiscite'.[33] In the midst of all these developments, Hunza, Gilgit, and Baltistan districts, which were part of the state of Jammu and Kashmir, announced their secession from the maharaja's Kashmir and joined Pakistan. Today this area is known as Gilgit–Baltistan, but earlier it was known as the Northern Areas of Pakistan. In reference to the proposed plebiscite, the Indian prime minister, Jawaharlal Nehru, on 31 October 1947, reiterated: 'We have given this pledge not only to Kashmir, not only to Pakistan, but to the whole world. We will not and cannot back out of it.'[34]

To resolve the Kashmir crisis, on 1 January 1948 India referred the issue to the United Nations under Article 35 (Chapter VI) of the UN Charter, charging that Pakistan had committed aggression. India demanded that Pakistan should deny access to 'invaders' through its territory and should stop assisting them; otherwise India might invade Pakistan in self-defence. Pakistan in response denied the Indian charges of complicity and accused India of illegally annexing Jammu and Kashmir, of committing genocide upon Muslims in the state of Junagadh, and of trying to throttle Pakistan in its infancy. The United Nations Security Council (UNSC) passed its first resolution on the matter on 17 January 1948, calling on both sides to ease tensions.[35] Three days later the UNSC passed another resolution to create the United Nations Commission for India and Pakistan (UNCIP) to investigate the facts and exercise a mediatory role.[36]

BACKGROUND

Led by the United States and Britain, the UN adopted a third resolution on 21 April 1948, with clear instructions that the commission should use its mediatory role to restore order and hold a plebiscite in cooperation with India and Pakistan. On 14 August 1948 the Commission presented its proposals simultaneously to the governments of India and Pakistan. Interestingly, the event marked the first time that Pakistan admitted that it retained three army brigades in Kashmir to defend its rivers flowing through the territory. The existence of the troops did not go unnoticed by the UNCIP. The Commission recommended that:

1. The government of Pakistan should withdraw its troops from the state;
2. The government of Pakistan should also use its best endeavor to secure the withdrawal of tribesmen;
3. Pending a final solution, the territory evacuated by Pakistani troops will be administered by the local authorities under the surveillance of the Commission; and
4. When the Commission shall have notified the government of India that the tribesmen and Pakistani forces have withdrawn, the government of India should begin to withdraw the bulk of their forces from the state.

However, rather than considering these recommendations, India and Pakistan continued with their limited and sporadic military offensives in this theatre. Meanwhile, Pakistan, which was required to act first, established and strengthened its control over about a third of Jammu and Kashmir and declared it 'Azad Kashmir' (Free Kashmir). The areas under Indian control continued to be called the state of Jammu and Kashmir. Later the Commission played a key role in bringing about a ceasefire, and both states finally agreed to allow UN observers to supervise the area from 1 January 1949. While this effort was instrumental in persuading the parties to cease fighting in Kashmir, it did not succeed in paving the way for the promised plebiscite.

As the political and military deadlock persisted, pressures came to the fore over the timing and schedule of the withdrawal of Indian and Pakistani forces from the area. On 30 August 1949 US President Harry S. Truman and British Prime Minister Clement Attlee suggested that the Kashmir issue be settled by arbitration by a high-profile and impartial person. Truman and Attlee recommended US Admiral Chester Nimitz for the post of mediator. India immediately rejected the proposal, and Nehru strongly asserted that the Anglo-American proposition was an 'unwarranted intervention'.[37]

In response, the Indian government announced steps for convening a constituent assembly in Jammu and Kashmir towards the end of 1950, and proclaimed that India would determine the future shape and affiliations of the region. Many thought that the constituent assembly, in effect, would streamline the ratification of the formal accession of Jammu and Kashmir to India. This Indian policy could have nullified the prospects of a plebiscite, and Pakistan brought this development to the UNSC's attention. Accordingly, the UNSC adopted a resolution on 30 March 1951, which stated that such a move on India's part would be contrary to the principles already agreed upon for the resolution of the conflict.[38] India ignored the UNSC resolution and went ahead with the elections, which resulted in Sheikh Abdullah's National Congress winning seventy-three unopposed seats in a house of seventy-five, due to an opposition boycott.[39] Abdullah, though friendly with the Indian leadership, proved to be a tough customer, as he was hoping to achieve independent status for Jammu and Kashmir within the Indian union. India found Abdullah's ambitions unacceptable, and not only dismissed him from office (8 August 1953) but also imprisoned him. An interim political set-up gave power to Bakhshi Ghulam Mohammad, which enabled India to attempt to bypass the UNSC again. In 1954 Mohammad passed a resolution in the Kashmir constituent assembly confirming the maharaja's decision to accede to India. It adopted a new constitution for the state of Jammu and Kashmir and declared it 'an integral part of India'. The question of Jammu and Kashmir's status was again referred back to the UNSC in 1956. The Council after a long debate adopted a resolution on 24 January 1957 wherein it refused to accept the assertions of the Indian leaders and reaffirmed its previous position on the need for a plebiscite.[40]

UN Representatives such as General A. G. L. McNaughton, Sir Owen Dixon, Dr Frank P. Graham, and Gunnar Jarring came up with various proposals to resolve the lingering crisis during the 1950–8 timeframe, but to little avail.[41] Instead, Nehru tried to wriggle out of the promised plebiscite in 1961 by categorically stating that 'there is no question of any plebiscite in Kashmir, now or later'.[42] From an Indian perspective, this tough line was a response to Pakistan's military alliance with the Western powers, especially the United States. At the same time, due to Cold War dynamics, the former Soviet Union was becoming more supportive of India, making it increasingly difficult for the UN to meaningfully contribute in its conflict-resolution efforts.[43]

Six rounds of bilateral talks with India at the ministerial level followed in 1960–5, but without breaking the impasse. In October 1963 Pakistan approached the UNSC again to plead for the implementation of its resolutions on Kashmir, but a Soviet veto blocked this effort. By this time India had become 'non-aligned'. The impending stalemate finally resulted in a war between India and Pakistan in 1965, which ended without a clear victory for either party. However, with Soviet mediation, both countries accepted a return to the negotiating table, and this resulted in the Tashkent Declaration of 10 January 1966. But other than re-establishing diplomatic channels, no significant headway was made towards resolution of the Kashmir dispute, and overall relations remained tense.[44]

From Pakistan's point of view, its legitimate and legal claim over Jammu and Kashmir was repeatedly met by hostile denials and rejections from India. Further, UN efforts to mediate and resolve the conflict bore no fruit. Pakistan's alliances with the West and attempts to take the area by force also failed to change on-the-ground realities, adding to its disappointment, frustration, and insecurity. Pakistan was convinced that it had been denied justice in the matter and that India could get away with it because of its size and military power, which Pakistan couldn't match. Indian oppression in Jammu and Kashmir also regularly reminded Pakistan of this 'unfinished business' of Partition.

The Rise of the Military and the Emergence of National Security State

Much like the rest of Pakistan, the military went through a dramatic transition after Partition took effect. The division of British India's assets in 1947 left Pakistan with one-third of the British Indian army and only 17 per cent of its revenues.[45] With such limited resources in terms of personnel and assets, Pakistan was under a military disadvantage compared to its rival India right from the start. Adding to its troubles was another unfriendly neighbour to the west. Pakistan shared a 1,500-mile border with Afghanistan, which was the only country that opposed Pakistan's admission to the UN. Grievances between Afghanistan and Pakistan stemmed from their disputes over the Durand Line (which divides the Pashtun tribes between the two countries). Pakistan's paranoia over its territorial security was an outcome of this set of factors—and these were largely legitimate concerns. In this regard, according to the eminent Pakistani scholar Ayesha Siddiqa, the centrality of the armed forces as the guardian of the state was intrinsic, as it compensated for the deep sense of insecurity that infested the state after its birth.[46]

In its first twenty-five years Pakistan resembled Jack Nelson-Pallmeyer's conception of a national security state.[47] Nelson-Pallmeyer identifies seven characteristics of a national security state, and these definitive features offer a strong understanding of what occurred within Pakistan from 1947 to 1972: (1) the first and most distinguishing feature of a national security state is the progression of the military to the highest authority, assuming power and leverage to determine the overall direction of the society; (2) democratic institutions are viewed with suspicion, even though the state often maintains an appearance of democracy through puppet institutions; (3) a national security establishment emerges where the military and its associated institutions wield substantial political and economic authority; (4) a psychological obsession with the state's enemies becomes pervasive, driving the creation of a distinct national identity; (5) viewing the enemy as cunning and ruthless, in turn justifying the utilization of any means available to counter the enemy; restrictions over public discourse limit popular participation; and lastly (6) the church is mobilized for financial as well as ideological support in service to the overarching mission of the state.

Each of these characteristics, in varying degrees, describes Pakistan between 1947 and 1972. As noted earlier, at the time of Partition the Pakistani army was in a lamentable state. It had a shortage of everything: men, defence stores, weapons, ammunition, and officers. Its higher-ranking officers consisted of one major-general, two brigadiers, and fifty-three colonels. The scarcity of a professional officer corps reflected the shortcomings in the military more broadly. For example, of the 600 officers required in the army corps of engineers, most were unqualified, according to Stephen P. Cohen, a leading American expert on Pakistan's military.[48] Startlingly, not a single complete regiment came to Pakistan from the British Indian army at the time of Partition. Though there were Sikh regiments, and many Hindu regiments, in the British Indian army, no regiment consisted of an all-Muslim unit. This 'oversight' had its roots in the War of Independence—or mutiny as per the British narrative—in 1857. At the time, while the British decided they needed Muslim soldiery, they could not trust it enough to form independent all-Muslim units. They therefore scattered Muslim soldiers and mixed them with other units to dilute their strength. This distrust for Muslim units hardly subsided over the next hundred years, leading to the location of the majority of military assets with what became the Indian side rather than a fairer distribution between the two newly created states.[49]

Pakistani hopes for fair allocation of the military assets rested with Field Marshal Auchinleck, the Supreme Commander of India and Pakistan, who was made responsible for the distribution of defence stores and materials between the two countries. His attempts at fairness were condemned as bias in favour of Pakistan by the senior Indian officers and political leaders. As a campaign of vilification built up against Auchinleck (by the Indians), he proposed that the Supreme Commanders' Headquarters in New Delhi cease operations six months early, in November 1947 rather than on the scheduled date of closure in April 1948. Pakistan protested against this proposal, but India supported it, and Mountbatten demonstrated little difficulty in going along with the Indian demand.[50] The premature shutting down of the Supreme Commanders' Headquarters dashed Pakistan's slender hopes for a fair share of military assets and produced a general sense of betrayal in Pakistan, seen as part of Indian efforts to sabotage Pakistan's security.

In light of the deficiencies in personnel and military assets, disputes with neighbours, rising insecurity, and inadequate state infrastructures and nascent political institutions, the Pakistani army was asked to shoulder critical responsibilities. Pakistan's concern over Kashmir and

India's hostility developed into the most immediate responsibility, and led to a mad rush to acquire military equipment from wherever possible. The military budget thus became a priority very early on, directly increasing the strength and power of the military and indirectly bolstering its influence. In the very first year the government allocated about 70 per cent of the budget to defence needs.[51] Such large expenditure surely reinforced an emphasis on security over social concerns. Meanwhile, Pakistan's first war with India in 1948 firmly established the primacy of the national security culture. Ayesha Siddiqa argues that this development was also accompanied by lax control of the management of the armed forces by the civilian leadership.[52] In part, this occurred because the political leadership, besides being busy in establishing new state institutions, possessed no experience in overseeing military operations, whereas senior army officers were more experienced, having been part of the well-organized and professional British India army.

In contrast to the army's rising significance, the feudalistic political leadership was losing legitimacy as it failed to devise a new constitution. Ethnic tussles and vested political interests stunted the growth and maturing process of a new nation which was trying to come to terms with immense challenges. Pakistan's political institutions also had to absorb the shock of the death of Jinnah in 1948 and the assassination of the first prime minister, Liaquat Ali Khan, in 1951. Consequently, for a brief period between 1954 and 1957, the British-trained bureaucracy dominated the political landscape. During these years, the army chief was inducted into the federal cabinet as defence minister, creating a bad precedent. The army, under Commander-in-Chief General Ayub Khan, finally moved in to take charge of the situation in 1958, and imposed martial law. From thereon all policy formulation and governance became the domain of the Pakistani army. This had significant implications for relations with India. This was the birth of the national security state.

In parallel to these developments, the US–Pakistan military partnership and cooperation grew, reinforcing the central role of the Pakistani army. The USA, in its efforts to build an alliance in the region to counter possible Soviet expansionism, signed several military agreements with Pakistan in 1953 and 1954, leading to Pakistan's joining the South

East Asia Treaty Organization (SEATO) and the Baghdad Pact (later called the Central Treaty Organization [CENTO]). General Ayub Khan had made an indirect commitment to the US assistant secretary of state, Henry Byroade, in 1953 in an attempt to draw in the USA: 'Our army can be your army if you want us.'[53] Consequently, major US military assistance flowed into the country, supplementing Pakistani investment and enabling it to modernize its armed forces capabilities in the face of the Indian military buildup. The net result was a powerful US–Pakistani relationship that served both states' interests. The USA had befriended another state to counter the Soviet Union, while for Pakistan, getting access to a supplier of military goods and professional training meant that it could have a shot at countering India effectively. The growth in military capabilities empowered the Pakistani military, which soon started setting its own rules of business outside the constitutional domain. The instructions given to Brigadier Ghulam Gillani, Pakistan's first military attaché to Washington, by General Ayub Khan in 1952 are truly insightful. Khan told Gillani that his main task was to procure military equipment from the Pentagon, and that he need not take either Pakistan's ambassador or foreign office into confidence, for in Khan's view 'these civilians cannot be trusted with such sensitive matters of national security'.[54] Without constitutional checks the military consolidated its power and focused the state's attention on the Indian threat and the simmering Kashmir conflict while artfully framing the security issues for American officials in terms of Pakistan's utility as a bulwark against the Soviet bloc. America did not consider it expedient to suspect Pakistan's intentions, while always stating on the record that US military hardware could not be used in any military confrontation with India. This was both American and Pakistani duplicity at its best.

General Ayub's rise to power as the head of state in 1958 ensured that the security interests of the state, as defined by the army, were to be served well. Ayub introduced a constitution in 1962 that was tailor-made for him and pushed the country further towards authoritarianism. Hostility with India fast turned into confrontation, providing an important stimulus for the emergence of Pakistan's military and national security state. In April 1965 the Pakistan army clashed with Indian forces in the Rann of Kutch area in Sind province, after the

Indian army invaded the disputed territory, eliciting an immediate response from Pakistan. Pakistan's army came off better in the ensuing battle, leading Pakistan to the conclusion that the time to take on the Indians had come.

More importantly, the international arbitration that followed the Rann of Kutch dispute (which found in favour of Pakistan) led Pakistan to assume that if the Kashmir problem was to be solved, the Rann of Kutch route would have to be replicated, in the sense of a limited armed conflict in Kashmir, leading to a threat of an all-out war, and then intervention and arbitration by the great powers.[55] At this stage there was considerable confidence in Pakistan about the strength of its arms, the capabilities of its military, and the determination in its resolve. Bolstered by the country's newfound friendship with China and supported by great emotional sympathy with the Kashmiris, the Pakistani army was now ready for a direct encounter. Zulfikar Ali Bhutto, Pakistan's foreign minister at the time, on 12 May 1965 sent a letter to President Ayub Khan, drawing his attention to the increasing Western military aid to India and how fast the balance of power in the region was shifting in India's favour as a result. He vociferously recommended that 'a bold and courageous stand' would 'open up greater possibility for a negotiated settlement', making a case that the time was ripe for a strategic military manoeuvre.[56]

A secret plan, Operation Gibraltar, was conceived at this juncture, calling for a sizeable armed force to infiltrate and cross the ceasefire line dividing Pakistani- and Indian-controlled parts of Kashmir. The purpose of the action included carrying out acts of sabotage in order to destabilize the government of Jammu and Kashmir and encourage the local Muslim population to rise up against the Indian occupation. The plan was put into action in August 1965, and India retaliated with a full-fledged military offensive against Pakistan, which Ayub and his colleagues apparently had not anticipated. A poor command decision at the height of the action—taking away command from the hands of brilliant Major-General Akhtar Hussain Malik and giving it to the ambitious Major-General Yahya Khan—was also a disaster. What little economic development and progress these very poor countries had achieved since their independence was frittered away in the space of seventeen days. But despite the failure of the original plan, Ayub's delusion was remarkably deep. Rather than acknowledging that his 'out-of-the-box' strategy to resolve the Kashmir dispute had not worked, he promoted himself to the rank of field marshal.[57] Power had gone to his head, and the military as an institution was going through a similar experience.

The Breakup of Pakistan: 1971

To be fair to Ayub, he modernized and professionalized the armed forces and improved the economic outlook of the country during his time in office (1958–69). His authoritarian rule, however, failed to resolve the major socio-political challenges that Pakistan faced. In fact, as the economist Omar Noman aptly contends, 'the policies of the Ayub regime had made a substantial and critical contribution towards Pakistan's political disintegration'.[58] Public disenchantment with the regime amid the frustration of political disorganization ultimately forced Ayub Khan to resign in 1969, but the damage was already done. Ayub did a further disservice to the country in bypassing the constitutional order that he had himself erected when he named a successor, handing over the reins of government to General Yahya Khan, the military commander-in-chief. He was required to invite the speaker of the National Assembly to take over, but Ayub, it seems, was more loyal to the army than the country.

Institutionalized discrimination was another aspect of Ayub Khan's legacy. In particular, the patronizing attitude of West Pakistan's political elite towards the people of the Bengal province in East Pakistan was striking. This prejudice played out in civil–military bureaucratic affairs, where the involvement of Bengalis was symbolic at best.[59] The Bengali share in various sectors of the economy such as revenue expenditure, development expenditure, and utilization of foreign aid remained most unsatisfactory and unjust.[60] Around the mid-1960s the Bengalis, after fully realizing that the deck was stacked against them, demanded complete autonomy under the leadership of Sheikh Mujib ur Rahman of the Awami League, a populist Bengali political party. This marked a significant shift in Pakistan's political and security culture.

General Yahya Khan, Pakistan's new military dictator, to his credit held free and open elections in 1970, in which the Awami League emerged as the majority party at the national level by virtue of winning all seats in East Pakistan (the larger wing), whereas in West Pakistan the Pakistan People's Party (PPP) won the majority of seats. However, neither party could win a single seat in the other wing. This was the end of a united Pakistan. The underlying sentiment that explained voting outcomes and seat allocations came from obvious regional disparities and class inequalities perpetuated by Ayub's dictatorship. Even winning an election was not sufficient for Bengalis, as power was withheld from them. They were enraged, and rightly so. When they voiced their concerns and protested against the injustices, the military, dominated by West Pakistani (mostly Punjabi) soldiers, moved to quell the growing separatist movement and crush the 'rebellion'. The failure to resolve the crisis through the use of force paved the way for East Pakistan to become Bangladesh on 16 December 1971. What cannot be ignored here is the fact that this turn of events was facilitated by an invasion by the Indian armed forces. Serious human rights violations were committed by the Pakistani security forces in the process, destroying any prospect of reconciliation.[61] The humiliation that the Pakistani army faced at the hands of both the Bengali resistance and Indian forces was immense. Nearly one hundred thousand Pakistani armed forces personnel fighting in Bengal surrendered to India as prisoners of war. In West Pakistan the whole episode was presented as an Indian conspiracy to hurt and divide Pakistan. To this day Pakistani textbooks attribute the 'fall of Dhaka' to the Indian military action.[62] In reality, it was only partly so. To a greater degree this was a self-inflicted wound—a fatal wound. A national security state was at work, and a different outcome would have been almost impossible.

This time around the military had to face the music. General Yahya Khan faced dissent within the military, and he was forced to hand over power to Zulfikar Ali Bhutto, the popularly elected PPP leader, in early 1972. Democracy finally returned to Pakistan, but it was a truncated Pakistan. Unaware of all the facts that had led to this divorce between the eastern and western wings of the country, most people blamed India for the tragedy, in turn keeping intact the hidden foundations of the wounded national security state.

Conclusion

From the very beginning, Pakistan was destined to base its security perceptions on a policy of countering India. India could have helped Pakistan to overcome this view but it too was hurt, and saw the creation of Pakistan as a mutilation of India—and a slur on its identity. In other words, as Ayesha Siddiqa aptly maintains, 'the popular perception amongst the decision-making elite makes the [India–Pakistan] rivalry akin to a battle between good and evil with the Indian "Goliath" forever trying to vanquish the Pakistani "David"'.[63] The ascendance of the military in Pakistan is a direct outcome of this worldview. Consequently, Pakistan's political and security structures took off on quite a different trajectory to those of its democratic neighbour India, exacerbating insecurity rather than resolving the multifaceted challenges that the country faced. Confusion about the role of religion in state affairs and ethnic cleavages further intensified the identity crisis.

Despite the conflict being territorial in essence, it increasingly took the shape of an ideological contest. Pakistan ignored the fact that there were almost as many Muslims living in India as in Pakistan. As for India, it struggled to accept Pakistan as a reality. Most Pakistanis believe that India still hopes that history can be reversed and that Pakistan can rejoin the mother country.[64] India appears to have developed some kind of an inferiority complex, and that may be why it did nothing to allay Pakistan's fears. In fact, India seldom missed the opportunity to provoke Pakistan. Pakistan, meanwhile, increasingly framed its rivalry with India in ideological terms, and this narrow vision coloured its strategic approach. Enhancing the capabilities of its armed forces—at any cost—was deemed absolutely necessary to ward off India's hegemonic designs. This tunnel vision seeped into an organizational culture. According to retired Pakistani soldier Brigadier Feroz Khan, Pakistan's military sector certainly examined and learned lessons from its failures in the 1971 war, but kept them internal and classified.[65] He further says that, in the army's view, their defeat was caused by bad luck or a unique situation, but not due to 'overall incompetence'. Power had changed hands from military to civilian rulers meanwhile, but the new leader, Zulfikar Ali Bhutto, was widely respected in the armed forces for his hawkish views about India.

Pakistan's experience with external alliances—with the United States and with China—was also less than satisfactory, as these connections proved to be of little help in safeguarding Pakistan's national security and integrity. It was also very conscious of its lack of strategic depth, especially in comparison to India. Hence, Pakistan's strategic thinking concluded that its survival could not be guaranteed by an outside power.[66] The natural corollary to this was emphasis on deterrence. It was a matter of time before deterrence through conventional military means would transform into a desperate need for a nuclear deterrent.

3

THE DEVELOPMENT OF PAKISTAN'S NUCLEAR WEAPONS PROGRAMME

If nuclear weapons can come to acquire the same 'profound value' as the sacred symbols that supposedly condense the meaning and purpose of a religion, and if the discourse surrounding them can seem as arcane and complex as the higher reaches of religious philosophizing can be for the ordinary believer of the uninitiated, then we have surely succeeded making the politics and ideology of the possession of nuclear weapons virtually incontestable.

Praful Bidwai and Achin Vanaik[1]

Pakistan carried out six nuclear test explosions between 28 and 30 May 1998 at the Chagai Hills site in the Baluchistan province. These were in reaction to five nuclear tests carried out by India just a few weeks earlier, on 11 and 13 May. India had provided Pakistan with a golden opportunity to demonstrate its nuclear capability; it was unthinkable that Pakistan would miss such a chance. India had also underestimated Pakistan. In March 1998 the Indian prime minister, I. K. Gujral, told a visiting Pugwash delegation in New Dehli that 'Pakistan was not capable of making atomic bombs'.[2] He had been convinced of this by both the Indian intelligence and people like Dr Raja Ramana, the former head of the Indian Atomic Energy Commission, who had even publicly claimed that nuclear weapons were beyond Pakistan's reach.[3]

On the eve of the tests Pakistani leaders openly confessed that its actions were reactive and necessary to ensure the security and survival of Pakistan. After the successful detonation, Pakistan's prime minister, Nawaz Sharif, summed up his sentiments in a nationally televised address, saying: 'Today, we have settled the score with India.'[4] This was not mere rhetoric meant for public consumption. This is exactly what inspired Pakistan to pursue nuclear weapons capability.

For the broader world, this was an alarming situation. The US president, Bill Clinton, openly remarked how 'Pakistan lost a priceless opportunity to improve its political standing in the eyes of the world'.[5] To expect restraint from Pakistan after the Indian nuclear tests was a asking too much. Pakistan's ambassador to the USA, Riaz Khokhar, justified the action by maintaining that Pakistan 'felt very threatened, not only because India exploded these devices', but also because, following their weapons tests, 'the Indian leadership had made very, very threatening statements directed at Pakistan'.[6] This is borne out by the fact that, soon after conducting its five tests, Indian officials maintained that they 'would begin fitting nuclear warheads on a range of missiles, including several developed specifically for targets in Pakistan'.[7] The provocation was intentional and well thought out—to put Pakistan on the spot. The Indian tests were certainly very alarming for Pakistan, and a tit-for-tat response was almost inevitable given the South Asian security dynamics. For Pakistan, the tests created a national sense of pride, significant achievement, and power.[8] It projected defiance.

Given the historically-laden hostilities, unresolved border disputes, and highly charged patriotic fervour coupled with ideological jingoism on both sides, international concerns about the prospect of catastrophic conflict in South Asia were legitimate and valid. Nuclear tests from both states naturally raised the stakes of nuclear confrontation. Neither country's nuclear programme was a secret, but the tests transformed the security environment.

There is no dearth of academic work about the nuclearization of South Asia, and on India's development of its nuclear plan in particular. Moreover, academics and experts have studied and researched India's decision to test its nuclear weapons at the time that it did, its second introduction of nuclear weapons onto the South Asia's strategic landscape.[9] However, in the case of Pakistan, other than limited scholarly treatment of its nuclear programme and how it overcame tremendous obstacles in achieving the nuclear fuel cycle, focus has lately shifted significantly towards its proliferation activities.[10] By analysing the history of Pakistan's nuclear programme, this chapter probes whether the processes involved in acquiring the technology are potentially linked to its later proliferation activities.

This chapter examines Pakistan's nuclear development, focusing on the sources and motivations of its nuclear policy since its early days. It argues that, although various factors influenced Pakistan's pursuit of its nuclear development programme in its initial phase (1950s and 1960s), it was national security concerns that played the most instrumental role in turning it to a weapons-focused project in the early 1970s. This argument is developed through the use of historical narrative to explain how Pakistan's nuclear policy has since evolved. It will illustrate how Pakistan moved from a civilian nuclear programme to a military one, and how the expertise and infrastructure developed in its early phases helped the weapons-directed programme in the later years. From successfully mastering the fuel-cycle technology to the designing of the bomb, and from skilfully developing a weapons-delivery system to the conducting of the nuclear explosion test, this journey required immense dedication and expertise, as well as ingenuity, sustained funding and political support. A range of institutions were involved in this herculean task, and contrary to general perceptions—both in Pakistan and abroad—it was the result of tremendous teamwork.

The contributions of A. Q. Khan in the overall project are also specifically covered here, including an exploration of how he created an import network for acquiring necessary components and became a critical player in the programme. Khan's politics within the nuclear programme, rivalries with other senior nuclear scientists of the Pakistan Atomic Energy Commission (PAEC), especially its talented chairman, Munir Ahmed Khan, and Khan's dealings with the military and political leadership are also discussed here.

Why did Pakistan Make the Bomb?

Political theorists propose four major contributing as well as competing factors that best explain why nations 'go nuclear' and build nuclear arsenals.[11] These are: (1) security challenges; (2) prestige and power; (3) technological imperatives; and (4) domestic push and pull factors.[12]

Beginning with security concerns, scholars note that when a state's physical security and survival is directly at risk, it may be driven to acquire nuclear weapons capabilities in order to protect its integrity and safeguard its people. Any state located in a dangerous region and threatened by an aggressive enemy is likely to be seriously concerned about its national security. Such fear often leads a state to develop methods to ensure its survival, in terms of both offensive and defensive policies, often resulting in the pursuit of strong military capabilities, a critical way to project power. In this sense, nuclear weapons empower states to feel secure. For instance, this theory argues that the 'first-generation' nuclear powers (the USA, the USSR, the UK, France, and China) and the 'second-generation' nuclear states (India, Pakistan, and Israel) acquired nuclear weapons because each faced a grave security threat from an adversary. Thus, developing nuclear weapons capability deters hostile action, enabling a state to effectively threaten that the consequences of an attack could be devastating for any aggressor.

A second view holds that the acquisition of nuclear weapons acts as a symbol of national prestige for any state. It also demonstrates technological sophistication, which creates a sense of pride not only in the abilities of its people but also of its state institutions. A nuclear weapons programme denotes a highly skilled industry requiring an extraordinary level of expertise, raising the standing of a state in the community of nations. Acquiring nuclear capability, according to this view, bestows great power status or global recognition upon a state. Britain, France, and India are often cited as examples of states for which prestige was an important factor in their decisions to acquire nuclear weapons.

A third motive behind a state's decision to develop a nuclear weapons programme is a logical and inevitable result of technological momentum created by civilian, purpose-driven nuclear research and development programmes.[13] This argument by Professor Matthew Fuhrman advances the notion that the successful implementation of nuclear programmes to foster greater knowledge of nuclear science and technology, as well as potential positive uses such as nuclear energy, naturally and logically drive further exploration into weapons programmes. His research concludes that 'on average, countries receiving higher levels of peaceful nuclear assistance are more likely to pursue and acquire the bomb—especially if they experience an international crisis after receiving aid'.[14]

The last basis for a nuclear weapons programme holds that domestic bureaucratic politics and the political calculus of leaders may lead a state to a nuclear path, as discussed above in the introduction. According to this view, bureaucrats inspired by their personal policy preferences and ideas, or bureaucracies carrying out their specific institutional interests, attempt to influence states' decision to go down the nuclear road. Homi Bhabha is often cited as an example in this category, as he played a central role in India's acquisition of nuclear weapons technology.

All of these theories can be considered relevant to Pakistan's pursuit of nuclear weapons technology. Lowell Ditmer's insights on Pakistan's motivations to develop a nuclear weapons programme in his 2001 *Asian Survey* review essay are noteworthy: 'Pakistan's motive for the acquisition of nuclear weapons is far less complex and more conventional and is merely about national security.'[15] Sumit Ganguly, a leading Indian-American scholar, concurs, making the case that the core aim of Pakistan's nuclear weapons programme is to prevent a repetition of the events of 1971 whereby direct Indian involvement facilitated the creation of a sovereign Bangladesh out of former East Pakistan. In this sense, according to Ganguly, a nuclear Pakistan would deter India strategically from further reducing Pakistan's territory.[16] Essentially, from a Pakistani point of view, nuclear weapons would significantly reduce the chances of any aggressive Indian manoeuvres threatening the territorial integrity of Pakistan.

Overwhelming evidence shows that India's nuclear activities shaped Pakistan's nuclear policy and postures. Samina Ahmed aptly remarks that 'every landmark in Pakistan's nuclear weapons program links closely to its troubled relationship with India and to Indian nuclear aspirations'.[17] There is a consensus in Pakistani policy circles that the decision to pursue nuclear weapons was a product of Indian-generated security imperatives. When India conducted a nuclear test in 1974, Pakistan was simply left with no other option but to aspire to do the same, according to this logic (whether we call it realism or neo-realism). It was a core security interest for Pakistan to pursue nuclear weapons. A similar dilemma was faced by Pakistan after the 1998

Indian nuclear tests. Any Pakistani leader would have decided to demonstrate Pakistan's capabilities in a similar way. As Shamshad Ahmad, Pakistan's foreign secretary in 1998, maintained in a *Foreign Affairs* article: 'to restore strategic balance to South Asia, Pakistan was obliged to respond to India's May 1998 nuclear blasts'.[18]

In 1998 the internal Pakistani debate was not really about whether to respond to Indian tests or not, but rather to what extent it should do so, and how best to weather the international sanctions that would surely follow.[19] Hence, not surprisingly, when India decided to unveil its nuclear capability, Pakistan followed suit shortly thereafter. Similarly, in 1972, the discussion among policy-makers was not whether to pursue the path to nuclearization, but how long it would take and how much it would cost. Stephen P. Cohen, a leading American scholar of South Asian studies, sums up Pakistan's security dilemma while comparing it with almost identical challenges faced by the state of Israel:

> Like Israel, Pakistan was founded by a people who felt persecuted when living as a minority, and even though they possess their own states (which are based on religious identity), both remain under threat from powerful enemies. In both cases, an original partition demonstrated the hostility of neighbors, and subsequent wars showed that these neighbors remained hostile. Pakistan and Israel have also followed parallel strategic policies. Both sought an entangling alliance with various outside powers (at various times Britain, France, China, and the United States), both ultimately concluded that outsiders could not be trusted in a moment of extreme crisis, and this led them to develop nuclear weapons.[20]

A renowned Pakistani nuclear scientist, Pervez Hoodbhoy, however, differs with these security-driven explanations, and believes that the prestige factor provides a pertinent basis for understanding Pakistan's pursuit of nuclear weapons. He also frames this issue in terms of the state's need to distract the public's attention away from other state failures. Hoodbhoy considers this as one of the three 'critically important' elements of the imperatives for the Pakistani bomb, the other two being the 'nuclear shield' doctrine and the military dominance of Pakistani decision-making structures.[21] Hoodbhoy finds:

> The growing institutional malfunction and a feeling of collective failure have understandably led to a steadily deepening crisis for the Pakistani

nation. Pride and confidence follow from real achievement; conversely absence of achievement inexorably leads to diminished self-esteem. ... The psychological anguish must somehow be made bearable. Enter the bomb.[22]

He further observed that the Khan Research Laboratories (KRL) helped create a 'sense of achievement' in an otherwise bleak environment, and many Pakistanis took 'mental refuge within its four walls'. No longer just a secret laboratory, KRL became a 'sacred symbol', in his words, which must be protected at all costs, as the atomic weapons produced there were 'glittering objects' symbolizing the mastery of the most sophisticated technology. He went on:

It is important to understand the extraordinary sense of desperation felt by most Pakistanis as they reel before the rapacity of political and economic elites. ... The bomb provides to the masses a refuge from reality and an antidote to collective depression.[23]

Another important Pakistani scholar, Professor Rasul B. Rais, in a 1985 *Asian Survey* article argued that, other than the security considerations, economic and political factors were important in Pakistan's pursuit of nuclear technology.[24] In terms of economic motivations, Rais suggested the desire and political will to resolve the energy crisis, which affected commerce and prevented many industrial sectors from growing. This line of argument followed the official Pakistani position of the time. Rais' second contention concerning political motivations stemmed from Pakistani perceptions about Western suspicions and hostility towards Islamic countries. Rais believed that the distrust engendered by the differences between Western and Islamic culture and the subsequent nature of international relations between these divergent societies played a role in formulating public policy to pursue nuclear weapons technology. He concluded that in reality it was the political dimension of the nuclear programme that sustained Pakistan's interest despite significant political changes such as the shift from democratic to military rule and back again.

In comparison, Feroz Hassan Khan, a retired Pakistani army brigadier now associated with the Center on Contemporary Conflict at the Naval Postgraduate School in Monterey, California, believes that a mix of realism and strategic culture explains Pakistan's nuclear pursuits, though he has a peculiar interpretation of the cultural context. He calls Pakistan's success in developing nuclear weapons a 'story of defiance and ingenuity' and claims that 'the Pakistani public eulogized every innovative method applied by A. Q. Khan to acquire Pakistan's nuclear capability'.[25] He aptly maintains that this norm-defiance was indeed a cultural trait, one that is hard for the West to comprehend. Besides Pakistan's insecurity, engendered by its structural inequality with India, another critical factor, in his words, has been 'the intrinsic belief that Pakistan has been used by the United States and then abandoned when those interests were served'.[26]

Each of these perspectives is valid and accurate, as all these factors contributed towards Pakistan's pursuance of nuclear weapons; but the most powerful driving factor was the motivation to construct a deterrent against India.

The Making of a Civilian Nuclear Programme: 1954–1965[27]

Pakistan's nuclear programme began in bits and pieces. Pakistan's premier educational institution, Government College in Lahore, served as the nursery for many physicists who played a critical role in the development of the programme. Among them was Professor Rafi Mohammad Chaudhry, who had earned his doctorate from University of Cambridge in 1929 under the guidance of the famous British nuclear physicist Ernest Rutherford. He migrated from India to Pakistan in 1948 and established the High Tension Laboratory (with particle accelerator) in Government College's physics department in the early 1950s to pursue nuclear research.[28] A dedicated teacher and highly committed to promote science education in nascent Pakistan, he trained many of the leading future nuclear scientists of Pakistan.[29] Renowned Pakistani nuclear scientist Samar Mubarakmand, who had successfully led the team that conducted the 1998 nuclear tests, calls Rafi Chaudhry 'the true father of the Pakistani nuclear programme'.[30] This was said in a major speech delivered in November 1998 at the Punjab University in Lahore. Addition of the word *true* here was probably a jibe at A. Q. Khan, a mere engineer, who was often referred to as the 'father of the bomb'.

Pakistan was struggling to survive in its formative years, so setting up a nuclear programme was not at the top of its agenda. It needed to build an infrastructure for industrial growth, and investment in physical sciences was deemed critical for that. The establishment of the Pakistan Council for Scientific and Industrial Research (PCSIR) in 1953 under noted scientist Salimuzzaman Siddiqui was an important step in that direction. An opportunity however presented itself in 1954, through the USA's Atoms for Peace proposal, which President Dwight Eisenhower announced in a speech to the UN General Assembly on 8 December 1953.[31] The initiative offered to transfer nuclear technology and materials to states that pledged not to use this support for building nuclear weapons programmes. In retrospect, it was a noble but also a naive expectation. Inspired by this idea, the government of Pakistan shortly thereafter constituted a committee of scientists to operate within the PCSIR to brainstorm the country's options on this front. This effort ultimately led to the creation of Pakistan Atomic Energy Commission (PAEC) in early 1956.[32]

The United States Information Agency (USIA) organized an Atoms for Peace exhibition in Bahawalpur in January 1955, attracting an estimated 50,000 Pakistanis, who were amazed to see pictures and documentaries showing the evolution and potential of nuclear energy.[33] It was good marketing. The US policy experts were seriously considering Pakistan in September 1954, alongside Japan, Korea, Brazil, and Israel, for further study into the relevance of their potential nuclear development. The sequence of events indicates that the PAEC was a project that was conceived as a follow-up to the Eisenhower's Atoms for Peace vision.[34] On 11 August 1955 the USA and Pakistan signed a five-year agreement entitled *Atomic Energy: Cooperation for Civil Uses*, enabling Pakistan to later obtain funding for a small research reactor and technical literature on nuclear science and engineering.

Dr Nazeer Ahmed, another Cambridge-educated scientist who worked at the Cavendish Laboratory under Rutherford, was appointed as the first chairman of the PAEC. Indeed, he was one of the handful of scientists in Pakistan who could pull this off. The PAEC was tasked with:

1. planning and developing peaceful uses of atomic energy with special reference to survey, procurement, and disposal of radioactive materials;

2. planning and establishing of the Atomic Energy and Nuclear Research Institute and the installing of research and power reactors;
3. negotiating with international atomic energy bodies; and
4. selecting and training personnel, application of radio-isotopes to agriculture, health, industry etc.[35]

These lofty goals were too ambitious for the young PAEC given its limited expertise and resources. This remained the case until 1961. Nevertheless, Pakistan received economic investment through the Atoms for Peace programme, which allowed Pakistani technicians and scientists to attain greater knowledge about nuclear science and technology. Earlier, in 1953, Pakistan's foreign minister, Sir Zafrullah Khan, had clearly stated that Pakistan was not interested in developing a nuclear bomb.[36] For Pakistan's military, different factors were at play. For instance, Major-General M. A. Latif, who assumed his responsibilities as the commandant of the military Command and Staff College at Quetta in 1954, later recalled:

> On taking over as Commandant I found that the study of the various operations of war under nuclear warfare conditions was carried out in an elementary form and ... this subject had not received the attention it deserved. The time had come for us to start making a serious study of fighting the next war which would, whether we liked it or not, be fought with nuclear weapons.[37]

Irrespective of such security analysis, the harsh reality was that Pakistan lacked financial resources to invest in this direction.

While the PAEC's long-term investment in human resource development was destined to produce dividends, poor management and bureaucratic hurdles created by other state institutions also came in the way of its organizational growth. By 1958 it had completed a technical evaluation report and draft proposal for the acquisition of a CP5-type heavy-water research reactor (for power generation as well as advanced scientific research) from the USA, but the finance ministry vetoed the proposal.[38] The PAEC was very disappointed but could do little. Subsequently, the USA became more careful and offered only a light-water reactor (with an upper budget limit of $350,000).[39] The by-products of a heavy-water reactor could have military applications, whereas a light-water reactor was more useful for research and training purposes. Pakistan approached Canada during the process, knowing that it had offered India a heavy-water reactor in 1955, but the price ($7 million) was too high for Pakistan's budget at the time. Dr Nazeer Ahmed, in an address to the Pakistan Institute of International Affairs in June 1958, rightly complained that the procurement of nuclear reactors was being delayed for 'non-technical' reasons.[40] He did his best.

Things started changing when Oxford- and Berkeley-educated Zulfikar Ali Bhutto took charge of the Ministry of Fuel, Power, and Natural Resources in October 1958. He was young, brilliant, and ambitious. Twenty years later, recounting his influence over the direction of Pakistan's nuclear programme, he maintained that it was twenty years behind that of India when he came onto the scene. Bhutto attributed the gap between India and Pakistan's programmes to 'internal opposition to the program within Pakistan ... from certain powerful ministers and bureaucrats'.[41] He was indeed instrumental in the development and progress of Pakistan's nuclear programme.

Bhutto is credited with getting approval for the setting up of the Pakistan Institute of Nuclear Science and Technology (PINSTECH) in 1961, which later emerged as an excellent research forum and spearheaded efforts to send hundreds of Pakistani students abroad to obtain degrees in physics and other nuclear science disciplines, including nuclear reactor engineering.[42] Foreign education opportunities had been open since 1955 thanks to the Atoms for Peace programme, but Bhutto encouraged this trend and helped in the expansion of the relevant programmes. By 1960 dozens of Pakistani students were already studying in higher-education institutions in the United States, France, Canada, the United Kingdom, the Soviet Union, and at the International Atomic Energy Agency (IAEA), headquartered in Austria.

Another very important figure for the struggling programme was yet another Cambridge-educated Pakistani physicist, Dr Abdus Salam. He was among those who laid the foundations of Pakistan's nuclear programme infrastructure, but he had left the country in the early 1950s after being disappointed by the state's lack of support for science education. He was also troubled by the poor treatment meted out to his minority religious community: the Ahmadiyya. The brilliant scientist won the Nobel Prize for physics in 1979, becoming the first Pakistani—and the first Muslim—to achieve this distinction. Though based abroad, he was in regular touch with PAEC and played a pivotal role in its growth. According to another PAEC stalwart, Dr Ishfaq Ahmad, 'Dr Salam was responsible for sending about 500 physicists, mathematicians and scientists from Pakistan, for Ph.D.'s to the best institutions in the UK and US.'[43]

In 1960 Dr Salam, who was now serving as the chief scientific adviser to President Ayub Khan, facilitated the appointment of Ishrat H. Usmani, an accomplished physicist, as the new chairman of the PAEC. Bhutto, who was overseeing the PAEC as a cabinet member and who had originally appointed Usmani to the PAEC as a senior member, also pushed for this appointment. Usmani's rise to the top was a boost for the PAEC, given that he was a former civil servant in British India and was known for his competence and professionalism.[44] He was rather aristocratic in style and attitude, and that too helped him, as the bureaucratic elite in Pakistan cherished its colonial past. Most importantly, he had earned his Ph.D. from Imperial College in London, for his research in atomic physics under the guidance of the Nobel laureate Professor Patrick Maynard Stuart Blackett. He focused his attention on institution building, and had two powerful supporters: Dr Salam, who opened doors for him in the international nuclear science arena; and the rising political star Bhutto, who was President Khan's right-hand man.

Usmani had little time to ruminate, so he quickly focused his attention towards (a) acquiring a research reactor; (b) gaining international recognition for Pakistan's nuclear programme (for peaceful purposes); (c) seeking international cooperation for nuclear technology procurement; and finally (d) enhancing training opportunities for Pakistani scientists.[45] He started off by setting up two research centres, the Atomic Energy Mineral Centre in Lahore (for uranium exploration) and a similar centre in Dhaka (East Pakistan) in 1961.[46] Around 1963 he started work on Pakistan's first civilian research reactor, PARR-1, gifted to Pakistan by the USA, and he initiated the mining of uranium.[47] By 1961 the PAEC had sponsored 144 scientists and engineers who had either completed or were undergoing foreign education in the nuclear science and technology sector.[48] Usmani was constantly on the lookout for bright science students he could recruit for higher education. He also commissioned a series of feasibility studies about the potential of nuclear energy in Pakistan. One of the products of this exercise was the 'Study of the Economic Feasibility of Nuclear Power in Pakistan', a report jointly produced by two American firms Gibbs & Hill and the Internuclear Company in 1961, which became a standard reference on nuclear policy.[49]

In the meanwhile, Bhutto moved on to become the country's foreign minister in 1963, attaining more influence and authority in the corridors of power. Within a year he had started 'lobbying in earnest to harness nuclear technology for weapons purposes', according to a well-researched 2007 report by the International Institute for Strategic Studies.[50] After the Chinese nuclear test in 1964 Bhutto had concluded that India would also go nuclear, leading Pakistan to follow suit.[51] While making this argument, he was also presenting himself as someone who military leadership could fully trust on national security issues. This strengthened his bona fides with army generals at a time of military rule. However, not all of the military ruling class subscribed to the idea of a nuclear weapons programme. President General Ayub Khan, the commander in chief, was in fact quite sceptical about nuclear weapons, an attitude that the US administration, through enticing security guarantees, helped to reinforce.[52]

Bhutto continued his efforts to expand Pakistan's civilian nuclear programme. He was convinced that it would need this capacity in the future. In 1964 the Executive Committee of the National Economic Council (ECNEC) approved a project to build a 137 MW nuclear power plant in Karachi with Canadian assistance, but negotiations over the sale of the plant from Canada stalled over the question of inspections.[53] Pakistan's Foreign Office argued that Canada had supplied a similar plant to India without any such condition. Canadian negotiators responded by saying that Pakistan must accept safeguards in order to obtain the reactors as part of a Canadian government aid package, but they were ready to drop the inspections clause if Pakistan paid for the reactors out of its own resources. This made sense, and Pakistan agreed. Perhaps it was forced to, given its financial constraints. It is interesting that during the tough negotiations with the Canadians, the PAEC pushed proposals for a nuclear fuel fabrication facility, a heavy-water plant, and a reprocessing facility—crucial elements of a proper nuclear programme infrastructure.[54] These requests, however, were made without the approval of President Khan, and had to be retracted later.[55]

Pakistan's negotiations with Canada clearly exposed differences between Ayub Khan and Z. A. Bhutto. President Ayub Khan certainly agreed with Bhutto about the seriousness of Indian military expansion and modernization, but he downplayed the prospect of an Indian nuclear arsenal. He believed that shoring up the military alliance with the USA and improving Pakistan's conventional capabilities, which greatly depended on US military aid, would be best for country's security.[56] The president pursued that path without hesitation until his last days in office.

Shifts in Nuclear Policy: 1965–1971

Even though Pakistan did not—and perhaps could not—convert its civilian nuclear programme into a weapons programme platform in 1965, India's conventional military superiority and apparent interest in nuclear weapons created the conditions for a serious debate about the need for and feasibility of nuclear weapons in Pakistan's corridors of power.

The catalyst for this discussion was public knowledge: China's first nuclear weapons test in late 1964 and its reverberations in Indian policy-making circles. Homi Bhabha, chairman of the Indian Atomic Energy Commission, gave a media interview in October 1964 in which he simply explained that 'atomic weapons give the state possessing them a deterrent power against attack from a much stronger state'.[57] Bhabha also talked about the remarkably low cost of a stockpile of fifty 'atomic bombs' at $21 million—his calculations—and referred in some detail to the benign uses of nuclear explosives as well.[58] Later, he would go on to claim that India could make a bomb in eighteen months if it wanted to.[59] Bhabha intended to reassure his domestic audience, which was a bit shaken by China's nuclear achievement. Indirectly, he was trying to convince the Indian political leadership to pursue nuclear weapons. Pakistan was of course listening very carefully.

Bhabha's comments attracted international attention. George Perkovich convincingly argues that Bhutto listened to Bhabha's broadcast and became convinced that 'India was going to build the bomb. Therefore Pakistan would have to follow suit in order to deter its more powerful neighbor.'[60] Perkovich references British journalist Patrick Keatley, who in early 1965 insightfully reported 'deep anxieties ... in the key ministries in Rawalpindi, particularly at Defence, over the possibility that 110 million Pakistanis will wake up one fine morning to learn from Radio Delhi of India's becoming the world's sixth nuclear power'.[61]

It was at this juncture that Bhutto famously declared that if India developed nuclear weapons, 'Pakistan will eat grass or leaves, even go hungry' in order to develop a programme of its own.[62] Within a matter of months Pakistan signed a contract with the Canadian General Electric Company (CGE) to build a 137 MW heavy-water nuclear power reactor on a turnkey basis at Karachi. The Canadian government offered Pakistan a soft loan of $33 million and a supplier credit of $24 million to finance the project.[63] It came to be known as Karachi Nuclear Power Plant (KANUPP). By this point PINSTECH had expanded from its humble beginnings in 1963 and was progressing well, later producing its first batch of radio-isotopes in 1967.

Against this backdrop, Bhutto's ally Usmani moved the PAEC to become more independent as it worked through the legal requirements, making it an autonomous statutory body, arming it with discretionary powers and avoiding bureaucratic hurdles. Usmani, as a former member of the elitist civil service, knew the art of finding his way through the bureaucratic jungle.

Pakistan was also becoming increasingly worried about Indian nuclear ambitions and what that would mean for Pakistan's security. It raised the issue of India's nuclear intentions during a 1964 visit by the American Atomic Energy Commission chairman Glenn T. Seaborg, who in response assured the Pakistani government that India was a long way from making a bomb.[64] Pakistan was hardly convinced, because it was looking at a different set of facts: the inauguration of the Canadian–Indian reactor and completion of the reprocessing plant in 1965.[65] Pakistan's war with India in 1965, discussed in an earlier chapter, naturally complicated Pakistan's security dilemma. In early March 1965 Ayub Khan and Bhutto had met Chinese leader Zhou Enlai in Beijing. According to the transcript of his 1977 trial (when he was prosecuted by the military dictator General Zia), Bhutto hinted that he had sought China's help in acquiring nuclear weapons capability during that trip.[66]

In parallel, Usmani's efforts started bearing fruit: international interest in Pakistan's civilian programme was growing as it offered a new market for business and investment. French nuclear engineering firm Société Générale pour les Techniques Nouvelles (SGN) offered to supply a 100-tonne nuclear fuel reprocessing plant to the PAEC, but the anti-nuclear weapons lobby in Pakistan, led by Ayub Khan's finance minister Mohammad Shoaib, rejected the proposal.[67] Shoaib was loyal to Ayub Khan and was very friendly towards the USA. A declassified CIA document of 10 December 1965, 'The President's Daily Brief', refers to Shoaib's views about the politics behind Ayub Khan's visit to the USA:

> Finance Minister Shoaib, who favors closer US ties, described Ayub yesterday as now realizing that the divisions in the cabinet run too deep and ... identified Foreign Minister Bhutto and the ministers of information and transport as the "three musketeers" who had tried to prevent the US visit and were against better relations with the US.[68]

Bhutto was indeed trying hard to convince Ayub Khan to pursue a nuclear weapons programme. He claimed that he was certain that India was determined to go nuclear when he met Indian prime minister Jawaharlal Nehru in 1960 at the United Nations. Bhutto apprised President Ayub and his cabinet of his conclusions and pleaded for a nuclear programme, but to no avail.[69] He continued raising the issue of India's potential to go nuclear in cabinet meetings, and arguing in favour of building a Pakistani nuclear weapons programme. Irritated at Bhutto's persistence, Ayub Khan snubbed him at one of the meetings, noting: 'If India went nuclear we [Pakistan] would buy a [nuclear] weapon off the shelf somewhere.'[70] Ayub's remarks, obviously, did not reflect Pakistan's financial situation, but he had made his point. It cannot be underestimated how India's nuclear leanings pushed Pakistan to view things more strategically and change its policies in imperceptible ways.

Among Bhutto's supporters were Aziz Ahmed and Agha Shahi, two clever diplomats who understood his worldview well. This was the initial core of the Pakistani 'bomb lobby'. A later arrival was Munir Ahmed Khan, a Pakistani physicist who was serving as director of the IAEA's Nuclear Power and Reactor Division in 1965. A student of Rafi Chaudhry at the Government College Lahore, he was awarded a Fulbright scholarship, which enabled him to earn a master's degree in electrical engineering from University of North Carolina in 1952. He later worked at the Illinois Institute of Technology in Chicago and the

International School of Nuclear Science and Engineering, Argonne National Laboratory (ANL), from which he earned a certificate in 1957.[71] He tried to approach Ayub Khan soon after the 1965 war to talk about Pakistan's nuclear programme (through his elder brother Khurshid Ahmed, who was serving in Pakistan's federal cabinet at the time) but the president's office referred him to Foreign Minister Bhutto. Bhutto and Munir were acquaintances, but a meeting in Vienna later that year led to friendship. What Munir told him was simply music to Bhutto's ears. Bhutto arranged a secret meeting between Munir Khan and President Ayub Khan to convince him about the need for acquiring a nuclear deterrent. Munir had added credibility given his intimate knowledge about India's nuclear programme: he had personally visited the Indian nuclear facilities in Trombay in 1964, consisting of a plutonium production reactor and a reprocessing plant.[72] In a public speech in 1999 Munir recalled that the said meeting was at the Dorchester hotel in London on 11 December 1965, where he told Ayub that 'there were no restrictions on nuclear technology, it was freely available, India was soaking it up, so was Israel'.[73] Ayub was totally unmoved. He told Munir almost exactly what he had told Bhutto earlier: 'Pakistan was too poor to spend that much money. Moreover, if we ever need the bomb, we will buy it off the shelf.'[74] According to another version, Ayub said that 'if needed, Pakistan could get [the bomb] from China'.[75] According to Munir Khan's first-hand account, Bhutto was pacing up and down in the hotel lobby waiting for Munir. When Munir shared Ayub's response with him, Bhutto quipped: 'Do not worry—our turn will come.'[76]

Political differences between President Khan and Bhutto were gaining momentum very quickly after 1965; Ayub Khan was becoming unpopular and Bhutto's star was rising. Their differences ultimately came to a head in June 1966, when Ayub dismissed Bhutto. He was a military ruler after all, and a politically ascendant Bhutto was a serious danger to him. Pakistan's civilian nuclear programme, moreover, was now firmly on course, and could survive Bhutto's departure from power.

Military circles were now also taking interest in the topic. In the spring of 1967 General Headquarters in Rawalpindi invited PAEC chairman Usmani to deliver a lecture to army officers entitled 'The Mysteries of the Atom'.[77] He explained the functioning of a nuclear reactor and the role of the nuclear fuel cycle in the nuclear weapons programme, generating further interest and appreciation for the work the PAEC was doing. The post-1965 US arms embargo was now hurting the Pakistan army, and it was willing to think out of the box.

In 1969 the PAEC signed a contract with the United Kingdom Atomic Energy Agency (UKAEA) for a downscaled nuclear fuel reprocessing plant that mirrored the one at Windscale. The plant had the capacity for extracting 360 g of weapons-grade plutonium annually. A team of PAEC scientists left for the UK to receive training in this regard, and on their return recommended to the PAEC leadership that they purchase only key parts, and manufacture others domestically. The team also believed that it would be possible to upgrade the plant to produce weapons-grade plutonium.[78] This episode shows that some scientists within the PAEC were already thinking about how to develop the extensive infrastructure necessary for a nuclear weapons programme. Up to this point, however, the main focus of acquiring nuclear scientific and technological capabilities had been for civilian purposes. By this point the PAEC had helped develop and sustain eight medical and agricultural centres that trained around 350 scientists.[79] It had begun to make its mark.

Between 1960 and 1968 Pakistan spent 324 million rupees (about $170 million at the time) on the development of nuclear technology, and allocated another 400 million rupees (about $210 million) for KANUPP.[80] The first reactor school, the Centre for Nuclear Studies (CNS), opened in 1969, training nuclear scientists and engineers, and becoming a hub for scientists returning to the country after studying abroad.[81] The Atoms for Peace programme had helped Pakistan tremendously in developing the know-how necessary for running a nuclear programme.

Bhutto continued to play a critical role in making a case for the bomb. After leaving Ayub's government he, along with a few like-minded people, formed a new socialist-oriented political party (the Pakistan People's Party (PPP). He was more open now about his passion to acquire nuclear weapons capability for Pakistan. He took his arguments to the streets and made a public case for nuclear weapons. In his book *The Myth of Independence*, published in 1969, he forcefully maintains:

> If Pakistan restricts or suspends her nuclear program, it would not only enable India to blackmail Pakistan with her nuclear advantage, but would

impose a crippling limitation on the development of Pakistan's science and technology … our problem in its essence, is how to obtain such a weapon in time before the crisis begins.[82]

During the next two years Pakistan encountered political turmoil, and was forced into the hands of yet another military ruler, General Yahya Khan, who replaced the weak and demoralized Ayub Khan. Pakistani perceptions about the nuclear option were gradually evolving meanwhile, and Bhutto's pro-bomb narrative was gaining currency. The transformation was consequential. The shift in public perception reflected policy decisions, including the decision not to sign the Nuclear Non-Proliferation Treaty in 1968. By refusing to abide by this international regime, Pakistan signalled that it was not ready to rule out anything.

In fact, as early as 1963 Bhutto had raised the issue of India's potential to go nuclear in a cabinet meeting, and had argued in favour of building a Pakistani nuclear weapons programme. But Ayub Khan had snubbed him at the time.[83]

Ayub's departure signified the end of the anti-bomb lobby. The new ruler, General Yahya Khan, was too busy overseeing the dismemberment of Pakistan to think about anything else. The time was ripe for the rise of Bhutto to power. He won the 1970 national election by a good majority in what remained of Pakistan, and in 1971 Yahya Khan resigned, turning the government over to him. His education, charisma, and experience in government were unmatched—and he made it a point to meet the US president, Richard Nixon, before assuming his responsibilities to allay any American concerns about his priorities. He was not a particular favourite with the Americans, but he was charming, and that worked—at least for the time being. Bhutto was also lucky to be dealing with an American president who was not only well disposed towards Pakistan but also had a 'raging dislike for India and the then Prime Minister Indira Gandhi'.[84]

The Making of the Bomb: The Critical Phase (1972–1984)

The 1971 war with India, leading to the split of Pakistan, had far-reaching consequences on the Pakistan psyche. The loss of half of the country's territory was devastating for public confidence in the state's capacity to manage its affairs. Bhutto wanted to build a 'new Pakistan', but knew that he could not accomplish it without lifting the nation out of its demoralized state. He ended up employing nationalist slogans to heal the people. They wanted to feel secure, and Bhutto had to come up with short-term solutions. During the 1970 election campaign, and in many of the anti-Ayub Khan rallies, Bhutto had publicly made the case for a nuclear bomb.[85] He reverted to this mantra, and it did indeed energize his audience.

The time for turning his commitments into reality had arrived, and it didn't take him very long to begin reorienting Pakistan's nuclear policy. He started off by taking three important steps in this direction. First, he personally took charge of the Division of Nuclear Energy Affairs and created a new Ministry of Science, Technology and Production to expedite scientific development in the country. Second, he brought the PAEC under his direct control.[86] Third, he called a meeting of several dozen scientists and officials in Multan in January 1972 where, after being provoked by 'nuclear enthusiasts', he asked them a simple question: How long will it take you to make a nuclear bomb?[87] Dr Abdus Salam and Ishrat Usmani were sharing the stage with him at this not-so-secret meeting. This daring query, coming directly from the head of the state, was a strong demonstration of Bhutto's intentions and mindset. Many local politicians, bureaucrats, and even some Western journalists were also among the audience. Various accounts of the event indicate that the scientists' responses to Bhutto's query were more passionate than professional, each speaker claiming that he could make the bomb even faster than the previous one. Young scientists were trying to 'outbid each other as though at an auction'.[88] Bhutto was intelligent enough to be aware that Pakistan's nuclear programme was in its infancy. An interesting debate ensued when Professor Rafi Chaudhry emphatically claimed that only experimental physicists could make the bomb, and Dr Salam intervened to say that the nuclear programmes of the USA, Britain, India, and various other countries had been headed by theoretical physicists.[89] Despite all the drama and absence of any structured discussion on the pros and cons of the path Pakistan was about to undertake, this was a watershed event in the country's nuclear history. While Bhutto promised the audience that he would arrange the requisite finances, he also gave them a deadline: 'I want the bomb in three years.'[90] He must have known that this was too ambitious a target, but he was determined to inspire them. Bhutto wasted little time in placing key players into roles that would support his vision. He announced his decision to appoint Munir Ahmed Khan as chairman of the PAEC, replacing I. H. Usmani, during this meeting.

Usmani was taken aback at this move, even though he was promoted to secretary of the Ministry of Science and Technology. Some writers argue that Usmani was removed because he had shown some reluctance to pursue the nuclear weapons programme on the grounds that it was beyond Pakistan's ability at that time.[91] He was quite right. A more serious charge made against Usmani later on was that he was working for the CIA, helping them collect Chinese nuclear test data.[92] He was cleared after an investigation, but the whole exercise left a very bitter taste. It is difficult to deny that Usmani not only helped build the foundations of a strong nuclear infrastructure in Pakistan but that he was fully cognizant of the fact that his efforts were leading Pakistan towards developing future nuclear weapons capabilities. After a somewhat unceremonious departure from Pakistan he first moved to a position at the United Nations in Kenya and then in 1978 joined the IAEA, where he briefly served as the chairman of the Board of Governors.[93] After leaving Pakistan, he openly claimed that he had been forced out because he was not willing to steer the nuclear programme towards military use. In the Bhutto camp, this was interpreted as a self-serving agenda.

Bhutto handpicked Munir Ahmed Khan—who was popular in IAEA circles, with the nickname Reactor Khan thanks to his interest and training—for the PAEC leadership position, for several reasons.[94] Bhutto was confident that Munir Khan was fully on board with his vision of developing a nuclear weapons programme, and had wide international contacts and exposure. Munir Khan's significant institutional knowledge of nuclear power programmes across the world was an asset.[95] Last but not least, he was a smooth operator with excellent interpersonal skills which were useful both with Bhutto and with his colleagues abroad.

Munir Khan had a gigantic mission to pursue. Pakistan had lost a significant number of trained Bengali scientists—estimated to be over 200—to the new state of Bangladesh. The PAEC was left with only 283 trained personnel on its payroll in early 1972.[96] KANUPP was still under construction and PINSTECH was not fully functional either. No fuel-cycle facilities were in operation anywhere in the country, and without them no progress could be made in the nuclear arena. Mastering the nuclear fuel cycle was the top priority now.

The Nuclear Non-Proliferation Treaty (NPT) meanwhile had been in effect since March 1970 and Pakistan had not signed it. A cautious approach was in order. Munir Khan sought approval for a long-term nuclear development plan in May 1972, which received Bhutto's endorsement the day it was submitted. The plan called for the acquisition of a range of facilities to pursue the complete nuclear fuel cycle— from uranium exploration, processing, and conversion to a fuel fabrication and reprocessing plan for plutonium production.[97] Various committees and study groups functioning under several ministries were abolished with one stroke of Bhutto's powerful pen, and the Finance Ministry was instructed to ensure the availability of funds for the PAEC on a priority basis.[98]

The strategic nuclear road map developed by the PAEC was to obtain IAEA-safeguarded nuclear fuel-cycle facilities and approach France, Canada, and West Germany to begin with. Munir used his IAEA contacts intelligently and, in consultation with the IAEA, embarked on an ambitious plan to construct fifteen new nuclear reactors over a period of twenty-five years in order to meet two-thirds of Pakistan's power requirements.[99] According to George Perkovich, 'Pakistan's initial plan was not to divert or misuse foreign supplied reactors and a reprocessing plant to produce nuclear weapon fuel, but rather to use the know-how gained from this cooperation to indigenously produce parallel capabilities that could yield a bomb.'[100]

Munir Khan also encouraged further exploration of uranium deposits discovered in the 1960s and the refining of uranium that had been acquired from earlier mining. Good news came in December 1973, when the PAEC announced the discovery of large uranium deposits in southern Punjab. Munir Khan's aggressive approach was inspiring for the PAEC. With Bhutto closely overseeing the direction of the organization, and with a highly motivated group of scientists supporting his goals, progress towards attaining nuclear weapons gathered steam. At the least the PAEC was now thinking about all aspects of the puzzle— from fuel cycle to weapons design and from a highly trained workforce to delivery systems.

Aware that nothing could be left to chance, Pakistan started planning to design a bomb with the creation of the Theoretical Physics Group in December 1972 within the PAEC, led by a theoretical physicist, Riazuddin. A student of Dr Abdus Salam, he had a Ph.D. from University of Cambridge, which produced so many Pakistani nuclear scientists. His 1968 book, *Theory of Weak Interactions in Particle Physics*, co-written with C. P. Ryan and Robert E. Marshak, is still very highly regarded among physicists.[101] Dr. Salam told Munir Khan that Riazuddin was the right person to lead a team that 'would explore various technical aspects: the conceptual design for a nuclear device, calculation of the critical size of the fissile core, working out of a triggering mechanism, and finding the explosive yield for a variety of theoretical designs'.[102] Riazuddin headed to Washington immediately, and gathered as much information as he could from the unclassified and declassified documentation about the Manhattan Project from the Library of Congress and Technical Information Service in Virginia. He was utterly committed to taking Pakistan's nuclear project to its logical end. With great help from his colleagues, especially Masud Ahmed and Tufail Naseem, he successfully completed the highly sensitive task of designing the bomb by early 1978. That was a huge achievement in itself. It is worth noting here that the team involved in bomb-design calculations were frequently invited to the International Centre for Theoretical Physics (ICTP) in Trieste, Italy, by Dr Salam to use its ample library and research facilities.[103] Salam had established ICTP in 1964 after his attempts to build such an institution in Pakistan did not work out.

The PAEC was now working on various fronts, as Bhutto was living up to his promise that he would guarantee the flow of funds to this national task. Around March 1974 the PAEC established another important group—known as the Wah Group—to work on a nuclear device. The group took its name from a small city in the vicinity of Islamabad where they convened and met for 'research'. Pakistan's scientists decided to start working towards developing an 'implosion' type of nuclear fission device for its nuclear reactors (in preference to the 'gun' type option, which would require a higher volume of fissile material). Dr Zaman Sheikh, a chemical engineer and explosives expert at the Defence Science Laboratories—a military weapons

development organization working under the Ministry of Defence—
was tasked with focusing on the critical components needed for the
proposed device.[104]

When India successfully conducted a nuclear test on 18 May 1974
the power dynamics in South Asia changed significantly overnight.
Pakistan's reaction was predictable. Bhutto called a press conference
the very next day and declared:

> There is no need to be alarmed over India's nuclear demonstration. ... I
> give a solemn pledge to all our countrymen that we will never let Pakistan
> be a victim of nuclear blackmail. ... In concrete terms, we will not com-
> promise the right of self-determination of the people of Jammu and
> Kashmir. Nor will we accept Indian hegemony or domination over the
> Sub-continent.[105]

Within weeks, on 15 June 1974, Bhutto presided over a formal
defence committee of the cabinet and made the decision to formally,
though secretly, launch Pakistan's nuclear weapons programme.[106] The
Indian test was indeed the tipping point that altered the earlier 'capability decision' into a 'proliferation decision'.[107] It couldn't remain a
secret for long. In December 1974 Pakistani newspapers carried the
headline, quoting Bhutto: 'Ultimately, if our backs are to the wall and
we have absolutely no option, in that event, this decision about going
nuclear will have to be taken'.[108] In official communications with the
USA, Pakistan continued to maintain that its nuclear programme was
geared towards civilian purposes. At times Bhutto gave contradictory
statements, even in public, to assure the outside world that Pakistan
was not pursuing a nuclear weapons programme and that its efforts to
obtain relevant technologies were meant purely to cater to its energy
needs. It must have been very difficult for him to argue that:

> For poor countries like us, [the] atom bomb is a mirage and we don't want
> it. In 1965, when I was the foreign minister, I said that if India had the
> atom bomb, we would get one too, even if we had to eat grass. Well, we
> are more reasonable nowadays.[109]

It sounds hypocritical, but he was performing his role as the patron of
Pakistan's core security needs.

To expedite its programme the PAEC had started working on the
most efficient pathway to nuclear weapons, which involved the produc-

tion of weapons-grade plutonium. This route was similar to India's, and was easier than utilizing uranium-enrichment technology. Also, weapons-grade plutonium provided a logical choice to follow, as, once a country possessed a civilian reactor, a chemical reprocessing plant was the only additional facility needed to recover the plutonium (Pu 239) produced by Uranium-238 capture of a neutron resulting from the fission process. Munir Khan also had a better understanding of the plutonium route. As Pakistan followed this route, many serious obstacles appeared, including the now operational KANUPP reactor, which fell under the IAEA safeguards. Western states also ensured that Pakistan's access to reprocessing technology remained very limited. As Pakistan's ability to acquire reprocessing technology for plutonium was being blocked by the West, few states knew that Pakistan was secretly pursuing the highly enriched uranium (HEU) track at the same time.

Despite many stumbling-blocks, Pakistan continued its efforts on the plutonium route, and entered into negotiations with France to acquire an industrial-scale reprocessing plant. Pakistan ambitiously hoped to obtain the facility free from international safeguards and oversight. The PAEC was now desperate to learn and develop the expertise to be able to construct parallel capabilities that could yield a bomb. Developing a large nuclear infrastructure with foreign help and then attempting to convert it into a weapons capability programme was near impossible with foreign governments' conditions about following IAEA guidelines and safeguards. The problems Pakistan faced in negotiations with France for acquiring a reprocessing plant in 1975 is a case in point here. Bhutto was becoming frustrated and impatient due to the roadblocks that the PAEC encountered in this journey. Canada and France had categorically refused to live up to the agreements they had with Pakistan; and Pakistan was convinced that US pressure was at work here, which was indeed the case. Pervez Butt, who later rose to the position of chairman of the PAEC, while analysing the situation in the mid- to late 1970s, maintains that the Western countries 'were not simply denying us technology, their aim was to cripple the existing nascent nuclear infrastructure'.[110] The perception that took root at the time was that the West was especially uncomfortable with a Muslim country developing nuclear weapons capability.

It was in these trying circumstances that, in late September 1974, Prime Minister Bhutto received a letter via Pakistan's ambassador in the Netherlands from a Pakistani nuclear scientist based in the Netherlands, A. Q. Khan. Khan offered his services for Pakistan's nuclear programme, especially for delivering on the uranium enrichment front. His credentials were very impressive, earning immediate attention. After his graduation from Karachi University in 1960, he had gone to Europe, where he earned an MS from the Technological University of Delft in 1967 and then a Ph.D. in copper metallurgy from the Catholic University of Leuven in 1972. The same year he had joined Fysisch Dynamisch Onderzoek (FDO), a subsidiary of Verenidge Machinefabrieken (VMF), which was working closely with Ultra-Centrifuge Nederland (UCN). UCN was the Dutch partner of the Uranium Enrichment Consortium (URENCO). Khan had gained crucial knowledge of centrifuge-based enrichment processes by working at the URENCO plant in Almelo in the Netherlands from 1973 to 1975, where his tasks included translating a classified and critical German report on centrifuge technology.[111] His fluency in German and French as well as English came in very handy.

Bhutto verified Khan's credentials, and invited him for a meeting in December 1974. Khan needed little effort to convince Bhutto that the uranium enrichment route provided the best option for Pakistan to pursue. Bhutto could see that Khan had the requisite experience and skills to deliver this for Pakistan. He interpreted Khan's offer as a patriotic act and a well-meaning effort to rescue his motherland. There is no record of the first meeting, but it is safe to assume that Khan had been following Bhutto's security-driven statements, and that must have given him a fair amount of idea about his worldview. Khan's thinking about the Indian threat was the same as that of Bhutto. A.Q. Khan was immediately referred to Munir Khan, as Bhutto wanted to keep him in the loop on all his efforts pertaining to the nuclear programme. Munir Khan apparently suggested that Bhutto advise A. Q. Khan to continue to work in Netherlands and gather more information on the subject. That's exactly what Bhutto told A.Q. Khan in their second meeting (probably in late December 1974), which was also attended by two very seasoned and influential bureaucrats who would become A.Q. Khan's strongest supporters in future: Ghulam Ishaq Khan, who was secretary of defence at the time (and later rose to become Pakistan's president), and the brilliant Agha Shahi, the foreign secretary (who later became General Zia's foreign minister).[112]

Bhutto was doing everything in his power to reduce the financial constraints that had marred Pakistan's nuclear programme in the past. According to Shahid-ur-Rahman, a resourceful Pakistani journalist, Bhutto approved a $450 million budget on 15 February 1975 for a nuclear weapons programme using the enriched uranium route.[113] This plan stipulated the setting up of a uranium yellowcake plant at Baghalchur, a chemical plant at Dera Ghazi Khan for producing natural uranium hexafluoride gas (UF6) as feedstock for enrichment, and the gas-centrifuge plant at Kahuta for the enrichment of UF6. The million-dollar question is the source of these funds. A significant chunk of this budget provision certainly came from Libya.[114] This assessment will be discussed in more detail in chapter 6, which deals with Pakistan and Libya's nuclear relationship. Bhutto's approach to the newly oil-rich Arab states was a well-planned effort to raise funds for the project, and it worked.

The PAEC's advice was sought before inviting A. Q. Khan to return to Pakistan and help the PAEC's modest uranium-enrichment programme. For Khan it was a dream come true to return to his homeland. He said goodbye to Netherlands with his Dutch wife Hendrina and two daughters, and reported for duty in Islamabad in early January 1976. Pakistan's plutonium programme was in the doldrums at the time.[115]

A. Q. Khan brought a wealth of knowledge to the PAEC in terms of experience, technical know-how, and, most importantly, access to a Western network of suppliers. As agreed with Bhutto, Khan had expanded his network aggressively at URENCO during 1975, gathering critical information for potential use in Pakistan.[116] He also met many Pakistani nuclear scientists to assess the status of Pakistani efforts and gauge what would be required once he returned to Pakistan. He had started passing on sensitive information to the PAEC, while still employed in Netherlands, so that it could begin acquiring necessary equipment.[117] His conduit for these undertakings was a physicist named Shafique Ahmed Butt (S. A. Butt), who was the PAEC's chief procurement officer posted at Pakistan's embassy in Brussels. Butt was an intelligent man and a savvy negotiator whose contributions to Pakistan's nuclear programme were considerable. He had been successfully serving the PAEC's procurement needs since 1972, and luckily for Pakistan, he and A. Q. Khan got on well from the start, doing wonders for Pakistan's nuclear ambitions. He was known as the 'tactical commander' of Pakistan's nuclear procurement network.[118]

When A.Q. Khan finally joined the PAEC in January 1976, a small uranium-enrichment programme code named Project 706 (also known as the Directorate of Industrial Liaison) had been in place under the management of Sultan Bashiruddin Mahmood since October 1974. Munir Khan was directly supervising the nascent project, but there is almost a consensus among experts that it was going nowhere before A. Q. Khan.[119] A. Q. Khan was asked to report to Mahmood as director of research and development, but was unhappy about that, given his vastly superior qualifications. Bhutto had already approved the construction of a centrifuge research and development laboratory under an unassuming title: the Aviation Development Workshop (ADW).[120] It was a good cover, as this was located in the old barracks at Chaklala Airport, between Islamabad and Rawalpindi.

Within a matter of months A. Q. Khan ran into trouble with Munir Khan and others involved in the project. One view is that personality clashes and a desire for more control over the project brought the two Khans and others into conflict. What is often ignored here is the fact that A. Q. Khan was used to working in environments where efficiency and discipline were valued very highly. He had risen in his professional career because of his hard work and professionalism. The PAEC was quite different, as he quickly found out. It was more individual driven, and A. Q. Khan found it difficult to adjust. Disappointed with the lack of support from Munir Khan, A. Q. Khan told the prime minister that he needed financial and administrative independence to be able to deliver. He bitterly argued that he 'could have contributed at least ten times more' if he had been allowed to operate the way he wanted to.[121] Bhutto appeared receptive to A. Q. Khan's demands, as he was well acquainted with bureaucratic culture in Pakistan. He could see that jealousies were at play. To remove the administrative hurdles and bickering that had developed between the two Khans, he decided to give A. Q. Khan independent control of the centrifuge project. He did so by administratively separating the centrifuge project from the PAEC; the new institution was named the Engineering Research Laboratories (ERL). It was inaugurated on 31 July 1976, under A. Q. Khan's direct command. The ERL project remained a well-kept secret and, other than the prime minister, only Ghulam Ishaq Khan knew the specifics of A. Q. Khan's operation. As is evident from A. Q. Khan's recent writings (as a columnist for *The News* since 2015), he had complete freedom to hire and make appointments in the organization—and he was able to attract the best scientific minds in the country.[122]

Pakistan was active on the diplomatic front also. Bhutto had even sent special emissaries to Washington after the Indian tests in 1974 to lobby for nuclear umbrella and security guarantees, but to little avail. Pakistan was surprised that India had faced almost no sanctions of any sort whereas Pakistan could see the walls rising. Agha Shahi, Bhutto's foreign secretary, argues that had there been a positive response from the USA, Pakistan would have not started its own nuclear weapons programme and the world 'would never have heard of A.Q. Khan'.[123] Instead, Henry Kissinger, US secretary of state, tried hard to convince Bhutto to avoid the nuclear path—and offered him some incentives to do so—but in private he honestly acknowledged: 'It is a little rough on the Pakistanis to require them to do what the Indians don't have to do.'[124]

Pakistan went through some tumultuous events in 1977 owing to political instability caused by controversial elections and resultant street protests, spearheaded by the right-wing religious parties, that mobilized thousands across the country. Bhutto's brilliance couldn't save him, and he fell to a military coup in July 1977. The overthrow was directed by the army chief, General Zia-ul-Haq, who was known for his conservative religious leanings and cleverness. Bhutto, from his jail cell, claimed that the USA had played a role in his removal from office and had facilitated the military coup as a punishment for the nuclear weapons programme.[125] It was true that America had recently not been comfortable with Bhutto.

Like his predecessor, Zia took direct control of the nuclear programme. Munir Khan's fate was hanging in the balance given his closeness with Bhutto, but A. Q. Khan, with no political baggage, decided to reach out to General Zia and explain the vital nature of his project.[126] He succeeded in convincing him to further reinforce the ERL's autonomy. The rivalry between Munir Khan and A. Q. Khan became more entrenched from then on, and A. Q. Khan left no stone unturned in his efforts to emphasize that only he could deliver. The personal rancour also generated stiff institutional competition within the Pakistani nuclear complex. It was not a healthy competition on the face of it, but Zia could see some benefits. He decided to make good use of this schism. A. Q. Khan's uranium-enrichment project became his Plan A, and Munir Khan's plutonium route was now relegated to Plan B. Zia had the added advantage that the USA could not treat him as they had done Bhutto, as Pakistan soon emerged as a frontline state challenging the 1979 Soviet invasion of Afghanistan. This provided an unexpected but highly valuable cover to Pakistan's nuclear programme.

A. Q. Khan worked day and night to reproduce his previous work in the Netherlands. He succeeded in enriching a small amount of uranium for the first time in April 1978. The Kahuta plant, which opened in 1979, began producing substantial quantities of enriched uranium within two years.[127] In May 1981 President Zia renamed the ERL the Khan Research Laboratories (KRL) to honour Khan's significant contribution. While the KRL achieved these milestones, the PAEC also made critical progress, especially on the management of nuclear reactors, the development of a fuel-fabrication plant, and the oversight of uranium conversion. Many of Khan's top team members at ERL/KRL originally belonged to the PAEC, including G. D. Alam, Anwar Ali, Ijaz Khokhar, and Javed Arshad Mirza.[128] The PAEC's progress, despite losing many of its highly skilled and trained professionals to Khan's operations, demonstrated how it too was making advancements. As mentioned earlier, the work on nuclear weapons design was being spearheaded by the PAEC, while the KRL led the charge on a critical component of the larger nuclear puzzle: enriching UF6 into weapons-grade material. The remainder of the big picture, from mining to yellowcake to gasification and back again from gas to metal to milling and weapons fabrication, fell under the domain of the PAEC.[129] According to US declassified documents it was in June 1982 that British intelligence shared with their counterparts in the USA that they were getting reports of 'significant' Chinese assistance to Pakistan for nuclear weapons design.[130]

During this critical phase of Pakistan's nuclear weapons programme, Zia was very skilfully pursuing a strategic posture of nuclear ambiguity, neither admitting nor denying the presence of a military nuclear programme. The Americans had a good idea of where things were headed, but Zia's vagueness was useful for keeping Pakistan–US cooperation in the Afghan jihad theatre intact, where Afghan *mujahideen* (religiously inspired soldiers) needed all the support they could muster to defy the Soviets. America's trusted friend in the region, the Shah of Iran, had also fallen. Zia accurately gauged that the USA could not afford to lose another ally in the region and that India was too friendly towards the Soviet Union for America to trust it.

American warnings kept on coming though, as its intelligence reports—probably from its moles within Pakistan's nuclear programme and government—were providing it pretty accurate assessments. In March 1979 Warren Christopher, the US deputy secretary of state, visited Islamabad to alert Zia to the possibility of a suspension of American economic aid under the Symington Amendment to the Foreign Assistance Act, unless Zia could assure the US administration that it was not pursuing nuclear weapons. Zia readily assured Christopher that the Pakistani nuclear programme was at least as 'peaceful' as India's. He avoided commenting on any other aspect of the programme. However, Zia categorically refused to accept international safeguards on Pakistan's nuclear facilities.[131] The USA opted to apply a variety of domestic anti-proliferation laws to compel Pakistan to abandon its nuclear ambitions—but these came across as half-hearted attempts at best. The obstacles America was creating for Pakistan's nuclear programme were unsuccessful partly because the extensive international network that Khan had nurtured remained a step ahead of the USA.

The regional political situation meanwhile was changing rapidly. Zia was also more confident of his power base in the country after hanging Bhutto in 1979 on dubious charges that were sanctified by a criminal court. Zia sent his close confidant General Khalid Mahmood Arif (vice chief of army staff) to accompany Foreign Minister Agha Shahi on his visit to Washington in 1981 for deliberations on security matters. They met secretary of state Alexander Haig, who gave them the impression that the new administration under President Ronald Reagan could live with Pakistan's nuclear programme, but warned them against testing a nuclear device, which would probably take matters out of the president's hands and place them in the lap of the United States Congress.[132] The US intelligence knew in 1981 that the PAEC was digging a tunnel in Chaghai area of Baluchistan, preparing for a nuclear test at short notice.[133] According to 2012 declassified US documents, the Reagan administration had sent former CIA deputy director General Vernon Walters to meet secretly with General Zia in July 1982 to share US concerns about Pakistan's nuclear programme developments.[134] Walters had a very interesting conversation with Zia, after which he concluded that either Zia 'did not know the facts' or was the 'most superb and patriotic liar I have ever met'.[135] At the end of the day the USA knew its limitations and realized that it was not in its best interest to put Pakistan to the test at that juncture. Pakistan had planned well to make the best use of this situation.

The Israeli air force's successful targeting of an Iraqi nuclear reactor in 1981, however, alerted Zia to a potential development for which they had no plan ready. It struck them that the Indian air force could have a similar plan. Pakistan's chief of air staff, Air Chief Marshal Anwar Shamim, relates that General Zia notified him that India was indeed up to something on those lines, according to 'solid evidence' he had received.[136] Shamim told Zia that Pakistan's air force was not strong enough to counter such a strike, and advised him to use Munir Khan to reach out to India via his connections and convey that such an attack would provoke a nuclear exchange.[137]

According to Pakistani journalistic accounts, both the PAEC and KRL succeeded in developing a deliverable nuclear weapon independent of each other at roughly the same time.[138] The PAEC developed its first nuclear weapon design using uranium-238 (U-238) as a reflector around 1978 and conducted its first cold test (triggering the device without the use of fissile material) on 11 March 1983 under the supervision of nuclear scientist Dr. Samar Mubarakmand. According to one of the leading Western experts on Pakistan's nuclear programme, Michael Krepon, Mubarakmand was probably 'the brightest light in Pakistan's nuclear firmament'.[139] A graduate of Government College in Lahore, and with a doctorate in experimental nuclear physics from University of Oxford, Mubarakmand was also the man who was tasked in 1981—as a member of the PAEC's secretive Directorate of Technical Development—with preparing the Chagai nuclear test site in Baluchistan. He ultimately led the team that conducted the 1998 nuclear tests at this site. He is also credited with developing and producing Pakistan's solid-fuel missiles. Dr Mubarakmand claims that the

PAEC had started work on developing a complete 'nuclear weapons system' with missile-delivery capability in 1988, and that this was successfully completed in 1995.[140] A Pakistan air force F-16 fighter aircraft had carried out a simulated nuclear bombing exercise as early as 27 July 1990, but it took time to add sophisticated features and safeguards. The size of the prototype bomb was too large for a plane to land if the mission had to be aborted without dropping it.[141]

In parallel, A. Q. Khan claims President Zia specifically directed him in 1982 in the presence of Lieutenant-General Syed Ali Zamin Naqvi, adviser to the president on nuclear affairs, also to start work on developing a nuclear device, in addition to the uranium enrichment for which he was initially commissioned. He was told to keep it a secret, even from Zia's own senior staff and other important officials involved with the nuclear programme.[142] In pursuance of this mission, Khan claims that KRL carried out its own independent cold test of a nuclear device in March 1984 (in the Kirana Hills near Sargodha) that was deliverable through a C-130 cargo aircraft. While reporting this feat to President Zia in writing on 10 December 1984 he said that 'everything was in place at Kahuta to detonate a real nuclear bomb'.[143] Zia was thrilled, but cautious, according to his close associate General Arif: 'He was eager to witness Pakistan's nuclear ascendency, but equally wary of losing the billions of dollars coming from the US.'[144] Khan was told to wait for further orders.

Intriguingly, Khan had alleged that General Arif, Zia's deputy, shared a KRL weapon design with the PAEC; and the PAEC made a similar claim, that another army general—Lieutenant-General Zamin Naqvi— had forwarded their design to KRL.[145] They were basically accusing each other of stealing their weapon designs. It was almost childish. Also, it is believed that China provided significant help to Pakistan at this stage of the programme, especially with Khan's bomb-design efforts. In June 1985 the US State Department reported that Pakistan was now able to produce a workable explosive triggering package.[146] Some time in 1994–5 Munir Khan had told Dr Pervez Hoodbhoy 'that the Americans had angrily told him that Pakistan possessed detailed Chinese blueprints and drawings'.[147] Judging from the various accounts, there is a strong possibility that A. Q. Khan had received Chinese help as early as 1981, but that Pakistani scientists both at KRL and especially at the PAEC made significant improvements in the design over time.

A. Q. Khan, meanwhile, had started losing his popularity within the corridors of power, as he was becoming increasingly boastful about his accomplishments. In January 1987 he really tested Zia's patience when he gave an interview to a renowned Indian journalist, Kuldeep Nayyer, claiming that Pakistan had already developed a nuclear capability. The comment was immediately reported in India, and a media report followed later in March, creating serious issues for the government. According to a senior Pakistani nuclear scientist I interviewed, Khan was told by Zia 'to grow up and start behaving like an adult' or prepare to see the worst side of Zia.[148] The same day, KRL was told to transfer the bomb design project to the PAEC at short notice. The PAEC–KRL rivalry had served its purpose, and had now become a liability. It didn't matter much to Khan, as he was generally seen as the man who had delivered for Pakistan. The PAEC, in comparison, remained low key, but its success on the plutonium route was also monumental—and no less in importance than that of the rival KRL.

Khan, to his credit, was able to pull it off because he was an excellent planner and a highly resourceful and well-connected person. The following features of his strategy are worth analysing to understand the dynamics involved in Pakistan's nuclear weapons programme:[149]

1. *Extensive use of professional connections*: After returning to Pakistan, Khan approached several former colleagues to obtain specific technical information, and offered them lucrative business contracts to join his project. His key associates included: Heinz Mebus, a German businessman who had been a college classmate; Henk Slebos, who had studied with him at Delft Technological University in Leuven in the late 1960s; Peter Griffin, whom he met in London in 1976; Paul Griffin, Peter's son, who ran Gulf Technical Industries, one of the main Dubai-based front companies; Urs Tinner, a Swiss national and long-time associate of Khan, who also oversaw the production of centrifuge parts in Malaysia as a consultant until 2003;[150] Friedrich Tinner (Urs' father), a Swiss engineer Khan had known since the 1970s; Gotthard Lerch, a German engineer he had also known since the 1970s; Marco Tinner (Urs' brother, president of the Swiss

firm Traco); and Gerhard Wisser, a German mechanical engineer and an old acquaintance of Lerch.

2. *No financial constraints*: Khan had huge funds at his disposal, and he often paid up to 50 per cent more than the market price.[151] There was no auditing of the funds he received till the late 1990s, when army chief General Jahangir Karamat asked for an audit (which Khan strongly resisted).

3. *Careful monitoring of export controls and their systematic abuse*: When internationally regulated export controls on nuclear weapons-related technology were effectively activated in the 1970s, Khan bypassed the measures by purchasing individual components of technology rather than entire units. Khan imported 'pre-forms' (unfinished products), which were not necessarily covered by export controls, and at times he ordered unnecessary and irrelevant parts in huge quantities, disguising the acquisition of a certain critical component. To evade national export controls and legal procedures established by various manufacturing companies, the network systematically falsified end-user certificates, and even forged order forms. South African court documents detailed how two South African-based members of the network, Gerhard Wisser and Daniel Geiges, forged order forms for flow meters and other special equipment from Leybold in Germany for Pakistan's gas centrifuge enrichment plants. KRL also developed industrial facilities to manufacture domestically the parts that could not be easily be acquired from abroad, and he managed to use certain states such as the UAE and Turkey which were under less international scrutiny as trans-shipment points.

4. *Focus on self-reliance*: As Khan put it: 'Once the Western propaganda reached its climax and all efforts were made to stop or block even the most harmless items, we said enough and started indigenous production of all sophisticated electronic, electrical and vacuum equipment.'[152] The organizing principle behind this mode of self-reliance effort was to procure critical technologies ahead of emerging supplier-control regimes and tightening global non-proliferation norms.

5. *Extensive use of front companies and renowned Pakistani businessmen*: The network created front companies in Pakistan, Europe, and North

America. Help from some leading Pakistani businessmen of the time, such as Seth Abid and BCCI founder Agha Hasan Abedi, was also sought. Khan used both financial and nationalist incentives to solicit the participation of foreign nationals of Pakistani origin, especially for the procurement of spare parts.

6. *Involving Pakistani embassies abroad*: From the early 1970s to the late 1990s, Pakistani embassies around the world, especially in Europe (Germany, the UK, and France), were key components of the Khan network. Various embassies arranged the covert purchase of equipment and material, including electrical inverters from Britain and Canada; stainless-steel vessels from Italy; aluminium rods and vacuum pumps from West Germany; and vacuum valves and evaporation and condensation systems from Switzerland.[153] For PAEC work especially, support and collaboration with West German companies proved to be the most beneficial.

7. *Use of media*: Khan extensively and effectively used his contacts in the Pakistani media to print misleading news stories to divert international attention from any issue on which he was focusing at a given time. This practice backfired occasionally, when some deception was exposed by the Indian and international media, but by and large it worked well for the programme.

8. *Secrecy, effective management, and financial benefits for employees*: Khan used all his political capital to acquire extraordinary benefits— mostly education and healthcare—for KRL employees. He was known as an efficient administrator and a 'go-getter'. On the administrative side, secrecy was also an important factor. He maintained compartmentalization within KRL and introduced separate chains of command for various projects with in the organization. The separation of PAEC and KRL management also significantly helped maintain the secrecy of many elements of the programme.

Khan's public acknowledgement of his strategy in a popular Pakistani talk show in August 2009 is instructive:

People accuse me of stealing lists of European suppliers, but that is rubbish. I would travel from one corner of Europe to the other. I knew the addresses of all the suppliers. When I came to Pakistan, I started purchasing equipment from them until they proscribed the selling of equipment to us. Then we started purchasing the same equipment through other countries, for example Kuwait, Bahrain, UAE, Abu Dhabi and Singapore. They could not outmaneuver us, as we remained a step ahead.[154]

A critical factor in all of this was emphasis and investment in developing a large team capable of handling this sensitive project. A recently declassified CIA assessment of Pakistan's nuclear programme, written in 1985, attests to the fact that Pakistan's nuclear programme had developed a highly professional and dedicated team:

> Senior scientists associated with the weapons effort make up a well-educated, committed cadre. Key personnel included physicists, engineers, and chemists, most of whom received their graduate education and training in the West. ... Most of Pakistan's second generation of nuclear scientists have been educated in Pakistan with some specialized training abroad.[155]

The brief history of Pakistan's nuclear programme shows that a variety of factors were at play behind Pakistan's strategic choices in the realm of nuclear policy.[156] Prime Minister Z. A. Bhutto and President General Zia as heads of state, and Munir Khan, Samar Mubarakmand, and A. Q. Khan as technical and administrative managers of the nuclear programme, played the most critical roles from the formative years of the programme to its maturity. They artfully responded to developments in line with both their personal inclinations and the state's strategic preferences. Such a situation is not unique to the international security system. These myth-makers, as Peter Lavoy calls them—and Feroz Hassan Khan has also borrowed this framing for his work—functioned within the parameters of both the international environment and their state's political context, but they acquired enough flexibility to reorient and tweak policies, and even goals, when needed. Pakistan undoubtedly acquired nuclear capability primarily to counter the Indian nuclear threat. The project, however, was spun as an 'Islamic bomb' to motivate scientists and generate requisite funds from wealthy Muslim states.

All these individuals faced stiff resistance from their colleagues (or competitors), as well as from powerful states, but they were undaunted by pressures, incentives, and blackmail. As the nuclear programme progressed, domestic politics and civil–military relations became important factors driving nuclear weapons acquisition. A narrative of Western (especially US) betrayal and a sense of injustice galvanized Pakistani scientists.[157] Pakistan's list of grievances increased after

European countries stopped assisting it while India pursued its programme with relative freedom. The larger context of Pakistan's nuclear weapons policy remained security driven.

4

PAKISTAN'S NUCLEAR PROLIFERATION LINKS WITH IRAN

The relationship in the field of nuclear technology between Pakistan and the Islamic Republic of Iran remained active from 1986 to 2001, during which Iran received nuclear assistance from Dr A. Q. Khan, the head of Pakistan's Khan Research Laboratories (KRL). This included nuclear plant designs, construction of components, technical consulting, and shipments of related equipment. These transfers certainly aided Iran in its efforts to enrich uranium, though Iranians maintain privately that Khan initially provided them with defective centrifuges.[1] This author also heard this complaint directly from a former deputy foreign minister of Iran.[2] The most critical question here is: why did Pakistan trade its expertise, and what did it have to gain by doing so?

Pakistani nuclear assistance to Iran for over a decade and a half is puzzling on many counts. First, it complicated Pakistan's security environment. Relations between the two states became unstable during the 1980s due to the conflict in Afghanistan, as the two countries supported rival Afghan factions (even though these were on the same side in their fight against the Soviets). Also, the growing Indo-Iranian entente during the 1990s added another dimension that proved disconcerting to Islamabad.

In comparison to Pakistan's nuclear dealings with Libya and North Korea, the engagement with Iran challenges the explanations of nuclear optimists such as Kenneth Waltz, who argues that good nuclear stewardship is based on a realistic faith in the rationality of a state not to devalue its immediate security concerns. He asserts that states are unlikely to 'run major risks for minor gains'[3] because doing so jeopardizes the security of the state. Pakistan's assistance to Iran contradicts this assumption, as Islamabad apparently had little incentive to share its nuclear technology with Iran. One may argue that Pakistan's actions followed the precedent of the former Soviet Union, which significantly aided the nuclear programme of the People's Republic of China from 1957 to 1960. Soviet perceptions about its security changed when China's goals to become a regional power became apparent, and the technology transfers stopped.[4]

Moreover, the potential international repercussions outweighed any likely financial or political dividends, as two of Pakistan's most important allies, Saudi Arabia and the United States, would have been disappointed and angered had its dealings with Iran been revealed. Yet despite such obvious reasons not to supply nuclear technology to Iran, Pakistan—or, more accurately, a group of influential Pakistanis—nevertheless did so. Why did Pakistan trade its expertise? The situation in the late 1980s and mid-1990s (when nuclear contacts between the two states were most active) was influenced by factors that were complex and intricate. What were those driving factors? How did this relationship start off? Who opened this avenue of 'cooperation' for Iran, and who were the Pakistani officials involved in making decisions in this regard? Who implemented the deals reached between the two parties? What motivations in Europe drove this development? It is necessary and worth probing these dynamics to understand why Pakistan would gamble its security for what Waltz calls 'small gains'.

To understand all these aspects, this chapter begins by looking at the history of bilateral relations between Pakistan and Iran, their security perspectives, and the geopolitical influences in the region at various periods. The purpose is to examine the basis for the two countries' friendly relations, analyse the changing perspectives, and relate these views to regional as well as global developments. An understanding of these historical experiences is critical in order to examine the motivations, ambitions, and goals of both countries for engagement in the realm of nuclear technology cooperation.

History of Pakistani–Iranian Relations 1947–1985

Cultural Linkages

Relations between the peoples of Iran and Pakistan date back more than a thousand years. The rich Persian culture greatly influenced the traditions and customs of South Asians, especially in Muslim-dominated areas. Geographical proximity, ethnic and linguistic links, shared and similarly held religious beliefs, and regional politics played a role in this long relationship. The extent of this influence can be gauged from the fact that in the eleventh century the eastern city of Lahore (now the capital of Punjab province in Pakistan) emerged as a centre of Persian culture, especially in the arts and in literature.[5] This enlightened period was recognized by many Indian rulers who adopted Farsi (Persian) as the administrative language in local government.[6] Pakistani scholar Suroosh Irfani captured the essence of this growing identity fusion, calling it the 'Indo-Persian cultural matrix'.[7] He argues that this matrix constitutes a 'foundational plank' of Muslim identity on the Indian subcontinent and that the cultural osmosis in fact gave rise to an influential Shia minority in the South Asian region.[8]

Also of significance is that a small but influential number of Persian speakers lived in Pakistan, largely located in the North West Frontier Province (now renamed Khyber Pukhtunkhwa Province) and Baluchistan. Within the literary and intellectual circles in the country, knowledge of the Persian language was, and still is, considered a sign of scholarship and sophistication.[9] Almost all of the leading Urdu poets in South Asia wrote poetry in Persian as well. Urdu, the national language of Pakistan, also derives considerably from Persian roots. Even Pakistan's national anthem is written with Persian grammar. The long-lasting cultural links between the two peoples played an important role in strengthening Pakistan–Iran relations. This bond goes beyond any sectarian connections, but the fact that Iran is a Shia-majority state, and that around 20 per cent of the population in Pakistan belong to the Shia sect, is also relevant here.

1947–1950

Iran was the first country to recognize the new state of Pakistan soon after its independence in 1947—acknowledging the common heritage and historical relationship between Iran and the Muslims of South Asia.[10] Baluchistan, Pakistan's largest province, has a 900-kilometre border along the eastern edge of the Iranian plateau, which connects this area, ethnically and linguistically, with Iranian Baluchistan. Apart from cultural values, Iran's recognition reflected political and strategic considerations. The creation of another Muslim state in the neighbourhood was seen by Iran as a positive development. Diplomatic relations between the two states were established in May 1948, and Pakistan's first prime minister, Liaquat Ali Khan, visited Iran in May 1949.[11] Shah Mohammed Reza Pahlavi, more commonly known as the Shah of Iran, was the first foreign leader to pay an official state visit to Pakistan, in March 1950. In the words of Pakistan's former foreign minister, Abdul Sattar, the Shah received 'a memorable welcome by enthusiastic crowds'.[12] A 'Treaty of Friendship' was then signed between the two states, which extended most-favoured-nation status in trade affairs to each other.[13] Both states were experiencing security problems at the time. Iran was in the process of recovering psychologically from the Soviet occupation of Azerbaijan in the immediate post-Second World War period and needed an outside power to guarantee security.[14] Iran's security interests were also linked to the Persian Gulf region, whereas the nascent Pakistan was struggling to stand on its own feet, and its principal security concerns revolved around India and, secondarily, Afghanistan. As neighbours, regional politics and security threats from the former Soviet Union were of serious concern to both states, which were looking towards the West for security alliances. However, as Barry Buzan maintains, security complexes play an important role in regional alliances, but are not permanent and unchanging.[15] Both Iran and Pakistan were too focused then on the immediate concerns of security and the future appeared too distant.

The 1950s

With weak state institutions, a shaky economic base, and an entrenched feeling of insecurity, Pakistan was convinced that a strategy of external alliances was essential in order to survive and meet its security challenges. Slowly and gradually Pakistan moved towards Western military alliances as the USA eyed it as a potential bulwark against Soviet expan-

sionism in the area.[16] For Iran, joining Western military alliances created a period of political turmoil. The Shah was firmly in the US camp,
given the threat posed by the Soviets, but his political standing within
Iran grew weak. Meanwhile, Mohammad Mossadegh, the elected
prime minister of Iran, became a rising star and quickly emerged as a
popular and strong leader compared to the Shah. The two leaders had
serious political differences in terms of both domestic policy and
external relations. In the midst of the political tussle between them,
the Mossadegh's decision in March 1951 to nationalize the Anglo-
Iranian Oil Company (AIOC), a British company, had serious consequences. The British viewed Mossadegh's actions as hostile and damaging to their political, strategic, and commercial interests in Iran, as the
British company enjoyed a monopoly over production, supply, pricing,
and distribution of oil from Iran. Pakistan officially—and rather coura-
geously—supported Mossadegh's move, though it was not in a position
to help Iran in any significant way in the event of conflict.[17] Soon a
British covert operation in collaboration with the USA overthrew the
Mossadegh popular government through a choreographed coup in
August 1953 and restored the monarchy and the leadership of the pro-
Western Shah.[18] Iran returned to being a staunch US ally. Around the
same time, political changes in Pakistan in the wake of the assassination
of the country's prime minister, Liaquat Ali Khan, brought in a pro-
Western government. The governments of both countries signed a
mutual defence assistance agreement with the USA in May 1954, and
in September 1954 joined the US-led South East Asia Treaty Organization (SEATO) in Manila, with the aim of containing communism. With
Iran and Pakistan clearly allied with the USA, in 1955 they both
entered the US-led Baghdad Pact, which included Iraq, Turkey, and
Great Britain. Renamed the Central Treaty Organization (CENTO) in
1958, it was intended to contain the Soviet Union's influence in South
and West Asia. Their interaction via this platform brought Pakistan and
Iran even closer to each other.

Arguably, the Shia factor also played a role in this bilateral relationship.
Muhammad Ali Jinnah, the founder of the country, was a Shia Muslim, as
were many leading members of the ruling Muslim League.[19] The last
governor-general of the Dominion of Pakistan and the first President of
the Islamic Republic of Pakistan, Syed Iskander Ali Mirza, played a crucial

role in bringing the two countries closer. Mirza was a Shia, and his wife, Naheed Amirteymour, was Iranian.[20] During Mirza's tenure as the chief executive, Pakistan signed a frontier agreement with Iran in 1956 to resolve an Iranian claim over some parts of Pakistani Baluchistan. Since that accord the border between the two countries has not been a subject of any dispute.[21] Following the military takeover of Pakistan in 1958 by General Ayub Khan, Mirza went into exile in London. When Mirza died in 1969, the then military ruler of Pakistan, General Yahya Khan, rejected his family's request to bury him in Pakistan. Iran came forward, and Mirza's body was flown to Tehran, where the Shah gave him a state funeral. The episode points to the nature of the historical relationship between the Pakistani and Iranian leadership.

Common views on regional and international issues also brought the two sides closer. For Pakistan, the Kashmir issue became a very important yardstick to judge friend from foe. Iran, despite its efforts to cultivate good relations with India, backed Pakistan by way of supporting the US resolution calling for a plebiscite in Kashmir (to decide whether Kashmir should go to India or Pakistan). Throughout the 1950s, when the Kashmir issue came up repeatedly at the UN, Pakistan could count on Iranian support both within the UN and outside it.[22] Iran's argument was clear: 'Ninety percent of the people of Kashmir are Muslims and possess ties of common culture, tradition and religion with Iran. As such, the Muslim world and in particular the people of Iran cannot remain indifferent to their lot.'[23]

The 1960s

In July 1964 Iran, Pakistan, and Turkey, the three influential US allies in the region, founded the Organization for Regional Cooperation and Development (ORCD), which increased the level of interaction between the governments of the three countries. The ORCD increased cooperation in the economic, technical, and cultural fields outside the existing framework of bilateral and multilateral collaboration, and fostered feelings of camaraderie, easing travel restrictions and improving communications between Iran, Pakistan, and Turkey.[24]

During the 1965 Indo-Pakistan war over the disputed Kashmir region, Iran proved to be a reliable ally for Pakistan. Iran supported Pakistan politically at international forums, and its military support came in the shape of permission to use its air bases in Zahedan and Mehrabad for refuelling and for protected parking.[25] Iran also helped Pakistan purchase used fighter aircraft from Canada soon after the war, while it was blocked from acquiring the fighter planes due to the UN arms embargo imposed during the war. Iran acquired the planes from Canada and then transferred them to Pakistan on the pretext of installing upgrades.[26] Pakistan's defence circles were truly indebted for this favour.

It is interesting to note that, despite having different policies towards the Arab states, the two states remained strategic allies. For the Shah of Iran the anti-Iran rhetoric of Arab nationalists was worrisome, whereas Pakistan's relations with the Arab world were getting warmer as it was trying to garner as much international support as possible vis-à-vis India.[27] Meanwhile, the relationship between the Shah and the Pakistani leadership strengthened to the point where the Iranian leader tried to mediate in the conflict between Pakistan and Afghanistan. The Shah played a critical role in the restoration of diplomatic ties between Pakistan and Afghanistan in 1963, ending a two-year break in relations. He could do so as his own relations with Mohammed Zahir Shah of Afghanistan had improved, enabling him to persuade the latter to soften his support towards the idea of a Pakhtunistan, which was unbearable for Pakistan.[28] This was a prerequisite for any rapprochement with Pakistan. In the early 1960s there even was some academic as well as media discussion about a potential confederation of Pakistan, Iran, and Afghanistan; but the idea fizzled out quickly.[29]

Iran's cordial relations with and political support for Pakistan, however, did not imply hostilities between Iran and India. Iran kept its diplomatic channels with India open in the hope of benefiting from India's good relations with the Arab states. The Indian prime minister Jawaharlal Nehru's special relationship with Colonel Nasser of Egypt could help moderate the anti-monarchy (and hence anti-Shah) policies of Egypt.

Regional leadership changes brought Iran and Pakistan yet closer. The change of regime in Iran's neighbour Iraq in 1958 and the new Iraqi government's growing relationship with the former Soviet Union exposed Iran to new pressures. Membership of CENTO and the bilateral agreements with the USA were important to Iranian security, and Iran, like Pakistan, had also renewed the mutual defence agreement with the USA.[30]

The 1970s

The 1970s changed the nature of the Iran–Pakistan relationship in many ways, as the increase in Iranian power and stature coincided with Pakistan's decline in the aftermath of the country's dismemberment in 1971. During the 1971 India–Pakistan tensions, the Shah of Iran even told India that an attack on Pakistan would involve Iran. Pakistan was no longer the largest Muslim state in the world, and its self-proclaimed stature as the 'fort of Islam' was also dealt a severe blow after the debacle. As Pakistan's strategic power in the region faltered, Iran's grew in strength. The withdrawal of Great Britain from the Persian Gulf in 1971, and the Shah's desire to replace the British as the guarantor of the status quo, enhanced Iran's geopolitical standing in the region. More significantly, the rising importance of oil as a crucial factor in international relations increased Iran's value in the comity of nations. The Arab–Israeli war of 1973 and the consequent Arab oil embargo further improved Iran's financial capabilities. As the price of oil rose, Iran's annual income from oil grew from $4.9 billion in 1973 to $25 billion in 1975.[31] The climbing oil revenues and consequent financial benefit to Iran helped the Shah pursue his goal of regional supremacy more effectively. Pakistan's prime minister, Zulfikar Ali Bhutto, while explaining his relationship with the Shah before and after 1973, somewhat sarcastically said: 'Before, when I talked with him, I used to talk to him as a brother. Now, I have an audience.'[32]

India's surprise nuclear test detonation, Smiling Buddha, in 1974 sent shudders through Pakistan and, as discussed in chapter 3, Pakistan started heavily investing in its clandestine nuclear programme. Bhutto was in constant need of financial and diplomatic support, and Iran always responded positively. Within a couple of months of the Indian nuclear test the Shah confirmed the strategic alliance with Pakistan, saying publicly that, if necessary, Iran would intervene militarily in case of a threat to Pakistan's integrity.[33] In addition, Iran came through with investment assistance, although it is not clear whether Bhutto had taken the Shah fully into his confidence about his nuclear plans. From 1974 to 1977 Iran extended over $800 million in credits and cash transfers to Pakistan, to offset the oil-price increase in the international market and for development projects.[34]

Despite signs of a strong alliance, some marginal conflict existed between Iran and Pakistan. The Shah disliked Colonel Muammar al-Qaddafi of Libya, whom he referred to as a 'crazy man'. In fact, it is believed that the Shah refused to attend the Islamic heads of state summit in Pakistan in 1973 as a snub to Pakistan for being close to Qaddafi.[35] However, the Shah's state visit to Pakistan in March 1976 shows that the relationship remained warm.

Important political changes in the region in the late 1970s, however, impacted on the relationship between the two neighbours. The imposition of martial law in Pakistan by General Mohammad Zia-ul-Haq in 1977, the invasion of Afghanistan in 1979 by the former Soviet Union, and the Islamic revolution in 1979, leading to the Shah's ignominious exit from Iran, changed the regional scene altogether. Pakistan was among the first countries to recognize the new government in Iran.

1980–1985

The Soviet invasion of Afghanistan and the subsequent regional instability raised similar concerns for both Pakistan and Iran, encouraging them to coordinate their response. Meanwhile, US–Iranian relations deteriorated significantly due to the anti-American tone of the Islamic revolution in Iran, and the hostage crisis at the American embassy in Tehran. In parallel, the US–Pakistan relations started warming up as their mutual interests in Afghanistan coincided.

Within Pakistan, religious political parties such as the Jamaat-e-Islami (the Party of Islam [JI]), started working with the Zia government to support the Afghan 'jihad'—a choreographed Afghan holy resistance, conceived by the Pakistani intelligence services, and fully sponsored and funded by the Americans and the Saudis. This campaign was anti-communist in essence, but religious motivation was deemed to be a critical element. Few could visualize how this approach would ignite sectarian tendencies in the long run; for the time being, relations between Sunni-dominated Pakistan and Shia Iran remained cordial.

In fact, Pakistan's Sunni religious parties, especially JI, had a good rapport with the Shia clergy in Iran. For instance, the condemnation of Salman Rushdie's *The Satanic Verses*, which led to an international diplomatic crisis, was in large measure precipitated by the JI. Ayatollah

Khomeini, the supreme leader of Iran, took notice of *The Satanic Verses* because of the JI's ability to mobilize resources in England, Saudi Arabia, and South Asia in protest against the book.[36] The founder and chief ideologue of the JI, Abul Ala Maududi, commenting on the Islamic revolution in Iran, said that he wished he had accomplished what Khomeini had, and that he would have liked to visit Iran to see the revolution for himself.[37] He could not visit Iran due to ill health, but sent a JI delegation soon after the revolution.

While revolutionary developments in Iran were being followed with alarm in the West, Pakistan under Zia gradually became more cautious about its relations with Iran so as not to raise suspicions in Washington. Zia's growing relationship with Saudi Arabia and warm relations with the USA were also not viewed positively by the new regime in Iran. Khomeini's denunciation of the West was however quite popular among sections of Pakistanis. Many Pakistani intellectuals felt genuinely inspired by the rise of an Islamic revolutionary state, and some began to investigate a trans-regional relationship between Muslim South Asia and Iranian revolutionaries. A few even argued that South Asian Muslim reformers such as Dr Mohammad Iqbal (1875–1938), the man who came up with the idea of Pakistan, had in fact provided the intellectual framework to Ayotallah Khomeini and another Iranian scholar-activist, Dr Ali Shariati, for the concept of an Islamic renaissance.[38] According to Nikki Keddie, a leading American scholar of Iran's history, there was a group in Pakistan 'mostly Shi'a, who admire Ayatollah Khomeini as a great leader who has stood up to the US and the West without falling under the Soviet Union'.[39]

Pakistan was trying to balance its relations with the USA and Iran. Abdul Sattar, former foreign secretary and foreign minister of Pakistan, explained that 'the Iranian media perception of Pakistan as a proxy for US interests in the region was painful to Pakistanis, who value Iran as a friend and a fraternal neighbor'.[40] Despite a fast-developing partnership with the USA, Pakistani officials felt compelled to criticize US actions against Iran in April 1980. It expressed 'shock and dismay' at the US assault on Iran to rescue its embassy staff from hostage takers and 'deplored this impermissible act which constitutes a serious violation of Iran's sovereignty'.[41] It was another matter that the US attack had failed. There was no condemnation of the hostage takers who had violated international law by forcibly holding diplomats.

For Pakistan, the Iraq–Iran War (1980–8) became the quintessential test case of maintaining a balance between Arab friends (especially Saudi Arabia, which was supporting Iraq) and Iran, since it could not please one side at the expense of the other. The dilemma that Pakistan faced concerned the substantial financial support Saudi Arabia was channelling for the Afghan jihad, as Iran routinely rebuked the Arab sheikhs and rulers as 'blots' on the Muslim character. While Pakistan never had a special relationship with Iraq, it did with Iraq's supporters: Jordan, Saudi Arabia, and the Gulf states. It was not easy to take sides. General Zia's modest efforts at arbitration between Iraq and Iran in the early 1980s were little more than superficial overtures. Ultimately, he opted to extricate himself from the quagmire by issuing a few moralizing statements on ending fratricide among Muslims.[42]

In 1985 the ORCD returned to life after a virtual shutdown in 1979. Resurrected as the Economic Cooperation Organization (ECO), it added seven new members in the early 1990s.[43] As this brought renewed interaction between the officials of these states, relations between Pakistan and Iran were becoming even more complicated due to the rise of sectarianism in Pakistan. Saudi Arabia, seriously concerned about the rising influence of the Shias in the region, was actively supporting anti-Shia militant groups in Pakistan around the mid-1980s. Conversely, some Shia groups started receiving funds from Iran.[44]

Relations between Pakistan's president General Zia and Iran's supreme leader Ayatollah Khomeini were also less than cordial. In fact, Zia knew well that Khomeini did not like him. Khomeini was aware that Zia had gone to Tehran in 1977, while the Shah was still the head of state, and had urged the Shah to crack down on revolutionary forces in the street.[45] Later, when Zia visited Iran to meet Khomeini, he was given a cold reception.[46] According to Pakistani journalist-turned-politician Mushahid Hussain, when the then US vice president George Bush visited Pakistan in 1984, he proposed an intriguing plan to General Zia. He offered US help for Pakistan to train some Afghan *mujahideen* in Baluchistan to destabilize Iran. Zia, however, was not ready to entertain this idea.[47] Pakistan's relations with Iran were by the mid-1980s still somewhat tepid.

Iran's Pursuit of Nuclear Technology

As discussed in chapter 3, Pakistan's nuclear programme, well established by 1985–6, drew from a network of nuclear material suppliers in the black market, local as well as international financiers, and various front companies that Pakistan had created to supply its nuclear requirements. A. Q. Khan's genius and expertise of course played a central role in developing an enterprise consisting of loosely connected intermediaries that gradually took a shape of its own to expand its reach and attract more customers. As David Albright and Corey Hinderstein argue, Khan and his associates slowly expanded their import operation into a transnational business network that 'exported gas centrifuges and production capabilities, as well as designs for nuclear weapons, to other, mostly Muslim countries to turn a profit and provide additional business for their international collaborators'.[48] Providing nuclear technology consulting services became a favourite sideline of Khan's, and Iran became his first client in 1987.

Before proceeding into further details about the nature of the 1987 collaboration, it is pertinent to briefly look at the history, nature, and status of Iran's nuclear programme in 1987 so as to fully understand the impact of this network's support to the Iranian programme. Iran had launched its pursuit of nuclear technology a quarter century before the 1979 revolution, and with significant support from the USA. Here is a glimpse of the basic facts in chronological order:[49]

1957: The First Step

The United States and Iran signed a civil nuclear cooperation agreement as part of the US Atoms for Peace programme, much like Pakistan. The agreement provided for technical assistance and the lease of several kilograms of enriched uranium for the purpose of research cooperation in pursuit of peaceful uses of nuclear energy.[50] CENTO's Institute of Nuclear Science moved from Baghdad to Tehran, and the Shah started taking special interest in nuclear energy, according to his memoirs.[51]

1960–7: Acquiring Research Reactor and US Support

Iran completed the formalities to purchase, from the USA, a 5 MW reacton for a nuclear research centre at Tehran University.[52] The USA supplied 5.545 kilograms of enriched uranium (93 per cent) to Iran for fuel in a research reactor. It also supplied Iran 112 grams of plutonium, for use as in the research reactor.[53]

1968–9: Signing the NPT

Iran signed the Nuclear Non-Proliferation Treaty (NPT) on 1 July 1968, the day it was opened for signatures. The USA extended the Iran–United States Agreement for Cooperation concerning Civil Uses of Atomic Energy of 1957 for another ten years.[54]

1972–3: Long-Term Plans and Outreach

After ratifying the NPT in 1970 the Iranian government announced that it intended to acquire nuclear power plants within the next ten years.[55] Secret nuclear collaboration between Argentina and Iran strengthened, and Argentinian scientists regularly visited Iran.[56]

1974: Aggressive Pursuit of Nuclear Technology

Iran provided a $1 billion loan to Commissariat à l'Énergie Atomique (CEA) to build a uranium enrichment plant at Tricastin in France for the Eurodif consortium. In return, Iran would receive a 10 per cent stake in the plant.[57] This deal was cancelled in 1979. Iran also announced the establishment of the Atomic Energy Organization of Iran (AEOI), with the Swiss-trained nuclear physicist Dr Akbar Etemad as its chairman, and set $30.8 million as the first year's budget. A communiqué was issued by the Indian prime minister, Indira Gandhi, during her visit to Iran, undertaking that contacts would be made 'between the atomic energy organizations in the two countries in order to establish a basis for cooperation in this field'.[58] Little came out of that exercise, but it showed that nuclear issues were on the agenda in all major meetings with foreign dignitaries.

In June that year the Shah stunned everyone by declaring that Iran would develop nuclear weapons 'without a doubt'; he had to back off later, reassuring everyone that 'not only Iran, but also other nations in the region should refrain from planning to gain atomic arsenals'.[59] In the same month, AEOI chairman Akbar Etemad and the Shah travelled to Paris, where France and Iran ratified a preliminary agreement for France to supply five 1,000 MWe reactors, uranium, and a nuclear research centre to Iran (though no progress was made on the agreement).[60] Similar contracts were signed with West Germany. Denmark also supplied Iran with 10 kilograms of highly enriched uranium (HEU) and 25 kilograms of natural uranium for research reactor fuel.[61] Formation of a US–Iranian joint commission was also agreed upon for enhancing cooperation in the field of nuclear energy and power generation.

1975: Developing Expertise and Infrastructure

Iran sent over a hundred students to Western universities for advanced training in nuclear science, and planned to send three hundred more in 1976 to West Germany, the United States, France, and the United Kingdom.[62] The Massachusetts Institute of Technology (MIT) signed a contract with the AEOI to provide training for Iranian nuclear engineers. The Atomic Energy Commissions of the ORCD (Pakistan, Iran, and Turkey) also decided to evaluate prospects for a joint atomic energy organization.[63] The Shah also remarked that Iran had no plans for acquiring nuclear weapons but that if small states (referring probably to Pakistan) began building them, then Iran might reconsider its policy.[64] Negotiations with the USA for acquiring nuclear reactors also continued, while the budget for the AEOI was increased to $1 billion for 1976.[65]

1976: Aggressive Investment in Developing Nuclear Infrastructure

In a secret arrangement, South Africa agreed to supply $700 million of yellowcake to Iran in return for Iran helping to finance an enrichment plant in South Africa.[66] Also, Kraftwerk Union of West Germany won a contract to construct nuclear plants in Iran (though the contract was later cancelled after the revolution).[67] The same year, AEOI signed an agreement with Kraftwerk Union of West Germany for the construction of the Bushehr nuclear power plant at a cost of DM7.8 billion.[68] While talks between Iran and the United

States on nuclear cooperation were suspended after a disagreement on safeguards issue, Iran signed another contract with France to purchase two reactors on short notice.[69]

1977: Purchase Deals Start Materializing

Iran finalized many deals to acquire uranium-enrichment services, nuclear plants, and nuclear power generators from France, West Germany, and the USA.[70] Iran also signed a contract with Austria for cooperation in nuclear waste storing, while France agreed to train 350 Iranian technicians.[71]

1978: Financial and Political Obstacles

Pending issues with the USA in relation to safety matters were resolved during the year, and the USA also agreed to sell Iran between six and eight light-water nuclear reactors.[72] Meanwhile, Akbar Etemad, director of the AEOI, was forced out due to charges of mismanagement and embezzlement which apparently also led to the cancellation of Iran's contract with Kraftwerk Union for four nuclear reactors. AEOI was then absorbed in to the Ministry of Energy to improve monitoring of the programme. Iran also diverted some of its resources from the nuclear programme to social spending, due to serious political problems faced by the Shah's regime.[73] Some analysts believed (based on US intelligence data) that the Shah had set up a clandestine nuclear weapons development programme.[74] The Tehran Nuclear Research Center (TNRC) was also tasked by the Shah to develop a nuclear weapons design at about this time. It is further confirmed by the Shah's close confidant Asadollah Alam in his memoirs that the Shah had envisioned Iran having nuclear weapons.[75]

According to newly declassified US documents pertaining to the US–Iran nuclear negotiations in the 1970s, both Presidents Ford and Carter—the two presidents who worked closely with the Shah of Iran on the subject—were quite concerned about proliferation potential and the Shah's possible desire to pursue nuclear weapons, and they framed their negotiating positions and relevant policies accordingly.[76]

1979: Nuclear Programme Rollback

The Islamic revolution in Iran changed the priorities of the new government; Prime Minister Mehdi Bazargan decided that Iran did not need nuclear energy, and the work at Bushehr was halted in February 1979.[77] The Bushehr nuclear power plant was worth $5 billion, and though not finished it was 85 per cent complete at that stage. Predictably, the USA immediately stopped its supply of HEU to Iran, while Iran also cancelled its contracts with France and the Eurodif consortium, demanding full repayment of the $1 billion loan it had provided for the construction of the Tricastin plant.[78] In April Fereydun Sahabi, Iran's deputy minister of energy and supervisor of the AEOI, stated that the AEOI was significantly cutting back its activities and that, except for the construction work on two power stations/nuclear facilities in Bushehr, all other nuclear power projects would be cancelled.[79] The number of AEOI employees was cut from an estimated 4,500 to 800.[80] All of this was directed by Ayatollah Khomeini, who declared nuclear weapons to be 'the work of the devil and un-Islamic'.[81] Rolf Mowatt-Larssen in his insightful report 'Islam and the Bomb: Religious Justification for and against Nuclear Weapons', establishes the authenticity of Khomeini's *fatwa* (religious edict) on the subject, which declared that:

> The Islamic Republic of Iran, based on its fundamental religious and legal beliefs, would never resort to the use of weapons of mass destruction. ... In contrast to the propaganda of our enemies, fundamentally we are against any production of weapons of mass destruction in any form.[82]

1980–3: Development of Nuclear Capabilities on the Back Burner

Though there are varying accounts of whether Iran was pursuing nuclear technology during the early 1980s, it is clear that the nuclear programme was not something that fascinated the Iranian government during this period. Iran appeared to be more interested in retrieving the financial investments it had made in this project.[83] Iran was also involved in various arbitrations during these years with countries and companies it had contracts with (for importing nuclear reactors, etc.) and there was certainly some interest in completing Bushehr, though hardly any progress was made. Iran even attempted—almost successfully—to hire the expertise of Indian scientists for the completion of the Bushehr project, but American pressure on India scuttled the prospects.[84]

1984–6: Nuclear Facilities under Attack

During its war with Iran, Iraq bombed the Bushehr site on six occasions (in March 1984, February 1985, March 1985, July 1986, and twice in November 1987), significantly damaging both reactor facilities under construction.[85] Iran meanwhile started work on a nuclear research centre at Isfahan with the assistance of China, but it was a small project with limited scope.[86] Before these Iraqi attacks, Iran had approached a West German company to discuss the acquisition of the remaining equipment for the Bushehr reactors.[87] In 1985 Iran had discovered 'high-quality uranium' in the Saghand region of the Yazd province after many years of exploratory work.

Four Phases of Pakistan–Iran Nuclear Cooperation

There is no doubt now that Iran revived its nuclear weapons programme after Iraq repeatedly used chemical weapons against it in the mid-1980s.[88] According to a Monterey Institute of International Studies report on the use of chemical weapons in the Iran–Iraq War, 'during the period 1984 to 1986, Iraq's use of CW [chemical weapons] was gradual, but from 1987 to 1988, Iraq intensified the tempo and scope of its chemical weapons … the major powers appeared disinterested or unwilling to recognize the gravity of Iraq's use of CW'.[89] Beside inflicting heavy casualties (around 60,000), the use of chemical weapons had a debilitating psychological impact on Iranian civilians as well as the military.[90] These horrible circumstances forced Iran to re-evaluate its security options and resurrect its nuclear programme. While some members of the Iranian clergy—in line with Khomeini's guidance—continued to argue that such weapons were against Islamic principles, various senior Iranian officials and clerics began to assert 'Iran's right to have nuclear weapons and … to produce weapons grade materials'.[91]

Incidentally, it is during this same period (late 1986–early 1987) that Pakistan's nuclear scientists belonging to Khan Research Laboratories (KRL) published some research papers describing the construction of more advanced centrifuges for uranium enrichment. A. Q. Khan also contributed to these papers. According to the *New York Times'* David Sanger, some of these papers published in 1987–8 even gave details of how to pursue the difficult steps in the construction of centrifuges, reaching beyond first-generation aluminium rotors to produce more efficient centrifuges out of maraging steel.[92] According to a 2007 study by the London-based International Institute of Strategic Studies (IISS), this boasting attracted the attention of Iranian intelligence operatives, who then 'entered into direct communications concerning possible business transactions with Khan and his cohorts'.[93]

Pakistan's nuclear links with Iran form a complex two-decade episode, and the relationship can be divided into four distinct phases, from 1986 to 2007:

1. The 1987 deal—access to Khan's expertise;
2. The 1988–92 phase—efforts to implement and expand the 1987 deal;
3. The 1993–5 phase—transfer of centrifuges and continued contacts between Khan and Iran until 2000;
4. Post-2004 phase—deterioration in Pakistan–Iran relations after the international exposure of the dangerous transfers, and allegations by both the states, blaming each other for divulging critical information about the secret deals to the IAEA.

The 1987 Deal

Iran reactivated procurement of nuclear programme-related items in 1985. For instance, in 1985 it acquired key 'flow-forming' equipment, useful in forming steel and aluminium centrifuge tubes, from the German firm Leifeld.[94] According to its 2003 declarations to the IAEA, it began its gas centrifuge programme in 1985 in order to make fuel for the German-supplied Bushehr power reactor, but this claim is doubtful as all the work on the said reactor was suspended at that time due to the ongoing war.[95] Iran had little expertise at the time to conceive the plan. Many Iranian scientists had left the country in the aftermath of the Shah's fall. On 6 November 1985 the foreign edition of the Iranian newspaper *Kayhan* (published in London) carried a government advertisement inviting nuclear scientists of Iranian origin to attend a nuclear science and technology conference in March 1986 in Iran. The results were not encouraging at all.

Iran was getting desperate, as Iraq's brutal military campaign, laced with chemical weapons and sponsored by many Arab neighbours and their Western allies, was becoming overwhelming. Iran approached the government of Pakistan in 1986, hoping to increase defence cooperation between the two countries. Iranian president Ali Khamenei's official visit to Pakistan in February 1986 was a step in this direction.[96] This led to an increased exchange of official delegations.[97] Some experts believe that A. Q. Khan visited Iran's Bushehr reactor to inspect the damage caused by Iraqi bombing of the facility in February 1986, but this claim lacks credibility.[98] Khan in his detailed 2011 statement about his nuclear proliferation activities claims that he never visited Iran.[99] Pakistan meanwhile started importing oil from Iran in 1986, which improved bilateral economic ties.[100]

Cooperation in the nuclear field began with a group visit of Iranian nuclear scientists to Pakistan in 1986 for training at the Pakistan Institute of Nuclear Science and Technology (PINSTECH).[101] Another group from Iran visited KRL in 1989. This training likely came in lieu of the technical cooperation agreement reportedly signed in 1987 between the Atomic Energy Commissions of the two countries. The arrangement set out to improve military and nuclear cooperation.[102] This agreement, given the sensitive nature of its contents, could not have been inked without the approval of the Pakistani president, General Zia. Also revealing was evidence that, after remaining neutral in the Iraq–Iran war for many years, General Zia had started tilting towards Iran in 1987. In an interview at the time about Pakistan–Iran relations, Zia took pride in Pakistan's 'fraternal and good-neighborly relations' with Iran and argued that the friendly ties between the two 'brought stability to the region'.[103] This tilt surprised the USA, and a senior State Department official soon declared this softening of policy 'troubling'.[104] It is worth remembering that Pakistan was concerned at the time that US sanctions could be forthcoming in response to its pursuit of a nuclear weapons capability. The Pakistani press had also reported in November 1986 that Zia had given the green light to an Iranian request for nuclear cooperation.[105] Sensitive nuclear policy decisions are usually not revealed through the press, and this could have been suicidal for the newspaper in question, especially in a country under military rule. Zia was indeed opening up to Iran—at least that was the impression he wanted to give to the Americans—but on the side, in his typical duplicitous style, he directed his nuclear scientists 'to play around' with the Iranians 'but not to yield anything substantial, at any cost'.[106] The 2007 IISS report *Nuclear Black Markets* also corroborates this by maintaining that 'Pakistani officials across the board insist that Zia did not approve any nuclear dealings with Iran that would involve the provision of sensitive technology'.[107]

Tanvir Ahmed Khan, Pakistan's ambassador to Iran from 1987 to 1989 and a seasoned diplomat, also has some important insights on the topic. He recounts a rare meeting with Iran's nuclear inner circle in January 1988: 'It was the only time I was allowed in the inner sanctum of the nuclear discussions. I was asked to a lunch ... they wanted to know whether Pakistan would help them on the nuclear side. They never said they wanted *nuclear* weapons. They said they wanted to master the nuclear [fuel] cycle.'[108] Tanvir Khan told the Iranians that it was unlikely that Pakistan would help out in this endeavour but he promised to relay the request to General Zia. When Tanvir Khan conveyed the message to Zia, he quipped: 'You gave them the right answer.'[109] An insightful editorial in the *Daily Times* also aptly explains the dynamics of the era:

> In April 1988, Gen Zia unleashed Sunni fanatics on the Shias of Gilgit and then calmly shrugged off the killing of Shia leader Arif ul Hussaini in Peshawar. If he was inclined to 'cooperate' with Iran with his nuclear programme in the beginning, he had plumped for the Arabs in his last days.[110]

Despite Pakistan's half-hearted response, Iran's leaders remained committed to acquiring nuclear technology, and they were able to make a 'significant breakthrough, obtaining a complete set of highly classified centrifuge drawings and some centrifuge components'.[111] There are many versions of how this transpired, but evidence clearly points towards A. Q. Khan and his European contacts who had earlier helped him in developing Pakistan's nuclear capabilities. Khan openly confessed such cooperation during an August 2009 television talk show in Pakistan where he explained the motivations behind this collaboration as well:

> Iran was interested in acquiring nuclear technology. Since Iran was an important Muslim country, we wished Iran to acquire this technology. Western countries pressured us unfairly. If Iran succeeds in acquiring nuclear technology, we will be a strong bloc in the region to counter international pressure. Iran's nuclear capability will neutralize Israel's power. We had advised Iran to contact the suppliers and purchase equipment from them.[112]

There was no Musharraf around at this time to force this confession. Once his house arrest restrictions were loosened around mid-2008, Khan had retracted his 2004 confession by claiming: 'It was not of my own free will. It was handed into my hand.'[113]

One of the most important players in these transactions was Gotthard Lerch, a German mechanical engineer.[114] He worked for many years for Leybold Heraeus, a German company that produced vacuum pumps and valves that were used in the centrifuge cascades.[115] This is the same company that shipped valves, vacuum pumps, and a gas purification system worth DM1.3 million to Pakistan in the 1980s.[116] Lerch left the company in the mid-1980s and moved to Switzerland. Soon afterwards, Leybold Heraeus discovered that trade secret and sensitive plans for important parts of the enrichment process were missing. What attracted their attention to Lerch was that, soon after he joined his new employers, they started producing gas ultracentrifuges remarkably similar to those featured in construction blueprints at Leybold Heraeus.[117] 'Business' relations between Khan and Lerch continued from Switzerland, and eventually Lerch moved on to establish his own business.

According to the research of Douglas Frantz and Catherine Collins, an Iranian nuclear scientist from the AEOI visited Lerch in Switzerland in 1987, looking for conventional weapons technology. Lerch agreed to help, but 'insisted that the Iranian watch a promotional film for his nuclear inventory'.[118] When Lerch called the Iranian scientists to receive feedback, he was told that Iran did indeed have an interest in nuclear technology. Another meeting was scheduled. It is interesting to note that these meetings took place in 1987, which was the year that Iran decided to pursue nuclear technology.

Lerch's known expertise among those interested in nuclear technology and the fact that Iran sent an AEOI official to talk to him, rather than an official from the Defence Ministry, is evidence that the purpose of the meeting was nuclear related right from the beginning. Consequently, Lerch met two nuclear scientists from Iran—Masud Naraghi and Mohammad Allahdad—and handed them a single-page proposal, which offered the following package:

1. drawings, descriptions, and specifications for manufacturing centrifuges;
2. one or two disassembled centrifuges to serve as prototypes;
3. sufficient components to build 2,000 centrifuges;
4. blueprints and specifications for a complete enrichment plant, including the full range of operating systems, provisions of auxiliary vacuum and electric drive equipment, and uranium hexafluoride re-conversion to metal and uranium casting capabilities (which can be used for nuclear weapons components, according to some experts).[119]

Lerch told them that most of the components were immediately available and the rest would be shipped later. Khan was to provide the centrifuges and components that were a key part of the deal.[120] Lerch asked for $20 million as a downpayment.[121] This proposal went up the chain of command in Tehran from the AEOI to the Ministry of Intelligence and Security, which submitted it to the country's top leadership.

According to David Armstrong and Joseph Trento, Masud Naraghi, a US-trained laser and plasma physicist, who in 1992 defected to the USA and now lives in New York State, claimed that A. Q. Khan's European suppliers 'initiated' the sales.[122] Naraghi, then the Iranian chief negotiator, maintains that that he only found out later that the European salesperson was offering Pakistani technology.[123] It is reasonable to assume that Naraghi conveyed the same information to US intelligence when he defected. It is probably the reason why US officials did not consider Khan to be directly involved in the nuclear proliferation at the time (1992)—or perhaps they did, and decided to watch Khan quietly in order to understand fully what was going on. Naraghi's assertion that Europeans organized the deal is indeed substantiated by the debriefing of the eight Pakistani nuclear scientists arrested and questioned by the

Pakistani authorities after the exposure of the A. Q. Khan network in 2004. One of them disclosed: 'We confided in them about the items needed to construct a nuclear bomb, as well as the makes of equipment, the names of companies, the countries from which they could be procured and how they could be procured.'[124]

The deal went ahead when Lerch and three Iranian officials met in Dubai in 1987. The secret meeting was also attended by Mohamed Farouq (not to be confused with Mohammed Farooq of KRL), an Indian-born Sri Lankan businessman (settled in Dubai) and a friend of A. Q. Khan and Heinz Mebus, who was one of his original suppliers for the Pakistani nuclear programme.[125] Khan did not attend the meeting. According to Douglas Frantz and Catherine Collins, it was Lerch who recruited Farouq and Mebus. Mebus had previously worked for Siemens and ironically, Lerch's one-page original deal was written on Siemens stationery.[126] Iran was only interested in parts of the offer.[127] It had financial constraints due to its ongoing war with Iraq, and Iranian officials instructed Naraghi to agree to an initial payment of $10 million, payable upon the delivery of the equipment.[128] The IAEA 'believes Iran outsmarted the dealers by buying much of the equipment and technology at lower prices from European, Russian and Chinese competitors during the early 1990s'.[129]

A. Q. Khan had sent two used P-1 centrifuges, and components for many more, through Farouq in Dubai for this deal with the Iranians.[130] Pakistan was already working on the more advanced P-2 centrifuges for its nuclear programme, and most P-1 machines in its stockpile were no longer of any use. The issue of who authorized Khan to 'export' this equipment is dealt with in more detail in later chapters, but it is suffice to say here that he was aware of the increasing Pakistan–Iran contacts in the defence sphere, and perhaps believed that selling the older P-1 version would fall within the ambit of the limited approval given by President Zia for bilateral nuclear cooperation.[131] According to some sources, Khan told military authorities that these transactions were of very limited significance, since these centrifuges were used and could be deemed obsolete equipment.[132]

As President Zia was very busy running the state affairs as well as managing the 'Afghan Jihad', Khan probably coordinated this with General Mirza Aslam Beg, who, as the vice chief of the army staff, was the most senior military official supervising Pakistan's nuclear programme.[133] According to estimates by Indian intelligence, first contact between Khan and Iranian nuclear scientists was established in 1984, but this is not corroborated by any other source.[134]

During the meeting, Lerch, Mebus, and Farouq handed over the equipment, drawings, and some technical plans to Naraghi and Allahdad, who were also accompanied by a third Iranian official named Hormoz Azodi.[135] The National Council of Resistance of Iran, an Iranian exile group, claimed that one of the Iranian representatives in this meeting was then-Brigadier-General Mohammad Eslami, in charge of the Iranian Revolutionary Guard's research centre. Eslami would later become a senior commander of the Revolutionary Guard. If he was indeed there, then it indicates that at this early stage this cooperation was certainly viewed as having military utility, or at a minimum that the state security apparatus needed to be present at the transaction.[136]

During the meeting Lerch provided the Iranian team with a fifteen-page document containing a detailed and extensive process for the production of uranium metal, which could be meant for use in forming the core of a nuclear device. This supports the notion that Iran was probably focused on developing nuclear weapons. IAEA director-general Mohamed El Baradei called this revealing information related to the production of nuclear weapons components a 'matter of concern'.[137] Iran, however, claims that though it did receive this document, it never asked for it.[138] In the February 2008 IAEA report on Iran, the agency restated Iran's claim that it never asked for the document. However, the IAEA never received any further details on this from Pakistan.[139]

Even if Iran never asked for the document, it apparently still had to pay for it. There are various reports about the sale price of the package ranging from $3 million to $10 million. According to Gordon Corera of the BBC, the deal was worth $3 million, of which Khan 'received less than a quarter', and the rest went to the European members of the network, leading Corera to conclude that 'it was the business network and not Khan who was driving the deal'.[140] Egmont Koch, a German journalist who has extensively covered the subject in his various writings and documentaries for many years, maintains that the Iranians paid $8 million for the package, with the largest single share of the money going to Gotthard Lerch.[141] In his documentary *Der Physiker der Mullahs* Koch maintains that 'Mebus was instrumental in scheduling and arranging the 1987 meeting in Dubai'—that it was an initiative of Khan's friends and not his. However, the documentary quotes Mebus' lawyer, who argues that Mebus started talking to Iran after Khan gave his name to the Iranians.[142] Of course, Khan's name recognition carried a lot of weight in terms of nuclear technology on offer. The third financial estimate of the deal, $10 million, comes from the investigation of Douglas Frantz and Catherine Collins. They maintain:

> Three million went to Lerch because he had originated the deal. Farooq [Farouq] and Khan received two million dollars each and Mebus received one million. Friedrich Tinner, the Swiss engineer, who like Khan had not attended the meeting, collected $500,000, while another million went into the BCCI account of an Islamabad dentist. The involvement of the dentist remains a mystery, but some intelligence officials have speculated that he passed on the money to the Pakistani government and military officials.[143]

The distribution of the final $500,000 remains unclear. The dentist was the late Dr Zafar Niazi, who was very close to the Pakistan People's Party (PPP) and Benazir Bhutto. Given his background and profile, it was unlikely that Niazi received money on behalf of the Pakistan army or intelligence services. In fact, the mention of Dr Niazi's name most likely came from preconceived plans to deceive Pakistani authorities should the network come under investigation or arrest. A senior Pakistani military official, closely involved with the 2004 investigations into A. Q. Khan, shared with me in an interview that, soon after his arrest, Khan tried to relay a message to Iran, which was intercepted by Pakistani intelligence. The message was short and clear: 'If asked about Pakistan–Iran nuclear collaboration, give out names of people who are dead—I will do the same.'[144] Intriguingly, the names of retired Major-General Imtiaz Ali and Dr Zafar Niazi soon appeared in some media reports in connection with the Pakistan–Iran nuclear contacts.[145] For instance, according to Gaurav Kampani, 'Khan has made the case that he was pressured to sell nuclear technologies to Iran by two individuals close to former Prime Minister Benazir Bhutto. The first, Dr Niazi, was a friend, while the latter, General Imtiaz Ali, served as military advisor to Benazir Bhutto.'[146] At the time of Zia's imposition of martial law in July 1977, Dr Niazi was arrested by the military due to his close association with the PPP. Interestingly, Niazi was released in 1981 as part of the al-Zulfiqar plane hijacking deal orchestrated by Benazir Bhutto's brother Murtaza Bhutto. Niazi was flown to Damascus.[147] Murtaza Bhutto and his associates conceived and implemented the hijacking of the Pakistan International Airlines plane in order to facilitate the release of PPP activists from Pakistani jails. Niazi later became a close associate of Benazir Bhutto and remained influential during her first stint as the prime minister (1988–90).[148] General Imtiaz Ali, the other person named in the news stories, served as a former military secretary to Prime Minister Zulfikar Ali Bhutto and later an adviser to Benazir on military affairs. In fact, Generals Imtiaz and Beg were not even on speaking terms, and it is highly unlikely that they would have worked together on this issue.[149] Both had died before 2004, and were both very close to the PPP. These names were given out as a cover-up to save the real wheeler-dealers.

The 1988–1992 Phase

The assassination of President Zia in August 1988 ushered in a new political era in Pakistan, while Ayotallah Khomeini's death in 1989 also changed the political dynamics in Iran. And in terms of strategic alliances, the end of the Cold War significantly changed the global scene. The new leaders of both countries renewed their relations more openly. In Pakistan, General Mirza Aslam Beg, became the chief of army staff (COAS), while Benazir Bhutto was elected as the prime minister in late 1988. The army remained the most influential organ of the state, and it only allowed Bhutto to take over the reins of government after she agreed to their terms and conditions. The conditions included assurance (a) that Bhutto would not interfere in Pakistan's nuclear programme; (b) that the Afghan policy of supporting certain militant factions would continue; and (c) that the army would manage its internal affairs independently.[150] In an interview with the author in early 2007 Bhutto maintained that during her first stint as prime minister, the president and the army chief declared the nuclear programme to be a 'no-go area' for her.[151] This is pretty well known. I remember the sadness in her eyes while she explained to me the trajectory of her relations with the military. After all, she was the daughter of the political architect of the nuclear programme and expected to be trusted to carry on her father's political legacy.

In any case, she had precious little time, as intelligence agencies and her political opponents—religious zealots of all stripes—forced her to spend most of her time trying to save her government. On one occasion when she tried to get involved in discussions about the future of the country's nuclear programme, she was snubbed. She recalled: 'I asked the army chief and he said, "It's got nothing to do with me. It's the president". I asked President Ishaq Khan, and he said, "There's no need for you to know."'[152] A. Q. Khan was fully aware of this situation, and it is inconceivable that he would have listened to her, or anyone close to her, in matters pertaining to the nuclear programme.

As Bhutto struggled to control the state, General Beg propounded the idea of a Pakistani–Afghan–Iranian (and possibly Turkish) alliance that could act in 'strategic defiance' to the West. The idea involved 'strengthening collective defenses of regional Muslim countries' through joint training, defence production, and collective defence arrangements.[153] Beg was also impressed by Iranian thinking on matters of international security.[154]

Initially (around December 1988), A. Q. Khan reached out to Prime Minister Benazir Bhutto with a request that the PAEC should also be brought under his command, but she declined and Khan moved even closer to General Beg and President Ghulam Ishaq Khan.[155] Clearly, Beg and Ishaq Khan were in control of both security and foreign policy issues. Iran re-energized its efforts to reach out to the new leadership in Pakistan via official channels, hoping for more support in the nuclear technology arena. Lieutenant-General Asad Durrani, who remained head of the Inter-Services Intelligence (ISI) from August 1990 to March 1992, shared with me in an interview that Mohsin Rezai, the head of the Islamic Revolutionary Guards Corps (IRGC), visited Pakistan to make a case for bilateral cooperation on 'peaceful uses of nuclear technology', but 'was politely told that it might not be possible'.[156] The Iranians are resilient, and were not disappointed at this response. They had decided by then to pursue this path, as is evident from a 1988 address by the Speaker of the Iranian parliament, Ali Akbar Hashemi Rafsanjani: 'We should at least think about [weapons of mass destruction] for our own defense. Even if the use of such weapons is inhuman and illegal, the

[Iran–Iraq] war has taught us that such laws are just drops of ink on paper.'[157] They were thinking hard about all options.

Kathy Gannon, a brave and highly respected journalist who has covered South Asia for decades now, interviewed General Beg in 2003, where he revealed that Iran had indeed approached him directly and offered 'upward of $10 billion for nuclear arms technology'.[158] Beg further mentioned that Iranian emissaries had also contacted Prime Minister Bhutto in this regard and that the two (Beg and Bhutto) played a game with them, sending them back and forth between the military chief's house and the prime minister's. One would say that the other had the authority to decide whether to share the technology, but neither would give the Iranians an outright refusal.[159]

While Benazir Bhutto denied General Beg's claim, she acknowledged that officials from the Iranian government approached her about help with nuclear technology in the autumn of 1989 when she attended a conference for Islamic heads of government in Tehran.[160] During a break in the conference, President Rafsanjani asked Bhutto go to a quiet corner to talk about a sensitive matter. He said, 'Our countries have reached an agreement on special defense matters' in recent years and 'I want us to reaffirm it as leaders of our governments.'[161] Unaware of any such arrangement, Bhutto asked him: 'What exactly are you talking about, Mr President?' President Rafsanjani, already having some idea about her ignorance in the matter said, 'Nuclear technology, Madam Prime Minister, nuclear technology.'[162] Iran offered $4 billion for the technology.[163] Bhutto, a diplomat par excellence, promised 'to get back to him' after consultations with the president and the army chief. On her return she discussed the issue with the two, who, according to her, claimed total ignorance and considered the matter closed.[164] Bhutto later said to Western media that she responded to this turn of events by ordering that 'no nuclear scientist was permitted to travel outside Pakistan without her approval'.[165] This executive order was a surprising initiative, as she knew well that she had limited say in anything related to the nuclear programme.

US–Pakistan relations began faltering in the late 1980s and early 1990s due to growing US concerns about Pakistan's advancing nuclear programme. The Soviet Union was no more, and American interest had shifted towards Eastern Europe while Pakistan was still hoping that the

USA would continue to ignore the issue just as it had during the Afghan engagement. But Washington had other ideas. When the USA finally threatened Pakistan with economic sanctions, the Pakistani military interpreted the threat as a significant shift in US policy. The former assistant secretary of defense for international security affairs, Henry Rowen, maintained that in January 1990 General Beg presented him with a very clear corresponding threat: 'If Pakistan was cut off [from US aid] it might be forced to share nuclear technology with Iran.'[166] Beg did not explicitly mention weapons technology, or perhaps he intentionally left it to Mr Rowen's imagination. When confronted with this statement in recent years, General Beg called Rowen's claim a 'blatant lie'.[167] Rowen's claim, however, appears more authentic, as two other senior US officials reported similar communications between General Beg and the US government. One was CENTCOM commander General Norman Schwarzkopf and the other was Robert Oakley, the US ambassador to Pakistan during the period when these conversations took place.[168]

Robert Oakley in a 2002 interview with prominent American journalist Steve Coll disclosed that Beg while visiting Tehran in February 1990 opened discussions with the IRCG about the possibility of Pakistani nuclear cooperation with Iran. Beg offered to trade Pakistan's bomb-making expertise for Iranian oil.[169] On his return, Oakley told Beg, 'What a disaster this would be, certainly in terms of the relationship with the United States.' Consequently, according to Oakley, Beg agreed to abandon the Iranian talks.[170] Oakley, however, gave a slightly different version of these discussions to Seymour Hersh. Oakley told Hersh that 'Beg on his return from Iran said to Oakley: "I am greatly reassured. … Now we're in good shape. With the support Iran promised me, we will win in case of war over Kashmir."'[171] In 1990 Pakistan's conflict with India over Kashmir heightened due to Pakistan's support for an insurgency in the disputed territory and, plausibly, Beg was interested in Iranian help in case of military confrontation with India. Beg must have offered something in return for such help. In the post-2004 scenario, when the A. Q. Khan excesses were exposed, Beg had this to say in his defence: 'It is not a crime. If I was in it and had the people contacted me, I would have told them to go to "such and such" supplier. I would not be committing a crime, in that I have not directly passed on any nuclear secrets or nuclear know-how.'[172] This sounds like more a defence of Khan than of himself.

President Ghulam Ishaq Khan, the other major power player in the Pakistani hierarchy, had strong ties to Beg, and he had also been deeply involved in the nuclear programme since its early phase. After General Zia's death in 1988, Ishaq was elevated from the chairmanship of the Senate to the presidency as per a constitutional provision. Upon assuming the role of acting president, Ishaq Khan immediately appointed Beg as the army chief. None of this was unconstitutional or unexpected, but it was not without a quid pro quo. General Beg later ensured that Ishaq became the elected president, not easy to achieve as only members of parliament and provincial assemblies could vote. Ishaq Khan had no political base to make it happen. Prime Minister Benazir Bhutto was forced to support Ishaq Khan as president as a part of a deal with the army leadership. Without General Beg, Ishaq Khan's career was almost over. Now they were in complete control as the constitution designed for General Zia gave all the crucial executive powers to the office of the president.

Ishaq Khan had an excellent rapport with A. Q. Khan, as he had worked closely with him since the early days of the nuclear programme. While paying tribute to him on the occasion of Pakistan's nuclear tests in 1998, A. Q. Khan recalled: 'Former president Ghulam Ishaq Khan was associated with it since Z. A. Bhutto's days. General Zia-ul-Haq also retained Ghulam Ishaq Khan. ... [He] took a very keen interest. He visited Kahuta every month and would see progress. ... Prime Minister Junejo also extended full support and allowed Ghulam Ishaq Khan to continue.'[173] In an opinion piece in 2015, A. Q. Khan praised Ishaq Khan's character and maintained that during Ishaq Khan's 'tenure of almost seventeen years as head of our nuclear programme, he never once recommended anybody for a job or promotion or asked for a favor'.[174]

Ishaq Khan's involvement enabled him to be privy to all the secret budgetary allocations for the nuclear programme. As the finance minister in the early 1980s he gave tax-free status to the BCCI Foundation, the non-profit branch of the now infamous BCCI bank. A. Q. Khan had routinely used BCCI for making payments to the international procurement network that he had developed. In return, BCCI provided

$10 million worth of grants to the Ghulam Ishaq Khan (GIK) Institute of Engineering Sciences and Technology in Swabi district, North West Frontier Province (now renamed as Khyber Pukhtunkhwa Province [KPK]). The GIK is a modern educational institution conceived and spearheaded by both A. Q. Khan and Ishaq Khan.[175] These contributions earned Ishaq Khan the title 'grandfather of Pakistan's nuclear bomb' in the eyes of many Pakistanis, since the title of the father of the bomb was already taken.[176]

As mentioned earlier, President Ishaq and General Beg kept Prime Minister Benazir Bhutto completely out of the loop on developments related to the nuclear programme. However, being on good terms with the US administration, Bhutto received a CIA briefing on the status of Pakistan's nuclear programme in June 1989 when she was visiting the USA. The brief was apparently intended to make her knowledgeable on the subject and to facilitate her participation in nuclear programme-related policy issues.[177] In the eyes of Beg and Ishaq Khan, this new knowledge was seen as threatening. They believed that she could not be trusted on this sensitive issue given her closeness with the USA. A. Q. Khan, still annoyed with her, harboured similar concerns. There were many factors at play, but scepticism about her views and interest in country's nuclear programme played a role in Ishaq Khan's decision to dislodge her twenty-month-old government on trumped-up charges of incompetence and corruption. The badly distorted constitution allowed it. Later, A. Q. Khan claimed that he had also advised the president to dismiss her government.[178] It was not surprising given his desire for political influence and a major role in policy making. After sacking the Bhutto government in August 1990, General Beg felt even more free to pursue his understanding with the Iranians.

A. Q. Khan, when confronted by Pakistani military interrogators in 2004 about his dealings with Iran, named General Beg as the one who 'urged him to share nuclear technology with Iran'.[179] When Beg was asked about Khan's statement, he surprisingly claimed that 'the security of the nuclear program had not been his responsibility' and that the president and prime minister were in control of the nuclear facilities.[180] This was a highly misleading statement as, besides shirking responsibility, he was not ready to blame A. Q. Khan at all.

Elected in November 1990, Prime Minister Nawaz Sharif was a close ally of the president and the Pakistan military. The military had ensured that Bhutto could not return to power in elections that were held after her unceremonious fall from power. Sharif had risen as a Zia protégé. His understanding about Pakistan's strategic considerations was minimal, which was a blessing for Beg, Ishaq Khan, and A. Q. Khan. Meanwhile, instability in the region reinforced Pakistan and Iran's strategic relationship. Iraq's invasion of Kuwait and the subsequent US-led military action in Iraq, and the US sanctions on Pakistan as a result of the Pressler Amendment further convinced General Beg of the need to be close to Iran. But in order to achieve this, he needed the political leadership to be on board. Interestingly, Sharif visited Tehran thrice in three years (1991–3), Ishaq Khan did so in 1991, and President Rafsanjani was welcomed in Islamabad on a return visit in 1992. The relationship was indeed warming up.

Beg was working on a twofold plan. First, he targeted important politicians close to Nawaz Sharif, in order to obtain their support and influence for developing and strengthening a strategic alliance with Iran. Two of them decided to publicly disclose these conversations with Beg. Chaudhry Nisar Ali Khan, who served as the federal minister for petroleum and natural resources (1990–3) representing Sharif's Muslim League was one. Nisar Ali Khan had not lost an election since 1985 and remained a powerful member of the cabinet during the 1997–9 Nawaz-led government as well as in the 2013–17 government. He maintained that Beg said to him: 'Iran is willing to give whatever it takes, $6 billion, $10 billion. We can sell the bomb to Iran at any price.'[181] The public nature of this allegation provides strong support for its authenticity. Given the sensitivity of the subject and the nature of civil–military relations in Pakistan, it is inconceivable for a politician to make such a claim against a former army chief without any evidence. It is also important to note that his father was a brigadier in the army and his brother retired as a lieutenant-general in the late 1990s.[182]

Another politician, Ishaq Dar, a former finance minister associated with Sharif's party (who again served as finance minister in the government formed after the 2013 elections), supported Nisar Khan's account.[183] Dar claimed in 2003 that General Beg had asked Sharif's government to transfer Pakistan's nuclear technology to a 'friendly' state for $12 billion but that Sharif had rejected that suggestion.[184] Dar further mentioned that an Iranian official was present when Beg made the offer to Prime Minister Sharif. Dar even raised this issue on the floor of Pakistan's Senate, the upper legislative chamber.[185] US Ambassador Oakley, who was closely monitoring these developments, urged Sharif to quash any such arrangement and Sharif, according to Oakley, agreed to speak to Iranian leaders on the subject.[186]

Beg's second line of action was to approach leading journalists in the country, especially those known for their expertise on national security issues. He wanted a media campaign in favour of an increase in defence collaboration with Iran, and told them in private that the purpose of this effort was to influence the government towards nuclear cooperation with Iran.[187] He genuinely believed that such an arrangement would serve Pakistan's security interests well. However, political support for the idea was not forthcoming, and even the president was no longer comfortable with Beg's strategic calculus. In fact, Beg's expanding political ambitions alarmed Ishaq Khan.

Before the end of Beg's three-year tenure as army chief (August 1988–August 1991) rumours started circulating that he was contemplating imposing martial law. Ishaq Khan, however, put an end to such speculation by nominating General Asif Nawaz as the next army chief ahead of time—almost six months before the expiration of Beg's term. Beg thus became a lame-duck army chief in the last few months of his tenure. No evidence exists that the proposed nuclear deal was completed at the time, and the subject was closed for discussion. But, as discussed earlier, limited cooperation had already taken place between the European network and the Iranian regime.

In 2011 A. Q. Khan came up with yet another public version of the events in the shape of a revised and detailed confessional statement shared with some US media outlets. In brief, he claimed that around 1989–90 General Beg 'promised to give the Iranians a few weapons in lieu of ten years of our defense budget. The Iranian Army chief, Shamkani flew to Islamabad to pick up the weapons and papers.'[188] He then claims that Beg pressurized Bhutto and others to deliver what had been committed, which was in his view insignificant, and here he again mentions the names of General Imtiaz and Dr Niazi, and even adds the name of another deceased person to the list: Mr Khokhar of KRL, who he alleged handed over the requisite equipment as A. Q. Khan himself was travelling.[189]

The Second Nuclear Deal: 1993–1995

In August 1991, during his last month in office, Beg did receive an Iranian delegation. General Asif Nawaz, Pakistan's COAS-in-waiting, was not invited to this meeting, which surprised him. This led Nawaz to send a message to Beg through the director-general of military intelligence (DGMI), Major-General Javed Ashraf Qazi, that 'all decisions taken in the meeting will be reviewed and any decision not in line with the national security objectives will be overturned'.[190] After this warning, the Iranian delegation visited him as well. The issue was deemed so important that soon after taking over the reins in October, General Nawaz visited Iran and met the president. At that meeting President Hashemi Rafsanjani asked Nawaz: 'When could we expect to receive the technology that your predecessor had promised us?'[191] General Nawaz 'feigned complete ignorance' and promised that he would check with the president and prime minister, and would follow up.[192] On his return to Pakistan, Nawaz was told by both President Ishaq Khan and Prime Minister Sharif that Beg had never received any authorization from them to carry on nuclear negotiations with Iran.

Beg's DGMI, Major-General Javed Ashraf Qazi, who later became director-general of Inter-Services Intelligence (ISI), corroborates Nawaz's interpretation of the events. Ashraf Qazi recalls that General Nawaz met with a delegation sent by Iranian minister Mohsin Rezai, which sought Pakistan's help with Iran's nuclear programme. In response, General Nawaz categorically maintained: 'Pakistan's nuclear programme is not for sale and no country on earth should think of acquiring the technology from Pakistan because Islamabad has made it a policy decision not to take part in proliferation of the technology since Pakistan has attained it for its own exclusive use.'[193] Zahid Hussain, a respected Pakistani journalist who writes for *Newsweek* and the *Wall Street Journal*, also recounts the episode in his book *Frontline Pakistan*. Hussain characterized General Nawaz as 'a moderate, Pro-West officer' who stopped the deal with Iran, which adversely affected Pakistan–Iran relations.[194] Also, Robert Oakley confirmed that Prime Minister Sharif and President Ishaq Khan conveyed their sentiments to Iranian president Hashemi Rafsanjani that the Pakistani government had no intention of carrying out any nuclear cooperation agreement.[195]

The 2007 IISS report on Pakistan's role in nuclear proliferation, however, maintains the opposite. It says that 'several sources have reported that an agreement was reached in 1991 between General Nawaz, Beg's successor as chief of army staff, Rafsanjani and General Mohsen Rezae, head of the Revolutionary Guard'.[196] The report claims that the said agreement involved Pakistani nuclear weapons-related technology in return for Iranian oil. It is striking that the report does not refer to any sources to substantiate this allegation, except an Indian news report, which was written by a journalist whose only story on the subject contained this revealing disclosure.[197] Beg had failed to obtain any political support for his nuclear collaboration plans, and clearly the military's institutional support for his endeavour was also lacking, especially after his departure from military command.

Consequently, A. Q. Khan's nuclear cooperation with Iran received a major setback with Beg's retirement. General Nawaz's tenure as army chief was brief, as he died suddenly in January 1993.[198] Shortly after being named as army chief, General Nawaz had said that the army had no role in politics other than to defend the civilian government and the country.[199] His widow later alleged that the then prime minister Nawaz Sharif was involved in the murder of her husband, and she even filed a police report against the chief of the intelligence bureau, a retired army officer.[200] On General Nawaz's death, Benazir Bhutto, then the leader of the opposition in the National Assembly praised him: 'He did what he said he would do—he kept the army out of politics.'[201]

General Abdul Waheed Kakar, the new army chief, generally known as a professional soldier, remained aloof from politics. Bhutto returned to power in October 1993 after a showdown between Prime Minister Sharif and President Ishaq Khan led to the fall of the Sharif government. Bhutto and Kakar had a good working relationship from the beginning as the general maintained a policy of non-interference. However, A. Q. Khan remained as powerful as before. Under Kakar's watch, from January 1993 to January 1996 Iran received a duplicate set of P-1 centrifuge designs along with components for 500 centrifuges from Khan.[202] It is believed that these components were from equipment that Pakistan had previously used in the uranium enrichment process, which explains the enriched uranium contamination found on the Iranian equipment.[203] These nuclear links also alerted Saudi intelligence, which was following Iran closely because of the rivalry between the two countries. Their information was so specific and credible that Saudi intelligence chief, Prince Turki al-Faisal, flew to Pakistan in early March 1995 to share it with Prime Minister Bhutto and try to convince her to call off any such cooperation.[204]

The usefulness of the components came into question as Iran blamed the technical difficulties they faced in setting up their centrifuge cascades on the poor quality of centrifuge components they had received from the A. Q. Khan network.[205] Thus, later in 1997 the network replaced previously supplied bellows because of their inferior performance.[206] The fact that the A. Q. Khan network was responding to Iranian complaints showed that indeed some form of contractual arrangement existed between the two.

In addition to securing P-1 centrifuge designs, Iran was now seeking more advanced designs. Having learned from the 1987 experience (when the quality of the centrifuges was found to be poor), Iran indeed received designs for the more advanced P-2 centrifuge between 1994 and 1996.[207] Despite obtaining the technology, Iran claims that it did not work on this design until early 2002, which is surprising.[208] Instead, it continued to focus on the P-1 designs. Iran's capabilities in the field and continuous investment are obvious from the fact that it was able to improve the functioning of the P-2 centrifuges after facing some problems in manufacturing those components.[209] Pakistan made P-2 centrifuges use maraging steel for the spinning rotors, while Iran developed a 'shorter, sub-critical carbon composite rotor', which makes the process more efficient.

Some experts believe that the Khan–Iran collaboration reached its peak during 1994–6.[210] Evidence shows that Iran continued to draw on the advice of the network until at least 1999.[211] Iran's nuclear project relied on more than Khan's personal expertise, as Iran admits that its officials met the network personnel thirteen times between 1994 and 1999.[212] Iranian authorities, however, say that these meetings were largely to complain about the quality of what was supplied, and Ali Akbar Salehi, a former Iranian ambassador to the IAEA, went as far as to say: 'They bought what they wanted to buy and unfortunately many of the things they bought were useless.'[213]

The transaction that occurred while General Abdul Waheed Kakar served as the army chief and while Bhutto led the country pointed to the direct role Khan had played as early as mid-1993. Douglas Frantz and Catherine Collins maintain that in the summer of 1994 Iran's defence minister travelled to Islamabad to persuade Khan to sell his country's most advanced nuclear technology to Iran and to reach out to some of his long-standing contacts.[214] The Iranians were now dealing directly with Khan. According to the 2007 IISS report, Bokhari Syed Abu Tahir, a close associate of Khan, had offered the equipment to an Iranian company, which led to these deliberations. Consequently, the report says: 'Rafsanjani sent Iranian officials to Dubai to meet with Tahir and Farouq. Surely Khan arranged for this meeting. A deal was struck for an initial payment of three million dollars to be paid, ensuring that the first deliveries would start in early 1994 using Iranian merchant ships.'[215] According to Gordon Corera, the cash was brought in two briefcases by Iranian officials and left at a lavish apartment that was used as a guesthouse by Khan during his frequent trips to Dubai.[216] That payment secured the delivery of P-1 and P-2 centrifuge designs to the Iranian regime. As Iran obtained P-2 centrifuge designs from Khan, it acquired component parts for P-2 centrifuges from other European sources.[217]

The relationship between Khan and Tahir is well established. IAEA investigations revealed a letter written by Khan to the president of Sri Lanka in 2003 that disclosed their collaboration regarding financial dealings and the first Iran deal of 1987. An excerpt from Khan's letter to Chandrika Bandaranaike Kumaratunga, the president of Sri Lanka, reads:

Excellency, I am venturing to write to you about a very serious case of fraud and extortion of money by one Mr. Harry Jayawardena, Chairman of Stassen Group of Companies from a dear friend (and like a son to me) Mr. Bokhari Syed Abu Tahir, a Sri Lankan national. ... Mr. Harry Jayawardena phoned Tahir in Dubai, who is now running a successful computer company (SMB Computer), and told him that Sri Lankan Intelligence (CID) was making inquiries about him and his connection with me. The fact is that I left the nuclear programme for more than 2 years and even before that the company, Bin Belilah Enterprises Ltd., for which Tahir was working, was owned by Col. Saeed Mattar Bin Belilah who fully knew the nature of our work and we never indulged in any illegal activities. Gen. Sheikh Butti Al-Maktoum, Commander of Dubai and brother-in-law of Gen. Shaikh Mohammad, was fully in the picture of our work and had given his blessing. ...Tahir's uncle, M. Farouq, an Indian national, ran away with a large amount of money to Singapore and got Singaporean nationality. The money belonged to a German engineer who was paid by us as advance money for certain equipment.[218]

Besides establishing the Khan–Tahir association, the letter indicates the involvement of influential people from Dubai in the transfer of nuclear-related technology to Iran. And it reveals internal differences over the distribution of the 1987 Iranian deal money. However, there is no smoking gun proving Pakistani authorization in the deals that Khan made with the Iranian officials.

Regardless of whether Khan had official authorization for his contacts with Iran between 1993 and 2000, it is unlikely that any political leader in Pakistan sanctioned the transfer of nuclear-related technology and expertise. Pakistan's deteriorating relations with Iran from the mid-1990s onwards—due to conflicting interests in Afghanistan—proved to be an impediment to any cooperation in the security arena. Also, by February 1997 Nawaz Sharif's political party had risen to power again and, judging from his views expressed in 1990–1, it was doubtful whether Khan or anyone else would have made another effort to persuade him on board with the project.

Another example of a lack of support for Khan came a year earlier. In January 1996 General Kakar completed his three-year tenure, and General Jahangir Karamat became the new army chief. Karamat, a well-read and intelligent general, was known for his professional approach. He was the first army chief who called for the auditing of the nuclear programme budget, which soured his relations with Khan.[219] Khan during his interrogations in and around 2004 mentioned General Karamat as one of the few who were aware of what he was doing, but this remains unsubstantiated.[220] It is more likely that Khan's second series of nuclear transactions with Iran (especially after Beg's retirement) were without any institutional support from the military.

Still a close aide to Khan at KRL, Mohammed Farooq, who was detained in the 2004 probe, was sent to Iran to help their scientists during this second phase, and for this Khan needed the approval of higher authorities.[221] It is unknown how Khan justified this to the army chief. Gordon Corera's conclusion in this regard appears rational: 'In essence, it appears that Khan could have received tacit approval and support from a small number of senior individuals but he may have continued and deepened the relationship on his—or network's—initiative.'[222] Douglas Frantz and Catherine Collins view this transaction as 'a private arrangement, which promised nothing to Pakistan and great wealth for Khan'. They believe it involved a downpayment to the tune of $6 or 7 million.[223] Friedrich Tinner, a Swiss engineer, and two Turkish businessmen played the central role in providing the equipment to Iran in this second deal.[224]

Another insightful disclosure indicates that some shipments to Iran possibly continued until as late as 2000. President Pervez Musharraf of Pakistan disclosed in a 2006 interview with the *New York Times* for the Discovery Times television documentary *Nuclear Jihad* that he fired Khan from his position at KRL in 2001 after discovering that he was trying to arrange a secret flight to the Iranian city of Zahedan.[225] He refused to discuss the flight even with Musharraf, saying that it was important and very secret. 'I said, "What the hell do you mean? You want to keep a secret from me?"' Musharraf recalled.[226]

The Post-2004 Phase

Since the unravelling of the A. Q. Khan network in late 2003 the Pakistan government had developed serious suspicions that Iran had given out crucial information about Pakistan–Iran nuclear cooperation to IAEA.[227] There was a strong feeling in Pakistan's corridors of power that Iran had put Pakistan in an awkward position.[228] The Iranian government had similar suspicions about Pakistan.[229] While talking about the need for nuclear disarmament in Middle East, Iran's former deputy foreign minister, Ambassador Sadegh Kharazi, mentioned Pakistan alongside India and Israel.[230] Pakistan's position is evident in this excerpt from a publication sponsored by a government research institute:

> The whole [nuclear] issue has caused a lot of resentment among [the] Pakistani public and official circles, who accuse Iran of buckling under international pressure and dragging Pakistan into this controversy. More so, because Pakistan was not under investigation, as it was not a signatory to the Nuclear Proliferation Treaty (NPT). Though the issue has not yet fully unfolded, and its long-term impact on Pak–Iran relations remains to

be seen, its immediate effect is clear: it will undermine those in Pakistan who had been advocating strategic relations with Iran.[231]

President Musharraf's comments on the subject in his memoirs further point to this view: 'The whole ugly episode leaked out and blew straight into Pakistan's face. Later, the IAEA's inspectors detected some contamination in the centrifuges in Iran, which Iranian officials conveniently deflected to the "outside source" providing the centrifuges.'[232]

Iran also became increasingly apprehensive of Pakistan's role in the US-led 'War on Terror'. Although both countries are looking for economic opportunities in the region, and efforts towards the Iran–Pakistan gas pipeline project reflects this trend, it is unlikely that they will even consider any collaboration in the nuclear field in the future.

In conclusion, there is no doubt that the A. Q. Khan network played a crucial role in Iran's nuclear programme. China's support was also very important for Iran, however.[233] The new components provided by the A. Q. Khan network in the 1994–6 phase especially helped Iran expand its testing. By 1999 Iran had tested its centrifuges with UF 6, and the construction of the Natanz nuclear enrichment facility began in 2001. By 2002 Iran was able to test a small cascade of centrifuges, and within a year of that threshold it started manufacturing centrifuges locally. By 2007 Iran had manufactured 3,000 centrifuges and had 100 kilograms of enriched uranium in storage, and by 2009 it had enough low-enriched uranium for a single nuclear weapon.[234] What also deserves due recognition here is the history of Iran's nuclear infrastructure, and the tough regional security context engendering insecurity. Like Pakistan, Iran was determined to acquire nuclear weapons technology by any means possible.

5

PAKISTAN'S NUCLEAR PROLIFERATION LINKS WITH NORTH KOREA

The controversy surrounding nuclear links between Pakistan and North Korea erupted in November 2002, when it was disclosed that 'Pakistan provided North [Korea] with many of the designs for gas centrifuges and many of the components it needed to make highly enriched uranium for the country's latest nuclear weapons project'.[1] According to the David Sanger of the *New York Times*, North Korea, with its long-range-missile expertise, provided Pakistan with ballistic missiles in exchange. The collaboration helped Pakistan 'build a nuclear arsenal capable of reaching every strategic site in India'.[2]

Initially, Pakistan dismissed the report as 'absolutely incorrect', but later in 2006 President Pervez Musharraf in his memoirs acknowledged that 'Pakistan had contracted a government-to-government deal with North Korea for the purchase of conventional ballistic missiles, including transfer of technology'.[3] As for the sharing of nuclear technology, Musharraf further added that 'A. Q. Khan transferred nearly two dozen P-1 and P-2 centrifuges to North Korea [along with] a flow meter, some special oils for centrifuges, and coaching on centrifuge technology, including visits to top-secret centrifuge plants'.[4] Musharraf strongly denied any direct link between the transfer of ballistic missiles and nuclear technology, but the possibility cannot be dismissed out of hand.

Whether an authorized barter deal occurred or not, the evidence suggesting that some kind of trade happened posed serious questions regarding the proliferation of nuclear technology and weapons. North Korea remains one of the world's most impoverished and isolated countries, with serious human rights issues. The spread of nuclear technology and weapons to such unstable states can have dire consequences.

Clearly, North Korea's determination in acquiring nuclear capabilities over forty years suggests that the issue remained one of the highest priorities for the country's national security and strategic considerations. As for Pakistan, nuclear proliferation or the sale of its nuclear expertise to North Korea did not constitute a threat to its sovereignty. But what occurred beneath the surface is critical. Information about the exact nature of the transactions between Pakistan and North Korea reveal a complex web that involves the A. Q. Khan network, the Pakistani military, and the government of Pakistan. But did Khan initiate and carry out the proliferation of nuclear technology on his own? Or, if authorization occurred, what was the role of the Pakistani government? In this regard, it will be important to distinguish between government policy per se and the Pakistani military; the latter manages and controls the nuclear programme, and at times operates exclusively outside the control of the political leadership.

There are various possibilities that explain the nuclear link between Pakistan and North Korea as reported in the 2002 *New York Times* article. But before continuing with our examination, a word must be said about the availability of information regarding nuclear technology exchange between Pakistan and North Korea. Pakistani–North Korean (Pak–DPRK) nuclear links, in comparison to evidence of Pakistan–Libya or Pakistan–Iran dealings, pose greater challenges to decipher due to the lack of information available on the subject. US officials have stated repeatedly that information on North Korea's centrifuge programme is limited.[5] Some of the latest books and trade publications have filled this void to some extent, but the level of information remains small compared to the Iranian and Libyan cases, where extensive IAEA reports provide useful details.[6] However, despite these difficulties, the author is confident of the conclusions presented here, which come after careful consideration and scrutiny of the literature, interviews, and evidence available publicly and off the record.

To understand the motivations behind nuclear exchanges between Pakistan and North Korea, it is best to first explore North Korea's motivations for developing nuclear capabilities. In this sense, similar to the Pakistan experience, neo-realism and strategic culture provide a framework to understand North Korea's actions.

One explanation is that the original Pakistan–North Korea deal was an official transaction in which Pakistan paid hard cash for long-range ballistic missiles in 1993, as claimed by the late prime minister Benazir Bhutto.[7] Then later, the A. Q. Khan network cut a separate deal with North Korea from 1997 to 1999 that involved the sale of centrifuge technology. According to this scenario, Khan acted outside his mandate and without government authorization. This explanation, however, fails to explain why Khan was permitted to host North Korean nuclear scientists at the Khan Research Laboratories (KRL) in 1999.[8] Permission for this would have had to come directly from the Pakistani military leadership managing the programme, since it exposed foreign nationals to highly sensitive information concerning national security. Moreover, the presence of North Korean nuclear scientists at KRL implies the sharing of information. Khan, in a 2011 statement, claimed that one of his two trips to North Korea was made at the request of General Musharraf himself.[9]

Some reports suggest that photographs taken by the US intelligence monitoring the Pakistani nuclear tests in 1998 reveal several North Korean military officers present at the detonations, further indicating the possible nature of strategic nuclear links between the two states.[10] Moreover, it is alleged that one of the tests Pakistan conducted on 30 May 1998 used plutonium, and was possibly carried out for the benefit of the North Korean visitors. This appears to be too risky an arrangement for Pakistan at the time, especially as the tests were conducted under the management of the PAEC, whereas the North Koreans had closer links with KRL. There is no evidence to back up this set of allegations.

In this overall context, this chapter first provides a brief sketch of North Korea's nuclear development, followed by an analysis of the historical nature of Pakistan–North Korea relations. Next, it charts out the nuclear links between the two countries. It further deliberates on the range of possibilities and theories that explain Pakistan–

North Korea nuclear trade and examines the potential motivations behind these transactions.

Why North Korea Sought the Bomb

As to what motivated North Korea to develop nuclear weapons, Daniel A. Pinkston argues that 'a strong military posture and advanced weapons systems not only help the leadership deal with external threats, but they are also popular among nationalistic citizens who are constantly reminded of the potential external threats to North Korea'.[11] Others argue that North Korea's historical animus against the USA specifically drives its nuclear weapons programme.[12] Since the 1953 Korean War 37,000 US troops have been stationed in South Korea, the U.S. had threatened nuclear attacks against both North Korea and China during the Korean War, and staged nuclear weapons in South Korea until 1991.[13] Hence, from the North Korean perspective the direct threat represented by the USA against its sovereignty constituted a national security concern necessitating that the regime develop capabilities to counter any potential American strike. Some newly declassified US documents (March 2017) via the National Security Archive showed that South Korean president Park Chung-hee had instructed his scientists to develop nuclear weapons by 1977, and that had created a stir when President Ford's administration learnt about it around 1974.[14] They were of course primarily concerned about provocation from North Korea. This explains the nature of mutual security threat assessments in the Korean Peninsula.

A second motivation for North Korea's acquisition of nuclear weapons involves its use as a negotiation tool, as this would strengthen its bargaining power. During talks with the USA and regional powers, North Korea's demands showed that the leadership used its nuclear weapons programme as leverage to extract economic concessions, as in 2012 when Pyongyang agreed to suspend nuclear tests, uranium enrichment, and long-range-missile tests in exchange for food aid from the USA.[15] It later backed out of that understanding, and conducted nuclear weapons tests in 2013 and twice in 2016.[16] It had conducted similar tests in 2006 and 2009. Investment in missile technology complements this strategy, as is evident from

North Korea's export of missiles to Egypt, Iran, Libya, Pakistan, Syria, and Yemen.

What Did North Korea Try in Order to Acquire the Bomb?

North Korea began its nuclear research programme around the mid-1960s, when Kim Il-Sung, father of Kim Jong-Il and grandfather of current leader Kim Jong-Un, began construction of an atomic energy research complex in the city of Yongbyon.[17] The facility underwent upgrades in the 1970s, enabling work to begin on a second reactor, which was completed in 1987. In the 1980s North Korea accelerated its efforts to produce plutonium fuel for nuclear weapons from these two facilities. International pressure on North Korea led to its signing of the Nuclear Non-Proliferation Treaty (NPT) in 1985, but it postponed signing a safeguards agreement with IAEA allowing inspections.

In the 1990s North Korea began building two larger reactors with expanded capacity to produce plutonium. When the Agreed Framework of 1994 'theoretically' stopped work on the plants, they were estimated to be about two years away from completion. Intelligence assessments at the time indicated that North Korea had developed the capacity to extract weapons grade plutonium from irridiated nuclear fuel.[18] According to US, Japanese, and South Korean intelligence reports North Korea had enough extracted plutonium for at least one or two nuclear weapons by 1990.[19] North Korea reportedly also bought plutonium on the Russian black market during the same period.[20] North Korea also sought to follow the enriched uranium route to nuclear weapons around the mid-1990s. In early 2002 an unclassified CIA report disclosed that North Korea 'has been seeking centrifuge-related materials in large quantities to support a uranium enrichment program. It also obtained equipment suitable for use in uranium feed and withdrawal systems.'[21] Meanwhile, as North Korea looked to develop nuclear weapons capabilities in the face of stiff international opposition, it had built up a significant stock of medium- and long-range missiles (e.g. No-Dong—1,300 km range; Taepo Dong I—1,500–2,200 km range; and Taepo Dong II—6,000 km range).[22] After successfully reverse-engineering Soviet-origin Scud missiles, North Korea became a leading exporter of ballistic missiles from the 1980s.

North Korea tested its first nuclear device on 9 October 2006 after expelling IAEA inspectors in December 2002 and withdrawing from the NPT in January 2003.[23] In October 1994 the USA and North Korea had signed the Agreed Framework, according to which North Korea had agreed to freeze its nuclear programme and allow IAEA inspections. In return, the USA, Japan, and South Korea agreed to provide it with a light-water nuclear power plant and heavy fuel oil as a compensation for giving up its plutonium production reactor. However, this agreement failed to halt North Korea's pursuit of nuclear weapons, and in 2003 six-party talks began between North Korea, South Korea, Japan, China, Russia, and the USA to address North Korea's nuclear ambitions. In February 2007 North Korea finally agreed to shut down its nuclear facility at Yongbyon in exchange for 50,000 tonnes of heavy fuel oil and the release of $25 million frozen North Korean funds that had been held in a Macao bank. Furthermore, according to the 2007 understanding reached between the parties, if North Korea provides an accurate declaration and disables all of its nuclear facilities, then it will receive an additional 950,000 tonnes of heavy fuel oil.[24] Since then there have been many ups and downs in negotiations, and in 2008 tensions resurfaced between North Korea and the USA due to disagreements over the six-party talks disarmament process. In October 2008 IAEA inspectors were forbidden by the North Korean government to conduct further inspections of the site, but within a couple of days the USA had removed North Korea from the US State Sponsors of Terrorism list and the Yongbyon deactivation process had resumed.[25] North Korea's 2016 claims about hydrogen bomb testing and development of miniature nuclear warheads that can fit on ballistic missiles explain the ambition and growth of its nuclear weapons programme. The 2017 crisis has further demonstrated Pyongyang's 'nuclear trajectory' mindset.

History of Pakistan–North Korean Relations

Pakistan's relationship with North Korea began with arms sales after its 1965 war with India, when the USA imposed sanctions on arms sales to Pakistan. The military embargo forced Pakistan to look for alternative sources of weapons and led it to purchase Chinese- and Russian-made weapons in the late 1960s. The Soviet Union's close relationship with India affected Pakistan's ability to do business with it, but an alternative arose when Pakistan discovered that North Korean weapons were generally compatible with Soviet-bloc weaponry, and were considerably cheaper.[26]

In 1971 Pakistan undertook its first diplomatic mission to the DPRK when Zulfikar Ali Bhutto, representing General Yahya Khan's government, visited Pyongyang with a shopping list of military equipment. Pakistan desperately needed the military hardware for a looming war with India. Prior to this Pakistan and North Korea had not had diplomatic relations. The visit led to the signing of an agreement on 18 September 1971, ten weeks before the outbreak of the war with India, for the supply of North Korean conventional weapons to Pakistan.[27] On the same day the two countries signed a second accord, setting up consular relations. Bhutto established full diplomatic relations with North Korea in 1976, and received an elaborate welcome in Pyongyang.

The relationship was indeed built on military-sector cooperation but, with the changing needs of Pakistan's security, other bilateral relations took precedence. In the 1980s Pakistan's relationship with the USA revived, as did U.S. attention to Pakistan's conventional military needs. Pakistan's security dynamics, however, faced another transition in the early 1990s, pushing it to look once more for non-Western military supplies. This renewed Pakistan's interest in North Korea. Pakistan was specifically seeking vehicles that could deliver its nuclear warheads. Overall four factors influenced Pakistan's priorities in terms of a renewed arms trade with North Korea:

1. Having developed the requisite levels of enriched uranium and nuclear weapons design, Pakistan was looking to improve its missile-based weapons-delivery system and obtain a reliable airborne nuclear delivery system. However, in 1989 the US Pressler Amendment effectively froze Pakistan's air force procurement, and consequently the delivery of F-16 aircraft that Islamabad had already purchased from the USA was stalled.[28]

2. The growing air-power imbalance with India was a concern for Pakistan. India had already test-fired its short-range Prithvi ballistic

missile in February 1988 and introduced Prithvi missile batteries into service with the army in 1994.[29]

3. Pakistan's relations with the U.S., in the aftermath of the Soviet withdrawal from Afghanistan in 1989, were deteriorating. At the same time, the emerging crisis in the wake of a renewed insurgency in the Indian-controlled part of Kashmir strained Pakistan's relations with India. The growing effectiveness of the Missile Technology Control Regime (MTCR), originally established in 1987, also had its impact on Pakistan. Most European suppliers were members of the MTCR group, and thus refused to supply Pakistan with the means to produce missile-delivery systems. Pakistan had acquired thirty-four solid-fuelled M-11 ballistic missiles from China in 1989, but these were short-range systems (300 km) and could not target locations throughout India.[30] Due to US pressure on China to comply strictly with the MTCR, China was reluctant to sell longer-range missiles in the M-series to Pakistan (though later it did).[31]

4. Rivalry between the PAEC and KRL was another crucial factor in the revival of Pakistan–North Korea security ties. The solid-fuel M-11 missiles from China went to the PAEC; KRL was responsible for the liquid-fuel missile programme, and it was lagging behind.[32] A. Q. Khan had a serious personal rivalry with the chairman of the PAEC, Munir Ahmed Khan, and wanted to be ahead of the PAEC at all costs in developing the nuclear weapons delivery system. North Korean No-Dong missiles were liquid-fuel generated, which attracted A. Q. Khan, who understood complex liquid handling systems.

Genesis of the Nuclear Connection: 1992–2002

In 1992 North Korean officials offered their long-range missile expertise to Pakistani officials who had travelled to North Korea to view a prototype of the No-Dong missile.[33] North Korea was of course more than willing to sell the missiles, but Pakistan insisted on purchasing the designs as well in a comprehensive package deal. At this juncture, A. Q. Khan was brought into the negotiations, which smoothed things significantly.

It is not too difficult to guess what Khan could offer to North Korea that the Pakistani military officials who had visited North Korea earlier could not: he promised them uranium-enrichment equipment and expertise. Pakistan was keen to have the designs of No-Dong because then they could produce the missile with a 'Made in Pakistan' tag, allowing it to show off its ability to produce long-range missiles, like India. Pakistan was ready to pay any price for the designs, both as a matter of necessity and of prestige.

According to Doug Frantz and Catherine Collins, Khan went to Prime Minister Benazir Bhutto in December 1993 and asked her to add a visit to North Korea on to her trip to China. Khan asked that Bhutto follow up with the North Korean leadership about a deal that he had negotiated regarding the purchase of No-Dong missiles, which could carry a nuclear payload.[34] Gordon Corera believes that Khan and the military involved Bhutto in the missile deal because of the pre-existing relationship between her late father, Z. A. Bhutto, and the North Korean leadership.[35] This is further substantiated by Bruno Tertrais, who maintains that Khan seems to have 'paved the way' for Bhutto's visit.[36] Benazir Bhutto corroborated this in one of her last interviews to the media:

> Concerning North Korea, the army and scientists came to me in 1993 and asked me to go to North Korea, which I did, to negotiate the exchange of nuclear delivery technology for cold cash. After we got the technology, they came to me again and said, 'Now we want to develop this updated missile technology.' I refused to give them the money to go forward because I was very clear at the time that I didn't want a missile race with India.[37]

Like Pakistan, North Korea was going through a severe economic crunch due to international sanctions imposed on it after the discovery of its nuclear activity in 1992. In her remarks given at a state dinner hosted by Kim Il-Sung (during her December 1993 visit), Benazir Bhutto said that Pakistan and North Korea 'shared the problem of American imposed sanctions'.[38] Kim Il-Sung, speaking earlier at the same event, had remarked that the 'technical know-how' acquired by Asian people was an important guarantee for the independence and prosperity of the continent based on cooperation.[39] Bhutto acknowledged this point, and added: 'Pakistan firmly holds the view that nuclear non-proliferation should not be made a pretext for preventing states from exercising fully their right to acquire and develop nuclear technology for peaceful purposes.'[40] Evidently, both leaders knew what was involved in the deal.

However, it is entirely possible that Bhutto was not fully aware of what exactly Khan had committed to North Korea because she had been told that Pakistan was paying hard cash for the transaction. Khan and military officials may have wanted her to believe that there was no underhand dealing involved. After all, they had previously declared her a security risk for the country, and never trusted her fully, thinking that she was too close to America.[41] They also thought that Bhutto was likely to share the details about this missile deal with the USA, especially if asked about it, which was indeed possible, given serious US apprehensions about North Korea. Hence, by convincing Bhutto about the nature of the transaction (i.e. cash for the missiles), the army was in turn trying to cover its back. Military leaders involved, and A. Q. Khan, knew that providing uranium-enrichment expertise to North Korea, if exposed, would not go down well with the USA at all, and thus it was crucial to hide these links by any means.

According to the 2007 IISS report *Nuclear Black Markets*, this North Korea–Pakistan deal called for between twelve and twenty-five No-Dong missiles.[42] These negotiations were conducted in 1995, and the contract included at least one mobile launcher; the delivery of all equipment was set to occur within the next couple of years. According to the North Korean Politburo defector Hwang Jang Yop, the deal was concluded in the summer of 1996.[43] Two years later, on 6 April 1998, the 1,500-kilometre-range Ghauri-1 missile, a liquid-fuelled No-Dong derivative, was flight-tested in Pakistan under the management of Khan's KRL. In parallel, the PAEC was also focused throughout the 1990s on acquiring a delivery vehicle, and it tested its product (Hatf IV—a derivative of a Chinese M-9 missile) in April 1999. Comparing the two missile flight tests Christopher O. Clary aptly remarks: 'Khan and KRL beat PAEC by more than a year.'[44] That was indeed Khan's goal here. The institutional rivalry between KRL and the PAEC was healthy for Pakistan's security goals in that sense.

Various reports indicate that Khan supplied North Korea with centrifuges and depleted uranium hexafluoride gas (UF 6) from late 1997 onwards. The frequency of cargo flights between North Korea and Pakistan reportedly increased from three per month in the autumn of 1997 to three times that in January the following year, indicating that air transportation was used extensively in the North Korea–Pakistan nuclear and missile transfers.[45] For transportation, C-130s belonging to the Pakistan air force or charter companies connected to it (e.g. Shaheen Air International) were used. Missile imports from North Korea through this mode was part of the deal, and it is near impossible that any KRL equipment was loaded onto these planes at Pakistan air force bases (which are strictly guarded and monitored) on their way to North Korea without authorization from the highest officials of the Pakistan air force or army. The IISS rightly maintains: 'It seems unlikely that they [the army] would have been unaware of the nuclear coopera-tion that was occurring at the same time.'[46] In addition, Khan, on a trip to North Korea in 1999, was given a tour of its nuclear facilities, which should have rung alarm bells, as transfer of missile technology and purchases had already been completed.[47] Exchange visits between the scientists of the two countries continued until 2001.[48]

President Pervez Musharraf in his memoirs acknowledges that in 1999 he 'received a report suggesting that some North Korean nuclear experts, under the guise of missile engineers, had arrived at KRL and were being given secret briefings on centrifuges, including some visits to the plant'.[49]

To be fair, Khan has repeatedly claimed that three different army chiefs were aware of his nuclear deals with Pyongyang: General Abdul Waheed Kakar (1994–6), General Jahangir Karamat (1996–8), and General Pervez Musharraf (1998–2007).[50] Gaurav Kampani supports this contention when he concludes that 'it is difficult to imagine how Dr. A. Q. Khan could have made such a momentous decision indepen-dently without the benefit of a debate, albeit a limited one, at the high-est levels of Pakistani government'.[51]

Pakistan had an incentive to provide evidence of financial transactions that might have come to light in its investigations of Khan because this would have helped to distance the government and the military from Khan's nuclear sales, but no such evidence has surfaced since 2004. Khan, meanwhile, came out with some specific allegations involving General Karamat in a 2011 statement shared with Western media. He claims to have 'shared' twenty P-1 centrifuges and four advanced P-2s with the North Koreans after clear approval from General Karamat (in fact, he sold them). He further maintains that he handed over $2.5 mil-lion to the general at his official residence, as he had demanded the amount for a secret army fund that he was managing.[52] The general, who enjoys a good professional reputation, denies this charge vociferously. Why Khan decided to target General Karamat, however, is worth probing. As mentioned earlier, Karamat was indeed the first to ask for an audit of the nuclear programme, and Khan was uneasy about it. A retired army general confirmed to me that 'Yes—a classified audit was ordered but only partially carried out because of various considerations that surfaced.'[53] It was called off, as the military hierarchy was convinced that records of some of the transactions involved intelligence assets who might be compromised in the auditing process.

Analysis and Conclusion

Various studies have analysed counter-arguments to many of the above assertions since the exposure of Pakistan–North Korea links between 2002 and 2004. The missile imports were discovered by the USA around 1997–8, and in April 1998 the US State Department applied sanctions against KRL.[54] When the USA discovered that Islamabad was possibly exporting nuclear technology to North Korea, President Clinton took up this issue with Prime Minister Nawaz Sharif in December 1998 and told him to cease such transfers; Sharif claimed complete ignorance in the matter.[55] However, when US deputy secretary of state Strobe Talbott followed up with Sharif later, Sharif made a commitment that 'no transfer of nuclear weapon or ballistic missile technology or data would go to the North Koreans'. Sharif however refused to commit to anything further, saying that Pakistan had 'legitimate defense requirements with regard to its conventional weaponry that it could meet only through trade with North Korea'.[56] Sharif must have discussed the issue with his chief of army staff, General Pervez Musharraf.

It is also plausible that A. Q. Khan extended and expanded the deal with North Korea on his own, as he did in the case of Iran. Another argument considers the financial circumstances in which Pakistan found itself around the mid-1990s. In the words of Sharon A. Squassoni, Pakistan's 'reserve crunch' might have prompted it to turn from cash to nuclear technology in return for missile technology.[57] It is a documented fact that in 1996 Pakistan's foreign exchange reserves were equivalent to only three weeks of imports and the country was only able to avoid default with help from the International Monetary Fund and by borrowing $500 million from domestic banks.[58] So this argument is not without its merits.

Christopher Oren Clary argues that there are five reasons to reject the theory that decision-makers in Pakistan had authorized a nuclear-for-missile technology exchange with North Korea. These are: (1) Benazir Bhutto had claimed that the missile cooperation was based on cash payment, rather than nuclear barter; (2) While it is true that Pakistan's foreign reserves sank to dire levels in 1996, it is a long leap to assume that Pakistan could find no other way to finance missile acquisitions than by a technology exchange—the estimated cost of No-Dong missiles (between twelve and twenty-five) was between $48 million and $100 million, which was a trivial amount for Pakistan given that its arms imports in 1995–6 were worth around $819 million; (3) Even if Pakistan's financial ability to compensate North Korea was limited, Pakistan did not have to trade the nuclear 'crown jewels' for decades-old liquid-fuel missiles. If North Korea had sold its missiles to Egypt, Iran, Libya, Syria, and Yemen for money, then why should Pakistan's case be any different; (4) Evidence of Pakistani–North Korean transactions is not clear evidence of nuclear collaboration, as for instance cargo flights between the two countries could have been indicative of collaboration on other military equipment, including surface-to-air missiles and artillery; (5) Pakistan's Inter-Services Intelligence (ISI) did apparently raid a North Korea-bound chartered aircraft in 2000 and did not find anything proving Khan's malfeasance.[59]

Though most of these matters have been discussed and analysed in the previous section, a couple of issues raised by Clary require some analysis. Clary is right that the cargo flights might have been carrying other, non-nuclear, military hardware. If that indeed was the case, then it would be in Pakistan's interest to provide specific information about the trade items (which must be on record) to the IAEA or international media, which would discredit at least one of the charges. That has not happened. Secondly, North Korea's transactions with Pakistan cannot be compared with its other business deals, as each case is unique depending upon its individual circumstances, the prevailing international political scenario, and the regional security scene. For instance, none of the other countries mentioned by Clary had nuclear technology or know-how at their disposal in the mid-1990s, and it was widely known that Pakistan had acquired the capability—hence the possible North Korean interest in such a barter deal. Finally, for the sake of argument, even if it was a solo venture by the A. Q. Khan network, the Pakistan government (especially its army) cannot escape the charge of criminal negligence. This last point is duly acknowledged by Clary in his analysis.[60]

Furthermore, as David Albright rightly contends, the IAEA is not involved in an active investigation of Khan's assistance to North Korea, and 'details remain sparse about who brokered the deals—and where and when key meetings took place'.[61]

According to Selig Harrison, director of the Asia Program at the Center for International Policy, when the USA questioned North Korean officials about their uranium-enrichment programme in the second half of 2007, they responded by saying: 'Why don't you invite A. Q. Khan to join the negotiations? ...Where is the invoice? Give us the evidence.'[62] Harrison considers various reasons why President Musharraf did not allow US officials to talk to Khan and get more information about the North Korean deal. He suggested as one possibility that Musharraf 'invented the "facts" in his memoir to curry favor with the Bush administration; by strengthening its case against North Korea, in this view, he hoped to offset dissatisfaction in Washington with his ineffectual performance in combating al-Qaeda and the Taliban'.[63]

However, Khan broke his silence on the issue in July 2008, when Musharraf was in deep trouble politically. Khan confessed in a media interview that he had provided centrifuges to North Korea in a shipment in 2000 that had been supervised by the army under Musharraf. In his own words: 'It was a North Korean plane, and the army had complete knowledge about it and the equipment.'[64] He further argued: 'It must have gone with his [Musharraf's] consent.'[65]

There are also questions about whether the nuclear weapons design was also given by Khan to North Korea, but evidence is lacking in this regard. It is also argued that two dozen centrifuges were insufficient to produce enough highly enriched uranium for a nuclear bomb, but if Khan also provided them with centrifuge designs (which is possible) then North Korea could use the actual centrifuges as a template and its scientists and engineers could build their own centrifuge production line. As with Iran, Khan also reportedly provided a 'shopping list' to North Korea, which enabled it to purchase additional components directly from other foreign suppliers.[66] According to the IISS report *Nuclear Black Markets*, North Korea had by 2000 begun to seek such materials in industrial-scale quantities from international market; this convinced many analysts that North Korea had progressed beyond the research and development stage in its uranium-enrichment centrifuge programme.[67] Pakistan's help thus played an important role in North Korea's clandestine uranium-enrichment programme, though it opted to use plutonium in the nuclear test it conducted in October 2006. Whether North Korea used plutonium or uranium as the starting material for the 2013 tests is unclear.[68] In 2016 international media reports indicated that India–North Korea nuclear cooperation is also something to monitor.[69]

6

PAKISTAN'S NUCLEAR PROLIFERATION LINKS
WITH LIBYA

The most well-documented case of nuclear proliferation emanating from Pakistan is that of Libya.[1] The A. Q. Khan network's wide-ranging sale of nuclear weapons technology began in 1997 and continued until 2003. The trade ceased shortly after the US invasion of Iraq, when Libyan president Muammar al-Qaddafi decided to completely, verifiably, and irreversibly dismantle its nuclear programme. Essentially, Libya traded away its nuclear programme for re-entry into the international community, and the decision to do so pulled the rug out from underneath the A.Q. Khan network. It led to the unexpected unravelling of this transnational nuclear technology sales enterprise.

In comparison to Iran and North Korea, the evidence of the A. Q. Khan network's nuclear cooperation and proliferation complicity with Libya is more definitive. Libya gave full disclosure to the IAEA inspectors in 2003.[2] The facts provide a telling story of proliferation.

The A. Q. Khan network had undertaken to supply Libya with a wide range of items, including a turnkey gas centrifuge plant, uranium hexafluoride (UF 6), and nuclear weapons designs, as well as transferring the expertise to make centrifuges, and the ability to produce UF 6. It also signed onto a clause to train the technical personnel necessary to maintain such an infrastructure. Libya was willing to pay $100 million for such a capability. Many of these items and equipment were in the pipeline when Libya decided to call it a day. Qaddafi confessed that he had sanctioned these procurements in contravention of Libya's international obligations under the Nuclear Non-Proliferation Treaty (NPT).

The giving up of the nuclear option by Libya, however, was not entirely voluntary. After secret negotiations with the USA and UK to lift sanctions implemented in response to the Lockerbie bombing, Libya contacted the British intelligence service MI6 in March 2003 to initiate talks on dismantling its strategic weapons programme in exchange for the removal of other sanctions. Libya was initially reluctant to acknowledge the full extent of its nuclear plans and deals in progress, until the German-registered vessel *BBC China*, bound for Libya with centrifuge equipment from the A. Q. Khan network, was discovered and impounded in a joint USA–UK–Germany–Italy operation. This showed Libya that its nuclear supply lines were compromised, and it then opted for complete disclosure.[3]

The Libyan–Pakistani nuclear trade case is important for two important reasons. First, it exposed the A. Q. Khan network's nuclear specialists, middlemen, and supplier companies from three continents. Second, it produced a previously unthinkable range of possibilities, especially in terms of the involvement of non-state actors in nuclear proliferation.

This chapter begins with a brief sketch of Libya's nuclear programme, its history and motivations, followed by a glance at historical Pakistan–Libya relations. It then delves into the details of the A. Q. Khan network's deal with Libya, and probes whether this was a private venture by the network or whether, as in the cases of Iran and North Korea, there was some level of involvement and sanction from other institutions and individuals in Pakistan.

A History of Libya's Nuclear Programme

The story of Libya's nuclear programme begins during the reign of the pro-Western king of Libya, Sayyid Muhammad Idris. He ruled Libya from 1951 to 1969, and aligned the country with the USA and the West.

Sayyid believed that nuclear weapons proliferation threatened global peace, and he signed the NPT in July 1968. However, his reign came to an end in 1969 when the Revolutionary Command Council headed by Colonel Muammar al-Qaddafi overthrew him. Qaddafi's rise to power was partly driven by resentment over the 1967 defeat of the Arabs by Israel, and he began seeking nuclear technology shortly after taking power despite Libya being a signatory to the NPT. Without a hint of shame, Libya ratified the NPT in 1975.[4] Qaddafi pursued nuclear weapons technology ambitiously but, due to the limited availability of scientific capabilities and an inadequate industrial base, many of his initial efforts came to nothing. Focus was soon shifted to foreign suppliers.

Qaddafi's nuclear technology pursuits effectively began in 1970, when he made an unsuccessful attempt to purchase nuclear weapons from China.[5] During the 1972–4 period, Qaddafi met Pakistan's prime minister Z. A. Bhutto on three to four occasions, and nuclear cooperation was discussed in detail.[6] In 1976 negotiations were held between France and Libya for the purchase of a 600 MW reactor. A preliminary agreement was reached, but strong objections by the international community led France to cancel the project.[7] In the 1970s (and also later) Libya discussed the construction of a nuclear power plant with the Soviet Union, and at one point the Belgian firm Belgonucleaire was in discussions with Libyan officials to provide engineering support and equipment for this proposed project, but US pressure led the firm to refuse the contract.[8] Qaddafi finally proceeded to make a deal with the Soviet Union—after negotiations with the American-based company General Atomics were cut off by the US Department of State—that would provide Libya with its first nuclear reactor.

In 1983 the Soviet-supplied 10 MW research reactor began operating at the Tajura Nuclear Research Centre, but it was subject to IAEA inspections.[9] However, in 2004 Libya admitted to the IAEA that it had also acquired a pilot-scale uranium conversion facility in 1984.[10] The relevant IAEA report does not identify the country that supplied Libya with this facility. It says that the plant was fabricated in portable modules, in accordance with Libyan specifications, and that these modules were received in 1986, but then placed in storage until 1998.[11] Libya has also admitted that during the 1980s it conducted undeclared laboratory-scale uranium-conversion experiments at the Tajura Nuclear Research Centre.[12] However, the official and public statements of the Libyan leader at this period had a different message. For instance, when asked by a *Time* magazine reporter in 1981 if he was developing an 'Islamic bomb', independently or in cooperation with Pakistan, he said:

> I have nothing but scorn for the notion of an Islamic bomb. There is no such thing as an Islamic bomb or a Christian bomb. Any such weapon is a means of terrorizing humanity, and we are against the manufacture and acquisition of nuclear weapons. This is in line with our definition of—and opposition to terrorism.[13]

Next, Libya tried to hire foreign nuclear experts, but these efforts produced few results. At some point in the 1980s, however, a foreign expert began a research and design programme at the Tajura Nuclear Research Centre, aimed at producing gas centrifuges for uranium enrichment.[14] The unknown foreign expert was reportedly a former employee of a German firm.[15] However, Libya told the IAEA that by the time the foreign expert concluded his work in 1992, Libya was not yet able to produce an operating centrifuge, and no centrifuge experiments involving nuclear materials had been conducted. However, some technical expertise useful for the next stage of centrifuge designing had been developed in the process. According to the same IAEA report, after the German expert left, the uranium-enrichment programme lost momentum. However, also in 1992, an official of the Kurchatov Institute in Moscow, a leading Russian nuclear research centre, claimed that Libya had unsuccessfully tried to recruit two of his colleagues to work at the Tajura Nuclear Research Centre in Libya.[16]

Libya's official position regarding its nuclear aspirations remained vague in the 1990s, and contradictory statements were a regular occurrence.[17] For instance, while Libyan officials continued with the mantra that Libya did not desire a nuclear weapon, Qaddafi repeatedly stated that Israel's nuclear capability justified Libya's pursuit of the nuclear technology.[18] He was hedging his bets in case his secret efforts were exposed. In 1996 Libya took a potentially constructive step when it signed the Pelindaba Treaty, declaring Africa a nuclear-free zone and prohibiting parties to the treaty from possessing nuclear weapons or materials.[19] However, the same year Qaddafi stated that Arab states should develop a nuclear weapon to counter Israel's nuclear weapons capability.

One of the reasons why Libya's nuclear programme could not really take off was the economic impact of US sanctions (for alleged involvement in international terrorism), initially imposed on Libya in 1984 and expanded in 1992 and 1996. Libya renewed its efforts to seek help from China as well as Russia in the early 1990s, but to no avail.[20] Libya also unsuccessfully sought help from Argentina, Bulgaria, and Japan in search of plutonium as a route to a nuclear bomb during the 1990s. Finally, it turned to its old friend Pakistan, and that worked. This was in pursuance of a Libyan decision in July 1995 'to reinvigorate its nuclear activities, including gas centrifuge enrichment'.[21] According to the 2007 IISS report *Nuclear Black Markets*, Libyan intelligence initiated contact with A. Q. Khan in 1997, and followed it up with a meeting in Istanbul later that year to conclude a comprehensive nuclear deal, which is discussed in some detail in this chapter.[22]

A History of Pakistan–Libya Relations

Though Pakistan had had diplomatic relations with Libya since its inception in 1952, it was the 1974 Islamic Summit in the Pakistani city of Lahore, organized by Prime Minister Z. A. Bhutto, that brought Pakistan and Libya closer to each other. A photograph of Bhutto and Colonel Qaddafi, standing arm in arm with clenched fists in a pavilion of the historic Shalimar Gardens in Lahore, remains a popular image in Pakistan. Observing Qaddafi's popularity there, Bhutto named Pakistan's premier cricket stadium in Lahore after him.[23] Suggestions of a name change after Qaddafi's tragic end in 2011 have failed to receive any support in Pakistan.

As discussed in earlier chapters, India conducted its nuclear explosive test in 1974, inspiring Bhutto to follow India's path to nuclear weapons technology with renewed vigour. It was a project that needed a lot of money, and Bhutto was looking to Libya and other oil-producing Arab states for financial backing. Bhutto's visit to Libya soon after his secret 1972 meeting with Pakistani nuclear scientists was also aimed at raising the requisite funds.[24] A Pakistani writer explains the Bhutto–Qaddafi relationship as follows:

> There is little doubt that Bhutto and Qaddafi shared a vision of reviving the glory of the Islamic world. Their notion of Pan-Islamism, however roman-tic or unrealistic in retrospect, did spawn a natural bond of camaraderie between them. That explained the rationale for Qaddafi helping Pakistan's nuclear programme, in its infancy, with injections of money.[25]

Though there is no official record setting out the nature of the understanding that the two leaders had reached about nuclear cooperation, it is believed by many Pakistani nuclear scientists that there was a tacit understanding that Pakistan would share its nuclear expertise, including weapons, the training of scientists, and the sharing of fuel with Libya after successfully acquiring the nuclear technology.[26] The US Department of State also believed so at the time, as one of its leaked cables refers to 'an intelligence report that Libya has agreed to finance the Pakistani reprocessing project in return for some unspecified future nuclear cooperation'.[27]

In addition to financial support, Libya tried to help Pakistan's nuclear programme in other ways. In the mid-1970s, for instance, Qaddafi passed 450 tonnes of yellowcake to Pakistan that Libya had obtained from Niger.[28] According to the scholar Bhumitra Chakma, however, Pakistan's former foreign secretary Niaz A. Naik had gone to Niger in the mid-1970s to arrange uranium import from there.[29] There is a consensus among writers (journalists as well as academics) that Libya certainly provided funds to Pakistan for its nuclear programme in the early 1970s. Estimates range between $100 million and $500 million.[30] As a goodwill gesture, Bhutto had sent some Pakistan air force pilots to Libya in the early 1970s to help the Libyan air force, along with a small contingent of officers from Pakistan's navy.[31]

Later, after the hanging of Bhutto by General Zia-ul-Haq, Qaddafi became so angry that he decided to expel 50,000 Pakistanis working in Libya. It took Zia's government months of frantic diplomacy to dissuade Qaddafi from implementing this decision. Zia had visited Libya in late 1977 to soften Qaddafi's anger towards him for overthrowing Bhutto's government.[32] The Pakistan–Libya nuclear cooperation at the government-to-government level ended at that stage, including the training facilities that Pakistan had been providing to Libyan scientists at PINSTECH, a nuclear research institution in Pakistan.[33]

During the late 1980s a few Pakistani nuclear scientists with experience working on Pakistan's nuclear programme were also hired by the Libyan nuclear programme, but they left Libya in frustration with the difficult work environment and lack of scientific facilities.[34] However, according to Egyptian nuclear scientists who worked in Libya from 1975 through the early 1980s, the number of Pakistani nuclear scientists visiting Libya steadily increased during that period.[35]

PAKISTAN'S NUCLEAR PROLIFERATION LINKS WITH LIBYA

The 1997–2003 Deal

By 1995 Libya had clearly decided to revive its nuclear programme, especially the uranium-enrichment efforts, and it started making contacts among Pakistani scientists and officials in this regard.[36] As mentioned earlier, in 1997 Libyan intelligence officials were successful in meeting A. Q. Khan in Istanbul. Bokhari Syed Abu Tahir, a Sri Lankan national who was a nephew of Mohamed Farouq (of the 1987 Iran deal fame) and a leading member of the A. Q. Khan network based in Malaysia, went to the meeting. Malaysian police had been tracking Tahir as part of an investigation. According to a Malaysian police report on the subject, the Libyans asked Khan to supply centrifuge units for their nuclear programme.[37] According to the deal, Libya purchased twenty complete P-1 (which Libya called L-1) aluminium centrifuges from the network, along with most of the components for an additional 200 L-1 centrifuges. The feed and withdrawal systems, the frequency converters for small cascades, and some of the centrifuge components were supplied by the network outside Pakistan. However, the network apparently was unable or unwilling to provide the aluminium rotors and magnets necessary for these 200 unassembled units.[38] A few of these centrifuges had been used in Pakistan until 1987.

In the next phase, in 2000, Libya purchased two P-2 (which Libya called L-2) maraging steel centrifuges from Pakistan. Both of these centrifuges had also been used in the Pakistani nuclear programme, and came contaminated with highly enriched uranium particles. Libya had also placed another order for 10,000 L-2 centrifuges (in late 1999 or 2000), with the first deliveries arriving in December 2002.[39]

Along with the staggering order for 10,000 L-2 centrifuges from the network, Libya paid for contract assistance to construct a sophisticated manufacturing centre, code-named Workshop 1001. This would allow Libya to make its own centrifuge components. According to the original plan, once the network delivered the first 10,000 centrifuges, the workshop would be set up so that Libya could replace and repair any damaged ones. The workshop also allowed Libya to expand its programme by producing more centrifuges. According to Albright and Hinderstein, a facility of this size would have been able to produce enough highly enriched uranium for more than ten nuclear weapons annually.[40]

To fulfil this massive Libyan order, the A. Q. Khan network decided to make the centrifuges and related equipment outside Pakistan. Since each P-2 (L-2) centrifuge contained roughly a hundred different components, this order translated into a total of about a million components, a staggering number of parts, reflecting the sophistication of gas centrifuge components. The network assembled an impressive cast of experts, companies, suppliers, and workshops to make these components. In addition to accessing a range of experts who would make the completion of this deal possible, the A. Q. Khan network promised to provide the Libyans with the necessary training to ultimately assemble and run the project on their own. The deal included ongoing technical assistance to help the Libyan nuclear programme tackle any future hurdles.

By late 2003 Libya had received an extensive collection of equipment and materials for Workshop 1001.[41] Importantly, most of the equipment for the centre came from Europe, particularly from or through Spain and Italy, as well as via Dubai. Dubai was indeed the hub of the A. Q. Khan network. Khan remained deeply involved in every stage of this process, as is evident from the fact that he made forty-four visits to Dubai between 1999 and 2003—many of these presumably for monitoring the implementation of the Libyan deal.[42]

In addition to the means of producing fissile material, the network also gave Libya the information necessary to build a nuclear weapon in the form of designs and blueprints. The documentation included assembly drawings and manufacturing instructions for the explosive parts of the weapon, the detonator and fissile materials, although it did not include the associated electronics and high-quality cables. Libya maintains that it received the relevant documentation in late 2001 or early 2002, but took no steps to act on the information. While the key documents and all the drawings were provided in English, a detailed look at the documentation raised another set of questions about the primary source of this vital information. The experts inferred that these designs originated from China, indicating China's help to Pakistan in its development of nuclear weapons design and configuration.[43] The bomb design provided the most complete declassified instructions available. It was about 95 per cent complete, and was far more detailed than anything that has been available on the internet or through other unclassified sources, according to the assessment of experts at the IISS. The material laid out a step-by-step process of casting uranium into a metal bomb core. More insightfully, the designs were for a 10 kilotonne implosion device, which resembled a late 1960s Chinese design, weighing 453 kilograms. The 2007 IISS report *Nuclear Black Markets* maintains that 'many of the bomb design documents were described as copies of copies, and included handwritten notes from lectures by Chinese weapons experts, that seemed to confirm that they had been reviewed by KRL'.[44] In January 2004 Libya turned over to the USA and UK (via the IAEA) the design documents in the form in which Libya said they had arrived, wrapped in two white plastic shopping bags with the logo of an Islamabad tailor's shop, which Khan use to visit regularly.[45] It would be hard to make up such a connection.

David Albright's assessment substantiates a Chinese link. He argues that the nuclear weapon design given to Libya was that of a Chinese warhead tested on a missile, with a mass of about 500 kilograms, and measuring less than a metre in diameter.[46] This design would not have fitted on Libyan Scud missiles. Albright maintains that it could have been air dropped, or intended for a more advanced missile Libya may have sought. The design, he believes, would have fitted on Iranian and North Korean missiles.[47]

Fulfilling such a complex order required ingenuity on the part of the Libyan–Pakistani deal-makers, especially to avoid detection by customs and immigration authorities at various ports. Khan's innovation and genius shone as he established factories in third-party states. Workshops in Turkey served as European mini-hubs, from which Khan's network could procure and supply centrifuge motors, power supplies, and ring magnets from partially within the web of pan-European export controls. Importing sub-components from Europe and elsewhere, these facilities assembled centrifuge motors and frequency converters necessary to drive the centrifuges.[48]

Khan utilized other regions of the world as well. In South Africa, the network drew upon firms and individuals with connections to the now-defunct South African nuclear programme. After South Africa had made a strategic decision to abandon its nuclear weapons programme in the early 1990s, some of its experts involved in that programme became available for contract services. Gerhard Wisser, a German

national living in South Africa, knew Khan intimately, as he had previously supplied vacuum pumps and other equipment to Pakistan in the
1980s. When a lucrative offer from B. S. A. Tahir presented itself to
Wisser in 1999 (for the manufacture of 'certain pipe work systems')
after their 'incidental' meeting in Dubai, Wisser jumped at the opportunity.[49] It requires no genius to figure out that Khan must have facilitated the contact between Wisser and Tahir. Wisser further expanded
the web as he engaged a former associate who worked for the South
African nuclear programme, Johan Meyer, owner of the engineering
firm TradeFin, based in Vanderbiljpark in South Africa. Along with a
third associate, Swiss citizen Daniel Geiges, they set out to build a
complex steel system to feed and withdraw UF 6 gas into a centrifuge
cascade. The massive system filled eleven 40-foot shipping containers
and was estimated to be worth $33 million.[50] Clearly, the nature,
reach, and level of expertise available to the A. Q. Khan network to
enable the Libya deal were quite amazing.

The most well-known facility operated by the A. Q. Khan network,
however, was located in Shah Alam in Malaysia. This factory, established
in 2001, only employed about thirty people. Khan selected Malaysia
primarily because of Tahir and his contacts. Tahir's wife, who is a
Malaysian citizen, belongs to an influential Malaysian family. The
A. Q. Khan network needed to evade export controls from members
of the Nuclear Suppliers Group (NSG), and hence political connections
in Malaysia came in handy in case of any unexpected probing.

Also, Tahir contracted Scomi Group Berhad, a Malaysian oil and gas
firm, to manufacture thousands of centrifuge components for the Libya
operation. Scomi set up a subsidiary, Scomi Precision Engineering
(SCOPE), with a small facility in Shah Alam, in which to do the manufacturing.[51] Scomi's complicity in proliferation, however, proved to be
less pervasive, as Scomi officials were cleared in 2008 of having known
that the components were destined for a nuclear weapons programme
in Libya.[52] The two-year $3.5 million contract was signed in the name
of a company owned by another member of the A. Q. Khan network,
Peter 'Maverick' Griffin—although Griffin later denied any involvement, arguing that Tahir had forged the documents.[53] The network was
certainly masterful when it came to forgery. At Tahir's request, Urs
Tinner, son of long-time Khan associate Friedrich Tinner, also began

consulting for the SCOPE factory, and arranged to import important materials needed for the project. Between December 2002 and August 2003 SCOPE manufactured and sent fourteen types of centrifuge components (of the approximately one hundred components needed in total) to Dubai.[54]

The *BBC China* interdiction finally compromised the A. Q. Khan network and, according to Clary, 'individuals associated with the network began a mad scramble to destroy evidence of wrongdoing, or possibly to sell it quickly to other interested customers', and valuable and sensitive materials disappeared in 2003, as the network was collapsing.[55] The A.Q. Khan network was finally nearing its end.

Analysis and Conclusion

The Libyan case clearly demonstrates the A. Q. Khan network's global reach, its sheer audacity and defiance of the international order. Libya was the network's biggest customer, paying it around $100 million, according to US estimates. The Pakistani nuclear connections with Iran and North Korea can be logically seen to be based on security compulsions and historical connections, but the network's cooperation with Libya is more puzzling. The IISS report *Nuclear Black Markets* argues that this puzzle cannot be resolved unless the venture can be 'viewed as a straight business deal'.[56] There was little commonality of interest between Pakistan and Libya in 1997, when the initial contact with Khan was made. There was no ongoing collaboration in military affairs, nor were there extensive trade relations between the two countries at the time. Such relations were present only during the early 1970s when Qaddafi and Z. A. Bhutto were close, as discussed earlier. This nuclear cooperation between the A. Q. Khan network and Libya reached its peak at a time when Pakistan had become closely allied with the USA in the aftermath of the 11 September 2001 terror attacks in the USA, and thus it appears unlikely that the government of Pakistan would have risked such an undertaking (or a continuation thereof) with a pariah country for such a sum.

Interestingly, however, the relationship between Pakistan and Libya had revived to a limited degree by the year 2000, when Pervez Musharraf (then the chief executive of the country) visited Libya.[57] The last meeting between Qaddafi and any Pakistani leader was in 1988 when Benazir Bhutto, after becoming prime minister for the first time, visited Libya. The primary purpose of her visit was to thank Qaddafi for his support to her family members during their years in exile in the 1980s and for trying his best to convince President Zia in 1979 to release Z. A. Bhutto, and relocate him to Libya if necessary.[58]

As to why General Musharraf visited Libya in 2000, Benazir Bhutto, in an interview in 2004, alleged that Musharraf had sanctioned Khan's nuclear collaboration with Libya.[59] In the interview she mentions that when she travelled to Libya in 1988 Qaddafi never even raised the issue of nuclear collaboration with her. She provides some insightful reasoning as to why Musharraf might have given Khan the go-ahead in this regard:

> Musharraf did go there in 2000. If he didn't go to sell a bomb dossier, as has been reported, then why did he go? What made Libya so suddenly interested in the bomb? ... My surmise is that Musharraf was trying to make himself strategically important after being virtually ignored by President Clinton—who met with him for only four hours on his visit to South Asia [earlier in 2000]. Musharraf wanted to send a message: pay attention to me or you might see the consequences.[60]

There is no evidence available so far to support this argument, and the fact that Bhutto was in the political wilderness in 2004 might have influenced this claim. Musharraf was also pursing various corruption charges (largely politically motivated) against her in Pakistani and Swiss courts at the time, and she had been in self-imposed exile since 1997. Nothing can be ruled out, but it is unlikely that Musharraf was involved in this proliferation scandal.

According to Bruno Tertrais, personal greed, and perhaps a temptation to give the bomb to a Muslim country that had helped Pakistan so much in the past, were in all likelihood the determining factors here.[61] Clary also concludes that 'it appears that Khan was primarily motivated by greed, and perhaps to a lesser extent out of some misguided desire by Khan for pan-Muslim comity'.[62] He further says that Khan's Swiss, South African, Turkish, and British partners seem to have been squarely and solely motivated by personal greed, which is a rational assessment.[63] From this, he logically infers that micro-level individual decisions and motivations may have had a decisive strategic effect in this episode. This view is also substantiated by the fact that Khan was removed from his important and influential KRL position in March 2001, whereas his nuclear business deal with Libya remained intact.[64] If government of Pakistan or army was complicit in the deal, then they would not have sidelined Khan at that critical juncture—especially as there was no international or domestic pressure to do so. Musharraf had received an alert from the USA about Khan's activities, but he ignored it.[65] Musharraf, in his memoirs, however, says that in the year 2000 it was becoming clearer that Khan was not 'part of the problem' but 'the problem' itself, and that's why he decided to retire him in March 2001.[66] The details of this case strongly show that at the least the Pakistan government had singularly failed in monitoring Khan and his illicit activities.

7

INVESTIGATING A. Q. KHAN'S PERSONAL MOTIVATIONS, RELIGIOUS ORIENTATION, AND ANTI-WESTERN WORLDVIEW

This chapter investigates the personal motivations, religious influences, and political views of A. Q. Khan and other Pakistani officials who were involved in the nuclear proliferation activities and sale of nuclear technology to Iran, Libya, and North Korea. Secondly, it examines the religious trends of the state and society during the years when proliferation took place, and lastly it evaluates Pakistan's relations with the West in general and the USA in particular to examine whether the anti-Western views of Khan as well as those of other influential state actors were influential in the process.

Nuclear proliferation in this case was an outcome of Pakistan's nuclear weapons programme, but this unfortunate result was neither the goal nor the purpose of the project. So, why did proliferation happen, and what were the motivations behind it? These factors are separate and distinct from why Pakistan pursued the acquisition of a nuclear bomb in the first place. The answer to these questions will come from careful analysis of motivations, influences, and political views held by the key individuals who directed Pakistan's weapons programme, and the subsequent proliferation.

A. Q. Khan was the central figure on the team that procured nuclear weapons technology for Pakistan. The state provided all the means and

151

resources for the programme. In the early phase of the project, serious obstacles such as a lack of scientific expertise, domestic political opposition, and international players effectively hampered progress. Khan possessed the knowledge and expertise to help Pakistan overcome the obstacles to its quest for nuclear weapons. As Khan's technical know-how was revealed as the main catalyst behind the success of Pakistan's nuclear weapons programme, he achieved a cult-like following. Many other scientists contributed towards the project in significant ways as well, but the name A. Q. Khan became synonymous with the project. This made him a member of the elite, which brought with it power, prestige, and influence. Khan's power derived from the support he received from other political elites, the military, the nationalists, and the religious conservatives. Even to this day, the unwavering support Khan enjoyed from these groups is among the reasons why he has not been prosecuted. Instead, the Pakistani regime placed him under temporary house arrest, which was relaxed with the passage of time, and today he is a free citizen again, with few restrictions and extensive security cover.

He remained under virtual house arrest after his 2004 confession, but from Musharraf's fall in 2008 he petitioned the Islamabad High Court for his release and the court obliged, as Musharraf had managed the whole affair via executive orders and there was no legal basis to restrict Khan's movements. There was palpable US pressure on Islamabad to keep restrictions in place on Khan. Thus, a secret deal between the government of Pakistan and Khan was brokered before the court released him in February 2009. Khan agreed that (a) he would not visit any nuclear programme-related organizations; (b) he would not contact any person in these organizations without prior government permission; (c) he would travel outside Islamabad only after sufficient notice, and guest lists for events at his home or at a restaurant/hotel would be cleared by local security beforehand, and no foreigners could be invited to these events.[1] The court further ordered Khan to cooperate in any investigations on nuclear proliferation, and especially to refrain from 'exploiting specific media personnel to influence public opinion on various national/international issues without government clearance' and to avoid any political involvement and 'high profile socialization'. According to the leaked communications between the government of Pakistan and the US embassy in Islamabad of early 2009, Pakistan's interior minister Kamal Shah expressed his hope to the US ambassador to Pakistan Anne Patterson that this arrangement 'would reassure the international community, especially the US, that Khan remained neutralized as a potential proliferation threat'.[2] Pakistan wanted to move on, but international concerns persisted given the scale of Khan's dangerous activities and, more importantly, because of a lack of knowledge about his motivations. It is critical to understand why he did what he did.

Khan had initially approached Pakistan's leadership to offer help with the nuclear programme simply out of nationalism and patriotic feeling. But his personal ambitions and rivalry with PAEC chairman Munir Khan added another dimension to A. Q. Khan's agenda, which seems to have slowly and gradually moved him away from his patriotic motivations. A. Q. Khan competed with Munir Khan and other PAEC officials for political influence and status as he sought to dominate all aspects of Pakistan's nuclear programme, including taking on projects out of his purview as the head of Khan Research Laboratories (KRL). For instance, A. Q. Khan became involved in bomb design and weapons procurement, both of which initially were beyond the scope of his organization. Thus, after KRL successfully mastered the operation of the nuclear fuel cycle, beating its rival the PAEC became an obsession. In the process, Khan's programme and personal ambitions went unchecked—not to mention his massive ego.

One perspective suggests that Khan's personal ambitions came into conflict with Pakistan's national motives as soon as the lure of lucrative clandestine dealings with Iran and Libya appeared. Another view holds Pakistani officials responsible for fostering Khan's excesses. Khan 'was encouraged to engage in parallel business dealings so that KRL could decrease its reliance on state funding', the argument goes.[3] One of the results of this was the diffusion of nuclear weapons technology. Of course, he was not the first to benefit from the illicit trade in weapons technologies in the international market, but Khan indeed took it to new heights. Prior to Khan, the German physicist Klaus Fuchs was known as the greatest source of proliferation by espionage.[4]

Khan, unsatisfied with his position as a national hero, spent significant time, energy, and money disseminating the story that he and he alone was the 'father of the Pakistani bomb'. The secretive nature of the Pakistani nuclear programme, which was by no means unique, meant that his achievements largely had to be kept hidden from the public eye. Yet, upon achieving his main aim Khan did not wait for the government to bestow a title and honours on him. He went ahead with a public image campaign, fearful that others might take credit for his accomplishments.[5]

Khan's motivations were also influenced by India's perceived hegemony over the subcontinent. He believed that he alone had saved Pakistan from subjugation by India. By sharing nuclear secrets with Iran, Libya, and North Korea, he thought that 'the emergence of more nuclear states would ease Western attention on Pakistan', an idea which possibly originated inside Pakistan's security establishment.[6]

Khan was also aspiring to defy the West, which in his view had portrayed him as a villain who had stolen centrifuge designs from Netherlands. He certainly felt insulted and humiliated by this charge. According to the 2007 IISS report *Nuclear Black Markets*, 'he may also have felt a genuine sense of injustice and a victim of hypocrisy given the high number of Western industrialists who were more than ready to do business with him and were never pursued effectively'.[7] He had to prove all the more now that he could deliver a nuclear bomb to Pakistan by outwitting the West and overcoming all obstacles.

Khan is known for his claim that he was 'helping the Muslim cause', which potentially explains his dealings with Iran and Libya on the surface, but obviously not North Korea—a non-Muslim country. However, linking his actions to his religious and political rhetoric obscures the financial motivation that appears to be a critical factor in his dealings with both Iran and Libya. Equally plausible is the theory that he was providing nuclear weapons technology to states that defied the West—especially the USA—in their nuclear pursuits. In the case of Libya, although his removal from the KRL leadership position may appear to suggest that he was seeking retribution, he had signed on to the project in 1997 when he was fully in command of KRL and there was no threat to his position. A constellation of diverse motivations may explain the various deals made by Khan—varying in intensity and significance, and depending on circumstances: personal ambition and ego, financial benefits, nationalism, anti-American feelings, and, last but not least, Islamic identity.

Also worth keeping in mind is that the A. Q. Khan network was not a hierarchically structured enterprise, but rather an umbrella group. With its associated businesses spread across the world, which sometimes operated in league with Khan and at other times functioned independently or with other similar ventures, the network resembled a loosely affiliated multinational corporation. At least thirty companies and middlemen sold nuclear-related goods or offered consulting through the network.[8] Khan was in many ways the fulcrum of this undertaking, and for many individuals involved in the proliferation schemes his name recognition mattered hugely. His European associates were also very resourceful and networked, but without Khan the network would have been less successful than it turned out to be.

A. Q. Khan's Motivations

India Today, a popular Indian magazine, described Khan as a cross between Dr Strangelove and an Islamic James Bond as early as 1987.[9] However, the question in the aftermath of the fall of the A. Q. Khan network is aptly framed by Douglas Frantz: 'what turned a proud and ambitious man from patriot to proliferator'.[10] A look at his personal life is instructive here.

Personal and Professional Life

A. Q. Khan was born in Bhopal, in what was then British India, on 27 April 1936. His grandfather and great-grandfather had both served in the army in junior ranks, while his father, Abdul Ghafoor, was an educationist.[11] In his early days he witnessed the communal violence generated by the partition of the Indian subcontinent into India and Pakistan, and that left an indelible mark on his memory; he often spoke of seeing trains packed with the corpses of Muslims killed by Hindus.[12] He migrated to Pakistan in 1952 along with his mother and siblings, but his father remained in India and lived there until his death in 1956.[13] As the family made its way to the new state of Pakistan, they experienced intimidation and humiliation. He recalls one specific incident that has continued to haunt him ever since: 'I had been traveling with [a gift], a pen that my brother gave me when I passed my exams. Just as I was crossing out of India, a border guard reached toward me and snatched it from my pocket. ... It was something I will never forget.'[14] This is what defined Khan's image of India in the formative years of his life. He has recounted this story many times during his interviews with Pakistani and foreign journalists. In an April 1984 article in *Defence Journal* (Karachi) he further explained his views about the Partition mayhem in these words: 'The mischief and humiliation to which we were subjected from Ajmer and Munabao by the Hindu Railway personnel, police etc. is still vivid in my memory. I had then realized the necessity of the creation of Pakistan. ...'[15] It is not easy to forget such experiences.

Khan's middle-class family settled in the port city of Karachi after arriving in Pakistan, like a majority of the migrants who were lucky enough to reach Pakistan alive. Khan was a bright student who was interested in pursuing higher education. He graduated in engineering from the University of Karachi with high marks, and moved to Europe for postgraduate studies. He earned a master's degree at the Technological University of Delft in the Netherlands and a doctorate in 1972 from Catholic University of Leuven in Belgium—no mean achievement for someone from Pakistan, where science education was below standard. His adviser at Leuven, Professor M. J. Brabers, who would later describe him as someone with a great knack for making friends, helped him get a job in Amsterdam at Physical Dynamics Research Laboratory (FDO).[16] Khan continued his relationship with his mentor, who helped him in the establishment of the GIK Institute of Engineering Sciences and Technology and became its first rector.[17]

An analysis of Khan's thirty-one-page official curriculum vitae provides insight into his perception of himself. He used to hand it out to visiting journalists, and it was previously linked to his website.[18] The following excerpt taken from a section of the CV entitled 'Brief Sketch of Dr. A. Q. Khan' reveals Khan as an egoist:

> As arrow of time moves, the Will of God prevails and is focused on the emergence of humans endowed with exceptional intellectual capabilities and creative abilities. Such are the men who, by their good deeds, fulfill the edict of God. ... By their deeds and actions such persons, though not prophets, demonstrate that they are an extension of the will of the transcendental. These are the people, who are destined to make history in the

elevation of nations. Such is the personality of Dr. Abdul Quadeer Khan.
… As the time has unfolded itself, the Godly qualities enshrined in the
words 'Quadeer' and 'Ghafoor', symbolized in the names of Dr. Abdul
Quadeer Khan and his father, Mr. Abdul Ghafoor Khan, have raised the
Pakistani nation to new heights in high technology.

The CV also mentions that Khan received honorary degrees of
Doctor of Science from six Pakistani universities between 1993 and
2001. In terms of his personality traits and religious inclinations, the
following statement in the CV is insightful:

> He is a person imbued with the spirit of serving the cause of Pakistan and
> Muslim Ummah through his able researches, high acumen, intellectual
> robustness and unwavering devotion. So numerous are his activities that
> every segment of society has praised him in different forms. He has been
> awarded 63 gold medals by various national institutions and organizations.

It is a well-known joke in Pakistani media circles that many of the said
gold medals were paid for by Khan himself. Indicating his interest in
charitable works, the document also provides a list of twelve mosques
(with addresses), one tomb, and five health-care centres that he supported financially. It also mentions fifteen research centres, four build-
ings, and fifteen scholarships/medals that are named after him.

Former ISI chief General Asad Durrani told me that what used to
bother him the most was Khan's 'propensity to self-project and his
fondness for the limelight'.[19] He further shared that Ghulam Ishaq
Khan, whom he called 'the main custodian of the programme', was
'aware of AQK's weakness but also acknowledged that since no one
else could have delivered on that front [making of the nuclear bomb],
we might have to accept this flaw as "part of the package"'.[20] This confirms the view that Pakistani leaders—both military and civilian—
were convinced that without Khan Pakistan's nuclear weapons programme could not proceed.

It is insightful that after relaxation of restrictions on him in 2009
(imposed since his house arrest in 2004), he contemplated running for
political office, and even launched a new political party in 2012, Tehrik-
i-Tahaffuz Pakistan (Movement for the Security of Pakistan).[21]
According to media reports at the time, he met retired General Aslam
Beg, presumably also inviting him to join his political movement.[22] This
political effort was geared towards participating in the 2013 national

and provincial elections, and for that purpose the party fielded a total of 111 candidates across Pakistan. Not one of them was elected, and that was the end of the party.[23]

Statements and Interviews of A. Q. Khan

Hardly any other eminent Pakistani has given as many interviews as has Khan, and his statements and interviews provide a window into his thinking and worldview. A few selected excerpts below are reflective of his opinions:

1979: In a letter to *Der Spiegel*, Khan questioned 'the bloody holier-than-thou attitudes of the Americans and the British' and said: 'These bastards are God-appointed guardians of the world, to stockpile hundreds of thousands of nuclear warheads and have the God-given authority of carrying out explosions every month. But if we start a modest programme, we are the Satans, the devils.'[24]

1984: 'By forming an exclusive club, they [the West] are monopolizing the transfer of nuclear technology to energy starved Third World countries under the pretext of containment of nuclear weapons or non-proliferation. The control or restriction is relative; when it relates to Israel, India, South Africa, Brazil and Argentina, all out assistance is provided at government level and no stories or leakages are provided to the national or international press. The situation is different when it concerns the Islamic countries. The world wide propaganda organized by the Western lobby in general, and the Jewish lobby in particular, against Pakistan, Libya and Iraq has put to shame the campaign carried out against Hitler in war days. ... Why this hypocrisy and double standard with us? The answer is simple. The crusade is still on....'[25]

1984: 'By God's grace, Pakistan is now among those few countries which have acquired mastery over uranium enrichment. Perhaps whenever Western countries think about us, they get visions of donkey-carts and *tongas*, etc. They could never have imagined that an undeveloped country like Pakistan can finish their monopoly forever. ... You can see for yourself, how could they tolerate a Muslim country becoming their equal in this [nuclear] field....'[26]

1984: 'The rumor about the "Islamic bomb" is the creation of the Zionist brain and the anti-Islam Western countries have adopted it. ... The perpetual propaganda against us is really aimed at creating fear and terror among the general public and trade circles in Western countries warning them that anything they sell to Pakistan will appear before them in the shape of an Islamic bomb ... all Western countries including Israel are not the enemies of Pakistan but in fact Islam; had any other Muslim country instead of Pakistan made this progress, they would have conducted the same poisonous and false propaganda against it. The example of Iraq and Libya is before you.'[27]

1985: 'Pakistan would definitely continue its [nuclear] cooperation for peaceful purposes with other Muslim countries under the control of an international organization. ... [US] Senator Alan Cranston is having this suspicion that Pakistan would offer its nuclear [technology] to anyone on a platter, for no reason. He is under great pressure from Jews and is concerned as their representative and that is why he always remains in forefront in any campaign in support of Israel.'[28]

1986: 'Under the pressure of the Israeli Prime Minister, Menachem Begin, and of other western countries, the Dutch Government initiated a false and concocted case against me. ... They were in a hurry and concluded the case in absentia. But I challenged them in Amsterdam High Court and the case was dismissed as illegal and unfounded.'[29]

1990: 'Kahuta is an all Pakistan effort and is a symbol of Pakistan's determination to refuse to submit to blackmail and bullying.'[30]

1994: 'With lines clearly drawn between the developed and underdeveloped countries, the latter have grown into consumer only societies. Import-based economies of the Third World have not only accentuated the dominance of the West, but have also been responsible for undermining the process of domestic technological and industrial growth.'[31]

1995: 'Not only have they [Muslims] been at the receiving end of numerous political, cultural and military assaults of the West and its local accomplices, but they have also suffered from the developed world's discriminatory policies in every sphere of life. They are being denied access to the scientific and technological developments which are the hallmark of the modern age.'[32]

1995: 'Is it logic and common sense to let a few have this advanced [nuclear] technology which can decide the fate of all humanity and call them members of Nuclear Club, while others live in fear under this hegemony? One of the major arguments propounded by these states in support of this nuclear apartheid is the supposedly irresponsible behavior expected from the less developed, fragile and relatively small states in case they obtained nuclear weapons. If history is anything to go by, then the only irresponsible, downright inhuman instance of the abuse of nuclear technology has been perpetrated by no other country than the leader of the non proliferation drive itself—USA.'[33]

1995: 'Another Muslim country accused of having stepped on this prohibited [nuclear] path was Iraq, whose nuclear installations were destroyed by two Israeli air attacks, an incident which caused little concern among the self appointed custodians of international law.'[34]

1995: 'Western governments repeatedly tried to prevent Pakistan from developing a nuclear weapon capability, but they were foiled by the greed of their own companies: Many suppliers approached us with the details of the machinery and with figures and numbers of instruments and materials ... they begged us to purchase their goods. ... We purchased whatever we required.'[35]

1995: 'Some academics have aired the proposition of Islamic Atomic Energy commission. ... I would like to emphasize here that the honorable survival of the Muslim world lies in joining hands for acquiring this mode of energy production which would also have its political and military advantages.'[36]

1997: 'The very word "restricted" reflects the self assumed monopoly of the West over certain branches of science, and especially, its efforts to curtail the development [of] the Muslim World which the Western powers unjustifiably see as potential threat to their monopoly. Development made by certain Muslim states in the "restricted" technologies does not trickle down to others because of international pressures and lack of coordination and cooperation among the Muslim countries.'[37]

1996: 'The Muslim world is forced to toe the line of the advanced world as the latter's technical expertise and scientific skills allow it to exclusively dominate international affairs. Our resources are being robbed by the advanced nations, our governments virtually becoming hostage to international agencies and from Afghanistan to Bosnia and from the Middle East to Somalia our lands are being converted into lucrative markets of the western manufactured arms.'[38]

1996: 'Probably no other nations are more dependent on the advanced countries as the Muslims are when it comes to safety and security. While most of the Muslim countries lack the infrastructures to develop even conventional arms, there has continuously been intense pressure from the advanced world to hinder the Muslim World from acquiring some advanced capability in this regard.'[39]

1998: 'It does not bother me what the Western press says about me. They dislike our God, they dislike our Prophet, they dislike our national leaders, and no wonder they dislike anybody who tries to put this country on an independent and self-reliant path.'[40]

2004: 'I am proud of my work for my country. It has given Pakistanis a sense of pride, security and has been a great scientific achievement.'[41]

These statements by Khan are particularly revealing three main trends in his worldview: (1) Pakistan was able to achieve nuclear weapons capability despite many hurdles created by the West; (2) the USA and Israel demonized him, and tried their best to halt Pakistan's nuclear programme development just because it is a Muslim country; and (3) he was under an obligation to help other Muslim countries develop nuclear technology. These were not one-off statements; they were repeated on many occasions and in different words, and hence reflect his overall opinions on the matter. Many of these perspectives, especially as regards Western efforts to block scientific learning, development, and research in Muslim states, are popularly held views in Pakistan and in many Muslim countries.

Local Biographies of A. Q. Khan

There are more biographies of Khan available in Pakistan's bookstores than of any popular political leader of the country, with the probable exception of the country's founding father Muhammad Ali Jinnah. Most of these books are based on detailed interviews with Khan, and many contain articles written by him. His collaboration with their authors is clear from the inclusion of his personal and family photographs, which are not available publicly. Khan has actually financed many works on Pakistan's nuclear programme and his contribution to it.[42] According to Pervez Hoodbhoy, 'Qadeer's insistence on his paternity of Pakistan's supreme status symbol did not come free. He had to buy the loyalty of journalists, military men, and scientists. His biographers and other syco-phants were amply rewarded.'[43] A brief look at sections of two Urdu-language biographies of Khan provides interesting information.

Muhsin-i-Pakistan Dr. Abdul Qadeer Khan
[The One Who Did a Great Favour to Pakistan][44]

The book contains pictures of ten mosques constructed with finance provided by Khan, and photographs of his close associates, including those who were later arrested and charged with participating in the Khan network. The author mentions that two popular Muslim generals who played an important role in bringing Islam to Central and South Asia, Mohammad Bin Qasim and Yusuf Bin Tashfeen, were Khan's role models from childhood. The work also talks about Khan's rival, PAEC chairman Munir Ahmed Khan, in a derogatory fashion, further proof that Khan himself was involved in the book's production. It quotes him as saying that Pakistan's humiliating defeat at the hands of India in 1971 and consequent disintegration inspired him to do something for Pakistan to make it secure.

In a detailed interview with the author of the book, Khan strongly criticizes Israel for attacking Iraq's nuclear plant in 1981, and alleges that French technicians working there must have given the necessary information to Israelis. He also mentions the gratitude that the government of Saudi Arabia showed when he conducted the Ghauri (No-Dong) missile tests. Interestingly, the book also contains a detailed, favourable article written by General Aslam Beg about Khan. Beg severely criticizes the notion (then put about by the new Musharraf government) that Khan's role in Pakistan's nuclear programme constituted barely 5 per cent of the total effort. Beg also confirmed that, when army chief in 1988, he had tasked Khan and KRL to start working on non-nuclear weapon systems too. Beg also condemned those Pakistanis who were involved in the character assassination of Khan in Pakistan.

Mohsin-e-Pakistan Dr. Abdul Qadeer Khan: Islami bomb kay Khaliq aur Ghauri Mizzile kay Mojid Ki Walwala Khez Dastaan-e-Hayat *[The Fascinating Life Story of the Creator of the Islamic Bomb and the inventor of the Ghauri Missile]*[45]

This book, released in 2003, provides the most detailed biographical sketch of Khan in print. Exhaustive information about his parents and grandparents indicate that Khan must have provided all of this personal information to the biographer. The book also provides specific information about his paltry salary packages during the different stages of his professional career.

Chapter 18 is called 'American Threats', and it explains how different US administrations since the mid-1970s tried to halt Pakistan's nuclear programme.[46] It also mentions various (presumed) attempts by the CIA and Mossad to disrupt Pakistan's nuclear plans in the 1980s. Another chapter profiles close associates of Khan, including Agha Hasan Abedi (the founder of BCCI), as well as Arshad Pervaiz and Brigadier Inam-ul-Haq, both of whom were jailed in Canada and America for trying to export nuclear technology-related materials to Pakistan.[47] The author also alleges (most probably on behalf of Khan) that Benazir Bhutto, during both her stints as prime minister (1988–90, 1993–6), was hand in glove with the USA to discontinue Pakistan's nuclear programme but that she failed to deliver to the Americans.[48] The book also alleges that PAEC chairman Munir Ahmed Khan was working for the USA, and was deliberately delaying Pakistan's progress towards acquiring nuclear weapons.

The most interesting disclosures in the book, however, are about Khan's removal from KRL in 2001.[49] Khan informs his biographer that:

1. President Pervez Musharraf had decided to retire Khan under instructions from the USA, and that it had something to do with the missile programme undertaken by KRL (Ghauri/No-Dong).
2. Musharraf created a new institution called the Strategic Planning Directorate (SPD) under Lieutenant-General Khalid Kidwai to 'contain the courage and activities of A. Q. Khan'.
3. The real purpose of establishing the SPD was to make way for US sanctions to stop Pakistan's uranium-enrichment programme.

The book reads like an autobiography rather than a biography, and it explicitly documents Khan's anti-Western views. The narrative also explains that the emergence of the SPD in February 2000 was especially distressful for Khan, as he could see it as a death knell for the considerable independence he was enjoying in managing the affairs of KRL.

This sufficiently explains Khan's mindset about the West in general and the USA in particular. This perspective can also be analysed within the context of the 'clash of civilizations' theory: as far as Khan was concerned, American worries about Pakistan's nuclear programme were solely a product of the presumed religious identity of the Pakistani state. His cooperation with the nuclear programmes of Iran and Libya was most likely a product of this worldview. He certainly made money from these dealings, but financial benefit does not appear to be the driving force behind his proliferation activities.

Benazir Bhutto, who Khan met many times while she was prime minister, insightfully says that he seemed to have acquired a religious aspect when she encountered him after she was returned to office in 1993: 'My first impression of him was that he was a nationalist. ... By the time I returned to office, I felt that he was an Islamist. Something made him change.'[50] Pervez Hoodbhoy, however, observed a slightly different trend in the development of Khan's motivations. He believes that Khan 'started out on an anti India track', and that 'selling nuclear stuff came later, when he developed a compulsion to be rich and powerful'.[51]

Nature of the Pakistani State and the Role of Religion

This section probes whether the religious orientation of the state during the times when nuclear proliferation took place (1987–2003) helps us understand the motivations behind Pakistan's nuclear cooperation with Iran and Libya. Analysing the influence of religious forces (political groups as well as militant ones) on the state institutions during this period sheds some light on this dynamic.

In 1987 the reins of government were in the hands of President Mohammad Zia-ul-Haq (1977–88). Zia had imposed martial law in July 1977, overthrowing the elected government of Prime Minister Z. A. Bhutto. Zia had initially moved to restore order in the country and hold new elections within three months. He was clear about the kind of state he wanted: 'Take Islam out of Pakistan, and make it a secular state; it will collapse.'[52] Zia was also clear about his own role, and soon after the military takeover he started projecting himself as the 'soldier of Islam' who had a 'mission to purify and to cleanse Pakistan'.[53] He hanged Bhutto in 1979, discarded the democratic constitution, and proceeded with the Islamization of laws to justify staying in power. In this endeavour, he co-opted religious parties to create a political constituency for himself, and steered the state towards authoritarianism and religious fundamentalism. This approach, coupled with Pakistan's support of the Afghan jihad in 1980–8, led to the emergence of radicals such as Hafiz Saeed, the founder of Lashkar-e-Taiba, who maintained: 'We believe in Samuel Huntington's Clash of Civilizations and we will not rest until Islam becomes the dominant religion.'[54]

Zia died in a mysterious plane crash in August 1988, and the state reverted to democracy for eleven years before another military ruler, General Pervez Musharraf, emerged on the national scene in October 1999. In comparison to Zia, Musharraf proved to be a liberal and progressive leader, but the policy of the state until 2003 largely remained the same—especially in the realm of cooperation with the religious forces. Zia's various religious 'initiatives', including the introduction of a distorted version of Islamic laws in the country and the sponsoring of militant groups in Kashmir had a tremendous impact on state and society in Pakistan. The influence of conservative religious forces on Pakistan's nuclear policy can be summed up and discussed within the scope of these four topics:

1. the status of religious militant groups in Pakistan;
2. the strength of religious political parties in the country;
3. seeking 'strategic depth' in Afghanistan and General Aslam Beg's 'strategic defiance theory;
4. religious trends in the PAEC and KRL—the 'Bashiruddin Mahmood' factor

Religious Militant Groups in Pakistan

Around 2003 Pakistan had twenty-four armed religious extremist groups, most of which were officially banned, but many of them continued to operate under new names and through underground networks.[55] The figure is roughly accurate for the 1987–2003 period, except for the fact that in the 1990s not a single militant group was banned. This is the era before the rise of the Pakistani Taliban and before suicide bombings created havoc in the country. Among the twenty-four groups operating during the years when nuclear proliferation was taking place, some were primarily focused on operations in the Indian-controlled area of Kashmir (their members consider themselves freedom fighters), whereas others aspired to make Pakistan a theocratic state by violent means. There are groups also that are purely sectarian in orientation. Within this spectrum, many groups, despite sharing sectarian goals, are rivals when it comes to recruitment drives and attracting funds, although in some cases they draw strength from each other in terms of ideology, logistics, and expertise.[56]

Various *madrassa* (seminary) networks were (and still are) intrinsically linked with the militant groups in the country. Such networks had expanded in the Afghan jihad era (the 1980s), largely financed by Saudi Arabia and other Gulf countries, to produce recruits for the Afghan battlefield. Children of these Afghan refugees and Pashtuns of the Pak–Afghan tribal belt were the prime target of such *madrassas*. According to a retired Pakistani general, Kamal Matinuddin, General Zia had 'established a chain of *deeni madaris* [religious schools] along the Afghan–Pakistan border ... in order to create a belt of religiously oriented students who would assist the Afghan Mujahideen to evict the Soviets from Afghanistan'.[57] Pakistan witnessed a major growth of such *madrassas* throughout the 1990s.

There is also evidence that Ahle-Hadith group, the South Asian version of Wahhabism, and those belonging to Deobandi school of thought, who together constituted not more than 30 per cent of Sunni Muslims in Pakistan, hugely benefited from this development. At the time of Pakistan's inception, it had only 136 *madrassas*, but by 2002 the number had risen to around thirty thousand.[58] According to another estimate, in 1947 West Pakistan (today's Pakistan) had only 245 *madrassas*. By 1988 they had increased to 2,861. Between 1988 and 2000 this increase comes out as 136 per cent. The largest number of seminaries are Deobandi, at 64 per cent, followed by Barelvi (Sufi-oriented), at 25 per cent. Only 6 per cent are Ahle-Hadith. But the increase in the number of Ahle-Hadith seminaries or *madrassas* has been phenomenal, at 131 per cent, going up from 134 in 1988 to 310 in 2000.[59] This gain as compared to other groups occurred due to the Saudi and Gulf support. In addition, millions of dollars were spent by Saudi Arabia in Pakistan to pay for new mosques, free hajj trips, the training of clerics in Saudi institutions, and the printing of sectarian literature.[60] Various Shia Muslim groups also expanded during these years, and their support came largely from Iran.

During the 1980s many militants from across the Muslim world arrived in Pakistan on their way to Afghanistan, and this process continued until the early 1990s. Many secular Arab regimes were more than happy to get rid of their own 'extremists'—mostly incarcerated for being part of political opposition to local regimes. Pakistan's Inter-Services Intelligence (ISI) became a central player in this game, and managed these elements for quite a while.[61] The Red Mosque crisis in Islamabad in 2007 showed that such elements survived many state clampdowns, showing both their resilience and their connections within the state apparatus.[62] In this regional power play, Pakistan itself became radicalized.

Another relevant example is that of the Saudi gift of the seed money for General Zia's Zakat Fund: it was made conditional on a significant bequest being made to the Ahle-Hadith seminary headquarters in Faisalabad, the city where al-Qaeda's Abu Zubaidah would be arrested in 2002. Army chief General Aslam Beg (1988–91) was the first to allow Deobandi *madrassa*s in Bahawalpur and Rahimyar Khan (cities in the Punjab) so that their armed youth could be used as 'second line of defence' against a possible Indian attack from Rajasthan.[63]

The Deobandi seminaries became powerful in the Pakistan–Afghanistan tribal areas at first, but at the same time they were expanding their networks in many cities in the Punjab, and in particular Karachi, where the Deobandi school had a centre at the Binori complex of *madrassa*s.[64] Mufti Nizamuddin Shamzai, a famous head of the Binori complex, was known as a very influential cleric during the rule of Mullah Umar in Afghanistan (1996–2001). Reportedly, Mullah Umar and Osama Bin Laden met for the first time in the Binori mosque under the tutelage of Shamzai.[65] Among Shamzai's 2,000 *fatwas* (religious edicts), the most well known is the one he gave against the USA in October 2001 declaring jihad in response to the US military campaign in Afghanistan.[66] In 1999 he deemed it within the rights of the Muslims to kill Americans on sight, though he later modified it under government pressure.[67] Increasingly, the youth joining these centres were made to feel that somehow Pakistan had not enforced true Islam and that Pakistanis were living like infidels.

Musharraf's arrival on the Pakistani political scene in October 1999 was initially a setback for militant groups in the country, and the 9/11 attacks further enabled him to pursue them. In a crucial policy speech on 12 January 2002 Musharraf announced that all the organizations with words such as *jihad*, *lashkar* (army), *jaish* (armed group), or *mujahideen* (holy warriors) in their titles would be banned. He said that 'there is no need for *Lashkars*, *Jaishs* and *Mujahideen* in the presence of a regular Army'.[68] However, Pakistan's religious parties remained very critical of Musharraf's 'U-turn' policy—taking away support from the Taliban in Afghanistan and becoming an ally of the USA in the War on Terror. By 2003 most militant groups operating in the Kashmir theatre of operations were by and large intact and active. Al-Qaeda was certainly targeted by the Pakistan military and intelligence services after 2001, but the same cannot be said about the Taliban and the sectarian militant outfits operating in the country. Lashkar-e-Taiba was banned officially in 2002, but its political wing, Jamaat-ud-Dawa (Party of the Proselytizers), survived and at its 2004 annual gathering Hafiz Saeed lavishly praised A. Q. Khan, and defended him by maintaining that he had not committed any crime by transferring nuclear technology to other Muslim countries: 'He shared the technology for the supremacy of Islam and he acted on the Allah's command.'[69] It is difficult to understand why Musharraf ignored such a statement.

Though the militant groups' activities and the mushrooming of the *madrassa* networks had no direct impact on Pakistan's nuclear policy, the close working relations between Pakistan's intelligence services (especially the ISI) and militant groups operating in Kashmir indicate that military stake-holders were supportive of the 'jihad culture' during the 1987–2003 period. In a *Foreign Affairs* article in 2000, Jessica Stern aptly argued: 'The government in Islamabad supports these militants and their religious schools as cheap ways to fight India and educate Pakistan's youth. But this policy is creating a culture of violence that exacerbates internal sectarianism and destabilizes the region.'[70] This policy choice also indicated that the military leadership was not shy to employ such controversial tools in pursuance of what they deemed to be in Pakistan's national interest. In 1999 the Pakistan military's Kargil operation—a military incursion into the Indian side of the Line of Control (dividing the two Kashmiri areas), which also involved members of militant groups alongside the regular army, without any concern for international obligations—is indicative of the general trend and policy orientation of Pakistan at the time.[71]

Religious Political Parties in Pakistan

There were around 250 religious parties registered in Pakistan in 2003, 215 with their own seminaries, according to the research of Amir Rana, a knowledgeable Pakistani journalist.[72] Of these, 28 were openly taking part in politics; 104 claimed to focus on jihad; 82 were driven by sectarian agendas; and 20 were oriented toward *tabligh* (preaching/proselytizing). However, Pakistan's Islamic groups are not monolithic; they include apolitical religious traditionalists, and moderate religious politicians, as well as religious extremists and militants inspired by and affiliated with al-Qaeda and the Taliban.

Religious parties have a long history in Pakistan, but their electoral performance has been generally poor. They do well, however, whenever they join other political forces through alliances. During the 1987–2003 time frame their influence on policy making was channelled through street power, threats, and alliances with mainstream political forces. The influence of these parties increased over time owing to regional conflict theatres where their 'voluntary' services were found to be useful.

The two most important religious parties and their influence in the corridors of power are relevant to the discussion here, as both of these parties remained allied with government in some form or the other during the years when nuclear proliferation took place. The two parties are Jamaat-e-Islami (JI—the Party of Islam) and Jamiat-i-Ulema-e-Islam Fazl group (JUI-F—the Council of Islamic Scholars).[73] Another faction of the latter led by Sami-ul-Har, known as JUI-S, is also important for this analysis.

JI was founded by Maulana Maududi in 1941, and is considered to be Pakistan's best-organized religious party. Its goal is to establish an Islamic state in Pakistan, and rid the country of corruption. JI wants to attain these goals through an Islamic revolution.[74] Jamiat-i-Ulema-e-Islam (JUI), a major Islamist party, originally founded in 1945, is associated with *madrassa*s that gave rise to the Afghan Taliban movement in 1994. JUI is an advocate of a central role for Islam and *sharia* (Islamic law) in national governance. It opposes Westernization in its socio-economic and cultural forms. Although both these parties enjoy considerable street power in urban centres of the country, and were strengthened by General Zia's policies of the 1980s, their electoral showing has been quite limited.[75] The following chart and explanation show their strength in national elections between 1987 and 2003.[76]

JI and JUI Elected Seats in the National Assembly*

	1988	1990	1993	1997
Jamaat-e-Islami	8	4	3	boycott
JUI (both factions)	9	6	4	2

*Total Number of Elected National Assembly Seats: 237

These numbers, however, are not reflective of the influence that these parties had during the 1990s, as JI remained a coalition member of the Nawaz Sharif government (1990–3) and JUI-F was a coalition partner in the second Benazir Bhutto government (1993–6). As part of different political governments in the 1990s, both JI and JUI had some influence over the security policy of the state. In 1991 JI influenced Prime Minister Sharif to introduce the Sharia Bill in the parliament, which he did, but the draft failed to live up to JI's expectations and it drifted away from Sharif's government.[77] JUI had an easier relationship with the Bhutto government, which enabled it to play a very important role in supporting the rise of the Taliban in Afghanistan. Thousands of JUI *madrassa* students (from both JUI factions) joined the Taliban in Afghanistan during the mid-1990s. This cooperation between JUI and the Bhutto government also worked because it had the support of Pakistan's military and intelligence establishment.[78] In the 2002 elections JI and JUI joined forces with four other religious parties under the banner of Muttihada Majlis-e-Amal (MMA—the United Action Front) and received 11 per cent of the national vote, which translated into 68 national assembly seats (in a house of 342). MMA also single-handedly formed the provincial government in the then North West Frontier Province (NWFP), and joined a coalition government in the Baluchistan province. In the centre, MMA sat on the opposition benches but supported Musharraf's controversial constitutional changes in 2003, substantiating rumours that it had the tacit support of the military. This earned MMA the nickname the Mullah–Military Alliance.[79]

On nuclear policy issues, JI's standard position throughout the late 1980s and 1990s was that Pakistan should not sign the Nuclear Non-Proliferation Treaty (NPT) and the Comprehensive Test Ban Treaty (CTBT). In 1996, JI's *majlis-i-shoora* (central consultative body) passed a resolution declaring that 'the nation should not be deprived of its right to protect itself against any nuclear blackmail, through the NPT or CTBT, or under the pressure of some global power'.[80] JI's influence on Pakistan nuclear behaviour was discussed in a conference at the Center for International Security and Cooperation (CISAC) at Stanford University in 2004, and the assessments of the conference participants are relevant to this discussion:

> On one hand, it is clear that the Jama'at [JI] strongly favors hawkish nuclear policies, and the party lobbied loudly for a Pakistani response to India's nuclear tests in 1998. Moreover, the Jama'at views Pakistan's nuclear arsenal as not merely a national security instrument but a force to serve the broader Muslim community worldwide. On the other hand, there is little evidence to suggest that the Jama'at, while the strongest Islamic party in Pakistan, holds any meaningful sway over Pakistani politics.[81]

Indeed, JI lacks significant support among the people, but it does have some influence. For instance, JI leader Qazi Hussain Ahmed had also confessed in 2006 that Osama Bin Laden had visited JI headquarters in Mansoora (near Lahore) in 1989 and was 'prepared to buy parliamentarians' loyalties to see Nawaz Sharif as prime minister' (by supporting a vote of no-confidence against Prime Minister Benazir Bhutto).[82] However, he also claimed that Bin Laden was interested in a deal with JI but that he had declined.[83]

It is also interesting that after A. Q. Khan's house arrest in 2004, MMA members were among his most vocal supporters. In February 2004 during a public rally MMA announced a countrywide strike to express solidarity with Khan and other nuclear scientists (in government custody) and to condemn government policies for humiliating them. On the occasion, Qazi Hussain Ahmed (also a leader of MMA), while criticizing the USA for attempting to thwart Pakistan's pursuit of nuclear weapons, said that 'it is an effort to disarm Muslim states' and 'America never wanted to see any Muslim country become a nuclear power'.[84] Sounds like a familiar narrative.

Seeking 'Strategic Depth' in Afghanistan and General Aslam Beg's 'Strategic Defiance' Theory

Pakistan's relations with Afghanistan, in terms of supporting its favoured factions in the Afghan civil war (1989–94) and support of the Taliban (1994–2001), remained a critical component of its foreign policy; relations with Iran and Saudi Arabia were its other important pillars. This was in line with the strategic interests and vision of Pakistan's military leadership. In particular, political leaders were not allowed to interfere with the policy orientation of Pakistan's military pertaining to Afghanistan and Kashmir. In Afghanistan the strategy of supporting the Taliban government (1996–2001) was in pursuance of ensuring strategic depth for Pakistan in case of an Indian assault—a policy first defined by General Mirza Aslam Beg (chief of army staff 1988–91) and Lieutenant-General Hamid Gul (ISI chief 1987–9). Even in the 1970s Pakistan was involved in supporting some Afghan political elements (Gulbuddin Hekmatyar and Ahmad Shah Masoud), but that was intended to counter Kabul's attempts to strengthen its links with Pakistan's Pashtun elements, especially those who were supportive of the idea of an independent Pashtunistan.[85]

General Aslam Beg's 'strategic defiance' theory played an instrumental role in Pakistan's foreign policy direction during the 1988–91 period, as discussed earlier in chapter 4.[86] General Beg announced his theory of 'strategic defiance' (of the USA) on the eve of the Gulf War in 1990. On 3 December 1990 Beg, while commending Saddam Hussein's strategy, added that 'such strategic defiance is very important for Pakistan, in view of the kind of threat we are facing today'.[87] He proposed a Pakistan–Iran–Afghanistan partnership to thwart what he thought was an impending American invasion of all three countries. According to Pervez Hoodbhoy:

> Both General Zia ul Haq ... and the succeeding Chief of Army Staff, General Mirza Aslam Beg ... subscribed to a pan-Islamic vision. Possessed by the idea of 'strategic defiance' of the US, and of turning Pakistan's nuclear capability to its full strategic and financial advantage, Beg in particular wanted strong defence ties with Iran.[88]

Beg, however, denies having helped Iran in its nuclear programme, and calls such charges a conspiracy by the Jewish lobby.[89] In some interviews he tried to disown his concept of 'strategic defiance', but an article on his own think tank's website published under his name explains his perspective. Though undated, it was clearly written after the US–India civil nuclear collaboration was finalized around 2005. The argument in fact broadens the span of his earlier theory, moving it a step closer to that of Samuel Huntington:

> A growing bond of friendship between Pakistan, Iran and China is the rational concomitant of the Indo-US defence pact. Hopefully, this would lead to an alliance of the three countries—later to be joined by Afghanistan as a formidable force, radiating power, to defy, deter and defeat the forces of aggression without fighting, thus giving a real meaning to the notion of Strategic Defiance, which flows from the 'Strategic Depth' of a group of nations, having common perceptions and orientation towards their security and well being.[90]

In the early 1990s Beg's views certainly had an impact on policy formulation in Pakistan. He continued to deny that he sanctioned any help to Iran in the nuclear field while he was the army chief, but also continued to defend A. Q. Khan. He has also persistently argued that Iran deserved help in its nuclear programme. Some excerpts from his interviews and media statements are instructive in this context:

1. 'My apprehension is that Iranians, maybe Libyans and North Koreans, would have known that Pakistan was stealing, buying and smuggling all the items which are needed for developing nuclear capability. So, they must have approached these scientists. And what they might have done is told them to go to certain companies for the equipment they needed. Now is that a crime? How can these scientists be penalised simply for identifying their sources? This is what has happened.'[91]

2. Beg wrote an opinion piece in one of Pakistan's leading English newspapers floating the notion that Pakistan and India should jointly provide nuclear weapons to Iran under some sort of custodial arrangement similar to that used within the North Atlantic Treaty Organization (NATO).[92]

3. When some Iranian officials came to Beg in 2006 to seek advice about their nuclear policy, he told them: 'Make it clear that if anything happens to Iran, if anyone attacks it, it doesn't matter who it is or how it is attacked, that Iran's answer will be to hit Israel; the

only target will be Israel.'[93] A little later Iran issued a similar statement.[94] It appears that Iranian officials regularly consulted General
Beg about their security-related issues.

The following excerpt from an editorial published in a leading
Pakistani weekly, *The Friday Times*, written by a well-known journalist,
Najam Sethi, is also relevant to the theme of this section:

> In the mid 1990s, following a series of carefully planted 'nationalistic' arti-
> cles in the press advocating sale of nuclear technology to offset American
> economic and military sanctions, a full-page advertisement appeared in a
> national daily hawking nuclear wares to the world at large. When the diplo-
> matic enclave in Islamabad erupted in protest, the nuclear rogues seemed to
> beat a hasty retreat. But now it transpires that in fact they did quite the
> opposite: they simply went underground with their business.[95]

Religious Trends in the PAEC and KRL: The 'Bashiruddin Mahmood' Factor

Very little public information is available about religious trends inside
the PAEC and KRL, but some well-informed experts have commented
on this issue. Pervez Hoodbhoy, in an interview with AFP, described
the atmosphere at the KRL as 'very religiously charged'.[96] About the
PAEC, he commented: 'They have, especially over the last decade or
so, become much more religious and their attitudes are considerably
more anti-Western than 30 years ago.'[97] Hoodbhoy also believed that
A. Q. Khan espoused Islamic nationalism: 'He thinks the bomb is essential to protect Islam against assault from those who hate Islam.'[98]
Religious ideology and slogans were routinely used to inspire and
motivate officials at the PAEC and KRL to make the bomb. It must be
noted that in itself this may not indicate that employees of these organizations were religious extremists. However, serious concerns came
to the fore in 2001 with the case of Sultan Bashiruddin Mahmood, a
former senior nuclear engineer at KRL who, along with another scientist, Chaudhry Abdul Majeed, was arrested for links with the Taliban
and al-Qaeda.[99] Both Mahmood and Majeed visited Afghanistan, pur-
portedly for charity work. They had founded Ummah Tameer-e-Nau
(UTN—Reconstruction of the Muslim Ummah) for conducting relief
and development work in Afghanistan. UTN was also found to be affili-

ated with the Al-Rasheed Trust, which is listed by the US State Department as a terrorist organization for its links with al-Qaeda.

Pakistan was alerted by US officials about this when they found evidence in Afghanistan that some Pakistani nuclear scientists had visited Taliban leaders, who then arranged a meeting between the scientists and Osama Bin Laden.[100] Mahmood was a chief designer and director of the country's Khushab atomic reactor. He was also a pioneer in Pakistan's efforts to enrich uranium (Project 706) and held a patent on a technique for stopping leaks of heavy water from heavy water production plants.[101]

What should have alerted the Pakistani intelligence and security services earlier was Mahmood's background. He had resigned (or was honourably retired ahead of time, according to some reports) from the PAEC in the spring of 1999 to protest at Pakistan's inclination to sign the CTBT, soon after conducting a series of underground nuclear tests in May 1998. Mahmood published various articles on the subject, arguing that joining the CTBT would impose huge political and military costs, and provide few rewards. He also said: 'If we keep developing nuclear technology on the path of self-reliance, and also extend cooperation to other countries in this field, shall we not be the gainers ultimately?'[102] According to the *New York Times* story that broke the news of Mahmood's activities in Afghanistan, he had been 'going around giving talks, meeting with university students and faculty, going to schools, colleges, wherever there are people who will listen to him, and arguing that the Taliban are the way, that they show the way for Pakistan'.[103]

Mahmood was known in Pakistani scientific circles as a fundamentalist Muslim with unorthodox scientific views, and he remained under some form of surveillance after his retirement. He had also described Pakistan's nuclear capability as 'the property of a whole [Muslim] Ummah [community]'.[104] His mindset and worldview can also be gauged from a press release issued by him on 22 October 1999, in which he proclaimed:

> The world is approaching a state of affairs whereby the entire Western world will invade the heart of Islamic world (i.e. the Arab world) in order to protect Israel—a rehearsal of which was witnessed in the Gulf War. At this crucial juncture in history, in light of the Prophetic traditions, it will

be none other than Pakistan and Afghanistan which will rise to the occasion and defend the Islamic world. Indeed, this is the main objective behind our emergence as a nuclear power.[105]

Interestingly, Mahmood was awarded the prestigious Sitara-e-Imtiaz (Medal of Distinction) in 1999 by the president of Pakistan, and was kept in the job despite being reportedly declared 'dangerous' by the country's intelligence agencies.[106]

Chaudhry Abdul Majeed, the other scientist investigated in the case, retired in 2000 after a thirty-year career in the Nuclear Materials Division of the Pakistan Institute of Nuclear Science and Technology (PINSTECH), an allied institute of the PAEC. In the 1960s Majeed trained at a plutonium facility in Belgium, and also did research in Dr Salam's institute in Trieste, Italy. According to David Albright, he is an expert in nuclear fuels, and published extensively on nuclear detectors and the use of X-ray diffraction.[107]

Pervez Hoodbhoy, in a 2002 media interview, provided a larger context to these disturbing developments when, in the process of referring to some religious conservatives in KRL and the PAEC, he maintained that 'these people are able to see all the faults of the US, but unable to see their own', and estimated that about 10 per cent of Pakistan's nuclear scientists hold such views, many of them his former students.[108]

In December 2001 the media also reported that two other Pakistani nuclear scientists with expertise in weapon designs, Suleiman Asad and Mohammed Ali Mukhtar, were wanted by the Americans for questioning about their possible links to Osama Bin Laden.[109] However, the government of Pakistan informed the USA that both these scientists had left for a research project in Myanmar, and Pakistan did not want to interrupt their work by having them return to Pakistan for questioning.[110] Nothing has been heard about the two since.

The evidence discussed in this section indicates that the role and influence of conservative religious forces between 1987 and 2003 created both complexity and instability in the country. Clearly, Pakistan and its intelligence outfits had significant influence over religious political parties as well as militant groups during the years under discussion, but in turn the army's own orientation was also affected by this relationship. The concepts of 'strategic depth' and 'strategic defiance' were in essence military- and security-focused strategies, but in both cases had religious connotations. 'Strategic depth' empowered a fundamentalist regime in Afghanistan, and 'strategic defiance' lauded the nuclear programme of a clergy-led government in Iran. It can be inferred from this discussion that the confusion engendered by the organized religious forces and insular religious worldview of influential elements within major state institutions exacerbated the nuclear proliferation risk.

Turbulence in US–Pakistan Relations

Some of the indicators discussed in the earlier sections of this chapter about the anti-Western and anti-American views of General Aslam Beg, A. Q. Khan, JI leaders, and some nuclear scientists show their entrenched feelings and concerns about the West in general and the USA in particular. A brief glance at the history of Pakistan–US relations (1987–2003) will contribute towards evaluating how the ups and downs in the relationship might have induced nuclear proliferation activities originating from Pakistan.

Pakistan's relationship with the USA since independence has been erratic.[111] Having been part of the US-led military alliances in the 1950s and 1960s, Pakistan had high expectations from America in its wars with India in 1965 and 1971. As far as the USA was concerned, however, its commitments were only in relation to potential threats from the Soviet Union, and Pakistan's problems with India were not covered under those security guarantees. In fact, different US administrations, due to their domestic legal requirements, were required to cut off military aid to Pakistan during the wars with India, which created disenchantment and disappointment in Pakistan. This grew in the 1970s, when America imposed sanctions on Pakistan as a result of Pakistan's nuclear programme development. Even as early as 1973, Prime Minister Z. A. Bhutto said: 'Pakistan was once called the most allied ally of the United States. We are now the most non-allied.'[112] Bhutto's overthrow in July 1977 was also attributed to the USA by his supporters, on the assumption that he was being punished for pursuing nuclear weapons. During the final months of Bhutto's government there were widespread riots and confusion in the country in reaction to rigged elections, and Bhutto started complaining in televised speeches and statements before the National Assembly that the CIA was behind the political turmoil because he had refused to compromise Pakistan's nuclear energy programme.[113] In his memoirs *If I am Assassinated*, written from his death cell in 1979, Bhutto again alleged that his decision to pursue nuclear weapons was the reason for the death sentence imposed on him, and he referred to a conversation he had with the US secretary of state Henry Kissinger, in which he was threatened with dire consequences if he failed to halt Pakistan's nuclear programme.[114] For the people of Pakistan these claims were credible and rational. Some indeed were, and the USA's poor handling of Pakistan is well documented. A quick glance at the history of nuclear-driven American sanctions targeting Pakistan explain the ups and downs over the years, and especially during the 1987–2003 period.[115]

1976 Congress amends the Foreign Assistance Act (FAA) of 1961 to bar aid to countries that transfer uranium-enrichment or reprocessing equipment, materials, or technology in violation of specified conditions (Symington Amendment, Sec. 669, FAA).

1977 Congress amends FAA to bar aid for countries that detonate a nuclear explosive (Glenn Amendment, Sec. 670, FAA, which also covers reprocessing transfers). Aid to Pakistan is suspended in September because Pakistan is found to be seeking reprocessing technology from French companies.

1978 Aid resumed in October after France cancels reprocessing deal.

1979 Aid cut off in April because of Pakistan's enrichment activities (Symington invoked).

1980 Negotiations to resume aid begin after Soviets invade Afghanistan.

1981 Aid resumed for Pakistan (Symington waived by Congress [Sec. 620E, FAA] of Sec. 669) but restrictions added for transfers of nuclear weapons and design information.

1985 Solarz Amendment (amends Sec. 670, FAA) bars aid for illegal export from the USA of any material, equipment, or technology that would contribute significantly to the ability of a country to build a nuclear explosive device. Pressler Amendment (Sec. 620E(e), FAA) prohibits the transfer of military equipment or technology to Pakistan specifically unless the president certifies to Congress that Pakistan does not possess a nuclear explosive device and that the proposed US aid programme would significantly reduce the risk that Pakistan will possess such a device.

1987 Symington waiver expires; renewed for thirty months. The CIA, according to its 2017 declassified records, was quite concerned in that Moscow had become very active in campaigning against Pakistan's nuclear weapons programme. CIA analysts were of the view that 'if the United States cuts aid to Pakistan as a result of Islamabad's nuclear procurement activities, Moscow probably will soften its criticism of Pakistan in an effort to exploit the strain in US–Pakistani relations'.[116]

1990 Aid suspended under Pressler Amendment. Symington waiver expires.

1995 Brown Amendment relaxes cut-off so that only military aid and transfers are barred (with very limited financial impact on Pakistan).

1998 May: all aid suspended after the nuclear tests. July: Congress provides waiver for wheat purchases only. Aid resumes for one year, except military assistance, dual-use exports, and military sales (India–Pakistan Relief Act of 1998 (Brownback I).

1999 Aid resumes permanently (Brownback II gives the president permanent waiver authority for proliferation sanctions). However, foreign debt arrears and a military coup bar aid to Pakistan.

2001 Presidential executive order lifts remaining restrictions (after Pakistan joins the US-led War on Terror in Afghanistan in October 2001).

Pakistan's leaders could see a pattern in these repeated aid cut-offs and resumptions. The most critical aid cut-off was in 1990, because it would have had a direct impact on Pakistan's nuclear proliferation activities. A brief look at the context of this episode explains the Pakistani perspective. By 1987, of 777 terrorist incidents recorded worldwide, 90 per cent had taken place in Pakistan, mostly orchestrated by the KGB and leftist Afghan supporters of the Soviet campaign.[117] From Pakistan's point of view, this was the price it was paying for its deep involvement in the Afghan jihad of the 1980s and its close alliance with the USA. With steady US financial and military support to the Afghan *mujahideen* through Pakistani channels, Soviet occupation of Afghanistan was increasingly becoming untenable. Faced with military humiliation and the increasing financial burden of the occupation, the Soviet leader Mikhail Gorbachev announced in 1987 that his forces would withdraw from Afghanistan within a year. At this point a divergence in Pakistan–US interests manifested itself, reflecting the different expectations of the two countries. The USA just wanted to see the USSR out of Afghanistan and was not much concerned about its future, as is evident from a statement by the State Department's Michael Armacost: 'Our main interest was getting the Russians out. Afghanistan, as such, was remote from US concerns. The United States was not much interested in the internal Afghan setup and did not have much capacity to understand this.'[118] As soon as the Soviets left Afghanistan (1989), American interest in Afghanistan and Pakistan declined sharply. As Pakistan saw things, it had helped America to sow the winds of change in Afghanistan, but when the time came to reap the whirlwind, it had to do it alone. Pakistan saw the decline in US interest as abandonment, which left it with more than three million Afghan refugees to care for; thousands of *madrassa*s funded by Saudi money; militarization of the youth; a Kalashnikov culture, such that one could rent an automatic weapon in Karachi for less than $2 an hour; and last but not least, a flourishing drug trade.[119]

In the midst of this transformative phase, General Zia—along with twenty other senior Pakistani army officials, Arnold Lewis Raphel, the US ambassador to Pakistan, and Brigadier-General Herbert Wasson, the US defence representative—died in a mysterious air crash in August 1988. The official American position remains that the crash was an accident, but an overwhelming view among Pakistanis is that it was an assassination. Also, one of the most popular conspiracy theories in the country is that the USA was involved in it, though the well informed also pointed fingers at elements within Pakistan's armed forces.[120] These divergent perceptions speak volumes about how most Pakistanis view the USA.

For Pakistan the 1990 aid cut-off was a breach of contract. Pakistan believed that it had fulfilled its part of the contract in supporting the Afghan jihad, and that it had been ditched by America when its interests were served.[121] As far as the USA was concerned, its intelligence reports showed that Pakistan was producing weapons-grade uranium, and would soon be ready for nuclear weapons manufacturing. The relationship between the two states remained cold during the 1990s, though Prime Minister Benazir Bhutto made two official visits to Washington DC, to a warm welcome. The nuclear policy of the state, however, was completely in the hands of the military, and they received no US military aid during the 1990s. The military-to-military relationship only revived in the aftermath of the 9/11 attacks.

A 2005 report for the Congressional Research Service (CRS) aptly sums up the nature of the Pakistan–USA relationship: 'In over fifty years, the United States and Pakistan have never been able to align their national security objectives except partially and temporarily.'[122] This was a hard truth. The way in which the two countries defined their relationship with each other varied sharply. Pakistan believed that America—as its friend—would stand by it irrespective of its own behaviour. That is what is expected of friends in Pakistani culture. For the USA, the Afghan project served mutual security interests, and nuclear non-proliferation goals were a separate and critical issue on which no compromise was possible.

After the May 1998 nuclear tests triggered international sanctions, the sense of anti-Western nationalism among Pakistan's nuclear establishment grew.[123] At that time, according to Hoodbhoy, 'people in PAEC were saying, "If the US imposes sanctions, and the economy collapses, why not sell our bomb and prevent economic collapse?"'[124]

One may argue that Pakistan's critical view of the USA was not necessarily a consequence of the post-1990 US aid cut-off. Professor Rasul Baksh Rais, a respected Pakistani political scientist, wrote in 1985:

> There is a common feeling among the political and bureaucratic elites in Pakistan about latent hostility on the part of the Western powers toward the Islamic countries. It is generally perceived that the Christian West would not allow the Islamic countries to emerge independent, self-reliant and powerful enough to pursue an effective role in world politics. It is generally argued that the proponents of nuclear proliferation, while acquiescing to the nuclear capabilities of India and Israel, have tended to discriminate against Pakistan.[125]

Thus, the apprehensions, fears, and grudges against the USA held by Pakistan's nuclear myth-makers—be they political or military leaders or part of the civilian bureaucracy—played an important role in the whole nuclear proliferation drama.

8

POLITICAL INSTABILITY, CIVIL–MILITARY TUSSLES, AND LOOSE CONTROLS OVER THE NUCLEAR PROGRAMME MANAGEMENT

Though the A. Q. Khan network's nuclear proliferation activities spanned roughly a decade and a half, there are three critical periods when important nuclear proliferation decisions were taken—1987–9 (Iran), 1993–5 (North Korea and Iran), and 1997–9 (North Korea and Libya). Given Pakistan's constantly changing political and regional security environment, the country was facing unique challenges at these three critical points. Arguably, decision-making processes at these points in time were influenced by political instability, transition from military to civilian rule, economic distress, and internal conflict. The A. Q. Khan network and its supporters within Pakistan's policy-making arena most likely took advantage of the environment of constant crisis to hide their activities; chaos and instability could provide an enabling environment for nuclear proliferation. This chapter studies political developments in Pakistan during the said three critical junctures. It also assesses the controls, management, and monitoring of Pakistan's nuclear programme and associated facilities during these times. Pakistan's official line has been that governments of the day were not aware of the true extent of Khan's activities, and that whatever was known about his shadow network was overlooked because of his political standing and his contribution to national security. This can be judged only by evaluating the command-and-control system governing Khan Research Laboratories (KRL) and other nuclear programme-related institutions, especially the Pakistan Atomic Energy Commission (PAEC). KRL and the PAEC had parallel programmes (even though pursuing separate tracts), and it is also useful to analyse why KRL became a proliferation hub while no such breaches occurred at the PAEC. A scholarly probe is critical for reaching definitive conclusions.

(A) The Greater the Internal Political Instability and Limited Civilian Control over the Military, the Greater the Proliferation Risk?

To probe this hypothesis in some detail, it is useful to examine the political situation and the security environment, both internal and external, at the three critical junctures between 1987 and 2003 are analysed.

1987–9

According to General Aslam Beg, the vice chief of army staff in 1987, Pakistan successfully experimented with dropping a dummy nuclear device from F-16 and Mirage fighter aircraft in November 1987.[1] These years also witnessed a transition from military to civilian rule after President General Zia-ul-Haq's assassination in August 1988. General Zia's last year in office was marred by political uncertainty in Pakistan, regional instability due to the Afghan jihad, and differences between Pakistan and the USA over the future of Afghanistan after the Soviet withdrawal.

After ten years of military rule, Zia's political support in the country was on the wane in 1987, and he was becoming uncomfortable with his handpicked prime minister, Mohammad Khan Junejo, who wanted to take Pakistan back to the 1973 constitution through extensive legislation.[2] Junejo's promise to review all the amendments made by the President Zia meant that many of the presidential powers that Zia had amassed would be removed. This led to tension between the two highest offices in the country. Appointments, transfers, and extensions of the services of important civil/military officials also became a bone of contention between the two.[3] However, the real locking of horns came over the terms on which each wanted to see an end to the Soviet occupation of Afghanistan. At the start of the Soviet campaign Zia would have considered himself blessed if the Soviets could be held on the Afghan side of the Pakistan–Afghanistan border. But as the war progressed and the USSR's failure to accomplish its mission in Afghanistan became obvious, Zia's ambitions began to expand. His associates began strategizing to place a firmly pro-Pakistan government in charge of affairs in Kabul (for strategic depth), so that Pakistan could feel more secure vis-à-vis India. Towards this end his government worked hard to position Gulbuddin Hekmatyar as the next ruler of Afghanistan.

As the Geneva talks (1982–88), sponsored by the United Nations to resolve the Afghanistan crisis, progressed, it seemed probable around 1987 that the Soviets might actually leave Afghanistan. Pakistan also wanted them out, but first it wanted a provisional government in Kabul made up of the Afghan *mujahideen* groups that had been supported by Pakistan throughout the war years. Zia could not agree to Mohammad Najibullah, the pro-USSR ex-head of the notorious Afghan secret service KHAD, staying on as the Afghan president. Zia also needed more time so that Pakistan's nuclear programme could reach a stage in development where it would find security as a *fait accompli*. While he was reading the situation accurately, the Americans were aware of his thinking. According to 2012 declassified US documents, senior State Department officials wrote in the spring of 1987 that Pakistan's nuclear programme was on a fast track and that Zia was nearing a 'threshold which he cannot cross without blatantly violating his pledge not to embarrass the [US] President'.[4]

Zia was not interested in the Geneva forum discussions. But Junejo was convinced that Pakistan needed a way out, and the Geneva talks provided a good opportunity. He wanted to be seen as an independent politician so, without taking Zia into his confidence, Junejo arranged an all-political parties conference to consider Pakistan's options at the Geneva forum. Receiving the requisite support, he decided to sign an accord with the Soviet Union without any conditions.[5] Zia was fuming. On 10 April 1988, four days before the accord was to be signed, there was a massive explosion at Ojhri Camp, midway between Islamabad and Rawalpindi. This was the depot where all ordnance coming in as aid for the Afghan *mujahideen* was stored. Rockets, missiles, and shells rained on the twin cities for a few hours, bringing death, destruction, and panic. Sabotage was strongly suspected. While Zia was more interested in getting the destroyed ammunition stores refurbished by the USA, Junejo started asking tough questions. He wanted to identify those responsible for having sited the huge ammunition dump in the middle of a densely inhabited area and hold them accountable.[6] This amounted to pointing a finger at Zia's close associate General Akhtar Abdur Rahman, the former chief of the ISI, who had since been promoted to full general and chairman of the Joint Chiefs of Staff Committee, as he was the one who had picked the location for these stores.[7] Junejo was now close to crossing Zia's red line.

Besides signing the Geneva accord, another of Junejo's 'crimes' was his attempt to slash the country's defence budget; that would have been the first time in its history. In May 1988 the finance minister in Junejo's cabinet announced that a special review committee of the government had decided to reduce defence expenditure. He added that the committee, composed of MPs and officials from the economic ministries, had also forwarded proposals for raising a small professional army, comprehensive training for all citizens, and setting up a National Defence Council functioning under the parliament to scrutinize defence spending.[8] The general wasted little time in making a categorical response: 'Pakistan cannot afford any cut or freeze in defence expenditure, since you cannot freeze threats to Pakistan's security.'[9]

The drama was becoming serious. On 29 May 1988 Zia appeared live on national television to address the nation, and announced the dismissal of Junejo's government on the grounds of 'corruption' and an inability to enforce Islamic law in the country. Zia didn't live long enough to enjoy the fruits of total power, as his fatal plane crash occurred in August 1988. However, the military dictator's death meant a revival of full-fledged democracy in the country. It opened the door for thirty-five-year-old Benazir Bhutto to emerge as the new prime minister. As mentioned earlier, General Aslam Beg became the new chief of army staff (COAS), and the office of president went to a former bureaucrat and one of the architects of Pakistan's nuclear programme, Ghulam Ishaq Khan. During his last days Zia had been afraid of this potential scenario, and had instructed the chief of the ISI to cobble together conservative political forces to compete with Bhutto's Pakistan People's Party (PPP). The plan was put into action, but in the absence of Zia there was nothing that could stop the popular Benazir from gaining power.[10] As briefly mentioned earlier, Bhutto was allowed to take the oath of office only after giving an assurance that she would not interfere in Pakistan's nuclear programme, its Afghan policy, or the promotions/transfers and the budget of the armed forces.[11]

Bhutto later disclosed that Pakistan had operational nuclear weapons in 1989, nearly a decade before it actually conducted nuclear tests.[12] In an interview she also confirmed that uranium enrichment had reached the critical 93 per cent by 1988, and Pakistan conducted cold tests between January and March 1989.[13] (Cold tests yield no critical mass of fissile material). She remained under intense US pressure to cap Pakistan's nuclear programme during her first stint in government, but lacked the de facto power to decide about that. Also, the country faced multiple challenges, ranging from ethnic conflict in Sind province to insurgency in Indian-controlled Kashmir, with implications for Pakistan.[14] She also mentions a sense of paranoia in security circles about the possibility of Pakistan's nuclear sites coming under attack in 1988–90:

> The Army was concerned, the president was concerned, the Pressler amendment was there. The Soviets were withdrawing from Afghanistan and there was concern that as soon as the Soviets withdrew we would no longer be a frontline state in the fight against Communism. And that is when our nuclear installations could come under attack. So we had a very narrow timeframe during which we could actually negotiate to satisfy international concerns.[15]

Her government was dismissed in August 1990, after a mere twenty months in power, by President Ghulam Ishaq Khan, with the support of General Aslam Beg, on charges of corruption. 'The Military Intelligence [MI] was conspiring against my government from the first day,' said Benazir to local and foreign correspondents a day after her dismissal.[16] A few days later A. Q. Khan in a lecture at the National University of Science and Technology in Rawalpindi, a military-run institution, disclosed to a selected audience that he had repeatedly asked General Beg to get rid of Bhutto as she was creating hindrances in the further development of Pakistan's nuclear programme.[17]

1993–95

Benazir Bhutto returned to power in late 1993, after two years of the Nawaz Sharif government. Like Bhutto's first government (1988–90) Sharif was also ousted by President Ghulam Ishaq Khan on charges of corruption and incompetence, although in reality he was also a victim of turbulent civil–military relations. Sharif had formed a government in 1990 after the ISI ensured that Bhutto could not return to power by investing around $6 million in Sharif's political campaign.[18] Soon after his arrival in the prime minister's office in late 1990 Sharif had appointed Lieutenant-General Javed Nasir, who was a religious fanatic and deeply involved in supporting armed groups in Kashmir and else-where, as ISI chief. Nasir also later confessed that, 'despite UN ban on supply of arms to the besieged Bosnians, he successfully air lifted sophisticated anti-tank guided missiles which turned the tide in favor of Bosnian Muslims and forced the Serbs to lift the siege'.[19] Sharif reluctantly dismissed him in April 1993, after receiving a warning from the US administration, and after Pakistan was put on the US State Department's watch list for terrorist states.[20]

The sudden death of COAS head General Asif Nawaz Janjua (General Aslam Beg's successor) also led to rifts between President Ishaq Khan and Sharif regarding the appointment of the next army chief.[21] General Beg had disclosed at the time that General Nawaz was planning to impose martial law before he died, giving rise to many conspiracy theories.[22] A. Q. Khan also jumped into the fray by siding with his guardian and friend, President Ishaq Khan, and proclaimed that the 'president was defending the nuclear program as a rock'.[23] Finally, the tussle between President Ishaq Khan and Prime Minister Sharif resulted in the ouster of both from their offices by the new army chief, General Abdul Waheed Kakar. As the civil–military rifts during the years disabled the decision-making processes in the country, it is hard to be certain whether there was any consensus on country's nuclear policy in those turbulent times.

With this troubled background, Bhutto became more cautious dur-ing her second stint in office (1993–6). She also had the luxury this time around to have a member of her own party, Farooq Leghari, elected as president. President Leghari started off by declaring: 'I won't be a President who encourages intrigues or subverts the democratic process.'[24] That was a good start, but other challenges were now haunting the country, in the shape of increasing ethnic and sectarian violence. The rise of the Taliban in Afghanistan in 1994 was yet another major development; it consumed much of the top policy-makers' time. While the Taliban were in the ascendant in Afghanistan, Pakistan also experienced its first brush with an indigenous Taliban-style movement in November 1994. This was the black-turbaned Tehrik-i-Nifaz-i-Shariat-i-Mohammadi (Movement for the Enforcement of Muhammad's Law—TNSM) led by Sufi Mohammad. The movement spread in the Malakand area of the North West Frontier Province (NWFP) of Pakistan bordering Afghanistan, with many of its members boasting about their participation in the jihad in Afghanistan. They occupied the local airport (Saidu Sharif), forced government offices to close down, and blocked traffic on all major roads in the area, demanding the enforcement of a very controversial and dogmatic version of Islamic law in Malakand. While the government used the Frontier Corps (a federal paramilitary agency) to arrest Sufi Mohammad and restore order, it succumbed to the TNSM's demand for the introduction of Islamic law in the area.[25]

The government had hardly recovered from the Malakand crisis when, in November 1995, an Arab-Afghan veteran of the Afghan jihad blew himself up at the Egyptian embassy in Islamabad. This was the first case of a suicide bombing in Pakistan, and was a warning sign from Arab volunteers from the Afghan jihad who were now roaming around in Pakistan and wanted to avoid being sent back to their home countries. Soon differences arose between Bhutto and President Leghari on governance issues, and simultaneously she locked horns with the country's judiciary. Her government was yet again dismissed before completing the stipulated five-year term.

During these turbulent years nuclear policy remained in the hands of the military leadership, and A. Q. Khan got an extension from Bhutto in 1996 to continue as head of the Khan Research Laboratories (KRL). She was in no position to confront Khan even if she had wanted to; she was never even allowed to set foot inside KRL.[26] There were some media rumours in 1996 claiming that India could conduct nuclear tests, to which Bhutto responded by declaring that if India were to conduct a nuclear test, Pakistan could be forced to 'follow suit', though she expressed the hope that 'the day will never arise when we have to use our knowledge to make and detonate a [nuclear] device and export our technology'.[27] It is surprising that she made a reference to the export of nuclear technology here, out of context.

She was dismissed later in 1996 by the president, due to differences over governance issues, corruption charges, and rifts with the intelligence services. Intriguingly, her brother Murtaza Bhutto was killed in an apparent clash with police in Karachi weeks before her dismissal. These were very unusual circumstances.

1997–99

Nawaz Sharif returned as prime minister in early 1997 after a major victory in national elections. Having a two-thirds majority in the parliament, he immediately moved to make his office supreme by limiting presidential authority. Sharif's leadership was sorely tested when India, out of the blue, conducted nuclear tests in May 1998. Predictably, Sharif came under immense public pressure to respond with tit-for-tat tests. The moment that the USA had dreaded had arrived. President Clinton called Sharif four times to urge restraint, promising that should Pakistan avoid going down that path, the USA would write off its loans to Pakistan, persuade Japan to do the same, have its repayments to international lending agencies rescheduled, and try to get through Congress a military aid package that would add considerable credibility to the country's conventional deterrent.[28] There was no reference to any roll-back of the nuclear programme, so this was an offer that at least deserved serious consideration.

Sharif, however, was a politician who couldn't disregard public opinion. The religious parties openly warned him that unless he put Pakistan on the nuclear map, now that India had become a nuclear power without any fear of or regard for international opinion, he would be considered a traitor to his country. Army chief General Jahangir Karamat told the author that first he had a personal discussion with the prime minister on the subject, where he:

> requested him to hold and chair a DCC [Defence Committee of the Cabinet] meeting so that the technical administrative and financial (espe-

cially post event) matters could be discussed and decisions taken and recorded. The PM agreed and this meeting was held on May 16. The pros and cons were discussed and decisions taken.[29]

The military approached the issue quite professionally, avoiding taking a strong position either way. Another army general familiar with the proceedings told the author that General Karamat 'gave only the defence point of view, and left the decision to the PM because it had economic, political, and psychological implications'.[30] It had become a national issue, and politicians were at least as hawkish as the military, so the army leadership needed no lobbying or pressure tactics to get what they wanted.

Two factors that weighed strongly in favour of the decision to proceed with the nuclear tests were a lack of faith in US promises and an apparent encouragement from the government of Saudi Arabia to go ahead. Sharif tasked the PAEC to prepare for the tests, which came as a serious setback to A. Q. Khan, who tried without success to convince the army and the prime minister that KRL should be given the responsibility.[31] While Pakistan celebrated on hearing about the tests on 28 May 1998, President Clinton's press secretary at least acknowledged that 'Prime Minister Nawaz Sharif was honest and straight forward in the description of his decision, and India was manifestly not', providing some solace to Sharif.[32]

Sharif was enjoying the limelight, and there had been no immediate negative reaction, but the euphoria turned out to be short lived. Sharif's problems with the military began when in early October— barely four months since the tests—army chief General Jahangir Karamat, while delivering a keynote lecture at the Naval War College in Lahore, made some slighting statements about politicians while making a case for the need for the creation of a national security council to help the government formulate security policy. The well-read and scholarly general perhaps was not impressed by the quality of discussions at the highest levels of government, and the publicity given to his comments offended the Sharif government. Pakistan now was a declared nuclear weapons state, and indeed it did need better decision-making processes. However, Sharif misread the incident as an attempt by the general to make a case for removing him from office. Karamat was not the kind of general who harboured political ambitions, but within forty-eight hours of making the statement, he was told to pack up;[33] army generals are not accustomed to taking orders from civilian leaders, but Karamat acquiesced out of respect for the democratic order. Many of the other generals were furious, and told themselves that Sharif would have to pay for doing this. Sharif picked Pervez Musharraf to be the next army chief. Musharraf belonged to the immigrant Urdu-speaking community and, in a military dominated by ethnic Punjabis, he was seen as potentially harmless and docile. Sharif obviously had little sense of the *esprit de corps* in the military rank and file.

The military's list of grievances started piling up when Sharif opened the door to diplomacy with India and welcomed the Indian prime minister, Atal Bihari Vajpayee, to Pakistan in February 1999. Vajpayee also paid a visit to the Minar-i-Pakistan, a national monument marking the site where in 1940 Pakistan's founding fathers had resolved to work towards the goal of a separate national homeland. This visit was widely interpreted as a profound gesture reflecting India's acceptance of the 1947 Partition and an indication that India wanted to bury the hatchet and move forward. In what came to be termed as Lahore Declaration, the two leaders expressed an agreement to 'intensify their efforts to resolve all issues, including the issue of Jammu and Kashmir'.[34]

This was discomfiting for General Pervez Musharraf who, soon after taking over command of the military, began secretly planning a military incursion in the Kargil sector of the Jammu and Kashmir area (under Indian control). Sharif was not fully informed about the adventure, and when the crisis erupted he cut a sorry figure in front of the Indian leadership with whom he was engaged in back-channel diplomacy to resolve the Kashmir conflict for good.[35] Timely intercession by America stopped India and Pakistan from plunging into a full-scale war over the issue, but Sharif's relations with the army deteriorated considerably as a result.[36] The political leadership of the country was again at loggerheads with the military leadership, giving birth to another period of military rule beginning in October 1999. The army had had enough of Sharif, who was caught in the middle while trying to fire another army chief. Pervez Musharraf was the new head of the state, and Sharif landed up in jail. This was of course not without precedent in Pakistan.

David Sanger, a *New York Times* correspondent who has written extensively on the A. Q. Khan network, maintains that 'it is clear that

Dr. Khan's proliferation business thrived when Pakistan's leadership was at its weakest and most corrupt'.[37] This brief historical review of civil–military relations and the political instability during the three critical periods of nuclear proliferation activities demonstrates that the military in Pakistan was operating quite independently of the political leadership. Secondly, political leaders had very little oversight capacity over the workings of either the military or the nuclear establishment. Hence, the unstable state structures and persistent civil–military tensions provided an enabling environment for the nuclear proliferation activities of the A. Q. Khan network.

(B) Did Nuclear Proliferation Activities Succeed Due to Loose Controls, Lax Monitoring, and Poor Accountability of A. Q. Khan and the Nuclear Enterprises under his Control?

To examine how Pakistan's nuclear programme was supervised and controlled, this brief segment analyses various points of view on the issue and then looks at the available evidence to make sense of the monitoring, management, and accountability processes in place between 1987 and 2003.

In his memoirs, Musharraf provides many important insights about the management of the nuclear programme. He discloses that the funds for KRL were placed at A. Q. Khan's disposal and 'no audits were carried out and security was left to A. Q. himself'.[38] This was not the case to begin with, as Z. A. Bhutto was particular about processes and an institutional approach. He had established a committee of senior cabinet ministers, bureaucrats, and scientists to follow the progress of the nuclear programme, advise him, and ensure that bureaucratic hurdles regarding financial issues were tackled smoothly. To ensure civilian control, the military leadership was not included in this forum, but military sources and assistance were available to the PAEC and KRL.[39] However, General Zia-ul-Haq brought the management of the nuclear programme under his direct control, and its main supervisor during these years was Ghulam Ishaq Khan, according to A. Q. Khan.[40] Zia also constituted a Power Development Coordination Cell (PDCC) in 1978—a military-heavy body led by a two-star army general who would keep Zia updated on the nuclear weapons-related activities of the PAEC and KRL.[41]

A. Q. Khan enjoyed almost total freedom in his management of the programme during the Zia years, as he had direct access to Ishaq Khan. In a 2015 opinion piece A. Q. Khan maintained that during these years Foreign Secretary-General Agha Shahi had deputed a brigadier from the army to serve as focal administration person to take care of all travel arrangements and needs.[42] This indicates that the military was always completely aware of his international travels.

After Zia's death in 1988, President Ishaq Khan brought the army chief General Aslam Beg into the loop, and according to Musharraf 'from then on the chief of the army staff started managing our nuclear development on behalf of the president, dealing directly with A.Q.'.[43] After the transition from military to democratic rule, in the late 1980s, the chain of command was altered to include the prime minister, but only nominally. On the military side, the army chief created the post of director-general of combat development (DGCD), to be held by a serving major-general, to deal directly with A. Q. Khan.[44]

Musharraf acknowledged that Khan became his direct responsibility when he became the army chief in October 1998, and he quickly recommended that prime minister Nawaz Sharif bring 'strategic organizations and nuclear development under custodial controls', and submitted a 'written plan calling for a National Command Authority and a new secretariat within the government that would take charge of operational, financial and security controls which so far had been left to the discretion of A.Q.'.[45] Musharraf also maintained that he recommended these changes because he observed 'complete lack of coordination' between KRL and the PAEC. A decision on the subject by Sharif remained pending, so Musharraf alone had to establish 'a rudimentary version' of his proposal to the prime minister in early 1999. This was the genesis of the Strategic Plans Division (SPD) within the army.[46]

Musharraf formalized the system soon after taking over the reins of government, and by February 2000 the 'strategic weapons program came under formalized institutional control and thorough oversight' according to Musharraf.[47] This new set-up started operating under the newly formed National Command Authority (NCA) comprising the president, the prime minister, key federal ministers, armed forces chiefs, and senior scientists. Musharraf maintained that the SPD under a director-general from the army was tasked to assist the NCA in the implementation of plans and oversight.[48]

William Milam, a thoughtful American diplomat who served as the US ambassador to Pakistan from 1998 to 2001, has some very interesting insights about the status of Khan during his time in Pakistan. He believed that Khan was under orders from the military not to meet any Americans at the time. He further asserts: 'A. Q. Khan was by that time a kind of institution to himself basically, with control of a lot of resources, and acting pretty independently of the government. He was already selling his nuclear secrets by then quite clearly. You know he traveled in a convoy which was longer than the prime minister's.'[49] As regards nuclear proliferation involving Pakistan and Khan, and how much America knew specifically, he said: 'By the end of my third year [2001] I was pretty sure they were [proliferating]. I was pretty sure A. Q. Khan was at the center of it. But we didn't have any evidence.'[50] The author's conversations with senior officials who served under General Musharraf suggest that the USA conveyed these apprehensions and concerns to Musharraf, who already held a poor opinion of Khan. Now he had more reasons to call for a discreet National Accountability Bureau (NAB) investigation into Khan's financial dealings in early 2000.[51] The swift investigation, involving scrutiny of a secret dossier prepared by intelligence and military officers who had served at KRL and monitored Khan from ISI headquarters, showed signs of financial mismanagement and proof of assets that were beyond Khan's means, but the NAB advised Musharraf not to pursue the matter via the NAB (which would have led to legal proceedings for corruption charges), keeping in mind Khan's stature and the NAB's limited capacity to manage such a high-profile case. The NAB was a new organization trying to build its profile and professional image under Lieutenant-General Amjad, who was a man of good character and high integrity. This undertaking could have compromised Musharraf's whole anti-corruption campaign, which was gaining traction at the time. Khan had tremendous respect among the people in all sectors of society, and pursuing corruption charges against him would have been a Herculean task even if the NAB had possessed the resources and access to original KRL records.[52]

Musharraf decided to follow a different path. He pushed Khan to retire on 30 March 2001 in order to effectively cut him off from his base, and he believed that, 'when A. Q. Khan departed, our scientific organizations started functioning smoothly'.[53] Musharraf conveniently claimed that 'neither the Pakistan Army nor any of the past governments of Pakistan was ever involved or had any knowledge of A. Q.'s proliferation activities'.[54] He laid all the responsibility at the feet of Khan, and absolved everyone else. This contradicts his contention that 'for years, A. Q.'s lavish lifestyle and tales of his wealth, properties, corrupt practices, and financial magnanimity at state expense were generally all too well known in Islamabad's social and government circles'.[55] If that was indeed the case, then those who overlooked Khan's excesses cannot be absolved of sheer negligence and severe dereliction of duty. Musharraf avoids blaming anyone for that.

According to politician Mushahid Hussain, a committee headed by Ghulam Ishaq Khan from 1975 to 1991 supervised the nuclear programme.[56] Mushahid also maintains that President Ishaq Khan in an October 1990 letter to President George Bush made a commitment 'not to export, share, transfer or assist any country in nuclear technology', indicating that the US administration must also have conveyed some concerns on this count.[57] Ishaq Khan was known as a thorough professional and a methodical person who was very particular about rules and regulations, and it is inconceivable that he did not follow up the matter by ensuring that effective checks were in place and that the system was functioning properly.

General Beg also confirms that there was a 'National Nuclear Command Authority' in place from 1975, headed by the chief executive of the country.[58] According to Beg, this was later transformed into a 'Nuclear Command Committee', which took the main policy decisions and comprised the prime minister, the president, the army chief of staff, the defence minister, and the navy and air force chiefs.[59] However, after President Ishaq Khan's departure in 1993, nuclear program-related policy making became in effect the province of the army chief.

According to Douglas Frantz, in early 2000 A. Q. Khan summoned the journalist Hamid Mir for an interview at KRL, in which he severely criticized Musharraf for cutting the funding for KRL's missile programme and said that Musharraf was 'trying to appease the Americans by stopping my missile program'.[60] However, a senior Pakistani military official told Frantz that Musharraf was 'actually trying to assert control over Pakistan's sprawling nuclear establishment, particularly Khan's operation'.[61] Another narrative that substantiates these assertions is discussed in chapter 7 in relation to a book that was sponsored by Khan. The author of the book, Imran Chaudhry, quoted Khan as saying that 'the real purpose of establishing SPD was to make way for US sanctions to stop Pakistan's uranium enrichment program'.[62] Khan was certainly annoyed at Musharraf for instituting monitoring mechanisms, probably because he had not previously been under such constraints.

When I asked former ISI chief Lieutenant-General Asad Durrani about the Musharraf–Khan dynamic, he framed the issue in a different light, which is also insightful:

> A. Q. Khan had violated no international law, did less than what many others do (including abducting nuclear scientists), but was indiscreet and "got caught". Pakistan indeed had much to complain against him (and much more to thank him), but he was humiliated to make the "West" happy. ... Remember, the real target was, and still is, Pakistan and its nuclear programme, and not A. Q. Khan.[63]

According to the 2007 IISS report on Pakistan's nuclear programme, A. Q. Khan enjoyed freedom of action during most of his working career in Pakistan, but there is evidence that Pakistan's security establishment was suspicious of his activities from as early as 1989. The ISI director-general reported to President Ishaq Khan that Khan was meeting 'suspicious characters' in Dubai, but, rather than intensifying the surveillance on Khan, the president warned him to be careful and stay clear of the ISI.[64] The report maintains that until 2001, 'A. Q. Khan's illicit activities were overlooked due to the importance of his laboratories to national security as well as his heroic status among the Pakistani populace'.[65]

Some members of the PAEC and KRL warned the government that A. Q. Khan would cause a huge embarrassment if left unchecked, and suggested a thorough examination of his financial accounts and foreign activities, but the government dismissed the allegations, believing them to be motivated by institutional rivalry. As mentioned earlier, General Jahangir Karamat's decision to conduct an audit of the nuclear programme also fizzled out quickly. In 1998, under heavy US pressure to investigate Khan, Prime Minister Sharif ordered a detailed audit of his finances and directed the ISI to reinvestigate Khan's previous suspicious financial transactions. The ISI investigation produced hundreds of pages of information on Khan's personal assets and bank accounts, but again, no significant measures against his onward proliferation activities were taken following this audit.[66]

Finally, in March 2000 the intelligence services conducted a comprehensive investigation into A. Q. Khan's foreign procurements and entrepreneurial activities. This effort resulted in a secret 120-page report detailing Khan's irregular financial practices, his $8 million in various bank accounts, and his $10 million hotel in Timbuktu. However, indicting a man seen as a national hero for corruption and financial embezzlement was beyond the investigative agency NAB's ability and purview.[67] There is no independent verification of these figures and the intelligence may be exaggerated.

The IISS report establishes that KRL and Khan were not working in a vacuum and that on various occasions there were efforts to monitor KRL and hold Khan accountable. It leads one to conclude that either there was criminal incompetence or that Khan's supervisors were committed to save him because he was obeying instructions. A counterargument is offered by retired brigadier Feroz Hassan Khan, who argues that the emphasis on secrecy seriously affected the management of the programme, while the methods of acquisition 'contributed to a remarkable lack of oversight'. He further adds:

> The nuclear program was considered a national jewel, and security was geared to protecting it from external spies. However, these security arrangements were not designed to monitor scientists, who were seen as national heroes and therefore above concern. Eventually, this unhealthy synergy of strategic culture, urgency, and secrecy caused the program to slip out of the state's control...[68]

Pervez Hoodbhoy contradicts this line of argument by mentioning the case of the French ambassador to Pakistan, whose diplomatic immunity could not save him from being roughed up by Pakistan's security services when he journeyed to a point several miles from the enrichment facility at Kahuta in 1979. Based on this and other similar instances, he aptly concludes: 'In such an extreme security environment, it would be amazing to miss the travel abroad of senior scientists, engineers and administrators, their meetings with foreign nationals, and the transport and transfer of classified technical documents and components, if not whole centrifuges.'[69] This is also substantiated by the assessment of another leading Pakistani scholar, Hasan Askari Rizvi, who argues that although it would have been possible for Khan and his aides to covertly divulge nuclear designs and share the names of nuclear component suppliers with other countries without the military knowing, 'if hardware is moved out of the country, then the army is directly involved'.[70] Centrifuge machines that Khan sold to Iran will certainly fall into this category, because unlike the case of Libya, in which Khan arranged to manufacture centrifuges in Malaysia, in the 1993–5 transaction with Iran, he took out old and used centrifuges machines from KRL. The case of North Korea is similar to that of Iran.

Another important indicator of the state of affairs at KRL is in reference to the Khan's Pakistani associates who were investigated by the authorities in 2004. According to Pakistani media reports, at least fifteen officials linked to KRL were questioned by the Pakistani authorities in late 2003 and early 2004; most were released within a few weeks, but three were held in custody for six months and then placed under house arrest.[71] These were retired Major Islam ul-Haq (A. Q. Khan's personal staff officer), Nazeer Ahmed (director-general of science and technology at KRL), and retired brigadier Sajawal Khan Malik (former head of security at KRL and director of the General Maintenance and Construction Division). Only one KRL official, Mohammed Farooq, Khan's principal deputy at KRL, remained in detention. He is believed to have helped Khan in nuclear transfers to Libya and Iran.[72] Besides Sajawal Malik, another former head of security at KRL, Brigadier Iqbal Tajwar, was also detained for a longer period of time.

Initially, when the military authorities picked up these officials without charging them, their families approached the courts for help. Interestingly, in a joint petition to the Lahore High Court, the family members of the detained officials made just one submission in defence of their dear ones: 'The nature of the KRL was such that no individual, either singly or with others, could transfer nuclear know-how to a third party.'[73] This is true, as security around Pakistan's nuclear installations was always very tight: scientists were carefully screened, visitors were barred, and foreigners who trespassed on KRL's outskirts were detained until their credentials could be thoroughly checked. Pakistan's nuclear infrastructure had an estimated 50,000 highly trained chemists, physicists, geologists, and other workers, around 7,000 of whom travelled to KRL on official transport (mostly buses) each working day.[74] Without an elaborate security system in place, it was impossible to secure the area.

Those who were employed to monitor and conduct surveillance of the KRL facilities and personnel were subordinate to Khan. A former KRL security official shared with me that some middle-ranking army officers were suspicious of what Khan was doing but were afraid to report their suspicions to their senior commanders. One of them even thought that Khan would have him killed if he investigated some of his activities.[75] The intelligence agencies, on the other hand, had very limited technical expertise to monitor what Khan was doing, and on some occasions they were simply told to look the other way. Brigadier Naeem Salik, who served in the SPD, believes that 'the army made an error of judgment in the selection of these [security] officers who were usually on the verge of retirement and were therefore tempted to associate themselves very closely to A. Q. Khan with a view to gain his favors for their post retirement settlement.'[76]

Lastly, it is intriguing that all the known nuclear proliferation activities from Pakistan were generated from KRL rather than the PAEC, which is a bigger set-up with more resources, expertise, and scientists. The question is whether there were different rules and regulations for the two organizations, or whether it all comes down to the types of individuals who spearheaded these institutions. The discussion suggests that loose controls, weak monitoring, and a lack of accountability at least enabled the nuclear proliferation activities.

9

CONCLUSION

POLICY IMPLICATIONS AND THE FUTURE
OF PAKISTAN'S NUCLEAR PROGRAMME

On many occasions during the period of proliferation the state exploited A. Q. Khan; at other times, he artfully deceived the state authorities. When the network was finally exposed in late 2003, President Pervez Musharraf refused to take any responsibility despite the fact that as per his own admission in his memoirs, he had first observed 'signs of some suspicious activities by A. Q.' as early as in 1999.[1] Khan, earnestly believing that he could manipulate the system, went too far in the process. It also shows that, in the absence of an established decision-making process and a clear chain of command, it was possible for a small team to hoodwink the government of Pakistan.

In a nutshell, the investigative study has found that Khan acted on behalf of the sovereign in the initial phase of nuclear proliferation (for example, making initial contact with Iran in 1987). In the second stage (contact with North Korea from 1992), Khan represented the government of Pakistan, and he was possibly in league with the military leadership in offering nuclear technology to North Korea while the civilian leadership was duped. During the third stage (beginning in 1997–9) Khan started operating independently, and the Libya deal was finalized during this period. He also probably continued to deal with North

Korea on his own. His organization, Khan Research Laboratories (KRL), and its independent security department supported his endeavours throughout these years.

Since the military rule of General Zia-ul-Haq (1977–88), the chief of army staff (COAS) became the de facto manager of the country's nuclear project. The COAS was not answerable to anyone. Pakistan's complex diplomatic relations with Iran had opened the door for Khan to develop contacts with Iranian officials in 1987. There is strong evidence to suggest that COAS General Aslam Beg (1988–91) authorized Khan to help the Iranian nuclear programme in response to Iranian requests. It seems entirely plausible that in certain instances Khan acted independently and, given his stature and role as manager-in-chief of the nuclear programme, no one could question or challenge him.

Once Pakistan mastered the nuclear fuel cycle and developed an indigenous capacity to produce centrifuges, Khan and his team of scientists, besides being overjoyed with their success, began imagining themselves as demigods who were above the system. There was no accountability mechanism in place and, when General Jahangir Karamat (COAS 1996–9) endeavoured to audit the nuclear programme budget, he was branded an American agent by Khan in one of his conversations with Prime Minister Nawaz Sharif.[2] The decision-making process was whimsical at best, and depended upon very few individuals. For instance, Pervez Musharraf maintains that when he was director-general of military operations (DGMO) as a two-star general in 1992 responsible for overseeing all military planning and operations, he was kept 'totally out of the nuclear circuit'.[3] Khan and his close associates believed that they had outwitted American intelligence and accomplished the task of acquiring nuclear weapons capability despite the massive obstacles created by the USA. Many senior Pakistani military and civilian officials, as well as a broad spectrum of politicians, continue to earnestly believe so. As a result, they also developed anti-US feelings, and this too motivated their activities to some degree. Few of them were ready to entertain an alternate view: that perhaps the US had showed considerable flexibility towards Pakistan's nuclear programme during the 1980s, given the strong US–Pakistan collaboration in Afghanistan. The USSR for one were of the firm belief that the USA was complicit in helping Pakistan develop nuclear weapons in return for the use of Islamabad as a supply base by the Afghan resistance.[4] In fact, the US administration, most likely on the CIA's advice, had decided not to cut off aid to Pakistan in 1987 as that would allow the Soviets to exploit the situation to their benefit in Afghanistan.[5] Based on a similar CIA assessment in 1985, the US opted not to consider any suspension of security assistance, fearing that 'Pakistan almost certainly would try to escalate its nuclear weapons development program' and would move towards testing a nuclear device in that eventuality.[6]

Senator Larry Presser in his 2017 book Neighbours in Arms interestingly claims that he had even confronted President Reagan in these words: "We are helping Pakistan get nuclear weapons—and in fact our Pentagon is helping Pakistan pay for its nuclear weapons!"[7]

Overall, the A. Q. Khan network's nuclear proliferation activities were the product of a combination of factors: his personal ambitions and inward-looking worldview; the Pakistan army's need to compete with Indian missile development; weak state institutions; fragmented decision-making processes; and compartmentalized authority structures. The political chaos in the country and the absence of civilian oversight and effective controls enabled the network to peddle its nuclear merchandise and expertise globally.

Despite publicly confessing in 2004 that Pakistan's help to the nuclear programmes of Iran, Libya, and North Korea was 'invariably initiated' at his behest, Khan recanted his confession in April 2008 and claimed: 'I saved the country for the first time when I made Pakistan a nuclear nation and saved it again when I confessed and took the whole blame on myself.'[8] In March 2008, with the winds of democratic change blowing across Pakistan, Khan's wife Henny Khan, had for the first time issued a direct threat to the government, saying that the time for 'low-profile, patriotism and national interest' was over and that if her husband's situation did not change then the family would take appropriate action.[9] She even disclosed that Chaudhry Shujaat Hussain was 'instrumental in negotiating the deal in which Dr Khan was to take the full blame on himself and, in return, was to be granted pardon with full freedom of movement and travel within Pakistan', but that the government had 'failed to fulfill the promises it made'.[10] Shujaat Hussain is a leading Pakistani politician who was close to Musharraf, and his political party, the Pakistan Muslim League, was famously known as the 'king's party' in the country during the Musharraf years. Interestingly, he chose not to refute Henny Khan's statement.

A. Q. Khan's disowning of his 2004 confessional statement was not surprising for many in Pakistan because there had been suspicions about the whole episode and the circumstances around it, right from the beginning. Firstly this was because few were ready to believe that the national hero who had achieved nuclear weapons capability for Pakistan could do anything to harm its reputation and credentials. This image was at least partly thanks to Khan's friends in the media, whom he had cultivated over the years. Secondly, few Pakistanis were ready to accept that Khan could have transferred nuclear technology to any country without the sanction and authorization of the army generals, who are seen as the guardians of the nuclear programme and very powerful. The Roman satirist Juvenal's phrase *quis custodiet ipsos custodies* ('Who guards the guardians?') is an apt metaphor to use here. The following comment from a columnist reflects the opinion of many Pakistanis:

> So if Qaddafi is guilty of leaving Pakistan in a lurch, the generals holding the Pakistanis in their thrall haven't behaved differently, either. When the moment of truth came they had no compunction in feeding Dr. Qadeer Khan and his acolytes to the wolves. They and Qaddafi are even. Both are secure, for the moment, behind their sandbags.[11]

However, a nuanced analysis of the available evidence produces a more complicated picture. Scholars and analysts are also divided in their opinions about what really transpired during the nuclear proliferation process involving Pakistan. David Albright and Corey Hinderstein, while acknowledging that questions remain about the exact involvement of Pakistani government officials in the network, maintain that 'the Pakistani government was not directing this network' and 'it was essentially a criminal operation, a more disturbing and dangerous operation than if it had been a secret government-controlled effort'.[12] Likewise, the IISS report *Nuclear Black Markets* argues that the official Pakistani line—that the exports to Iran, North Korea, and Libya were the work of one errant man and his duped associates—cannot be taken at face value, and neither does the claim that Khan was a front, doing the government's bidding in each of these cases, appear valid. The report concludes by asserting that 'a careful analysis shows that most of Khan's dealings were carried out on his own initiative'.[13]

My research has a different emphasis. First, it highlights the linkage between the growth of Pakistan's nuclear programme, benefiting from an existing international network catering to global needs, and the extension of that network's proliferation activities involving Iran, Libya, and North Korea. Second, it establishes how much Pakistan was dependent on the expertise and connections of Khan to make quick progress in acquiring the nuclear weapons technology, as the country's previous efforts, pursuing the plutonium route to the bomb, were proving to be slow and cumbersome. International pressures and checks, especially from the USA, were mounting with the passage of time, and Pakistan was going through severe stress and strain in the regional security context. Z. A. Bhutto was also in a hurry because he wanted to cut the defence budget to minimize the influence of the army in politics, and he could only do so if he could claim that Pakistan had achieved a credible nuclear deterrent and so a large standing army was no longer required. Khan was his best bet.

Evidence indicates that it is difficult to make generalizations about the whole nuclear proliferation episode involving Pakistan, as different sets of motivations, circumstances, and players were involved in the three cases under discussion. Even the different stages of each case require separate treatment—for example, both Iran and North Korea did nuclear deals with the A. Q. Khan network in two separate stages, with a gap in between. For instance, the circumstances under which Pakistan helped Iran in 1987 were markedly different from the A. Q. Khan network's nuclear cooperation with Iran in 1993–4. In the first phase, Khan's half-hearted and duplicitous dealings with Iran were in line with the instructions he had received from Zia and his coterie, and General Aslam Beg had most probably been fully informed. Beg certainly shielded Khan during the Zia years. After the rise of Beg as army chief in August 1988, the policy regarding nuclear cooperation with Iran was streamlined. Beg was of the view that the global spread of nuclear weapons could lead to a multipolar world that would suit Pakistan's interests better than a bipolar or unipolar world dominated by the United States.[14] Khan had until then carefully handled the relationship with Iran via third parties. In the second stage of Pakistan's nuclear links with Iran (1993–4), both the political situation and the regional security context had changed significantly. Iran and Saudi Arabia were fighting a proxy sectarian war in Pakistan, leading to significant violence, and Pakistan and Iran had developed divergent interests in Afghanistan (with Islamabad supporting the Taliban and later the

Northern Alliance). Pakistan's military could not support Iran's nuclear ambitions in this new situation. Moreover, Aslam Beg had already retired from the army in 1991 and was no longer in a position to support and provide cover for Khan's activities. However, Khan responded positively when approached by Iran through third parties with financial interests. He could pursue such interests knowing that Pakistan's army was beholden to him for his efforts to procure the No-Dong missile from North Korea, and thus he was immune from any questioning.

By the mid-1990s Khan had also developed detailed brochures and packages containing key information, equipment, and documentation, often digitized, sufficient to attract the attention of prospective customers, aimed at maximizing his profits and satisfying his desire for proliferation. As David Albright aptly maintains, Khan's accomplices in these nuclear sales were European engineers and ambitious businessmen out to get rich quick: 'urbane and educated, they stashed millions of dollars in secret bank accounts' and 'they also drove the business by always being on the lookout for promising new markets'.[15] The second phase of Pakistan–Iran nuclear links was a product of such motivations.

Pakistan's nuclear cooperation with North Korea was entirely different from that with Iran. Pakistan desperately needed the No-Dong missile technology, and North Korea was initially hesitant. Finally Khan got involved, and the deal was done around 1994. However, as in the Iran case, the second phase of this interaction was different from the first. No third party was involved in this case but Khan, likely on his own accord, continued helping North Korea in the late 1990s and early 2000s. Evidence, however, is a bit murky in this second phase on many counts as hard information is missing. Libya, in comparison to the other situations, is an open-and-shut case, as there is growing evidence that Khan's international network was fully involved, but in an independent capacity. Some confusion remains as to why President Musharraf visited Libya in 2000 and how the trip coincided with the publication of an advertisement in Pakistani newspapers regarding procedures to be followed for the exports of nuclear material.

In terms of what inspired and motivated Khan and his supporters within the Pakistani nuclear establishment to transfer nuclear technology abroad, Khan's phobia about the USA and Israel trying to destroy Pakistan's nuclear programme was a factor, as was his sense of self-imposed obligation to help other Muslim countries acquire nuclear technology. The insecure nature of the Pakistani state and the religious worldview of influential elements within its important institutions exacerbated the nuclear proliferation risk. The three critical periods when nuclear proliferation took place witnessed severe civil–military tensions, political instability, and mounting internal and regional security threats, in turn creating an enabling environment for a relatively small group of influential people to pursue proliferation activities. Even though an elementary nuclear command system was in place from the early days of the programme, loose controls and absence of monitoring mechanisms significantly helped the A. Q. Khan network. Weak institutional management and political polarization generated chaos and confusion that allowed Khan and company to operate freely.

General Beg and Khan proved to be 'proliferation nationalists', as set out in the introductory chapter. Inspired by a burning desire to defy the West in general and America in particular, their ideological leanings revolved around their perceptions about a clash between the Muslim world and the West. They both employed 'myth-making' strategies to achieve their goals—they supported Iranian and Libyan nuclear programmes with a vision of helping other Muslim countries in need of nuclear weapons technology. They had a well-defined agenda to transfer nuclear technology and their influential positions meant that they needed to co-opt only a few others. Khan was held in such high esteem that he could operate without raising many red flags.

This study also provides a large set of data for the optimist–pessimist debate. The optimist argument is premised on rationality, the unitary nature of a nuclear weapons state, and a relative ease of control over nuclear technology. The three cases studies in this work challenge all of these notions. Rationality becomes subjective when ideological motivations become dominant. Secondly, in states where democratic institutions are weak and authoritarianism is the governing reality, individuals can take vital decisions secretly—unchallenged by any other stakeholders. There are limits to how useful 'the state' is as an analytical concept. In the realm of safety issues, it needs to be recognized that decision making on critical and especially national security-related issues in Pakistan is personalized and often secretive. Secrecy comes into conflict with security, as enforcing checks on a secret project is extremely difficult, and confidentiality can eliminate consultation. Information is often compartmentalized for security and secrecy reasons, allowing a small number of people to manoeuvre and manipulate. The optimist argument also maintains that the barriers to entry of nuclear acquisition will automatically screen out the least stable states. The A. Q. Khan network proved exactly the opposite.

For the USA and its non-proliferation partners, the rise of non-state actors on both the supply and demand sides of the nuclear proliferation equation is the toughest challenge. The A. Q. Khan network more than anything else has shown that non-state actors can penetrate deep into the proliferation business, which in the past has largely been dominated by state actors.

In terms of lessons learnt from the study of the A. Q. Khan network, there are five ideas that can reinforce prevention and pre-emption of any nuclear proliferation venture: (1) timely intelligence sharing to track illicit smuggling networks in nuclear materials and technology; (2) effective monitoring of front companies and subsidiaries of quasi-governmental organizations in states known to be circumventing export controls for their indigenous nuclear programmes; (3) strengthening and empowering of the IAEA—in particular, requiring countries to implement the advanced safeguards provided by the Additional Protocol as a necessary condition for supplying equipment and materials for civilian nuclear programmes; (4) sustained diplomatic and political engagement with states of concern; and (5) improving capacity to understand the political dynamics of countries that are marred by regional insecurity, internal ethnic and religious conflict, and political instability.

Future Trends and Critical Issues

Pakistan–Saudi Nuclear Collaboration: Myth and Reality

The prospect of a nuclear Iran terrified Saudi Arabia. Even the US-brokered P-5 nuclear arrangement with Iran in 2015 hardly soothed its concerns, and Saudi Arabia refuses to believe that the threat from the Iranian nuclear weapons programme has subsided permanently. This insecurity inspired Saudi Arabia to improve its ties with

Israel, and secret communications over the years brought the two states onto the same page with regard to developing a joint strategy to counter Iranian moves in the region.[16] For the House of Saud, which is empowered by petrodollars, security is of utmost value, and it would even be prepared to pay an exorbitant price for nuclear weapons. The challenge is that buying nuclear weapons is quite different from buying any other military hardware. The idea of a nuclear umbrella sounds more plausible, and might be the best bet for the Saudis. But it is hard to find a provider—except Pakistan, which might be attracted to such an undertaking under special circumstances and for a very high price, while ensuring that it would control the weapons even in that eventuality. But this is mere speculation, as there is no hard evidence to suggest that such a secret understanding exists. More likely, in terms of the logistical needs of such an arrangement, is that Pakistan will lose control of its weapons, which will not be acceptable to its nuclear command and control managers today. There is no dearth of rumours, however, and the most referred to is a statement from Amos Yadlin, a former head of Israeli military intelligence, who argued that if Iran acquires the bomb, 'the Saudis will not wait one month. They already paid for the bomb, they will go to Pakistan and bring what they need to bring.'[17] Israeli media also claim that many Pakistani nuclear scientists have visited Saudi Arabia and met Prince Bandar ibn Sultan, the head of the National Security Council.[18]

In reality, the Pakistani parliament's refusal of an official Saudi request in 2015 for support in the Saudi military offensive against Yemen is indicative of Pakistan's thinking.[19] Pakistan's military leadership is also sceptical, and it was the military that received the initial Saudi request but decided to pass it over to the civilian side, knowing quite well the most likely outcome. Pakistan's unwieldy military and political entanglements abroad had only brought misery to the country in the shape of radicalization, sectarian bigotry, and violence—and finally it appeared that it had started learning from its past mistakes.

One must appreciate, however, the Saudi tenacity when it comes to the belief that money can buy you anything, any time, and anywhere. Perhaps not the bomb—but almost everything else. The Saudis were able to creatively engage Pakistan by offering the retired army chief General Raheel Sharif, a job as the first commander-in-chief of the

Islamic Military Alliance to Fight Terrorism (IMAFT)—also dubbed the 'Muslim NATO'—with its headquarters in Riyadh.[20] By March 2017 a Pakistan army brigade was in place in the south of Saudi Arabia to defend its border against any Yemeni incursions or retaliation.[21] This is indeed instructive.

And this is also not surprising given the close ties between the two states. Pakistani politicians, generals, and other influential citizens travel to Saudi Arabia more frequently than anywhere else—for pilgrimage, with a begging bowl in times of financial crisis, and occasionally seeking refuge. The Saudi footprint in Pakistan is also tangible. Saudi military officers routinely attend Pakistani defence academies. The Pakistan air force helped establish the Royal Saudi Air Force, and its pilots flew combat missions during the Saudi tensions with South Yemen in the early 1970s. It is well recorded that Pakistan's military units remained stationed in Saudi Arabia during the 1980s, but what is relatively unknown is that Pakistan's military intelligence also helped set up the modern Saudi intelligence infrastructure. In the aftermath of the Indian nuclear tests in 1998, Saudi support in the shape of free oil and other financial commitments helped Pakistan decide in favour of tit-for-tat nuclear tests. Prince Sultan ibn Abdulaziz, then the Saudi defence minister, was accorded a tour of nuclear programme facilities around the time of the tests, as the government's special guest.[22]

Despite these close links and influence, direct transfer of nuclear weapons from Pakistan to Saudi Arabia is extremely unlikely. Saudi Arabia signed the Nuclear Non-Proliferation Treaty (NPT) in 1988, which is also a barrier. In June 2011 Saudi Arabia announced plans to construct nuclear power plants over a period of twenty years at the cost of over $80 billion, and the plans are still in place, even though progress appears to be slow.[23] In October 2016 it announced that selection of the site for the first of these reactors was near.[24] Given its resources, it can hire the services of nuclear engineers and scientists with expertise in nuclear weapons development from many places, including Pakistan. However, there are no signs yet of anything happening along these lines. According to the credible assessment of the Nuclear Threat Initiative (NTI), there is nothing to substantiate the allegations that Pakistan and Saudi Arabia are collaborating in the nuclear weapons arena.[25] However, Saudi Arabia is still investing in developing a vast infrastructure for producing nuclear energy, which continues to draw scepticism.[26] It is worth quoting the scholar Matthew Fuhrman, whose research findings conclude that

> civilian assistance and weapons proliferation are linked because the former leads to the supply of technology and materials that have applications for nuclear energy and nuclear weapons, and because civilian assistance establishes an indigenous base of knowledge in nuclear matters that could be useful for a weapons program.[27]

Safety and Security of Nuclear Weapons

As of 2017, Pakistan is estimated to have around 125 nuclear weapons. Based on broader security trends in South Asia and anticipated weapons deployments, some Western experts believe that Pakistan's 'stockpile could potentially grow to 220–250 warheads by 2025, making it the world's fifth-largest nuclear weapon state'.[28] This may sound a bit exaggerated, but there is no denying that Pakistan's nuclear programme has expanded vastly over the last decade and a half. This assessment corroborates the 2016 statement by Dr Samar Mubarakmand, a leading and highly informed Pakistani nuclear scientist, that only China, France, Russia, and the United States have more nuclear weapons than Pakistan.[29] According to an assessment of the Arms Control Association, the UK today has 120 operational nuclear weapons.[30] In terms of the range of weapons available in Pakistan's nuclear arsenal, Dr Mubarakmand states that 'Pakistan has over fifteen types of nuclear weapons, from large weapons that can be carried on fighter jets to small ones that can be loaded onto ballistic missiles, and even smaller warheads for cruise missiles and tactical nuclear weapons'.[31]

Pakistan indeed made tremendous progress in operationalizing its nuclear capability. While it was developing several land-based platforms to deliver warheads, it successfully modified some of its F-16s and Mirage 5s for weapons delivery as well. Its ballistic missile arsenal includes the longer-range, solid-fuelled Shaheen-III, with a range of 2,750 kilometres, capable of reaching any target in India, including the most distant Indian islands in the Bay of Bengal. Besides many short-range missile options (ranging from 300 to 2,000 kilometres) it invested significant resources and expertise in developing its version of a nuclear-capable cruise missile named Babur with an estimated range of 700 kilometres. Pakistan also tested an air-launched cruise missile version known as Ra'ad, with a range of 350 kilometres in January 2016, and is working hard on developing sea-launched versions of the Babur and Ra'ad to add to its naval capabilities.[32]

This is an impressive accomplishment, and for Pakistan a matter of great pride, but for India and many in the West, a matter of concern. Indian too has been modernizing and updating its delivery systems quite aggressively, but without raising comparable alarm. For Pakistan, nuclear weapons are its best bet against any Indian aggression and hence to serve as a deterrent. Preserving territorial integrity, preventing military escalation, and neutralizing Indian conventional superiority were the central goals of Pakistan's nuclear policy—and it made sense, given its entrenched rivalry with India.[33] That was the justification for pursuing nuclear weapons in the first place. Credible minimum deterrence was the mantra emanating from Islamabad, and it sounded rational. That, however, seems to be a thing of the past, and a nuclear race appears to have ensued lately. The 2005 US–India Civil Nuclear Agreement was highly distressing for Pakistan, which felt provoked to do all in its power to compete with the Indian nuclear programme. It was ready to punch above its weight, whatever the cost. Pakistan's increased investment in missile development is arguably a consequence of US—India nuclear cooperation. (It is another matter that the implementation of the said US—India arrangement encountered many obstacles and is yet to bear fruit for both states).

Pakistan argues that India's 'Cold Start Doctrine'—an offensive 'limited-war strategy designed to seize Pakistani territory swiftly without, in theory, risking a nuclear conflict' as a punitive action in response to Pakistan's support for militant organizations conducting attacks in India—forced it to adjust its deterrence posture.[34] Pakistan responded by testing a short-range—60 kilometre—nuclear tactical weapon in April 2011, and General Kidwai, who was in charge of Pakistan's nuclear policy, declared that 'by introducing the variety of tactical nuclear weapons in Pakistan's inventory, and in the strategic stability debate, we have blocked the avenues for serious military operations by the other side'.[35] Strategists in Pakistan's nuclear policy-making arena presented this as a necessity, and a move that would make war with

India less likely.[36] This should not be surprising for anyone who has followed the growth of Pakistan's nuclear programme.

Pakistan's Strategic Plans Division (SPD) meanwhile emerged as an effective and responsible institution managing Pakistan's nuclear and missile programmes. The ten-member National Command Authority (NCA), led by the president (with the prime minister as its vice chairman), is responsible for devising the nuclear policy of the state (including decisions relating to possible deployment and use of nuclear weapons), but it is the SPD that directly oversees the nuclear arsenal. Agencies administered by the SPD include the National Engineering and Scientific Commission (NESCOM), the Space and Upper Atmosphere Research Commission (SUPARCO), the Pakistan Atomic Energy Commission (PAEC), Khan Research Laboratories (KRL), and the National Development Complex (NDC).

Along with the SPD, the Pakistan Nuclear Regulatory Authority (PNRA) controls, regulates, and supervises all matters related to nuclear safety and radiation protection in Pakistan. In late 2006 the PNRA initiated a five-year National Nuclear Safety and Security Action Plan (NSAP) to establish a more robust nuclear security regime seeking capacity building in Pakistan's ability to plan for, respond to, and recover from terrorist incidents in collaboration with other government agencies. IAEA guidelines are adhered to in this field, according to PNRA publications.[37]

Pakistan's nuclear safeguards have improved in the process. In recent years the USA is also reported to have aided and assisted Pakistan financially as well as technologically securing its nuclear arsenal. Admiral Mike Mullen, chairman of the US Joint Chiefs of Staff, had publicly maintained in February 2008 that in his assessment Pakistan's weapons were well protected and he saw little chance of them falling into terrorist hands.

General Kidwai, who remained at the helm of affairs at the SPD until 2013, in a rare briefing to foreign media in early 2008 said that about 10,000 soldiers were deployed to secure the nuclear facilities and provide intelligence to the NCA.[38] He added that his organization had developed plans for any contingency and had reassessed the militant threat in the light of escalating attacks on the security forces and intelligence personnel. In the same briefing, while commenting on the media reports that the Pentagon has contingency plans for seizing Pakistan's nuclear facilities if they should fall into the hands of extremists, he argued that such an operation would be very unlikely to succeed.[39] However, such rumours are known to have negatively impacted on Pakistan's cooperation with Western states (especially the USA and UK) in terms of sharing of security- and safety-related information, as it fears that any such knowledge about its nuclear infrastructure could be used by the USA if it decided to rid Pakistan of its nuclear capabilities.

The SPD officially acknowledges that foreign assistance helped it to acquire surveillance cameras, special locks, specialized perimeter fencing, and patrol vehicles. Pakistan has developed personnel and human reliability programmes to screen military and civilian personnel involved in the strategic programmes, and has instituted two-man— and, according to some, three-man—rules for handling nuclear materials, and it has developed some sort of permissive-action-link technology (sometimes referred to as PakPALs).[40] The SPD also acknowledged that about 2,000 scientists working in particularly sensitive areas were subject to intense scrutiny throughout their lives, including regular surveillance of their political and financial activities, as well as medical and psychological fitness tests. Sharing of this information indicates that the Pakistan military is very concerned about the international scepticism regarding the safety of its nuclear arsenal.

Pakistan's nuclear weapons are reportedly in a disassembled form for security purposes.[41] Theoretically, nuclear weapons on the move are inherently less secure than nuclear weapons at heavily guarded storage sites, and are also more susceptible to 'insider' security threats. Hence, unless there is a crisis situation with India, Pakistan's nuclear arsenal, though dispersed, remains more secure. Arguably, any rise in Pakistan–India tension and a consequent regional conflict scenario that would lead to the movement of nuclear weapons (in order to avoid possible enemy surveillance) is potentially alarming in this context.

A hasty deployment and rapid movement of nuclear arsenal—especially tactical warheads—in times of frenzied India-Pakistan tensions presents a really frightening scenario. Nuclear safety will surely be more vulnerable in such circumstances. Terrorists or even any extremists within Pakistan's security infrastructure can attempt to hijack or divert weapons during a chaotic situation. There are also serious concerns about further innovations in Pakistan's nuclear weapons capabilities; for instance placement of nuclear land mines on Pakistan-India border to deter advancement of Indian ground troops on Pakistani territory in a worst case scenario where Pakistan's conventional forces are overpowered or decimated.[42] Some of these fears as unlikely or as exaggerated as they may appear are quite plausible in the eyes of western nuclear security experts.

For Pakistan's nuclear managers today, matching Indian nuclear capabilities is all that matters. Brigadier Zahir Kazmi, Director at the Arms Control and Disarmament Affairs Branch of SPD laments that, "while the Indian strategy for waging conventional war under the nuclear threshold is accepted, the Pakistani countermeasures are considered 'at odds with responsible nuclear behavior.'"[43] Whether it is about prospects of admission into Nuclear Supplier Group or gaining access to western technology useful for civilian nuclear purposes, Pakistan feels that it is treated unfairly vis-à-vis India. On the side, Pakistan is also aggressively investing in developing nuclear reactors capable of yielding weapon-grade plutonium with China's help.

It needed little help however in repositioning its emphasis from maintaining credible minimum nuclear deterrence to employing "full spectrum deterrence." In any case it remains a challenge on how to interpret Pakistan's nuclear doctrine and attendant posture. It is hard to guess what is Pakistan's exact threshold that would trigger use of nuclear weapons. The ambiguity appears to be both intentional and strategic but the crux of the matter is that Pakistan wants India to positively understand that it is not only ready for a tit for tat response to any Indian military offensive but can afford to be provocative in pursuing its security interests. It has made it clear on more than one occasion that it reserves the right of "first use" to safeguard Pakistan's integrity in the face of a massive Indian conventional military campaign.[44] The simmering Kashmir dispute continues to drive Pakistan's security perspective and it considers all means—including use of any proxy militant groups—as legitimate. Pakistan is unlikely to budge from this posture in foreseeable future.

India is obviously not impressed with this state of affairs and its calculus also involves following China's nuclear capabilities and policies. India's nuclear posture naturally corresponds to its status as a rising global power; it pledges "no first use" but also promises a massive retaliation against an adversary that strikes first with nuclear weapons.[45] There is some speculation that India is revising its options and it "may abandon its no first use policy and launch a preemptive counter-force strike against Pakistan if it believed that Pakistan was going to use nuclear weapons (likely tactical nuclear weapons) against it."[46] This only further complicates the South Asian security scene that has already yielded to a deadly nuclear arms race with India having built its own "triad" of land, sea and air forces equipped with nuclear weapons with the latest addition of its nuclear ballistic-missile submarines and Pakistan having developed nuclear second strike capability.[47]

There are strong indicators that nuclear decision-making processes in Pakistan are being streamlined. Pakistan's strategic culture, however, is in need of reform and readjustments, which can only happen under a sustainable democratic dispensation. Civilian oversight of the nuclear programme in the real sense of the word will be a positive step in this direction. Pakistan needs to relocate its identity through religious accommodation and internal political reconciliation. It will have to invest more in domestic security through effective counter-terrorism strategies, building counter-narratives to religious extremism, and reforming its criminal justice system. Building more nuclear bombs is no substitute for these inadequacies.

In the prevailing security milieu of Pakistan, there is an entrenched and widely held belief that the Western world, and especially the USA, aspires to deprive Pakistan of its nuclear weapons. For instance, Pakistan received but never used many specialized vehicles and other equipment provided by the USA, suspecting that these are meant to monitor movement of nuclear weapons in the country.[48] This feeling of perpetual insecurity and distrust is a very dangerous factor, which could push Pakistan in a wrong direction.

As aptly framed by Toby Dalton and Michael Krepon, 'it is in Pakistan's national security interest and the interests of the international community to find ways in which Pakistan can enjoy the rights and follow the obligations of other nuclear weapons states recognized by the NPT'.[49] Pakistan has indeed learnt its lessons the hard way, but its well-meaning and concerted efforts towards enhancing the security of its nuclear infrastructure since the A. Q. Khan episode also deserve credit.

Nuclear safety concerns are of paramount importance, but that is not an end in itself. A call for 'a world without nuclear weapons' made by the former US president Barack Obama in May 2016 while he was visiting Hiroshima, the site of the first nuclear detonation, deserves appreciation.[50] One must hope that some day the possession and pursuit of this despicable weapon will be seen globally as a symbol of indignity rather than a matter of pride.

NOTES

1. INTRODUCTION: FRAMING THE QUESTIONS

1. Rafaqat Ali, 'Dr. Khan Seeks Pardon; Cabinet Decision Today; Meets Musharraf; Admits Error of Judgment', *Dawn* (Karachi), 5 February 2004, http://www.dawn.com/2004/02/05/top1.htm (accessed 5 November 2007). It was reprinted in full in *Disarmament Diplomacy* 75 (January/February 2004), 42.

2. 'A. Q. Khan "Covered up" for Musharraf: Benazir', *Daily Times* (Lahore), 6 March 2004.

3. 'Pakistani Scientist Tied to Illicit Nuclear Supply Network', *Washington Post*, 5 February 2004.

4. Esther Pan, 'Nonproliferation: The Pakistan Network', Council on Foreign Relations, 12 February 2004, http://www.cfr.org/publication/7751#12.

5. Christopher Oren Clary, 'The A. Q. Khan Network: Causes and Implications', Master's thesis, Naval Postgraduate School, Monterey, December 2005, http://www.fas.org/irp/eprint/clary.pdf (assessed 3 January 2008).

6. Pervez Musharraf, *In the Line of Fire: A Memoir*, London and New York: Simon & Schuster/Free Press, 2006, 294.

7. Peter R. Lavoy, 'The Strategic Consequences of Nuclear Proliferation: A Review Essay', *Security Studies* 4, 4 (Summer 1995), 696.

8. Clary, 'The A. Q. Khan Network'.

9. Ibid.

10. See Simon Henderson, 'Link Leaks', *National Review Online*, 19 January 2004.

11. Rana Qaiser, 'Musharraf Pardons Qadeer on Cabinet Nod', *Daily Times*, 6 February 2004.

12. Ibid.

13. 'Pakistani Govt Not Involved in Proliferation: US', *Daily Times*, 5 February 2004.

14. Kamran Khan, 'Business in Timbuktu: Conflict Views about Army's Awareness

of Qadeer's Engagements', *The News* (Islamabad), 1 February 2004; Kamran Khan, 'Foreign Accounts Having Proceeds from N-Technology Transfer Found', *The News* (Islamabad), 25 January 2004.

15. David Albright and Corey Hinderstein, 'Unraveling the A. Q. Khan and Future Proliferation Networks', *Washington Quarterly* 28, 2 (Spring 2005), 117.

16. William Broad, David E. Sanger, and Raymond Bonner, 'A Tale of Nuclear Proliferation: How Pakistani Built his Network', *New York Times*, 12 February 2004, A1.

17. Richard P. Cronin, K. Alan Kronstadt, and Sharon Squassoni, 'Pakistan's Nuclear Proliferation Activities and the Recommendations of the 9/11 Commission: US Policy Constraints and Options', CRS, Library of Congress, 25 January 2005, http://www.fas.org/spp/starwars/crs/RL32745.pdf

18. Clary, 'The A. Q. Khan Network'.

19. Seymour Hersh, 'The Deal: Why is Washington Going Easy on Pakistan's Nuclear Black Marketers?' *New Yorker*, 8 March 2004, http://www.newyorker.com/fact/content/?040308fa_fact

20. Quoted in Nick Schifrin and Habibullah Khan, 'Pakistan Nuke Proliferator Released, Says, "I Damn Don't Care" What Critics Think', ABC News, 6 February 2009.

21. Quoted in Hersh, 'The Deal'.

22. John Lancaster and Kamran Khan, 'Musharraf Named in Nuclear Probe', *Washington Post*, 3 February 2004.

23. Ibid.

24. William Langewiesche, 'The Point of No Return', *Atlantic Monthly* 297, 1 (January/February 2006), http://www.theatlantic.com/doc/200601/aq-khan

25. 'No More Details about A. Q. Khan to be Provided: Pakistan', *The News* (Islamabad), 17 October 2006.

26. Ibid.

27. 'A. Q. Khan Satisfied with Court Verdict', *Daily Times*, 7 February 2009.

28. Quoted in Joby Warrick, 'Nuclear Scientist A. Q. Khan is Freed from House Arrest', *Washington Post*, 7 February 2009.

29. 'A. Q. Khan a Closed Chapter, says FO', *Daily Times*, 7 February 2009.

30. For background see Kenneth N. Waltz and Scott D. Sagan, *The Spread of Nuclear Weapons: A Debate Renewed*, New York: W. W. Norton, 2003; John Mearsheimer, 'The Case for the Ukrainian Nuclear Deterrent', *Foreign Affairs* 72, 3 (Summer 1993); Sumit Ganguly and Devin T. Hagerty, *Fearful Symmetry: India–Pakistan Crisis in the Shadows of Nuclear Weapons*, Seattle: University of Washington Press, 2005; Benjamin Frankel, 'The Brooding Shadow: Systemic Incentives and Nuclear Weapons Proliferation', in Zachary S. Davis and Benjamin Frankel, eds., *The Proliferation Puzzle: Why Nuclear Weapons Spread and What Results*, London: Frank Cass, 1993; Stephen M. Meyer, *The Dynamics of Nuclear Nonproliferation*, Chicago: University of Chicago Press, 1984.

31. Bernard Brodie (ed.), *The Absolute Weapon: Atomic Power and World Order*, New York and Manchester, NH: Harcourt, Brace & Co./Ayer, 1946. Other important comparable works are John H. Herz, *International Politics in the Atomic Age*, New York: Columbia University Press, 1959; Robert Jervis, *The Meaning of the Nuclear Revolution: Statecraft and the Prospect for Armageddon*, Ithaca: Cornell University Press, 1989.

32. Deterrence theory is a military strategy developed during the Cold War, especially with regard to the use of nuclear weapons. Generally, it refers to being prepared to inflict unacceptable damage on an aggressor, and making sure that a potential aggressor is aware of the risk so that he refrains from aggression. Simply, the idea of deterrence is to strong enough to frighten the enemy— to deter him from aggression. See Patrick M. Morgan, *Deterrence Now*, Cambridge: Cambridge University Press, 2003.

33. Quoted in Fred Charles Iklé, 'Nth Countries and Disarmament', *Bulletin of the Atomic Scientists* 16, 10 (December, 1960), 391.

34. Waltz and Sagan, *The Spread of Nuclear Weapons*, 10.

35. Waltz and Sagan, *The Spread of Nuclear Weapons*.

36. Robert Jervis, 'Rational Deterrence: Theory and Evidence', *World Politics* 41, 2 (January 1989): 183–207.

37. See Bruce de Mesquita and William H. Riker, 'An Assessment of the Merits of Selective Nuclear Proliferation', *Journal of Conflict Resolution* 26, 2 (June 1982), 283; John J Mearsheimer, 'Back to the Future: Instability in Europe after the Cold War', *International Security* 15, 1 (Summer 1990): 5–56.

38. John Mearsheimer, 'The Case for the Ukrainian Nuclear Deterrent', *Foreign Affairs* 72, 3 (Summer 1993), 50–66.

39. Peter Lavoy, 'Civil–Military Relations, Strategic Conduct, and the Stability of Nuclear Deterrence in South Asia', in Scott D. Sagan (ed.), *Civil–Military Relations and Nuclear Weapons*, Stanford: Stanford Center for International Security and Arms Control, June 1994.

40. Ashley J. Tellis, C. Christine Fair, and Jamison Jo Medby, *Limited Conflicts under the Nuclear Umbrella: Indian and Pakistani Lessons from the Kargil Crisis*, RAND Monograph Report, Santa Monica: RAND Corporation, 2002, 78–9, http://www.rand.org/pubs/monograph_reports/MR1450/.

41. Ashley J. Tellis, *Stability in South Asia*, Santa Monica: RAND Corporation, 1997, 30–3.

42. Ganguly and Hagerty, *Fearful Symmetry*.

43. Rajesh Rajagopalan, *Second Strike Arguments about Nuclear War in South Asia*, New Dehli: Viking Penguin Books India, 2005.

44. Namrata Goswami, 'The Essence of the South Asian Nuclear Debate', *Strategic Analysis* 30, 3 (July–September 2006), 664. Also see Michael Walzer, *Just and Unjust Wars: A Moral Argument with Historical Illustrations*, New York: Basic Books, 1992, 269–86. Walzer maintains that nuclear deterrence works primarily because it is a strategy based on bluff.

45. Graham Allison, *Essence of Decision*, New York: Scott, Foresman & Co., 1971; Graham Allison and Philip Zelikow, *Essence of Decision*, 2nd edn, New York: Longman, 1999.

46. Allison and Zelikow, *Essence of Decision*, 255–324.

47. The idea is explained in detail in Peter Lavoy's Ph.D. thesis, 'Learning to Live with the Bomb? India and Nuclear Weapons, 1947–1974', University of California, Berkeley, 1997. The theory is further refined in Peter R. Lavoy, 'Nuclear Proliferation over the Next Decade: Causes, Warning Signs, and Policy Responses', *Nonproliferation Review* 13, 3 (November 2006): 434–54. The expression 'nuclear myths' is also used by Kenneth Waltz, but in a different context with a different meaning. See Kenneth N. Waltz, 'Nuclear Myths and Political Realities', *American Political Science Review* 84, 3 (September 1990): 731–45.

48. For background see Peter R. Lavoy, 'Nuclear Myths and the Causes of Nuclear Proliferation', in Zachary S. Davis and Benjamin Frankel (eds.), *The Proliferation Puzzle: Why Nuclear Weapons Spread (And What Results)*, London: Frank Cass, 1993; Peter R. Lavoy, 'Pakistan's Strategic Culture: A Theoretical Excursion', *Strategic Insights* 6, 10 (October 2005).

49. Lavoy, 'Nuclear Proliferation over the Next Decade', 435.

50. Lavoy, 'Pakistan's Strategic Culture'.

51. Ibid.

52. Bernard Lewis, 'The Roots of Muslim Rage', *Atlantic Monthly* 266, 3 (September 1990).

53. Samuel P. Huntington, 'The Clash of Civilizations?' *Foreign Affairs* 72, 3 (1993).

54. Samuel P. Huntington, *The Clash of Civilizations and the Remaking of World Order*, New York: Simon & Schuster, 1998 [1996].

55. Quoted in Edward Said, 'The Clash of Ignorance', *The Nation*, 4 October 2001.

56. Huntington, *The Clash of Civilizations*, 64.

57. Samuel P. Huntington, 'Try Again: A Reply to Russett, Oneal & Cox', *Journal of Peace Research* 37, 5 (2000), 609.

58. Amartya Sen, 'What Clash of Civilizations? Why Religious Identity isn't Destiny', *Slate*, 29 March 2006. Also see Matthew Price, 'Re-clash of Civilizations', *Boston Globe*, 15 February 2004.

59. Sen, 'What Clash of Civilizations?'

60. A search for the term 'clash of civilizations' in the database of *Dawn* newspaper (www.dawn.com), the country's most respected and comparatively liberal newspaper, produces more than three hundred articles/news stories where this idea is discussed or referred to—almost always in negative and critical terms.

61. 'We Need Atomic Weapons and Mujahideen, says Daawa', *Daily Times*, 6 February 2004.

62. Ibid.

63. Quoted in Zahid Hussain, 'Inside Jihad', *Newsline*, February 2001, 22.

64. Nathan Gardels, 'Musharraf Knew about A. Q. Khan's "Private" Proliferation', *New Perspectives Quarterly* 21, 2 (Spring 2004): 39–43, http://www.digitalnpq.org/archive/2004_spring/bhutto.html.

65. Graham Evans and Jeffrey Newnham, *Penguin Dictionary of International Relations*, 1st edn. London: Penguin, 1998, 346.

66. See Charles Hauss, 'Nationalism', *Beyond Intractability*, University of Colorado, Conflict Research Consortium, September 2003, http://www.beyondintractability.org/essay/nationalism.

67. Michael Hechter, *Containing Nationalism*, Oxford and New York: Oxford University Press, 2000.

68. Hans J. Morgenthau, *Politics Among Nations*, 7th edn., rev. Kenneth W. Thompson and W. David Clinton, New York: McGraw-Hill, 2006, 118.

69. For an overview see Eric J. Hobsbawm, *Nations and Nationalism Since 1780: Programme, Myth, Reality*, 2nd edn., Cambridge: Cambridge University Press, 1992; Ernest Gellner, *Nations and Nationalism*, Ithaca: Cornell University Press, 1983; Paul Gilbert, *The Philosophy of Nationalism*, Boulder, CO: Westview Press, 1998. For summaries of major works on the subject see the *Nationalism Project*, at http://www.nationalismproject.org/books.htm (accessed 5 January 2008).

70. Quoted in Praful Bidwai, 'Indian Left Embraces Nuclear Nationalism', https://www.tni.org/es/node/13138.

71. Pervez Hoodbhoy, 'The Nuclear Noose around Pakistan's Neck', *Washington Post*, 1 February 2004.

72. See Zia Mian, 'Nuclear Nationalism', Nuclear Age Peace Foundation, 5 May 1999, https://www.wagingpeace.org/nuclear-nationalism/; David Ignatius, 'The New Nationalism', *Washington Post*, 20 April 2005; Hugh Purcell, 'Alone against India's Nuclear Nationalism', BBC, 12 August 2003, http://news.bbc.co.uk/2/hi/south_asia/3142039.stm; Haider K. Nizamani, 'Whose Bomb is it Anyway? Public Opinion and Perceptions about Nuclear Weapons and Policy in the Post-Explosions Phase in Pakistan', Social Science Research Council, http://programs.ssrc.org/gsc/gsc_activities/nizamani/ (accessed 6 December 2007).

73. Douglas Frantz, 'From Patriot to Proliferator', *Los Angeles Times*, 23 September 2005.

74. Jacques E. C. Hymans, *The Psychology of Nuclear Proliferation: Identity, Emotions and Foreign Policy*, Cambridge: Cambridge University Press, 2006.

75. Ibid., 2.

76. 'A. Q. Khan, Godfather of the Islamic Bomb: Hero or Proliferator?' AFP, 30 January 2004, available at http://www.spacewar.com/2004/040130110728.yxbeuoad.html.

77. Bruno Tertrais, 'Pakistan's Nuclear Exports: Was there a State Strategy?' in Henry D. Sokolski (ed.), *Pakistan's Nuclear Future: Worries beyond War*, Washington, DC and Carlisle Barracks, PA: Strategic Studies Institute Publications Office/ United States Army War College, 2008).

78. The books are Zahid Malik, *Mohsin-e-Pakistan ki de-briefing* [The debriefing of Pakistan's benefactor], published by Hurmat Press in October 2004; Imran Hussain Chaudhry, *Dr. Abdul Qadeer Khan: Islami bomb ke khaliq aur ghori mezail ke mojid ki walwala khez daastan-e-hayat* [Dr Abdul Qadeer Khan: fascinating life story of the creator of the Islamic bomb and the inventor of the Ghori missile], published by Ilm-o-Irfan press in 2003; Shahid Nazir Chaudhry, *Dr. Abdul Qadeer Khan aur atomi Pakistan* [Dr Abdul Qadeer Khan and atomic Pakistan], published by Fatima publications in 2001; Mobeen Ghaznavi, *Islami bomb ka khaliq kon* [Who Created the Islamic bomb?], Lahore: Ilm-o-Irfan, 2011.

79. Zahid Malik, *Dr A. Q. Khan and the Islamic Bomb*, Islamabad: Hurmat, 1992.

80. See Shaun Gregory, 'The Terrorist Threat to Pakistan's Nuclear Weapons', *CTC Sentinel*, 15 July 2009.

81. Quoted in Hassan Abbas, 'Pakistan 2020: A Vision for Building a Better Future', *Asia Society Pakistan 2020 Study Group Report*, May 2011. For the complete report see https://asiasociety.org/files/pdf/as_pakistan%202020_study_group_rpt.pdf

2. BACKGROUND: PAKISTAN–INDIA RIVALRY AND THE MAKING OF A NATIONAL SECURITY STATE (1947–1972)

1. This chapter borrows some ideas and language from this author's earlier work, *Pakistan's Drift into Extremism: Allah, the Army and America's War on Terror*, New York: M. E. Sharpe, 2004.

2. Nayef al-Rodhan, 'Strategic Culture and Pragmatic National Interest', Geneva Centre for Security Policy, July 2015, http://www.gcsp.ch/News-Knowledge/Publications/Strategic-Culture-and-Pragmatic-National-Interest.

3. Jack Snyder, *The Soviet Strategic Culture: Implications for Nuclear Options*, R-2154-AF, Santa Monica: RAND Corporation, 1977, 8.

4. See Stephen M. Walt, *The Origins of Alliances*, Ithaca: Cornell University Press, 1990; Stephen M. Walt, 'Alliance Formation and the Balance of Power', *International Security* 9, 4 (Spring 1985): 3–43.

5. Lavoy, 'Pakistan's Strategic Culture'.

6. Stanley Wolpert, *Jinnah of Pakistan*, New York: Oxford University Press, 1984, 1.

7. See Ayesha Jalal, *The Sole Spokesman: Jinnah, the Muslim League and the Demand for Pakistan*, Cambridge: Cambridge University Press, 1994; Abbas, *Pakistan's Drift into Extremism*, 3–15.

8. For details see Chaudhry Muhammad Ali, *Emergence of Pakistan*, New York: Columbia University Press, 1967, chaps. 1–3.

9. See Jalal, *The Sole Spokesman*.

10. Ali, *Emergence of Pakistan*, 372.

11. See Sudeepta Adhikari, 'Some Aspects of Indian Federalism: A Study in Political Geography', *Singapore Journal of Tropical Geography* 7, 1 (1986): 1–11.

12. Sugata Bose and Ayesha Jalal, *Modern South Asia: History, Culture, Political Economy*, London and New York: Routledge, 1998, 190.

13. Quoted in H. M. Seervai, *Partition of India: Legend and Reality*, Bombay: Emmenem Publications, 1990, 131. Original source: Viceroy's Personal Report No. 11, 4 July 1947, in Nicholas Mansergh et al. (eds.), *Constitutional Relations between Britain and India: Transfer of Power 1942–47*, vol. XI, London: Her Majesty's Stationery Office, 1982, 899–900.

14. Seervai, *Partition of India*, 131–2.

15. For a first-hand account see Ali, *Emergence of Pakistan*.

16. For details see Husain Haqqani, *Pakistan: Between Mosque and Military*, Washington, DC: Carnegie Endowment for International Peace, 2005, 1–51.

17. Liaquat Ali Khan (the first prime minister), leading financiers of the freedom movement Mohammad Amir Ahmed Khan (Raja Sahib of Mahmudabad) and M. A. Ispahani, and Khawaja Nazimuddin (the second prime minister) were all from the Shiite community. See Vali Nasr, *The Shia Revival: How Conflicts within Islam Will Shape the Future*, New York: W. W. Norton, 2006, 87–8.

18. For a complete transcript of the speech see www.pakistani.org/pakistan/legislation/constituent_address_11aug1947.html (accessed November 2007).

19. Pakistan in 1947 comprised six major ethnic groups: Bengali, Punjabi, Pashtun, Sindhi, Baloch, and Mohajir (Muslim migrants from India).

20. For details see Hassan Abbas, *Poleaxe or Politics of the Eighth Amendment 1985–97*, Lahore: Watandost Press, 1997.

21. 'A Report to the National Security Council by the Executive Secretary on the Position of the United States with Respect to South Asia (declassified)', 5 January 1951, NSC 93.

22. For a detailed analysis see Seyyed Vali Reza Nasr, *Mawdudi and the Making of Islamic Revivalism*, New York: Oxford University Press, 1995.

23. Ibid.

24. For details about JI see Vali Nasr, *The Vanguard of the Islamic Revolution: The Jama'at-i Islami of Pakistan*, Berkeley: University of California Press, 1994.

25. Haqqani, *Pakistan: Between Mosque and Military*, 15.

26. Samuel M. Burke, *Mainsprings of Indian and Pakistani Foreign Policies*, Minneapolis: University of Minnesota Press, 1974, 16.

27. Alastair Lamb, *Kashmir: A Disputed Legacy 1846–1990*, Hertingfordbury and Karachi: Roxford Books and Oxford University Press, 1991, 9–10.

28. For further details and analysis of the award see Victoria Schofield, *Kashmir in the Crossfire*, London: I. B. Tauris, 1996, 125–31.

29. For more details on the accession controversy see Alexander Rose, 'Paradise Lost', *The National Interest* (Winter 1999).

30. Lamb, *Kashmir*, 123. Pakistan also believed that people of Poonch were in fact celebrating the independence of Pakistan on 14 August 1947 when the maharaja ordered the clampdown.

31. Ibid.

32. Prem Shankar Jha, *Kashmir 1947: Rival Versions of History*, Dehli: Oxford University Press, 1996, 12.

33. Victoria Schofield, *Kashmir in Conflict*, London: I. B. Tauris, 2000, 153.

34. Mustaqur Rahman, *Divided Kashmir: Old Problems, New Opportunities for India, Pakistan and the Kashmiri People*, London: Lynne Rienner Publishers, 1996, 87.

35. UN SC Resolution 38 (1948).

36. UN SC Resolution 47 (1948).

37. Quoted in Rahman, *Divided Kashmir*, 89.

38. UN SC Resolution 9 (1951).

39. Schofield, *Kashmir in Conflict*, 171.

40. UN SC Resolution 122 (1957).

41. For a summary of the crucial conflict-resolution attempts see Robert G. Wirsing, *India, Pakistan and the Kashmir Dispute*, New York: St Martin's Press, 1994, Annexure 1.

42. The statement appeared in *The Times of India* (New Delhi), 20 July 1961.

43. For detailed analysis of this aspect see Surendra Chopra, *UN Mediation in Kashmir: A Study in Power Politics*, Kurukshetra: Vishal Publications, 1971, 133–57.

44. Owen Bennett Jones, *Pakistan: Eye of the Storm*, New Haven: Yale University Press, 2002, 80–1.

45. Husain Haqqani, 'The Role of Islam in Pakistan's Future', *Washington Quarterly* 28, 1 (Winter 2004–5), 87.

46. Ayesha Siddiqa, *Military Inc.: Inside Pakistan's Military Economy*, London: Pluto Press, 2007, 62.

47. See Jack Nelson-Pallmeyer, *Brave New World Order: Must we Pledge Allegiance*, Maryknoll, NY: Orbis Books, 1992.

48. Stephen P. Cohen, *The Pakistan Army: 1998 Edition with a new Foreword and Epilogue*, Karachi: Oxford University Press, 1998, 7.

49. For further details see Abbas, *Pakistan's Drift into Extremism*, 32–54.

50. Hasan Askari Rizvi, *Military, State and Society in Pakistan*, London: Macmillan, 2000, 55.

51. Stephen P. Cohen, *The Idea of Pakistan*, Washington, DC: Brookings Institution, 2004, 105.

52. Siddiqa, *Military Inc.*, 63.

53. Dennis Kux, *The United States and Pakistan, 1947–2000: Disenchanted Allies*, Washington, DC: Woodrow Wilson Centre Press, 2001, 57.

54. Mushahid Hussain and Akmal Hussain, *Pakistan: Problems of Governance*, Lahore: Vanguard Books, 1986, 30.

55. Sir Morrice James, *Pakistan Chronicle*, New York: St Martin's Press, 1993, 129–30.

56. Ibid., 128.

57. On Ayub Khan see Altaf Gauhar, *Ayub Khan: Pakistan's First Military Ruler*, New York: Oxford University Press, 1996; Mohammad Ayub Khan, *Friends Not Master: A Political Autobiography*, Oxford: Oxford University Press, 1967.

58. Omar Noman, *Pakistan: Economic and Political History Since 1947*, 2nd edn, London: Kegan Paul International, 1990, 32.

59. For details see Mehrunnisa Ali, *Politics of Federalism in Pakistan*, Karachi: Royal Book Company, 1996, 68–9.

60. G. W. Choudhary, *The Last Days of United Pakistan*, Karachi: Oxford University Press, 1993, 143.

61. For details see Richard Sisson and Leo E. Rose, *War and Succession: Pakistan, India and the Creation of Bangladesh*, Berkeley: University of California Press, 1990.

62. For instance, textbooks of grades 9 and 10 published by Punjab Text Book Board, provide this perspective.

63. Ayesha Siddiqa, 'Pakistan's Security: Problems of Linearity', *South Asian Journal* 3 (January–March 2004).

64. For an interesting brief discussion on the topic see Shivam Vij, 'Congratulations Pakistan', *Express Tribune*, 24 May 2014.

65. Feroz Khan, 'Comparative Strategic Culture: The Case of Pakistan', *Strategic Insights* 4, 10 (October 2005).

66. Ibid.

3. THE DEVELOPMENT OF PAKISTAN'S NUCLEAR WEAPONS PROGRAMME

1. Praful Bidwai and Achin Vanaik, *South Asia on a Short Fuse: Nuclear Politics and the Future of Global Disarmament*, New Delhi: Oxford University Press, 1999, 1–2.

2. Pervez Hoodbhoy, 'The Flight to Nowhere: Pakistan's Nuclear Trajectory', Heinrich-Böll-Stiftung, November 2009, 7, http://in.boell.org/sites/defualt/files/downloads/The_Flight_To_Nowhere_by_Pervez_Hoodbhoy_GE.pdf

3. Ibid.

4. Nawaz Sharif quoted in 'Defiant Sharif Prepares for Fallout', UPI, 28 May 1998.

5. Quoted in 'Pakistan may be Preparing for New Nuclear Test', CNN.com, 28 May 1998.

6. 'Going Nuclear', The Newshour with Jim Lehrer, transcript, 28 May 1998,

http://www.pbs.org/newshour/bb/asia/jan-june98/nuclear_5–28.html (accessed 18 November 2008).

7. John F. Burns, 'Nuclear Anxiety: The Overview; Pakistan Answering India, Carries out Nuclear Tests; Clinton's Appeal Rejected', *New York Times*, 29 May 1998.

8. For an overview of international reactions to the Indian and Pakistani nuclear tests, see 'India and Pakistan Nuclear Tests', *Disarmament Diplomacy* 26 (May 1998): 2–21.

9. See George Perkovich, *India's Nuclear Bomb*, Berkeley: University of California Press, 2001; Sumit Ganguly, 'India's Pathway to Pokhran II: The Prospects and Sources of New Delhi's Nuclear Weapons Program', *International Security* 23, 4 (Spring 1999): 148–77; Jasjit Singh, ed., *Nuclear India*, Delhi: IDSA, 1998; K. Subrahmanyam, 'India and the International Nuclear Order', in D. R. SarDesai and Raju Thomas (eds.), *Nuclear India in the Twenty-First Century*, New York: Palgrave, 2002, 63–84; Jaswant Singh, 'Against Nuclear Apartheid', *Foreign Affairs*, (September–October 1998); Stephen Cohen, 'Nuclear Weapons and Conflict in South Asia, http://www.brookings.edu/views/articles/cohens/1998TSP.htm (accessed 5 November 2007); Raj Chengappa, *Weapons of Peace*, Delhi: HarperCollins, 2000; Scott Sagan, 'Why Do States Build Nuclear Weapons? Three Models in Search of the Bomb', *International Security* 21, 3 (Winter 1996–7): 54–86.

10. Samina Ahmed, 'Pakistan's Nuclear Weapons Program: Turning Points and Nuclear Choices', *International Security* 23, 4 (Spring 1999): 178–204; Samina Ahmed and David Cortright, eds., *Pakistan and the Bomb: Public Opinion and Nuclear Options*, South Bend, IN: University of Notre Dame Press, 1998; Zia Mian, *Pakistan's Atomic Bomb and the Search for Security*, Lahore: Gautam Publishers, 1995; Lowell Ditmer, 'South Asia's Security Dilemma', *Asian Survey* 41, 6 (November–December 2001): 897–906.

11. This section greatly benefits from Bhumitra Chakma, 'Road to Chagai: Pakistan's Nuclear Programme, its Sources and Motivations', *Modern Asian Studies* 36, 4 (2002): 871–912. Also benefited from, Rabia Akhtar, "Bhutto and US Nuclear Politics," *Dawn*, June 20, 2016).

12. For a general discussion on the causes of nuclear weapons proliferation see William Epstein, 'Why States Go—and Don't Go—Nuclear', *Annals of the American Academy of Political and Social Science* 430 (March 1977): 16–28; Lewis A. Dunn, *Controlling the Bomb*, New Haven: Yale University Press, 1982; Scott D. Sagan, 'The Causes of Nuclear Proliferation', *Current History* 96, 609 (April 1997): 151–6.

13. See Matthew Fuhrman, *Atomic Assistance: The Causes and Consequences of Peaceful Nuclear Cooperation*, New York: Cornell University Press, 2012.

14. Quoted from description of his book page at Cornell University Press: http://www.cornellpress.cornell.edu/book/?GCOI=80140100285320

15. Ditmer, 'South Asia's Security Dilemma', 900.

16. Ganguly and Hagerty, *Fearful Symmetry*, 123.

17. Samina Ahmed, 'Pakistan's Nuclear Weapons Program: Moving Forward or Tactical Retreat', Kroc Institute Occasional Paper no. 18:OP:2, Notre Dame, IN: Kroc Institute, February 2000.

18. Shamshad Ahmad, 'The Nuclear Subcontinent: Bringing Stability Back to South Asia', *Foreign Affairs* 78, 4 (July/August 1999): 123–5.

19. Hasan Askari Rizvi, 'Pakistan's Nuclear Testing', *Asian Survey* 41, 6 (November/December 2001): 943–55.

20. Stephen P. Cohen, *India: Emerging Power*, Washington, DC: Brookings Institution Press, 2001, 204.

21. See Pervez Hoodbhoy, 'Pakistan's Nuclear Future', in Samina Ahmed and David Cortright (eds.), *Pakistan and the Bomb: Public Opinion and Nuclear Options*, South Bend, IN: University of Notre Dame Press, 1998, 70–4.

22. Ibid., 73.

23. Ibid.

24. Rasul B. Rais, 'Pakistan's Nuclear Program: Prospects for Proliferation', *Asian Survey* 25, 4 (April 1985): 458–72.

25. Khan, 'Comparative Strategic Culture'. He expanded his arguments in his book *Eating Grass: The Making of the Pakistani Bomb*, Stanford: Stanford University Press, 2012.

26. Khan, 'Comparative Strategic Culture'.

27. A informative and well-referenced chronology of the early years of Pakistan's nuclear programme is available at the Nuclear Threat Initiative (NTI) website, http://www.nti.org/e_research/profiles/pakistan/nuclear/5593.html (accessed 10 July 2008).

28. 'Nucleus of a Nuclear Power', *Daily Times* (Lahore), 12 January 2004.

29. His students included Munir Ahmed Khan, Ishfaq Ahmad, Javed Arshad Mirza, G. D. Alam, Tahir Hussain, Pervez Butt, and Samar Mubarakmand.

30. See Dr Samar Mubarakmand, 'A Science Odyssey: Pakistan's Nuclear Emergence', text of speech delivered at the Punjab University, Lahore, 30 November 1998; full text available at http://pakdef.org/a-science-odyssey-pakistans-nuclear-emergence/

31. An American Atoms for Peace team visited Pakistan in 1954, highlighting the benefits of nuclear technology in the fields of energy, agriculture, and medicine. For Eisenhower's speech, see US Department of State, *Documents on Disarmament, 1945–1959*, Washington, DC: Department of State Publication, 1960, 393–400.

32. Salimuzzaman Siddiqui, 'The Pakistan Council of Scientific and Industrial Research: A Review of its Activities', *Pakistan Quarterly* 7, 4 (Winter 1957): 42–5. See the history section of the PAEC website, http://www.paec.gov.pk/

33. Zia Mian, *Nuclear Passions and Interests: The Founding of Atomic Pakistan*, Washington, DC and Amsterdam: Social Science Research Council and

International Institute of Social History, 2005, 16–17. Also see 'Atoms for Peace Exhibit Popular at Bahawalpur', *Dawn*, 1 February 1955.

34. For more details see Zia Mian, 'Fevered with Dreams of the Future: The Coming of the Atomic Age to Pakistan', https://www.princeton.edu/sgs/faculty-staff/zia-mian/Fevered-with-Dreams-of.pdf

35. Nazeer Ahmed, 'The Atomic Energy Commission', *Pakistan Quarterly* 7, 3 (Autumn 1957), 14.

36. Ashok Kapur, *Pakistan's Nuclear Development*, New York: Croom Helm, 1987, 34.

37. See Major-General M. A. Latif Khan, 'The Staff College as I Saw it', in *Command and Staff College Quetta 1905–1980*, ed. and comp. Command and Staff College, Quetta, Quetta: Command and Staff College, 1982, 139–40.

38. Shahid-ur-Rehman, *Long Road to Chagai*, Islamabad: Print Wise Publications, 1999, 23.

39. Kapur, *Pakistan's Nuclear Development*, 42.

40. *Asian Recorder* (New Delhi) 4, 24 (7–13 June 1958), 2095.

41. See Zulfikar Ali Bhutto, *If I am Assassinated*, New Delhi: Vikas, 1979, 137.

42. 'Nuclear Black Markets: Pakistan, A. Q. Khan and the Rise of Proliferation Networks—A Net Assessment', *IISS*, 2 May 2007.

43. Zainab Mahmood, 'Dr. Salam—The Mystic Scientist', *Chowk*, 26 November 2004.

44. For background on Usmani see Suhail Yusuf, 'Dr I. H. Usmani', *Dawn*, 16 June 2011.

45. Kapur, *Pakistan's Nuclear Development*, 53, 70–1.

46. M. A. Chaudhri, 'Pakistan's Nuclear History: Separating Myth from Reality', *Defence Journal* (Karachi) 9, 10 (May 2006).

47. Ibid.

48. Mian, *Nuclear Passions and Interests*, 71.

49. Khan, *Eating Grass*, 53.

50. Mark Fitzpatrick, *Nuclear Black Markets: Pakistan, A. Q. Khan and the Rise of Proliferation Networks—A Net Assessment*, IISS Strategic Dossier, 2 May 2007, 15.

51. Ibid. For background see Lorne J. Kavic, *India's Quest for Security: Defence Policies, 1947–1965*, Berkeley: University of California Press, 1967.

52. See Peter R. Lavoy and Robin Walker, 'Conference Report: Nuclear Weapons Proliferation: 2016', Center on Contemporary Conflict, Naval Postgraduate School, Monterey, California, 28–29 July 2006, http://calhoun.nps.edu/bitstream/handle/10945/30509/2006–07_Nuclear_Weapons_Proliferation_2016.pdf?sequence=1.

53. Rehman, *Long Road to Chagai*, 24.

54. Ibid., 25.

55. Interview with a senior member of Pakistan's Foreign Office, August 2007.

56. Lavoy, 'Nuclear Proliferation over the Next Decade', 441.

57. Perkovich, *India's Nuclear Bomb*, 68.

58. Ibid.

59. George Perkovich, 'Could Anything be Done to Stop them? Lessons from Pakistan's Proliferating Past', in Henry D. Sokolski (ed.), *Pakistan Nuclear Future: Worries Beyond War*, Carlisle and Washington, DC: Strategic Studies Institute, 2008, 61.

60. Ibid.

61. Perkovich, *India's Nuclear Bomb*, 108.

62. Fitzpatrick, *Nuclear Black Markets*, 15.

63. Rehman, *Long Road to Chagai*, 24.

64. V. V. R. Sharma, 'India's Capability to Produce Nuclear Weapons Haunts Pakistan', *The Times of India* (New Delhi), 9 November 1964.

65. Munir Ahmed Khan, '1993—Crucial for Nuclear Proliferation in South Asia', *The Muslim*, 10 January 1993.

66. Perkovich, 'Could Anything be Done to Stop them?' 62.

67. Ziba Moshaver, *Nuclear Weapons Proliferation in the Indian Subcontinent*, London: Macmillan, 1991, 31. For Muhammad Shoaib's anti-nuclear-weapons-programme views see Farhatullah Babar, 'Bhutto's Footprints on Nuclear Pakistan', *The News*, 4 April 2006.

68. CIA, 'The President's Daily Brief 10 December 1965', http://www.foia.cia.gov/sites/default/files/document_conversions/1827265/DOC_0005968042.pdf

69. See Mansoor Ahmed, 'Pakistan's Nuclear Programme: Security, Politics and Technology', Ph.D. thesis, Quaid-i-Azam University, Islamabad, 2012, citing 'When Munir Ahmad Khan Presented his Nuclear Plans', *Pak Atom* (May 1974).

70. 'Statement of the Prime Minister of Pakistan Regarding the Indian Nuclear Explosion', *Pakistan Horizon* 27, 2, 19 May 1974, 133, quoted in Chakma, 'Road to Chagai', 879.

71. Haris N. Khan, 'Pakistan's Nuclear Programme: Setting the Record Straight', *Defence Journal* (Karachi) 14, 1 (August 2010.)

72. Text of Munir Khan speech at the Chagai Medal Award Ceremony, Pakistan Nuclear Society, PINSTECH Auditorium, Islamabad, March 20, 1999, http://www.nuclearfiles.org/menu/key-issues/nuclear-weapons/issues/policy/pakistani-nuclear-policy/munir%20ahmad%20khan%27s%20speech.html

73. Ibid.

74. Ibid.

75. Quoted in Babar, 'Bhutto's Footprints on Nuclear Pakistan'.

76. Ibid.

77. Khan, *Eating Grass*, 80.

78. Rehman, *Long Road to Chagai*, 35–36. The five scientists who recommended this option were Dr S. M. Bhutta, M. T. Ahmad, Abdul Majid, Dr Mohammad Afzal, and Dr Ehsan Mubarak.

79. Moshaver, *Nuclear Weapons Proliferation in the Indian Subcontinent*, 100.

80. Chakma, 'Road to Chagai', 877.

81. Ibid.

82. Zulfikar Ali Bhutto, *The Myth of Independence*, Karachi: Oxford University Press, 1969, 117–18.

83. 'Statement of the Prime Minister of Pakistan Regarding the Indian Nuclear Explosion', 133.

84. Arthur J. Pais, 'Bangladesh War: "Nixon, Kissinger Let Personal Judgements Cloud their Thinking"', *Rediff News*, 13 December 2013.

85. For details see Zulfikar Ali Bhutto, *Awakening the People: Speeches of Zulfikar Ali Bhutto, 1966–1969*, comp. Hamid Jalal and Khalid Hasan, Rawalpindi: Pakistan Publications, 1970, 21.

86. Chakma, 'Road to Chagai', 886.

87. Steve Weissman and Herbert Krosney, *The Islamic Bomb: The Nuclear Threat to Israel and the Middle East*, New York: Times Books, 1981, 45. See also Khan, *Eating Grass*, 86–7. Another relevant reference is Munir Ahmed Khan, 'Nuclearisation of South Asia and its Regional and Global Implications', *Focus on Regional Issues*, Islamabad: Institute of Regional Studies, 1998, 11. The conference was held at the residence of the Punjab chief minister, Nawab Sadiq Qureshi, in Multan. Key invitees included scientists from PINSTECH, the PAEC, Quaid-i-Azam University in Islamabad, Government College in Lahore, and the Defence Science and Technology Organization (DESTO).

88. Quoted in Pervez Hoodbhoy, 'The Man Who Designed Pakistan's Bomb', *Newsweek*, Pakistan, 30 November 2013, http://newsweekpakistan.com/the-man-who-designed-pakistans-bomb/

89. Ibid.

90. Weissman and Krosney, *The Islamic Bomb*, 46.

91. Ibid.

92. Khan, *Eating Grass*, 89–90.

93. Yusuf, 'I. H. Usmani'.

94. 'Reactor Khan' is mentioned in Mansoor Ahmed, 'Pakistan's Nuclear Odyssey: An Organizational and Bureaucratic-Politics Perspective', in Karthika Sasikumar (ed.), *Organizational Cultures and the Management of Nuclear Technology: Political and Military Sociology—An Annual Review*, vol. 39, New Brunswick, NJ: Transaction Publishers, 2012, 65.

95. At the IAEA, Munir Khan's responsibilities included developing major international programmes relating to thermal and fast-breeder reactors, and heavy-water and gas-cooled reactors. He also studied research reactor utilization in developing countries, review of design, construction, and operation of dem

onstration power reactors in North America. He was also responsible for coordinating programmes for research contracts for theoretical estimation of uranium depletion and plutonium build-up in nuclear power reactors in developed states. Conducting market surveys for nuclear power plants were also part of his overall responsibilities. For further details see Mansoor, 'Pakistan's Nuclear Programme'.

96. Text of Munir Khan's speech at the Chagai Medal Award Ceremony, Pakistan Nuclear Society, PINSTECH Auditorium, Islamabad, 20 March 1999. See also Munir Ahmed Khan, 'Significance of Chashma Plant', *Dawn*, 8 August 1993.

97. Munir Khan, speech at the Chagai Medal Award Ceremony.

98. Ibid.

99. See 'Pakistan Nuclear Chronology' on the Nuclear Threat Initiative website, http://www.nti.org/media/pdfs/pakistan_nuclear.pdf?_=1316466791

100. George Perkovich, 'Could Anything be Done to Stop them? Lessons from Pakistan', Nonproliferation Policy Education Center, 26 July 2006, www.npec-web.org/Essays/20060726-Perkovich CouldAnythingBeDone.pdf

101. See Hoodbhoy, 'The Man Who Designed Pakistan's Bomb'.

102. Ibid.

103. Ibid.

104. Rehman, *Long Road to Chagai*, 40.

105. See full text at 'Documents: Government of Pakistan Statements and Interviews', *Pakistan Horizon* 27, 2 (1974): 115–64.

106. Rehman, *Long Road to Chagai*, 43.

107. Feroz Hassan Khan, 'Nuclear Proliferation Motivations: Lessons from Pakistan', *Nonproliferation Review* 13, 3 (November 2006), 503.

108. Reported on the front page of *The Pakistan Times*, 27 December 1974.

109. *Morning News*, Karachi, 22 October 1975, quoted in Samina Ahmed, 'Franco-Pakistan Relations-II: The Issue of the Nuclear Reprocessing Plant', *Pakistan Horizon* 31, 1 (First Quarter, 1978), 36.

110. Quoted in Khan, *Eating Grass*, 128.

111. For details see Michael Laufer, 'A. Q. Khan Nuclear Chronology', Carnegie Endowment for International Peace, 7 September 2005, http://carnegieendowment.org/2005/09/07/a.-q.-khan-nuclear-chronology

112. Khan, *Eating Grass*, 141.

113. Rehman, *Long Road to Chagai*, 50.

114. Khan, *Eating Grass*, 111, 172.

115. Fitzpatrick, *Nuclear Black Markets*, 17.

116. For details see Gordon Corera, *Shopping for Bombs: Nuclear Proliferation, Global Insecurity and the Rise and Fall of the A. Q. Khan Network*, Oxford: Oxford University Press, 2006, 14–16.

117. Ibid., 15.

118. Fitzpatrick, *Nuclear Black Markets*, 46.
119. Khan, *Eating Grass*, 143.
120. Rehman, *Long Road to Chagai*, 50.
121. Ibid., 51.
122. See A. Q. Khan, 'Unsung Heroes', *The News*, 12 January 2015, https://www.thenews.com.pk/print/17884-unsung-heroes
123. Adrian Levy and Catherine Scott-Clark, *Deception: Pakistan, the United States, and the Secret Trade in Nuclear Weapons*, New York: Walker & Co., 2007, 14.
124. Ibid., 14.
125. Bhutto, *If I am Assassinated*, 118.
126. Interview with a former colleague of A. Q. Khan, 23 November 2007.
127. Fitzpatrick, *Nuclear Black Markets*, 20.
128. Khan, 'Pakistan's Nuclear Program'.
129. Clary, 'The A. Q. Khan Network', 35.
130. Central Intelligence Agency, '"Significant" Chinese Aid on Nuclear Design', 4 June 1982, https://www.documentcloud.org/documents/347024-doc-11-6-4-82.html
131. Kux, *The United States and Pakistan 1947–2000*, 239.
132. Ibid., 257–8.
133. David K. Wills, 'Pakistan: Crash Program, Secret Bids for Nuclear Technology', *Christian Science Monitor*, 30 November 1981.
134. 'New Documents Spotlight Reagan-era Tensions over Pakistani Nuclear Program', National Security Archive, George Washington University, 27 April 2012, http://nsarchive.gwu.edu/nukevault/ebb377/
135. Ibid.
136. Anwar Shamim, *Cutting Edge PAF: A Former Air Chief's Reminiscences of a Developing Air Force*, Islamabad: Vanguard Books, 2010, 320–51.
137. Ibid.
138. See Munir Ahmed, *How We Got It! A True Story of Pakistan's Nuclear Programme*, Lahore: Shaam-Kay Baad, 1998; Chaudhri, 'Pakistan's Nuclear History'; Rehman, *Long Road to Chagai*.
139. Michael Krepon, 'A.Q. Khan and Samar Mubarakmand', Arms Control Wonk, 2 July 2009, http://www.armscontrolwonk.com/archive/402371/aq-khan-and-samar-mubarakmand/
140. Mansoor Ahmed's interview with Samar Mubarakmand, quoted in Ahmed, 'Pakistan's Nuclear Programme', 301.
141. Ibid., 301–3.
142. Rehman, *Long Road to Chagai*, 104.
143. Levy and Scott-Clark, *Deception*, 112.
144. Ibid.
145. Rehman, *Long Road to Chagai*, 6.
146. Fitzpatrick, *Nuclear Black Markets*, 22.

147. Quoted in Hoodbhoy, 'The Man Who Designed Pakistan's Bomb'.

148. Interview conducted in October 2007.

149. The list is drawn from information gleaned from Fitzpatrick, *Nuclear Black Markets*; Douglas Frantz and Catherine Collins, *The Nuclear Jihadist: The True Story of the Man who Sold the World's Most Dangerous Secrets—And How we Could Have Stopped him*, New York: Twelve, 2007; Corera, *Shopping for Bombs*; Levy and Scott-Clark, *Deception*.

150. Interview with a senior Pakistani military officer, September 2006.

151. Interview with S. H., a senior official at the PAEC, July 2008, Islamabad.

152. Quoted in Muhammad Aslam, *Dr. A. Q. Khan and Pakistan's Nuclear Programme*, Rawalpindi: Diplomat Publications, 1989, 33, 57–8.

153. Zafar Iqbal Cheema, *The Domestic Governance of Nuclear Weapons: The Case of Pakistan*, Case Report, Geneva: Geneva Centre for the Democratic Control of Armed Forces (DCAF), February 2008.

154. Khan, *Eating Grass*, 164, citing translated excerpts from *Islamabad Tonight*, a talk show hosted by Nadeem Malik, Aaj News Network, 31 August 2009.

155. Central Intelligence Agency, 'Pakistan's Nuclear Weapons Program: Personnel and Organizations', Research Paper, Directorate of Intelligence, November 1985, http://nsarchive.gwu.edu/nukevault/ebb423/docs/8.%20pakistan%201985.pdf

156. Lavoy, 'Pakistan's Strategic Culture'.

157. For developments that convinced Pakistan about Western obstructionism see 'Non-Paper and Demarches: US and British Combined to Delay Pakistani Nuclear Weapons Program in 1978–1981, Declassified Documents Show', National Security Archive Electronic Briefing Book No. 352, posted on 27 July 2011, http://nsarchive.gwu.edu/nukevault/ebb352/index.htm

4. PAKISTAN'S NUCLEAR PROLIFERATION LINKS WITH IRAN

1. Ivanka Barzashka and Ivan Oelrich, 'Figuring out Fordow', *Nuclear Engineering International*, 20 May 2010, http://www.neimagazine.com/story.asp?sc=2056428

2. Conversations with a former deputy foreign minister of Iran, Boston, September 2006.

3. Kenneth Waltz, *The Spread of Nuclear Weapons: More May be Better*, Adelphi Papers 171, London: International Institute for Strategic Studies, 1981, available at https://www.mtholyoke.edu/acad/intrel/waltz1.htm

4. John Wilson Lewis and Xue Litai, *China Builds the Bomb*, Stanford: Stanford University Press, 1988, 60–72.

5. Muzaffar Alam, Françoise Nalini Delvoye, and Marc Gaborieau (eds.), *The Making of Indo-Persian Culture*, New Delhi: Manohar, 2000.

6. Ibid.

7. Suroosh Irfani, 'Pakistan's Sectarian Violence: Between the "Arabist Shift" and

the Indo-Persian Culture', in Satu P. Limaye, Mohan Malik, and Robert Wirsing (eds.), *Religious Radicalism and Security in South Asia*, Honolulu: Asia-Pacific Center for Security Studies, 2004, 147–71.

8. Ibid., 151.

9. Joan Weeks, 'Aspects of Persian Culture: Professor Discusses 8,000-Year Legacy', *Library of Congress Information Bulletin* 54, 16 (4 September 1995).

10. Kaveh Afrasiabi, 'The Iran–Pakistan Nexus', *Asia Times*, 13 January 2006.

11. Shah Alam, 'Iran–Pakistan Relations: Political and Strategic Dimensions', *Strategic Analysis* 28, 4 (October–December 2004).

12. Abdul Sattar, *Pakistan's Foreign Policy: 1947–2005*, Karachi: Oxford University Press, 2007, 18.

13. Ibid.

14. Shirin Tahir-Kheli, 'Iran and Pakistan: Cooperation in an Area of Conflict', *Asian Survey* 17, 5 (May 1977), 474.

15. Barry Buzan, *People, States, and Fear: The National Security Problem in International Relations*, 2nd edn., Boulder: Lynne Rienner, 1991, 193–200.

16. For instance, see 'A Report to the National Security Council by the Executive Secretary on the Position of the United States with respect to South Asia (declassified)', 5 January 1951, NSC 93, NND867400, available at Digital National Security Archive.

17. Tahir-Kheli, 'Iran and Pakistan', 475.

18. For details see Stephen Kinzer, *All the Shah's Men: An American Coup and the Roots of Middle East Terror*, New York: John Wiley & Sons, 2003.

19. Wolpert, *Jinnah of Pakistan*, 4.

20. This was his second marriage. See Ian Talbot, *Pakistan: A Modern History*, New York: St Martin's Press, 1998, 146.

21. Sushil K. Pillai, 'Border Conflicts and Regional Disputes', in Monique Mekenkamp, Paul van Tongeren, and Hans van de Veen (eds.), *Searching for Peace in Central and South Asia: An Overview of Conflict Prevention and Peace Building Activities*, Boulder: Lynne Rienner Publishers, 2002.

22. Tahir-Kheli, 'Iran and Pakistan', 475.

23. *Sadai Mardun*, Iran, 6 March 1955.

24. For details see Nurul Islam, 'Regional Co-operation for Development: Pakistan, Iran and Turkey', *Journal of Common Market Studies* 5, 3 (March 1967).

25. Safdar Mahmood, *A Political Study of Pakistan*, Lahore: Mohammed Ashraf Publishers, 1972, 272.

26. For details about the indirect sale see 'Pakistan Air Force: The Canadair Sabre Goes to War', http://www.pakdef.info/pakmilitary/airforce/ac/sabre.html

27. Marvin Weinbaum and Gautam Sen, 'Pakistan Enters the Middle East', *Orbis* 22, 3 (Fall 1978): 595–612.

28. The idea of a separate Pashtun land comprising Pashtuns of the North West Frontier Province and Baluchistan had been widely promoted by some Pashtun

elements since Pakistan's creation. The Afghan government went a step further, claiming that in fact Afghanistan had rights over the Pashtun-dominated
areas of Pakistan.

29. For instance, see L. Dupree, 'A Suggested Pakistan–Afghanistan–Iran
    Federation', *Middle East Journal* 17 (1963): 383–99.
30. Tahir-Kheli, 'Iran and Pakistan', 476.
31. Shirin Tahir-Kheli, 'The Foreign Policy of "New" Pakistan', *Orbis* 30, 3 (Fall
    1976), 754–5.
32. Quoted in Tahir-Kheli, 'Iran and Pakistan', 481.
33. *Christian Science Monitor*, 29 July 1974.
34. Tahir-Kheli, 'Iran and Pakistan', 480.
35. Ibid., 485.
36. S. V. R. Nasr, 'Democracy and Islamic Revivalism', *Political Science Quarterly*
    110, 2 (Summer 1995), 268.
37. Nasr, *The Shia Revival*, 138.
38. Suroosh Irfani, *Revolutionary Islam in Iran: Popular Liberation or Religious
    Dictatorship?* London: Zed Books, 1983.
39. Joe Stork and Eric Hooglund, 'Nikki Keddie: Pakistan's Movement against
    Islamization', *MERIP Middle East Report* 148 (September–October 1987), 40–1.
40. Sattar, *Pakistan's Foreign Policy*, 159.
41. Ibid., 160.
42. Iftikhar H. Malik, 'Pakistan's National Security and Regional Issues: Politics
    of Mutualities with the Muslim World', *Asian Survey* 34, 12 (December 1994),
    1083–4.
43. In 1992 the ECO was expanded to include seven new members, namely
    Afghanistan, Azerbaijan, Kazakhstan, Kyrgyzstan, Tajikistan, Turkmenistan, and
    Uzbekistan. For details see the ECO's official website: http://www.ecosec-
    retariat.org/
44. For details see Mariam Abou Zahab and Olivier Roy, *Islamist Networks: The
    Afghan–Pakistan Connection*, New York: Columbia University Press, 2006.
45. Nasr, *The Shia Revival*, 161.
46. Ibid.
47. Mushahid Hussain, 'Pakistan–Iran Relations in the Changing World Scenario:
    Challenges and Response', in Tarik Jan et al. (eds.), *Foreign Policy Debate: The
    Years Ahead*, Islamabad: Institute of Policy Studies, 1993, p. 216; see also Alam,
    'Iran–Pakistan Relations', 531.
48. Albright and Hinderstein, 'Unraveling the A. Q. Khan and Future Proliferation
    Networks', 112.
49. This chronology relies heavily on the document created by the Nuclear Threat
    Initiative (NTI) at http://www.nti.org/media/pdfs/iran_nuclear.pdf?_=
    1316542527/, IAEA reports, and Mohammad Sahimi's series of three arti-
    cles covering Iran's Nuclear Program in *Payvand*, published in 2003–4, avail-

able at http://www.payvand.com/news/04/dec/1186.html; see also Mustafa Kibaroglu, 'Iran's Nuclear Ambitions from a Historical Perspective and the Attitude of the West', *Middle Eastern Studies* 43, 2 (March 2007), 223–45, available at http://mustafakibaroglu.com/sitebuildercontent/sitebuilderfiles/Kibaroglu-MES-March2007-IranNuclear.pdf

50. Daniel Poneman, *Nuclear Power in the Developing World*, London: George Allen & Unwin, 1982, 84.

51. Reza Shah Pahlavi, *Mission for my Country*, London: Hutchinson, 1961, 307–8.

52. David Albright and Mark Hibbs, 'Spotlight Shifts to Iran', *Bulletin of the Atomic Scientists* 48, 2 (March 1992), 9–11.

53. 'US Supplied Nuclear Material to Iran', Digital National Security Archive, 29 January 1980, http://nsarchive.chadwyck.com

54. 'Proposed Agreement for Cooperation between the US Government and the Government of Iran concerning the Civil Uses of Atomic Energy', Memorandum, 13 March 1969, in Digital National Security Archive, http://nsarchive.chadwyck.com

55. 'Nuclear Plant Study Started', *Kayhan International*, 19 December 1972.

56. For instance, see James F. Clarity, 'Iran Negotiates for Nuclear Energy Aid', *New York Times*, 27 May 1974.

57. Clyde H. Farnsworth, 'France Gives Iran Stake in Uranium', *New York Times*, 4 January 1975.

58. 'Full Text of Iran–India Joint Communiqué', *Iran Almanac*, Tehran: The Echo of Iran, 1974, 176.

59. John K. Cooley, 'More Fingers on Nuclear Trigger?' *Christian Science Monitor*, 25 June 1974; 'The Shah Meets the Press', *Kayhan International*, 5 October 1974.

60. Poneman, *Nuclear Power in the Developing World*, 88.

61. Mark Hibbs, 'Bushehr Construction Now Remote after Three Iraqi Air Strikes', *Nucleonics Week*, 26 November 1987, 5–6.

62. See 'Iran Profile: Nuclear Chronology 1957–1979', NTI, http://www.nti.org/media/pdfs/iran_nuclear.pdf?_=1316542527.

63. Irfan Parviz, 'Regional Atom Chiefs in Talks on Three-Country Organization', *Tehran Journal*, 27 January 1975.

64. *Der Spiegel*, 8 February 1975.

65. Leslie H. Gelb, 'US Nuclear Deal with Iran Delayed', *New York Times*, 8 March 1975.

66. Leonard S. Spector, with Jacqueline R. Smith, *Nuclear Ambitions: The Spread of Nuclear Weapons, 1989–1990*, Boulder: Westview Press, 1990, 205.

67. 'Italy: Referendum Approval Uncertain', *Nucleonics Week*, 29 October 1987, 13.

68. For details see Morteza Gharehbaghian, 'Oil Revenue and the Militarisation of Iran: 1960–1978', *Social Scientist* 15, 4/5 (April–May 1987): 87–100.

69. 'US, Iran Resume Atom Power Talks', *Washington Post*, 9 August 1977.
70. For details see *New York Times*, 12 April 1977; *Washington Post*, 2 May 1977.
71. See *Washington Post*, 3 October 1977; *Wall Street Journal*, 13 September 1977.
72. 'Carter will Visit Sadat to Discuss Mideast Diplomacy', *Washington Post*, 1 January 1978.
73. *Wall Street Journal*, 11 October 1978.
74. Leonard S. Spector, *Going Nuclear: The Spread of Nuclear Weapons 1986–1987*, Cambridge: Ballinger Publishing Company, 1987, 50–1.
75. Mohammad Sahimi, 'Iran's Nuclear Program. Part I: Its History', *Payvand*, 2 October 2003.
76. William Burr (ed.), 'US–Iran Nuclear Negotiations in 1970s Featured Shah's Nationalism and US Weapons Worries', National Security Archive, George Washington University, 13 January 2009, http://nsarchive.gwu.edu/nukevault/ebb268/
77. Sahimi, 'Iran's Nuclear Program. Part I'.
78. Ann MacLachlan, 'Eurodif's Balance Sheet Threatened by Iranian Problem', *Nuclear Fuel* 16, 12 (10 June 1991), 4–5.
79. 'Iran Profile: Nuclear Chronology 1957–1979', NTI. See also William Branigin, 'Iran Set to Scrap $34 Billion Worth of Civilian Projects', *Washington Post*, 30 May 1979, A22.
80. Corera, *Shopping for Bombs*, 61.
81. Ibid.
82. Quoted in Rolf Mowatt-Larssen, 'Islam and the Bomb: Religious Justification for and against Nuclear Weapons', Belfer Center for Science and International Affairs, Harvard Kennedy School, January 2011, 51, http://www.belfercenter.org/sites/default/files/legacy/files/uploads/Islam_and_the_Bomb-Final.pdf
83. For instance see Kevin Done, 'German Group Nears Deal in Iranian Power Station Dispute', *Financial Times*, 31 March 1982, 20; 'Iran Won't Allow 62 French Citizens to Leave the Country', *New York Times*, 7 August 1981; 'Iran to Restudy A-Power', *New York Times*, 18 March 1982, A7.
84. Mark Hibbs and Neel Patri, 'US to Ask New Delhi to Back Off on Research Reactor Offer to Iran', *Nucleonics Week*, 21 November 1991, 2–3.
85. Sahimi, 'Iran's Nuclear Program. Part I'.
86. 'Proliferation: Pulling a Bomb Apart', *The Economist*, 14 March 1992, 46.
87. 'Iran Seeking Way to Finish Bushehr Plant but Bonn Denies Exports', *Neuclonics Week*, 30 October 1986, 4–5.
88. Anthony H. Cordesman and Khalid R. Al-Rodhan, *Iranian Nuclear Weapons? The Uncertain Nature of Iran's Nuclear Programs*, Washington, DC: Center for Strategic and International Studies, 2006, 24.
89. Javed Ali, 'Chemical Weapons and the Iraq–Iran War: A Case Study in Noncompliance', *The Nonproliferation Review* 8, 1 (Spring 2001), 50–1.

90. Ibid., 52.

91. Cordesman and Al-Rodhan, *Iranian Nuclear Weapons?*, 24–5.

92. For details see David Sanger, 'The Khan Network', paper presented at the Conference on South Asia and the Nuclear Future held at Stanford University on 4–5 June 2004, http://fsi.stanford.edu/sites/default/files/evnts/media//Khan_network-paper.pdf

93. Fitzpatrick, *Nuclear Black Markets*, 67.

94. David Albright and Corey Hinderstein, 'The Centrifuge Connection', *Bulletin of the Atomic Scientists* 60, 2 (March/April 2004), 62.

95. Ibid.

96. On the death of Ayatollah Khomeini in 1989, President Ali Khamenei became the supreme leader of Iran.

97. Eliza Van Hollen, 'Pakistan in 1986: Trials of Transition', *Asian Survey* 27, 2 (February 1987), 153.

98. Spector, *Nuclear Ambitions*, 212.

99. See 'A.Q. Khan's Thirteen-Page Confession', Fox News, 15 September 2011, http://www.foxnews.com/world/2011/09/15/aq-khans-thirteen-page-confession.html

100. Corera, *Shopping for Bombs*, 64.

101. Safdar Mahmood, *Pakistan: Political Roots and Development 1947–1999*, Oxford: Oxford University Press, 2000.

102. Farzad Bazoft, 'Iran Signs Secret Atom Deal', *The Observer*, 12 June 1988.

103. Elaine Sciolino, 'US sees Troubling Tilt by Pakistan to Iran', *New York Times*, 1 November 1987, http://www.nytimes.com/1987/11/01/world/us-sees-troubling-tilt-by-pakistan-to-iran.html

104. Ibid.

105. Fitzpatrick, *Nuclear Black Markets*, 67.

106. John Lancaster and Kamran Khan, 'Pakistanis Say Nuclear Scientists Aided Iran', *Washington Post*, 24 January 2004, A1.

107. Fitzpatrick, *Nuclear Black Markets*, 67.

108. Kathy Gannon, 'Iran Sought Advice in Pakistan on Attack', *Washington Post*, 12 May 2006.

109. Ibid.

110. "EDITORIAL: GIK: Has he Taken a Big Secret to his Grave?' *Daily Times*, 29 October 2006.

111. Albright and Hinderstein, 'The Centrifuge Connection', 62.

112. 'Pakistan: Dr Abdul Qadeer Khan Discusses Nuclear Program in TV Talk Show—Karachi *Aaj News Television* in Urdu 1400 GMT 31 Aug 09', https://fas.org/nuke/guide/pakistan/aqkhan-083109.pdf

113. Quoted in Declan Walsh, 'Disgraced Atomic Scientist Disowns Confession', *The Guardian*, 29 May 2008, https://www.theguardian.com/world/2008/may/30/pakistan.nuclear

114. Frantz and Collins, *The Nuclear Jihadist*, 155.

115. In the early 1990s Leybold Heraeus and its sister companies had been major suppliers to many secret nuclear weapons programmes, including those in Iraq, Iran, South Africa, and Pakistan. See Albright and Hinderstein, 'Unraveling the A. Q. Khan and the Future Proliferation Networks', 118.

116. Jürgen Dahlkamp, Georg Mascolo, and Holger Stark, 'Network of Death on Trial', *Der Spiegel*, 13 March 2006.

117. Ibid.

118. Frantz and Collins, *The Nuclear Jihadist*, 156.

119. Ibid., 157. Iran also provided these details to IAEA. See Pierre Goldschmidt (deputy director-general, Head of Department of Safeguards, IAEA), 'Statement to the IAEA Board of Governors, 1 March 2005, http://www.iaea.org/NewsCenter/Statements/DDGs/2005/goldschmidt01032005.html. Iran also maintains that it has no accompanying documentation of this meeting besides the one handwritten note. See International Atomic Energy Agency, 'Implementation of the NPT Safeguards Agreement in the Islamic Republic of Iran', report by the director-general to the Board of Governors, GOV/2005/67, 2 September 2005, 13.

120. Ibid.

121. Frantz and Collins, *The Nuclear Jihadist*, 156.

122. See David Armstrong and Joseph Trento, *America and the Islamic Bomb: The Deadly Compromise*, Hanover, NH: Steerforth Press, 2007, 160. This is further confirmed in Egmont Koch, *Der Physikar der Mullahs*, a film broadcast on German Public Television (WDR) on 22 February 2007, available at https://www.youtube.com/watch?v=G0uTiRSuKcQ.

123. Koch, *Der Physikar der Mullahs*.

124. Massoud Ansari, 'Nuclear Scientists from Pakistan Admit Helping Iran with Bomb-Making', *The Telegraph*, 25 January 2004.

125. Dafna Linzer, 'Iran was Offered Nuclear Parts: Secret Meeting in 1987 May Have Begun Program', *Washington Post*, 27 February 2005.

126. Ibid.

127. See International Atomic Energy Agency, 'Implementation of the NPT Safeguards Agreement in the Islamic Republic of Iran', report by the director-general to the Board of Governors, GOV/2006/15, 27 February 2006, 3.

128. Frantz and Collins, *The Nuclear Jihadist*, 158.

129. Linzer, 'Iran was Offered Nuclear Parts'.

130. See ibid. and International Atomic Energy Agency, 'Implementation of the NPT Safeguards Agreement in the Islamic Republic of Iran', report by the director-general to the Board of Governors, GOV/2004/83, 29 November 2004, 6.

131. Lancaster and Khan, 'Pakistanis Say Nuclear Scientists Aided Iran'; John Wilson, 'Iran, Pakistan and Nukes', Observer Research Foundation, 2005,

available at http://www.washingtontimes.com/news/2004/oct/4/20041004-015707-2087r/.

132. See John Lancaster and Kamran Khan, 'Musharraf Named in Nuclear Probe', *Washington Post*, 3 February 2004; Mubashir Zaidi, 'Scientist Claimed Nuclear Equipment Was Old, Official Says', *Los Angeles Times*, 10 February 2004.

133. Interview with a retired Pakistan army major-general, October 2007.

134. See Dalip Singh, 'Delhi Dossier on Pak Bomb Daddy', *The Telegraph* (India), 8 February 2004.

135. Frantz and Collins, *The Nuclear Jihadist*, 160.

136. 'Iranian Dissident Fires Ukraine, Iran Charges on Tehran's Nuclear Program', AFP, 26 August 2005.

137. IAEA, 'Implementation of the NPT Safeguards Agreement in the Islamic Republic of Iran', GOV/2006/15, 5, paras. 20 and 22.

138. Fitzpatrick, *Nuclear Black Markets*, 69.

139. 'Why Not Just Blow your Whistle', *The Economist*, 28 February 2008. According to this report, the IAEA showed some evidence (originally provided by the USA) to Iran in February 2008, reportedly recovered from an Iranian defector's laptop, suggesting that Iran had conducted work on uranium conversion, missile-warhead design and high-explosives testing—all potentially linked to nuclear weapons, but Iran called the allegations baseless and the supporting documents forged.

140. Corera, *Shopping for Bombs*, 66.

141. Koch, *Der Physiker der Mullahs*. See also Tom Bielefeld and Hassan Abbas, 'The Khan Job', *Bulletin of the Atomic Scientists*, 63, 4 (July/August 2007): 72–3.

142. Ibid.

143. Frantz and Collins, *The Nuclear Jihadist*, 161.

144. Interview with a military officer who served in the Strategic Plans Division, Joint Staff Headquarters in Rawalpindi, May 2006.

145. For instance, see David Rohde, 'Pakistanis Question Official Ignorance of Atom Transfers', *New York Times*, 3 February 2004; David Armstrong, 'Khan Man', *The New Republic*, 9 November 2004.

146. Gaurav Kampani, 'Proliferation Unbound: Nuclear Tales from Pakistan', CNS Research Story, Monterey: Center for Nonproliferation Studies, Monterey Institute of International Studies, 2004, http://cns.miis.edu/pubs/week/040223.htm (accessed 2 November 2008).

147. Raja Anwar, *The Terrorist Prince: The Life and Death of Murtaza Bhutto*, Lahore: Vanguard, 1997, 27.

148. See Aitzaz Ahsan, 'In Memoriam: Benazir Bhutto', *Daily Times*, 29 January 2008.

149. E-mail interview with retired Brigadier Naeem Salik, May 2016.

150. Hussain and Hussain, *Pakistan: Problems of Governance*, 39. See also *The Economist*, 3 December 1988.

151. Interview with Benazir Bhutto, May 2007.

152. Benazir Bhutto, interview with Douglas Frantz and Catherine Collins, quoted in *The Nuclear Jihadist*, 164.
153. *The Muslim* (Pakistan), 4 December 1990, quoted in Brian Cloughley, *A History of the Pakistan Army: Wars and Insurrections*, New York: Oxford University Press, 1999, 310. For more on strategic defiance see Kux, *The United States and Pakistan, 1947–2000*, 312–13.
154. Clary, 'The A. Q. Khan Network'.
155. Chaudhri, 'Pakistan's Nuclear History'.
156. E-mail interview Lieutenant-General Asad Durrani, May 2016.
157. Quoted in Borzou Daragahi, '1987 Chemical Strike Still Haunts Iran', *Los Angeles Times*, 19 March 2007.
158. Kathy Gannon, 'Explosive Secrets from Pakistan', *Los Angeles Times*, 30 January 2004.
159. Ibid.
160. Interview with Benazir Bhutto, Boston, May 2007.
161. Douglas Frantz and Catherine Collins, 'A Tale of Two Bhuttos', *Foreign Policy*, November 2007.
162. Ibid.
163. According to General Beg, Benazir Bhutto directly told him about this offer. Most probably this offer was made when she met Rafsanjani in 1989. See Gannon, 'Iran Sought Advice in Pakistan on Attack'.
164. Interview with Benazir Bhutto, Boston, May 2007.
165. Frantz and Collins, 'A Tale of Two Bhuttos'.
166. Farhan Bokhari et al., 'Pakistan's "Rogue Nuclear Scientist": What Did Khan's Government Know about his Deals?' *Financial Times*, 6 April 2004; also Matt Kelley, 'Pakistan Threatened to Give Nukes to Iran', *Washington Post*, 27 February 2004.
167. 'Beg Denies Involvement in N-Tech Transfer', *Dawn* (Karachi), 29 February 2004.
168. Corera, *Shopping for Bombs*, 76.
169. Steve Coll, *Ghost Wars: The Secret History of the CIA, Afghanistan, and Bin Laden, from the Soviet Invasion to September 10, 2001*, New York: Penguin, 2004, 221.
170. Ibid.
171. Seymour Hersh, 'On the Nuclear Edge', *New Yorker*, 29 March 1993.
172. Zahid Hussain, 'There is a Conspiracy against Me by the Jewish Lobby: General Aslam Beg', *Newsline*, Karachi, February 2004, http://www.newsline.com.pk/Newsfeb2004/cover3feb2004.htm (accessed 18 January 2008).
173. 'Interview with Abdul Qadeer Khan', *The News* (Islamabad), 30 May 1998, http://nuclearweaponarchive.org/Pakistan/KhanInterview.html.
174. A. Q. Khan, 'An Indomitable Man: Part III', *The News*, 2 February 2015, https://www.thenews.com.pk/print/21756-an-indomitable-man
175. The institute's website is at http://www.giki.edu.pk/. Previously, this offi-

cial website mentioned the role of A. Q. Khan as a project director of the institute, but lately this reference has been deleted. However, the older version is available at http://www.fas.org/nuke/guide/pakistan/agency/giki.htm (accessed 5 November 2007).

176. Kamran Khan, 'Dr Qadeer's Fate Hangs in the Balance', *The News* (Islamabad), 24 January 2004.
177. Hersh, 'On the Nuclear Edge'.
178. Abbas, *Pakistan's Drift into Extremism*, 142.
179. Rohde, 'Pakistanis Question Official Ignorance of Atom Transfers'; Lancaster and Khan, 'Musharraf Named in Nuclear Probe'; Armstrong, 'Khan Man'.
180. Rohde, 'Pakistanis Question Official Ignorance of Atom Transfers'.
181. Gannon, 'Explosive Secrets from Pakistan'.
182. Interview with Nisar Ali Khan, January 2004, Islamabad.
183. See Zahid Hussain, 'Nuked', *Newsline*, January 2004.
184. Shaukat Piracha, 'Beg Asked Nawaz to Give Nuclear Technology to a "Friend", says Ishaq Dar', *Daily Times*, 25 December 2003.
185. Dar mentioned that army chief General Mirza Aslam Beg had in 1991 pressurized Nawaz Sharif to sell nuclear technology to Iran. See *The News*, 28 February 2004.
186. David Rohde, 'Nuclear Inquiry Skips Pakistani Army', *New York Times*, 30 January 2004.
187. Interview with a senior Pakistani journalist who was invited to such briefings, April 2007, Washington, DC.
188. 'A.Q. Khan's Thirteen-Page Confession'.
189. Ibid.
190. Interview with Shuja Nawaz, younger brother of General Asif Nawaz, Washington, DC, 25 February 2008. Shuja Nawaz has served in the IMF and IAEA in senior positions, and also worked for the *New York Times*. His 2008 book *Crossed Swords* also discusses nuclear proliferation issues.
191. Shuja Nawaz, *Crossed Swords: Pakistan, its Army and the Wars Within*, Karachi: Oxford University Press, 2008, 448–9.
192. Ibid.
193. Muhammad Saleh Zaafir, 'Gen. Asif had Refused Nuclear Assistance to Iran, Says Javed', *The News*, 14 February 2004.
194. Zahid Hussain, *Frontline Pakistan: The Struggle with Militant Islam*, New York: Oxford University Press, 2007, 167.
195. Lancaster and Khan, 'Pakistanis Say Nuclear Scientists Aided Iran'.
196. Fitzpatrick, *Nuclear Black Markets*, 70.
197. Udayan Namboodiri, 'Dr Khan's Story: Thy Hand, Great Gen!' *Pioneer*, 6 February 2004.
198. Nuzhat Janjua, the widow of General Asif Nawaz, suspected that her husband had been poisoned by arsenic administered in a cup of tea served to him at a meeting of the Joint Chiefs of Staff Committee.

199. 'Gen. Asif Nawaz of Pakistan, 56, a Champion of Democracy, Dies', *New York Times*, 9 January 1993.

200. Khaled Ahmed, 'Second Opinion: Decline of the Army Chief in Pakistan—Khaled Ahmed's Review of the Urdu Press', *Daily Times*, 9 June 2006; Bidanda M. Chengappa, 'The ISI Role in Pakistan's Politics', *Strategic Analysis* (New Dehli) 23, 11 (2000): 1857–78.

201. Ibid.

202. IAEA, 'Implementation of the NPT Safeguards Agreement in the Islamic Republic of Iran', GOV/2004/83, 6; see also Royal Malaysian Police, 'Press Release by Inspector-General of Police in Relation to Investigation of Alleged Production of Components for Libya's Uranium Enrichment Programme', 20 February 2004, http://www.rmp.gov.my/rmp03/040220scomi_eng.htm.

203. Albright and Hinderstein, 'Unraveling the A. Q. Khan and Future Proliferation Networks', 115; see also IAEA, 'Implementation of the NPT Safeguards Agreement in the Islamic Republic of Iran', GOV/2004/83, 9-10, 23.

204. 'Pakistan Cracks Down on al-Ansar', 30 March 1995, https://www.intelligenceonline.com/threat-assessment/1995/03/29/pakistan-cracks-down-on-al-ansar,65330-ART.

205. International Atomic Energy Agency, 'Implementation of the NPT Safeguards Agreement in the Islamic Republic of Iran', report by the director-general to the Board of Governors, 10 November 2003, GOV/2003/75, 8.

206. IAEA, 'Implementation of the NPT Safeguards Agreement in the Islamic Republic of Iran', GOV/2004/83, 8.

207. Ibid, 10–11.

208. Ibid.

209. Ibid.

210. Clary, 'The A. Q. Khan Network', 40–2.

211. Bill Powell and Tim McGirk, 'The Man who Sold the Bomb', *Time*, 6 February 2005.

212. Ibid.

213. *Iran's Nuclear Programme*, BBC Two, 3 May 2005.

214. Frantz and Collins, *The Nuclear Jihadist*, 203, 211.

215. Fitzpatrick, *Nuclear Black Markets*, 70.

216. Corera, *Shopping for Bombs*, 69.

217. IAEA, 'Implementation of the NPT Safeguards Agreement in the Islamic Republic of Iran', GOV/2004/83, 11, para 45.

218. The copy of the letter is acquired from Farhan Raza, a Pakistani journalist investigating the A. Q. Khan network.

219. Interview with a former senior army official, September 2007.

220. 'Pakistan Said to Know of Nuclear Transfer', *New York Times*, 3 February 2004.

221. Ibid.

222. Corera, *Shopping for Bombs*, 73.

223. Frantz and Collins, *The Nuclear Jihadist*, 210–11.

224. Ibid.

225. William J. Broad and David E. Sanger, 'Iran Claims Nuclear Steps in New Worry', *New York Times*, 17 April 2006.

226. Ibid.

227. Interview with a federal minister of Pakistan deemed close to President Musharraf, November 2007.

228. Tariq Butt, 'Iran, Libya Role Disappoints Islamabad', *The News*, 7 February 2004.

229. Interview with Abbas Maleki, former deputy foreign minister of Iran, Cambridge, September 2007.

230. 'Q & A', Asia Source, 20 June 2007.

231. Ahmed Montezeran and Kashif Mumtaz, 'Iran–Pakistan: Cooperation for Regional Stability and Peace', *Strategic Studies*, 24, 1 (Spring 2004).

232. Musharraf, *In the Line of Fire*, 293.

233. Mehdi Mohammadi, 'God's Hand Was at Work', interview with Dr Mohammad Sa'idi, Atomic Energy Organization of Iran deputy for planning and international affairs, *Kayhan*, 27 April 2005, quoted in Clary, 'The A. Q. Khan Network: Causes and Implications', 48.

234. 'Iran's Nuclear Capabilities: Fast Facts', CNN Library, updated 27 March 2017, http://www.cnn.com/2013/11/07/world/meast/irans-nuclear-capabilities-fast-facts/

5. PAKISTAN'S NUCLEAR PROLIFERATION LINKS WITH NORTH KOREA

1. David E. Sanger, 'Threats and Responses: Alliances; in North Korea and Pakistan, Deep Roots of Nuclear Barter', *New York Times*, 24 November 2002.

2. Ibid.

3. Musharraf, *In the Line of Fire*, 288.

4. Ibid., 296.

5. David Albright, 'The A. Q. Khan Illicit Nuclear Trade Network and Implications for Nonproliferation Efforts', *Strategic Insights* 5, 6 (July 2006); repr. in James A. Russell and James J. Wirtz (eds.), *Globalization and WMD Proliferation: Terrorism, Translational Network and International Security*, New York: Routledge, 2008, 49–62.

6. For details see Corera, *Shopping for Bombs*, 86–102; Frantz and Collins, *The Nuclear Jihadist*, 193–8, 206–10, 231–2; Levy and Scott-Clark, *Deception*, 244–50, 256–61, 277–82.

7. Corera, *Shopping for Bombs*, 89.

8. The North Korean nuclear scientists' visit to KRL in 1999 is mentioned in Pervez Musharraf's memoirs. See Musharraf, *In the Line of Fire*, 288–9.

9. 'A.Q Khan's Thirteen-Page Confession'.

10. Frantz and Collins, *The Nuclear Jihadist*, 231.

11. Daniel A. Pinkston, 'Domestic Politics and Stakeholders in North Korean Missile Development Program', *Nonproliferation Review* 10 (Summer 2003), 2, https://www.nonproliferation.org/wp-content/uploads/npr/102pink.pdf

12. Benjamin Friedman, 'Fact Sheet: North Korea's Nuclear Weapons Program', Center for Defense Information, 23 January 2003 (link no longer available).

13. Pinkston, 'North Korean Motivations for Developing Nuclear Weapons'.

14. William Burr (ed.), 'Stopping Korea from Going Nuclear', National Security Archive, George Washington University, 22 March 2017, http://nsarchive. gwu.edu/nukevault/ebb582-The-U.S.-and-the-South-Korean-Nuclear-Program,-1974-1976,-Part-1/

15. Steven Lee Myers and Choe Sang-hun, 'North Koreans Agree to Freeze Nuclear Work; US to Give Aid', *New York Times*, 29 February 2012.

16. Nuclear Threat Initiative, 'North Korea Profile', updated February 2017, http://www.nti.org/learn/countries/north-korea/

17. 'Nuclear Weapons Program—North Korea', Federation of American Scientists, http://www.fas.org/nuke/guide/dprk/nuke/index.html (accessed 4 April 2017).

18. Ibid.

19. 'DPRK Nuclear Program', Global Security.org, http://www.globalsecurity. org/wmd/world/dprk/nuke.htm (accessed 17 January 2008)

20. Larry A. Niksch, 'North Nuclear Weapons Program', Congressional Research Service, 27 August 2003, 8, http://fas.org/spp/starwars/crs/IB91141.pdf (accessed 18 January 2008).

21. Central Intelligence Agency, Unclassified Report to Congress on the Acquisition of Technology Relating to Weapons of Mass Destruction and Advanced Conventional Munitions, July 1 through December 31, 2001, http://www.cia.gov/cia/publications/bian/bian_jan_2003.htm#5 (accessed August 2007).

22. For details see http://www.fas.org/nuke/guide/dprk/missile/index.html (accessed 7 March 2017).

23. For details see Larry A. Niksch, *North Korea's Nuclear Weapons Program*, Congressional Research Service Report, Washington, DC: Library of Congress, 5 October 2006.

24. Nuclear Threat Initiative, 'North Korea Profile'.

25. Demetri Sevastopulo, 'Bush Removes North Korea from Terror List', *Financial Times*, 11 October 2008.

26. Fitzpatrick, *Nuclear Black Markets*, 73.

27. B. Raman, 'The Pakistan–North Korea Nexus', 8 April 2003, http://www. rediff.com/news/2003/apr/08spec.htm.

28. For details see Kux, *The United States and Pakistan, 1947–2000*, 309–10.

29. For details see 'Missile Overview: India Profile', NTI, http://www.nti.org/e_ research/profiles/India/Missile/index.html (accessed 2 January 2017).

30. Gordon Oehler, 'Proliferation of Chinese Missiles', Testimony to the Senate Foreign Relations Committee, 11 June 1998.
31. 'Pakistan and North Korea: Dangerous Counter-Trades', *International Institute for Strategic Studies Strategic Comments* 8, 9 (November 2002), 1.
32. Fitzpatrick, *Nuclear Black Markets*, 24.
33. Ibid.
34. Frantz and Collins, *The Nuclear Jihadist*, 207.
35. See Corera, *Shopping for Bombs*, 87.
36. Tertrais, 'Khan's Nuclear Exports', 24.
37. *Gardels,* 'Musharraf Knew about A. Q. Khan's "Private" Proliferation'.
38. Frantz and Collins, *The Nuclear Jihadist*, 208.
39. Quoted in Corera, *Shopping for Bombs*, 86.
40. Ibid.
41. For details see Abbas, *Pakistan's Drift into Extremism*, 133–42.
42. Fitzpatrick, *Nuclear Black Markets*, 74.
43. Ibid.
44. Clary, 'The A. Q. Khan Network', 61.
45. 'Pakistan and North Korea: Dangerous Counter-Trades', 1–2.
46. Fitzpatrick, *Nuclear Black Markets*, 75.
47. Powell and McGirk, 'The Man who Sold the Bomb'.
48. Albright, 'The A. Q. Khan Illicit Nuclear Trade Network and Implications for Nonproliferation Efforts'.
49. Musharraf, *In the Line of Fire*, 288–9.
50. For instance, see Lancaster and Khan, 'Musharraf Named in Nuclear Probe'.
51. Gaurav Kampani, 'Second Tier Proliferation: The Case of Pakistan and North Korea', *Nonproliferation Review* 9, 3 (Fall–Winter 2002), 111–12.
52. 'A. Q. Khan's Thirteen-Page Confession'.
53. E-mail interview with a retired Pakistani four-star army general, June 2016.
54. See Andrew Koch, 'Pakistan Persists with Nuclear Procurement', *Jane's Intelligence Review* 9, 3 (March 1997); and Kux, *The United States and Pakistan 1947–2000*, 343.
55. Strobe Talbott, *Engaging India: Diplomacy, Democracy and the Bomb* (Washington, DC: Brookings Institution Press, 2004), 150.
56. Ibid., 150–1.
57. Sharon A. Squassoni, *Weapons of Mass Destruction: Trade between North Korea and Pakistan, CRS report for Congress, RL 31900, Washington, DC:* Congressional Research Service, 28 November 2006, 15.
58. Ibid.
59. Clary, 'The A. Q. Khan Network', 63–5.
60. Ibid., 71.
61. Albright, 'The A. Q. Khan Illicit Nuclear Trade Network and Implications for Nonproliferation Efforts'.

62. Selig S. Harrison, 'What A. Q. Khan Knows: How Pakistan's Proliferator Could Help in Pyongyang', *Washington Post*, 31 January 2008, A21.

63. Ibid.

64. *Munir Ahmad, 'Scientist: Pakistan Knew of N. Korea Nuke Deal'*, Associated Press, 5 July 2008, available at http://www.heraldnet.com/news/scientist-pakistan-knew-of-north-korea-nuke-deal/.

65. Ibid.

66. Fitzpatrick, *Nuclear Black Markets*, 73.

67. Ibid.

68. 'North Korea's Nuclear Programme: How Advanced is it?' BBC, 6 January 2017, http://www.bbc.com/news/world-asia-pacific-11813699

69. For details see 'India's Embarrassing North Korea Connection', al-Jazeera, 21 June 2016, http://www.aljazeera.com/indepth/features/2016/06/india-embarrassing-north-korean-connection-160620195559208.html

6. PAKISTAN'S NUCLEAR PROLIFERATION LINKS WITH LIBYA

1. For an overall view see Wyn Q. Bowen, *Libya and Nuclear Proliferation: Stepping Back from the Brink*, Adelphi Papers 380, New York and Abingdon: Taylor & Francis/Routledge for the International Institute of Strategic Studies, 2006.

2. For details see 'Implementation of the NPT Safeguards Agreement of the Socialist People's Libyan Arab Jamahiriya', report by the director-general to the Board of Governors, GOV/2004/12, 20 February 2004.

3. Fitzpatrick, *Nuclear Black Markets*, 76.

4. 'Libya Profile: Nuclear Overview', NTI, http://www.nti.org/e_research/profiles/Libya/3939.html (accessed 5 December 2007)

5. Joseph Cirincione, with Jon Wolfstahl and Miriam Rajkumar, *Deadly Arsenals: Tracking Weapons of Mass Destruction*, Washington, DC: Carnegie Endowment for International Peace, 2002, 307.

6. For details about the 1974 meeting see Frantz and Collins, *The Nuclear Jihadist*, 22.

7. Frank Barnaby, *The Invisible Bomb: The Nuclear Arms Race in the Middle East*, London: I. B. Tauris, 1993, 98.

8. Anthony Cordesman, 'Weapons of Mass Destruction in the Middle East', Center for Strategic and International Studies report, 1 January 2000, https://www.csis.org/analysis/weapons-mass-destruction-middle-east-0.

9. For details see 'Libya's Nuclear Update—2004', *Wisconsin Project on Nuclear Arms Control* 10, 2 (March–April 2004).

10. IAEA, 'Implementation of the NPT Safeguards Agreement of the Socialist People's Libyan Arab Jamahiriya', GOV/2004/12, 4.

11. Ibid.

12. Ibid.

13. Quoted in 'An Interview with Gaddafi', *Time*, 8 June 1981, http://content. time.com/time/magazine/article/0,9171,922551–1,00.html (accessed 3 March 2017).

14. IAEA, 'Implementation of the NPT Safeguards Agreement of the Socialist People's Libyan Arab Jamahiriya', GOV/2004/12, 5.

15. Peter Slevin, 'Libya Made Plutonium, Nuclear Watchdog Says', *Washington Post*, 21 February 2004, A15.

16. Jack Kelley, 'Russian Nuke Experts Wooed', *USA Today*, 8 January 1992.

17. For details about Libyan nuclear posture in 1990s see Joshua Sinai, 'Libya's Pursuit of Weapons of Mass Destruction', *Nonproliferation Review* 4 (Spring–Summer 1997), 97.

18. 'Libya's Nuclear Update—2004'.

19. For details of the Pelindaba Treaty see http://www.nti.org/e_research/official_docs/inventory/pdfs/anwfz.pdf (10 accessed December 2007).

20. See R. Jeffrey, 'US Complains to China about Libyan Arms Shipment', *Washington Post*, 28 April 1992; Lee Michael Katz, 'Nuclear Threat Different, Not Gone, Panel Warned', *USA Today*, 23 January 1992.

21. International Atomic Energy Agency, 'Implementation of the NPT Safeguards Agreement of the Socialist People's Libyan Arab Jamahiriya', report by the director-general to the Board of Governors, GOV/2004/33, 28 May 2004, 2–4.

22. Fitzpatrick, *Nuclear Black Markets*, 76.

23. See Karamatullah K. Ghori, 'Did Libya Stab Pakistan in the Back?', *Chowk*, 21 February 2004.

24. Details of Z. A. Bhutto's visit to Libya in 1972 are recounted in Weissman and Krosney, *The Islamic Bomb*, 54–5.

25. Ghori, 'Did Libya Stab Pakistan in the Back?'

26. Frantz and Collins, *The Nuclear Jihadist*, 22.

27. Department of State, Memorandum of conversation, Subject: Proposed Cable to Tehran on Pakistani Nuclear Reprocessing, Secret, 3, National Security Archive Electronic Briefing Book No. 268, 12 May 1976, available at http://nsarchive.gwu.edu/nukevault/ebb268/doc17.pdf. This document first came to light when the US embassy in Iran was ransacked by Iranian revolutionaries in 1979 and many secret communications stored in the embassy records were made public by Iran. Later it was declassified as part of the National Security Archives.

28. Fitzpatrick, *Nuclear Black Markets*, 76; *The Bangladesh Observer* (Dhaka) also reported this matter on 8 June 1977.

29. Chakma, 'Road to Chagai', 892.

30. Figure quoted in Fitzpatrick, *Nuclear Black Markets*, 76.

31. Mehdi Hassan, 'The Man Who Stooped to Conquer', *Chowk*, 8 September 1998.

32. Ibid.

33. Ibid.
34. Interview with I.S., a Pakistani scientist who worked in the Libyan programme briefly, December 2007.
35. Shyam Bhatia, *Nuclear Rivals in the Middle East*, London: Routledge, 1988.
36. For details see Bowen, *Libya and Nuclear Proliferation*, 30–43.
37. Royal Malaysian Police, 'Press Release by Inspector-General of Police'.
38. Albright, 'The A. Q. Khan Illicit Nuclear Trade Network and Implications for Nonproliferation Efforts'.
39. IAEA, 'Implementation of the NPT Safeguards Agreement of the Socialist People's Libyan Arab Jamahiriya', GOV/2004/33, 5–7.
40. Albright, 'The A. Q. Khan Illicit Nuclear Trade Network and Implications for Nonproliferation Efforts'.
41. Ibid.
42. Corera, *Shopping for Bombs*, 118.
43. Albright, 'The A. Q. Khan Illicit Nuclear Trade Network and Implications for Nonproliferation Efforts'.
44. Fitzpatrick, *Nuclear Black Markets*, 79; see also Joby Warrick and Peter Slevin, 'Libyan Arms Designs Traced back to China: Pakistanis Resold Chinese Provided Plans', *Washington Post*, 15 February 2004.
45. Albright, 'The A. Q. Khan Illicit Nuclear Trade Network and Implications for Nonproliferation Efforts'.
46. David Albright and Corey Hinderstein, 'Uncovering the Nuclear Black Market: Working Toward Closing Gaps in the International Nonproliferation Regime', *ISIS*, 2 July 2004, http://www.isis-online.org/publications/southasia/nuclear_black_market.html (accessed 19 December 2007).
47. Ibid.
48. Ibid.
49. Clary, 'The A. Q. Khan Network', 78.
50. Fitzpatrick, *Nuclear Black Markets*, 80–1.
51. Scomi Group Berhad, 'SCOPE's Press Statement on its Contract in Dubai', news release, 4 February 2004, http://www.scomigroup.com.my/publish/04news008.shtml (accessed 15 December 2008).
52. Ibid.
53. Griffin has vehemently denied any role in the endeavour, and successfully sued the *Guardian* in Great Britain. See Jan Colley, 'Libel Damages for Engineer', Press Association, 3 May 2005.
54. Clary, 'The A. Q. Khan Network', 78–9.
55. Ibid., 79.
56. Fitzpatrick, *Nuclear Black Markets*, 82.
57. Ibid.
58. Interview with a senior Pakistani diplomat, Islamabad, July 2008.
59. Gardels, 'Musharraf Knew about A.Q. Khan's "Private" Proliferation'.

60. Ibid.
61. Bruno Tertrais, 'Not a "Wal-Mart", but an "Imports–Exports Enterprise": Understanding the Nature of the A. Q. Khan Network', *Strategic Insights* 6, 5 (August 2007).
62. Clary, 'The A. Q. Khan Network', 81.
63. Ibid.
64. A. Q. Khan was forced into retirement in March 2001. He refused the compensatory position of 'Advisor to the Chief Executive' and was later given the ceremonial title of 'Special Adviser to the Chief Executive on Strategic and KRL Affairs'.
65. Interview with a senior military officer who served under General Musharraf in 2000–1, Islamabad, July 2004.
66. Musharraf, *In the Line of Fire*, 290.

7. INVESTIGATING A. Q. KHAN'S PERSONAL MOTIVATIONS, RELIGIOUS ORIENTATION, AND ANTI-WESTERN WORLDVIEW

1. Nirupama Subramanian, 'A. Q. Khan's "Secret Agreement"', *The Hindu*, 25 May 2011, http://www.thehindu.com/news/A.Q.-Khanrsquos-lsquosecret-agreementrsquo/article13738344.ece
2. Ibid.
3. Fitzpatrick, *Nuclear Black Markets*, 85.
4. Jeremy Bernstein, *Physicists on Wall Street and Other Essays on Science and Society*, New York: Springer, 2008, 55.
5. Interview with A.H., who worked closely with A. Q. Khan at KRL, June 2008.
6. David Rohde and David E. Sanger, 'Key Pakistani is Said to Admit Atom Transfers', *New York Times*, 2 February 2004.
7. Fitzpatrick, *Nuclear Black Markets*, 85. See also Kenley Butler, Sammy Salama, and Leonard S. Spector, 'Where is the Justice?' *Bulletin of Atomic Scientists* 62, 6 (November/December 2006).
8. Fitzpatrick, *Nuclear Black Markets*, 80.
9. 'Pakistan's Nuclear Bombshell', *India Today*, 31 March 1987.
10. Frantz, 'From Patriot to Proliferator', A1.
11. A. Q. Khan, *Dr. A. Q. Khan on Pakistan Bomb*, ed. Sreedhar, New Delhi; ABC Publishing House, 1987, 10.
12. Frantz, 'From Patriot to Proliferator'.
13. Syed Asif Jah, *Muhsin-i-Pakistan Dr. Abdul Qadeer Khan*, 3rd edn, Multan: Sohni Dharti Publishers, 2000, 71.
14. Frantz, 'From Patriot to Proliferator'.
15. Khan, *Dr. A. Q. Khan on Pakistan Bomb*, 10.

16. Frantz, 'From Patriot to Proliferator'.

17. Rauf Klasra, 'Nuclear Scientist Blasts HEC's Outgoing Chairman', *The News*, 17 October 2008.

18. The document was acquired from a journalist who had received this from Khan in 1998. Parts of this CV are still available http://www.draqkhan.com.pk/about.htm (accessed 2 April 2017).

19. E-mail Interview with Lieutenant-General Asad Durrani, May 2016.

20. Ibid.

21. Zahid Gishkori, 'A. Q. Khan Set to Launch Own Political Party', *Express Tribune*, 27 August 2012.

22. Ibid.

23. 'Abdul Qadeer Khan Dissolves Political Party', *Dawn*, 14 September 2013.

24. Quoted in 'A. Q. Khan Thought he could Defy the World: The Rediff Interview/Gordon Corera', Rediff.com, 22 September 2006, http://ia.rediff.com/news/2006/sep/22inter.htm (accessed 7 March 2017).

25. Abdul Qadeer Khan, 'An Analysis of Propaganda against Pakistan's Peaceful Nuclear Programme', *The Muslim* (Islamabad), 16 March 1984.

26. Translated excerpt from A. Q. Khan's interview published in Urdu newspaper *Nawa-i-Waqat*, Lahore, 10 February 1984.

27. Ibid.

28. Translated excerpts from A. Q. Khan's interview given to Zahid Malik (his biographer), published in the Urdu-language magazine *Hurmat*, 14 March 1985.

29. Interview given to *Arab News*, reproduced in Khan, *Dr. A. Q. Khan on Pakistan Bomb*, 97.

30. S. Shabbir Hussain and Mujahid Kamran (eds.), *Dr. A. Q. Khan on Science and Education*, Lahore: Sang-e-Meel Publications, 1997, 120. The quotation is from A. Q. Khan's lecture at a meeting organized by the Pakistan Institute of National Affairs on 9 September 1990 in Lahore.

31. Ibid., 150. These excerpts are from A. Q. Khan's keynote address at 'The First National Workshop on Magnets and Magnetic Materials', held in Islamabad on 20 April 1994.

32. Ibid., 171. Excerpts from A. Q. Khan's speech at the 'International Conference on Science in Islamic Polity in the Twenty First Century' held on 26–30 March 1995, Islamabad.

33. Ibid., 172.

34. Ibid., 173.

35. Rajesh Kumar Mishra, 'Pakistan as a Proliferator State: Blame it on Dr. A. Q. Khan', paper no. 567, South Asia Analysis Group, 20 December 2002.

36. Hussain and Kamran (eds.), *Dr. A.Q. Khan on Science and Education*, 180.

37. Ibid., 1, quoted as the theme statement.

38. Ibid., 190. This is an excerpt from A. Q. Khan's speech at the Islamic Development Bank's Headquarters, Jeddah, 19 May 1996.

39. Ibid., 203.

40. Quoted in Kara J. Peterson, 'Abdul Qadeer Khan Brings Nuclear Bomb to Pakistan', *World Press Review*, 1 September 1998.

41. 'Profile Abdul Qadeer Khan', BBC, 20 February 2004, http://news.bbc.co.uk/2/hi/south_asia/3343621.stm (accessed 18 January 2008).

42. For instance, Douglas Frantz also maintains that 'Khan gave money to charities and to people who might help him, including journalists, recycling his wealth to hedge against being marginalized'. See Frantz, 'From Patriot to Proliferator'.

43. Pervez Hoodbhoy, 'Pakistan: Inside the Nuclear Closet', Open democracy.com, 3 March 2004, http://www.opendemocracy.net/conflict-iraqwarafter/article_1767.jsp (accessed 9 January 2008).

44. Jah, *Muhsin-i-Pakistan Dr. Abdul Qadeer Khan*.

45. Imran Husain Chaudhry, *Mohsin-e-Pakistan Dr. Abdul Qadeer Khan: Islami bomb kay Khaliq aur Ghaui Mizzile kay Mojid Ki Walwala Khez Dastaan-e-Hayat*, Lahore: Ilm-o-Irfan Publishers, 2003.

46. Ibid., 161.

47. Ibid., 164–7.

48. Ibid., 224–6.

49. Ibid., 228–36.

50. Frantz, 'From Patriot to Proliferator'.

51. Ibid.

52. 'An Engaging Dictator Who Wants to Stay that Way', *The Economist*, 12 December 1981, 48.

53. Quoted in Haqqani, *Pakistan: Between Mosque and Military*, 133.

54. Hussain, 'Inside Jihad', 22.

55. Saeed Shafqat, 'From Official Islam to Islamism: The Rise of Dawat-ul-Irshad and Lashkar-e-Taiba', in Christophe Jaffrelot (ed.), *Pakistan: Nationalism Without a Nation?* London: Zed Books, 2002, 133.

56. See Nicholas Howenstein, 'The Jihadi Terrain in Pakistan: An Introduction to the Sunni Jihadi Groups in Pakistan and Kashmir', PSRU Report no. 1, Bradford: University of Bradford, 5 February 2008, http://spaces.brad.ac.uk:8080/download/attachments/748/resrep1.pdf (accessed 8 January 2008).

57. Kamal Matinuddin, *The Taliban Phenomenon: Afghanistan, 1994–1997*, Karachi: Oxford University Press, 1999, 14.

58. Vali Nasr, 'Islam, the State and the Rise of Sectarian Militancy in Pakistan', in Christophe Jaffrelot (ed.), *Pakistan: Nationalism without a Nation?* London: Zed Books, 2002.

59. Figures quoted in the *Herald*, Karachi, November 2001.

60. Stephen Schwartz, *The Two Faces of Islam: The House of Saud from Tradition to Terror*, New York: Doubleday, 2002, 184–6.

61. Mahmood Mamdani, *Good Muslim, Bad Muslim: America, the Cold War and the Roots of Terror*, New York: Doubleday, 2004, 119–77.

62. For details about the Red Mosque crisis see Hassan Abbas, 'The Road to Lal Masjid and its Aftermath', *Terrorism Monitor* 5, 14 (19 July 2007): 4–7.

63. Renowned Pakistani journalist Khaled Ahmed's conversation with a retired senior army officer quoted in Khaled Ahmed, 'Islamic Extremism in Pakistan', *South Asian Journal* 1, 2 (October–December 2003).

64. John K. Cooley, *Unholy Wars: Afghanistan, America and International Terrorism*, London: Pluto Press, 1998. Cooley maintains that during the 1980s Osama Bin Laden's Karachi connections included the Binori mosque, later recognized as one of the Jamiat-i-Ulema-e-Islam (JUI)–Taliban strongholds in Pakistan.

65. Interview with Khaled Ahmed, Washington, DC, 14 April 2007.

66. According to *Nawa-e-Waqt* (18 October 2007), a popular right-wing Urdu newspaper, Mufti Shamzai issued a fatwa decreeing that when the Americans landed in Pakistan, his followers should immediately take over the country's airports.

67. Ahmed, 'Islamic Extremism in Pakistan'.

68. For details see 'In Musharraf's Words: "A Day of Reckoning"', *New York Times*, 12 January 2002, http://www.nytimes.com/2002/01/12/international/in-musharrafs-words-a-day-of-reckoning.html

69. 'We Need Atomic Weapons and Mujahideen, says Daawa', *Daily Times*, 6 February 2004.

70. Jessica Stern, 'Pakistan's Jihad Culture', *Foreign Affairs* 79, 6 (November/December 2000); see also Stephen P. Cohen, 'The Jihadist Threat to Pakistan', *Washington Quarterly* 26, 3 (Summer 2003).

71. For details about the Kargil episode see Abbas, *Pakistan's Drift into Extremism*, 169–76.

72. Amir Rana, *A to Z of Jihadi Organizations in Pakistan*, Lahore: Mashal Books, 2004. See also Amir Rana, '245 religious parties in Pakistan', *Daily Times*, 13 April 2003.

73. The JUI was founded by Maulana Mufti Mahmud in 1945. After Mahmud's death in 1980, his son, Maulana Fazlur Rehman, took over JUI. The party split into two factions in the mid-1980s—JUI (F), led by Maulana Fazlur Rehman, and JUI (S), led by Maulana Samiul Haq, following disagreements over political strategy.

74. For details see JI's website: http://jamaat.org/ur/

75. K. Alan Kronstadt, 'Pakistan's Scheduled 2008 Election: Background', Congressional Research Service Report, 24 January 2008, 9, https://fas.org/sgp/crs/row/RL34335.pdf.

76. 'The First 10 General Elections of Pakistan', PILDAT, May 2013, http://

www.pildat.org/publications/publication/elections/First10GeneralElectionsof Pakistan.pdf; see also Nasr, *The Vanguard of the Islamic Revolution*.

77. For details see Abbas, *Pakistan's Drift into Extremism*, 146–8.

78. For details see Ahmed Rashid, *Taliban: Militant Islam, Oil and Fundamentalism in Central Asia*, New Haven: Yale University Press, 2001, 41–66, 157–69.

79. Kronstadt, 'Pakistan's Scheduled 2008 Election: Background', 9.

80. 'Our Perception of the Situation', Majlis-e-Shoora Resolution, Jamaat-e-Islami Pakistan, 6–7 November 1996, available at http://archive.li/eUu0f

81. For details see Todd S. Sechser (ed.), 'South Asia and the Nuclear Future: Rethinking the Causes and Consequences of Nuclear Proliferation', Conference Brief, Center for International Security and Cooperation, Stanford University, http://www.strategicstudiesinstitute.army.mil/pdffiles/pub688.pdf (accessed 19 January 2008).

82. 'Bin Laden Had Visited Mansoora: Qazi Hussain', *The Nation*, 18 March 2006; see also 'Osama–Nawaz ties to haunt PML-N', *The News*, 11 May 2011, https://www.thenews.com.pk/archive/amp/613747-osama-nawaz-ties-to-haunt-pml-n

83. 'Bin Laden Had Visited Mansoora: Qazi Hussain'.

84. Mohammad Kamran, 'MMA Vows to Wage Jihad for Kashmir and N-Defence', *Daily Times*, 6 February 2004.

85. Major-General Naseerullah Khan Babar, Inspector-General of the NWFP Frontier Corps, played a central role in 1973 in organizing and grooming Afghan resistance forces opposing President Sardar Mohammad Daud Khan. Babar (who became the federal interior minister in 1993–95 and is known for galvanizing and supporting the Taliban) publicly acknowledged that Gulbuddin Hekmatyar and Ahmad Shah Masoud were among the Afghans who were first recruited as Frontier Corps personnel (on paper) and then trained by the Pakistani military's Special Services Group. For details see Hassan Abbas, 'Transforming Pakistan's Frontier Corps', *Terrorism Monitor* 5, 6 (29 March 2007).

86. Zahid Hussain, 'Pakistan Targets Nuclear Scientists for Selling Nuclear Secrets', *Wall Street Journal*, 26 January 2004, A3; Piracha, 'Beg asked Nawaz to Give Nuclear Technology to a "Friend"', says Ishaq Dar'.

87. 'Pakistan Rejects Aid Ultimatum on Nuclear Program', *Japan Economic Newswire*, 8 December 1990. This statement was also carried by *Dawn* on 7 December 1990.

88. Pervez Hoodbhoy, 'For God and Profit', *Newsline*, Karachi, February 2004. See also Khaled Ahmed, 'The Death of Zia', *Criterion Quarterly* 2, 2 (May 2007), http://www.criterion-quarterly.com/the-death-of-zia-ul-haq/.

89. Hussain, 'There is a Conspiracy against Me by the Jewish Lobby: General Aslam Beg'.

90. Mirza Aslam Beg, 'Indo-US Defence Pact: Challenge and Response', http://

www.friends.org.pk/Beg/Indo%20US%20Defence%20Pact%20Challenge%20
and%20Response.htm (accessed 12 February 2008).

91. Hussain, 'There is a Conspiracy against Me by the Jewish Lobby: General
    Aslam Beg'.

92. Mirza Aslam Beg, 'South Asian Nuclear Security Regime', *Dawn* (Karachi),
    7 March 2005; see also Mirza Aslam Beg, 'Outside View: Nuke Proliferators
    can't be Stopped', United Press International, 7 March 2005, http://www.
    upi.com/Outside-View-Nuke-proliferators-cant-be-stopped/659411102
    30694/?spt=su.

93. 'Beg's Advice to Iran: Scare the Enemy', *The News*, 14 May 2006.

94. For the Iranian statement see Gannon, 'Iran Sought Advice in Pakistan on
    Attack'.

95. Najam Sethi, 'Nuclear Shenanigans: Najam Sethi's Editorial', *Friday Times*,
    15, 49, 30 January–5 February 2004.

96. 'A. Q. Khan: Hero or Proliferator?', *Daily Times*, 26 January 2004.

97. Ibid.

98. Ibid.

99. Dennis Overbye and James Glanz, 'A Nation Challenged: Nuclear Fears;
    Pakistani Atomic Expert, Arrested Last Week, Had Strong Pro-Taliban Views',
    New York Times, 2 November 2001; see also David Sanger, Douglas Frantz,
    and James Risen, 'Nuclear Experts in Pakistan May Have Links to Al Qaeda',
    New York Times, 9 December 2001.

100. For details see David Albright and Holly Higgins, 'A Bomb for the Ummah',
     Bulletin of the Atomic Scientists 59, 2 (March–April 2003).

101. Steven Mufson, 'US Worries about Pakistan Nuclear Arms', *Washington Post*,
     4 November 2001.

102. Sultan Mahmood and Muhammad Nasim, 'CTBT: A Technical Assessment',
     7 January 2000, http://www.Pakistanlink.com/Opinion/2000/Jan/07/02.
     htm (accessed September 2008).

103. Overbye and Glanz, 'A Nation Challenged'.

104. Asmir Latif, 'Two Pakistani Atomic Scientists Arrested', IslamOnline,
     24 October 2001, www.islam-online.net/English/News/2001–10/25/arti-
     cle3.shtml.

105. Quoted in David Albright and Holly Higgins, 'Pakistani Scientists: How Much
     Nuclear Assistance to Al Qaeda?', Institute for Science and International
     Security, 30 August 12 2002, http://www.exportcontrols.org/pakscientists.
     html (accessed 12 January 2008).

106. Ibid.

107. Albright and Higgins, 'A Bomb for the Ummah'.

108. Elizabeth Neuffer, 'A US Concern: Pakistan's Arsenal: Anti-American Mood
     Poses a Security Risk', *Boston Globe*, 16 August 2002, A1.

109. Albright and Higgins, 'A Bomb for the Ummah'.

110. Ibid.

111. For a detailed account of Pakistan–US relations see Kux, *The United States and Pakistan, 1947–2000*; Cohen, *The Idea of Pakistan*.

112. Quoted in the *New York Times*, 6 July 1973.

113. G. S. Bhargava, 'The Bomb for Pakistan: Ambitions and Constraints', *The Statesman*, 13 March 1982.

114. Bhutto, *If I am Assassinated*, 118.

115. Details are from Sharon Squassoni, 'Closing Pandora's Box: Pakistan's Role in Nuclear Proliferation', *Arms Control Today* 34, 3, Washington: Arms Control Association, April 2004.

116. Central Intelligence Agency, 'PAKISTAN/USSR: The Soviet Campaign against Pakistan's Nuclear Program', Declassified, 7 August 1987, https://www.cia.gov/library/readingroom/docs/CIA-RDP90T00114R000700470001-0.pdf

117. Mary Anne Weaver, *Pakistan: In the Shadows of Jihad and Afghanistan*, New York: Farrar, Straus & Giroux, 2002, 8.

118. Quoted in Kux, *The United States and Pakistan 1947–2000*, 287.

119. See Abbas, *Pakistan's Drift into Extremism*, 89–132.

120. Ibid., 124–32.

121. Khan, 'Comparative Strategic Culture'.

122. Richard P. Cronin, Alan Kronstadt, and Sharon Squassoni, 'Pakistan's Nuclear Proliferation Activities and the Recommendations of the 9/11 Commission: US Policy Constraints and Options', Congressional Research Service Report RL32745, 25 January 2005.

123. See 'A. Q. Khan, Godfather of the "Islamic Bomb": Hero or Proliferator?'

124. Ibid.

125. Rais, 'Pakistan's Nuclear Program', 461.

8. POLITICAL INSTABILITY, CIVIL–MILITARY TUSSLES, AND LOOSE CONTROLS OVER THE NUCLEAR PROGRAMME MANAGEMENT

1. Mir Jamil ur Rahman, 'Issues that Haunt', *The News*, 10 July 2006, http://www.thenews.com.pk/print1.asp?id=27346 (accessed 17 August 2008).

2. A statement on this subject by Prime Minister Junejo that was part of a speech to the National Assembly is covered in detail in *The Nation* (Lahore), 14 March 1987.

3. For details see Ikramullah, 'Shrinking Stature of Parliament and Prime Minister', *The Nation* (Lahore), 8 August 1991.

4. 'New Documents Spotlight Reagan-era Tensions over Pakistani Nuclear Program'.

5. For the reasons behind Junejo's decision see Cohen, *The Idea of Pakistan*, 145.

6. George Crile, *Charlie Wilson's War: The Extraordinary Story of the Largest Covert Operation in History*, New York: Atlantic Monthly Press, 2003, 491–2.

7. *Jang*, Rawalpindi, 5 March 1993.
8. Hussain and Hussain, *Pakistan: Problems of Governance*, 93.
9. Ibid.
10. See Hasan Askari Rizvi, 'Civil–Military Relations under General Beg', *Defence Journal* 7, 6 and 7 (August 1991): 17–21.
11. Hussain and Hussain, *Pakistan: Problems of Governance*, 39. See also *The Economist*, 3 December 1988.
12. 'A. Q. Khan "Covered up" for Musharraf: Benazir', *Daily Times*, 6 March 2004.
13. Ibid.
14. For details see Maleeha Lodhi and Zahid Hussain, 'The Night of the Jackals', *Newsline*, October 1992, 32–3.
15. 'A.Q. Khan "Covered up" for Musharraf: Benazir'.
16. *Dawn* (Karachi), 9 August 1990.
17. See Abbas, *Pakistan's Drift into Extremism*, 142. Various sections of this chapter borrow language and materials from the author's earlier works, especially *Pakistan's Drift into Extremism*.
18. Ardesher Cowasjee, 'We Never Learn from History', *Dawn* (Karachi), 21 July 2002.
19. Statement submitted by Lieutenant-General Javed Nasir in Lahore High Court in December 2002. See 'Ex-ISI Chief Reveals Secret Missile Shipments to Bosnia Defying UN Embargo', *South Asia Tribune* 22, 23–29 December 2002.
20. Ibid.
21. Haqqani, *Pakistan: Between Mosque and Military*, 225.
22. For a complete statement of Beg's disclosure see *The News* (Lahore), 10 August 1994.
23. See A. Q. Khan's statements in *The Frontier Post* (Lahore), 13 March 1993 and *The Nation* (Lahore), 12 March 1993.
24. See the statement by President Farooq Leghari in *The News*, 14 November 1993.
25. For details see Hassan Abbas, 'The Black-Turbaned Brigade: The Rise of TNSM in Pakistan', *Terrorism Monitor* 4, 23 (30 November 2006): 1–4.
26. Hoodbhoy, 'The Nuclear Noose around Pakistan's Neck'.
27. Ahmed Rashid, 'Bhutto Warns India against Testing Nuclear Device', *Daily Telegraph*, 6 January 1996.
28. Kux, *The United States and Pakistan, 1947–2000*, 345.
29. E-mail interview with General Karamat, July 2016.
30. E-mail interview with a retired Pakistani lieutenant-general with extensive service in intelligence organizations, July 2016.
31. See Rai Mohammad Saleh Azam, 'When Mountains Move: The Story of Chagai', *Defence Journal* (June 2000), http://www.defencejournal.com/2000/june/chagai.htm (accessed 17 February 2008); see also M. A. Chaudhri, 'The Unsung Nuclear Hero', *The Nation*, 22 April 2006.

32. John F. Burns, 'Pakistan, Answering India, Carries Out Nuclear Tests; Clinton's Appeal Rejected', *New York Times*, 29 May 1998.

33. For more details of the episode see Tim McGirk, 'General Speaks Out', *Time*, 19 October 1998, http://content.time.com/time/world/article/0,8599,205 4276,00.html

34. 'The Lahore Declaration', available at http://peacemaker.un.org/sites/peace-maker.un.org/files/IN%20PK_990221_The%20Lahore%20Declaration.pdf

35. For details see Robert Wirsing, *Kashmir in the Shadows of War: Regional Rivalries in a Nuclear Age*, New York: M. E. Sharpe, 2003, 25–36.

36. For a detailed analysis of the Kargil conflict see Tellis et al., *Limited Conflicts under the Nuclear Umbrella*.

37. David Sanger, 'So What about Those Nukes?', *New York Times*, 11 November 2007. He also covers this topic in a later book. See David Sanger, *The Inheritance: The World Obama Confronts and the Challenges to American Power*, New York: Harmony, 2009.

38. Musharraf, *In the Line of Fire*, 287.

39. Feroz Hassan Khan, 'Political Transitions and Nuclear Management in Pakistan', http://www.npolicy.org/books/Security_Crises/Ch5_Khan.pdf

40. A. Q. Khan, 'An Indomitable Man: Part II', *The News*, 26 January 2015, https://www.thenews.com.pk/print/20506-an-indomitable-man

41. Naeem Salik, *The Genesis of South Asian Nuclear Deterrence: Pakistan's Perspective*, Karachi: Oxford University Press, 2009, 265–7.

42. Khan, 'An Indomitable Man: Part II'.

43. Musharraf, *In the Line of Fire*, 287.

44. Ibid.

45. Ibid., 288.

46. Ibid.

47. Ibid., 289.

48. Ibid.

49. 'Ambassador William B. Milam: Interviewed by Charles Stuart Kennedy', Association for Diplomatic Studies and Training Foreign Affairs Oral History Project, 29 January 2004, http://adst.org/wp-content/uploads/2013/12/MIlam-William-B.pdf

50. Ibid.

51. The author served in the NAB in Islamabad as deputy director of investigations from November 1999 to January 2001, and this information is based on his interviews with relevant officials and on personal recollections.

52. Author's personal notes from service in National Accountability Bureau, 1999–2000.

53. Musharraf, *In the Line of Fire*, 290–1.

54. Ibid., 294.

55. Ibid., 296.

56. See Mushahid Hussain, 'Media off Target with Pakistan Nuclear Scare', *Asia Times*, 7 November 2001, http://www.atimes.com/ind-pak/CK07Df01.html (accessed 3 March 2008).

57. Ibid.

58. Quoted in Bennett Jones, *Pakistan: Eye of the Storm*, 210.

59. Ibid. See also Ahmed Rashid, 'Bare All and Be Damned: Ex-Army Chief Reveals Nuclear Secrets', *Far Eastern Economic Review*, 5 May 1994, 23.

60. Quoted in Frantz, 'From Patriot to Proliferator', A 1.

61. Ibid.

62. For details see Chaudhry, *Mohsin-e-Pakistan Dr. Abdul Qadeer Khan*.

63. E-mail interview with Lieutenant-General Asad Durrani, May 2016.

64. Fitzpatrick, *Nuclear Black Markets*, 94.

65. Ibid.

66. Ibid.

67. Ibid., 96.

68. Khan, 'Nuclear Proliferation Motivations', 504.

69. Hoodbhoy, 'The Nuclear Noose around Pakistan's Neck'.

70. Quoted in Rohde, 'Pakistanis Question Official Ignorance of Atom Transfers'.

71. 'Three KRL Officials Released', *Dawn*, 25 July 2004.

72. Khalid Hasan, '*Washington Post* Names Dr Khan and Farooq as Those who Sold N-Technology', *Daily Times*, 29 January 2004.

73. Amnesty International, 'Pakistan: Open Letter to President Pervez Musharraf', 3 February 2004, http://www.amnesty.org/ar/library/asset/ASA33/003/2004/en/tVEIgb1kvUAJ (accessed 2 March 2008).

74. Neuffer, 'A US Concern', A1.

75. Interview with a senior security official involved in KRL security, Islamabad, June 2008.

76. Salik, *The Genesis of South Asian Nuclear Deterrence*, 267.

9. CONCLUSION: POLICY IMPLICATIONS AND THE FUTURE OF PAKISTAN'S NUCLEAR PROGRAMME

1. Musharraf, *In the Line of Fire*, 288.

2. Interview with a senior bureaucrat who served on Nawaz Sharif's in 1997–9, Islamabad, July 2004.

3. See Musharraf, *In the Line of Fire*, 287.

4. CIA, 'PAKISTAN/USSR'.

5. Ibid.

6. Central Intelligence Agency, 'US–Pakistan: Implications of an Aid Cutoff', 15 July 1985, Declassified, 30 October 2009, https://www.cia.gov/library/readingroom/docs/CIA-RDP85T01058R000506640001–5.pdf

7. Quoted in Verghese K. George, "A Timely History Lesson," The Hindu,

September 2, 2017. Also see, Rabia Akhtar, "The Correct Narrative on Pressler", Dawn, May 29, 2017.

8. 'Dr Khan Says He Confessed to Save Pakistan', Dawn, 8 April 2008; For A. Q. Khan's confession see Rafaqat Ali, 'Dr Khan Seeks Pardon; Cabinet Decision Today; Meets Musharraf; Admits Error of Judgment', Dawn (Karachi), 5 February 2004.

9. Rauf Klasra, 'A. Q. Khan's Family Threatens Direct Action', The News, 12 March 2008.

10. Ibid.

11. Ghori, 'Did Libya Stab Pakistan in the Back?'.

12. Albright and Hinderstein, 'Uncovering the Nuclear Black Market'.

13. Fitzpatrick, Nuclear Black Markets, 93.

14. Corera, Shopping for Bombs, 74.

15. David Albright, 'Nuclear Black Markets: Pakistan, A. Q. Khan and the Rise of Proliferation Networks', Testimony before the House Committee on Foreign Affairs' Subcommittee on the Middle East and South Asia and the Subcommittee on Terrorism, Nonproliferation, and Trade, 27 June 2007.

16. Editorial Board, 'Can Israel and the Arab States be Friends?', New York Times, 27 August 2016, https://www.nytimes.com/2016/08/28/opinion/sunday/can-israel-and-the-arab-states-be-friends.html?_r=0

17. Quoted in Mark Urban, 'Saudi Nuclear Weapons "On Order" from Pakistan', BBC, 6 November 2013, http://www.bbc.com/news/world-middle-east-24823846

18. Yossi Melman, 'In Face of Iran Threat, Saudi Arabia Mulls Nuclear Cooperation with Pakistan', Haaretz, 8 September 2011, http://www.haaretz.com/blogs/the-arms-race/in-face-of-iran-threat-saudi-arabia-mulls-nuclear-cooperation-with-pakistan-1.383153

19. Mohammad Mukashaf, 'Pakistan Declines Saudi Call for Armed Support in Yemen Fight', Reuters, 10 April 2015, http://www.reuters.com/article/us-yemen-security-idUSKBN0N10LO20150410

20. Jon Boone, 'Former Pakistan Army Chief Raheel Sharif to Lead "Muslim Nato"', The Guardian, 8 January 2017, https://www.theguardian.com/world/2017/jan/08/former-pakistan-army-chief-raheel-sharif-lead-muslim-nato

21. David Hearst, 'EXCLUSIVE: Pakistan Sends Combat Troops to Southern Saudi Border', Middle East Eye, 17 March 2017, http://www.middleeasteye.net/news/exclusive-pakistan-sends-combat-troops-saudi-southern-border-248886071

22. Pervez Hoodbhoy, 'The Bomb: Iran, Saudi Arabia and Pakistan', Express Tribune, 22 January 2012.

23. For details see 'Nuclear Power in Saudi Arabia', World Nuclear Association, updated on 27 March 2017, http://www.world-nuclear.org/information-library/country-profiles/countries-o-s/saudi-arabia.aspx

24. Angelina Rascouet and Wael Mahdi, 'Saudi Arabia to Select Nuclear Power-

Plant Site "Very Soon"', Bloomberg, 20 October 2016, https://www.bloomberg.com/news/articles/2016–10–20/saudi-arabia-to-select-nuclear-power-plant-site-very-soon

25. Nuclear Threat Initiative, 'Saudi Arabia: Nuclear', updated July 2016, http://www.nti.org/learn/countries/saudi-arabia/nuclear/

26. James M. Dorsey, 'Saudi–Iran Rivalry Fuels Potential Nuclear Race', 5 April 2017, available at http://mideastsoccer.blogspot.com/2017/04/saudi-iranian-rivalry-fuels-potential.html

27. Matthew Fuhrman, 'Spreading Temptation: Proliferation and Peaceful Nuclear Cooperation Agreements', *International Security* 34, 1 (Summer 2009): 7–41.

28. Hans M. Kristensen and Robert S. Norris, 'Pakistani Nuclear Forces, 2016', *Bulletin of the Atomic Scientists* 72, 6 (2016): 368–76, http://thebulletin.org/2016/november/pakistani-nuclear-forces-201610118

29. Shahid Javed Daskavi, 'If Nuclear Program Were under Supervision of Political Governments, God Knows What Would Have Happened: Samar Mubarakmand', *Jehan Pakistan*, 5 February 2016.

30. Jefferson Morley, 'UK Downsizes Its Nuclear Arsenal', Arms Control Association, March 2015, https://www.armscontrol.org/ACT/2015_03/News-Brief/UK-Downsizes-Its-Nuclear-Arsenal.

31. Quoted in Paul K. Kerr and Mary Beth Nikitin, 'Pakistan's Nuclear Weapons', Congressional Research Service report RL34248, 1 August 2016, 6, https://fas.org/sgp/crs/nuke/RL34248.pdf

32. Ibid.; see also Christine Fair, 'Pakistan's Nuclear Program: Laying the Groundwork for Impunity', 21 November 2016, SSRN, https://ssrn.com/abstract=2946051

33. For instance, see Naeem Salik, 'Minimum Deterrence and India Pakistan Nuclear Dialogue: Case Study on Pakistan', Landau Network–Centro Volta South Asia Security Project Case Study, January 2006, http://www.centrovolta.it/landau/South%20Asia%20Security%20Program_file%5CDocumenti%5CCase%20Studies%5CSalik%20-%20S.A.%20Case%20Study%202006.pdf; 'Tactical N-Arms to Ward off War Threat, Says FO', *Dawn*, 20 October 2015.

34. See 'What is India's "Cold Start" Military Doctrine?', *The Economist*, 31 January 2017, http://www.economist.com/blogs/economist-explains/2017/02/economist-explains

35. Quoted in 'US–Indo Ties Not a Matter of Concern for Pak: Sartaj Aziz', Asian News International (ANI), 3 July 2016, available at http://indianexpress.com/article/india/india-news-india/indo-us-ties-not-a-matter-of-concern-for-pakistan-sartaj-aziz-2890921/.

36. For details see 'Transcript: A Conversation with Gen. Khalid Kidwai', Carnegie International Nuclear Policy Conference 2015, 23 March 2015, http://carnegieendowment.org/2015/03/23/conversation-with-gen.-khalid-kidwai-pub-58885

37. For details see http://www.pnra.org/ (last accessed 29 March 2009).

38. 'Pakistan Tightens Security at N-Facilities', *The News*, 27 January 2008.

39. Ibid.

40. Christopher Clary, 'Command and Control Trends and Choices for the Next Decade in South Asia', in Feroz Hassan Khan, Ryan Jacobs, and Emily Burke (eds.), *Nuclear Learning in South Asia: The Next Decade* (Monterey, CA: Naval Postgraduate School, June 2014), 95.

41. See 'Bhutto Death Threatens Democracy, Security', CBS, 27 December 2007, http://www.cbsnews.com/stories/2007/12/27/eveningnews/main3651630.shtml (last accessed 19 December 2008).

42. Interviews with U.S. security experts, Washington DC, November 2016.

43. Zahir Kazmi, "Normalizing Pakistan," IISS Voices, May 21, 2014; available at https://www.iiss.org/en/iiss%20voices/blogsections/iiss-voices-2014-b4d9/may-5382/normalising-pakistan-a5df

44. J. N. Dixit, *India and Pakistan in War and Peace* (New York: Routledge, 2002), 343.

45. Abhijnan Rej, "India is not changing its policy on no first use of nuclear weapons," War on the Rocks, March 29, 2017; available at https://warontherocks.com/2017/03/india-is-not-changing-its-policy-on-no-first-use-of-nuclear-weapons/

46. Views expressed by MIT's Professor Vipin Narang as summarized in "#Nukefest2017 Hot Takes: Potential Indian Nuclear First Use?," *South Asian Voices*, March 20, 2017; available at https://southasianvoices.org/sav-dc-nuke-fest2017-potential-indian-nuclear-first-use/#sthash.UpDMprdP.dpuf

47. For Indian nuclear capabilities, see Kyle Mizokami, "This is Why the World Should Fear India's Nuclear Weapons," The National Interest, May 27, 2017; and for Pakistan's nuclear developments, see, Tyler Rogoway, "Pakistan Closer To Nuclear Second-Strike Capability After Sub Missile Test," *The Drive*, January 13, 2017; available at http://www.thedrive.com/the-war-zone/6959/pakistan-closer-to-nuclear-second-strike-capability-after-sub-missile-test

48. Interview with a US expert on Pakistan's nuclear programme, Washington, DC, September 2016.

49. Toby Dalton and Michael Krepon, 'A Normal Nuclear Pakistan', Stimson and Carnegie Endowment for International Peace, 2015, https://www.stimson.org/content/normal-nuclear-pakistan-0

50. David Nakamura, 'In Hiroshima 71 Years after First Atomic Strike, Obama Calls for End of Nuclear Weapons', *Washington Post*, 27 May 2013, https://www.washingtonpost.com/politics/obama-visits-hiroshima-more-than-seven-decades-after-the-worlds-first-atomic-strike/2016/05/27/c7d0d250-23b6-11e6-8690-f14ca9de2972_story.html?tid=a_inl&utm_term=.fcd866a20b66

BIBLIOGRAPHY

'A. Q. Khan: Hero or Proliferator?' *Daily Times*, 26 January 2004.

'A. Q. Khan "Covered up" for Musharraf: Benazir'. *Daily Times*, 6 March 2004.

'A. Q. Khan's Thirteen-Page Confession'. Fox News, 15 September 2011, http://www.foxnews.com/world/2011/09/15/aq-khans-thirteen-page-confession.html.

'A. Q. Khan Thought He could Defy the World: The Rediff Interview/Gordon Corera'. Rediff.com, 22 September 2006, http://ia.rediff.com/news/2006/sep/22inter.htm.

Abbas, Hassan. *Pakistan's Drift into Extremism: Allah, the Army and America's War on Terror*. New York: M. E. Sharpe, 2004.

————. *The Taliban Revival: Violence and Extremism in the Pakistan—Afghanistan Frontier*. New Haven: Yale University Press, 2015.

Abbasi, Rizwana. 'Nuclear Energy Security: Emerging Trends and Pakistan'. *Policy Perspectives* 13, 2 (2016): 167–92.

Abraham, Itty. *The Making of the Indian Atomic Bomb: Science, Society, and the Postcolonial State*. London: Zed Books, 1998.

Achen, Christopher, and Duncan Snidal. 'The Rational Deterrence Debate: A Symposium Rational Deterrence Theory and Comparative Case Studies'. *World Politics* 41, 2 (1989): 143–69.

Afrasiabi, Kaveh. 'The Iran–Pakistan Nexus'. *Asia Times*, 13 January 2006.

'After the Quaid-i-Azam, Dr. Abdul Qadeer Khan is the Greatest Benefactor of this Nation'. *Nawai-i-Waqt* (Rawalpindi), 9 January 1990.

Ahmad, Munir. 'Scientist: Pakistan Knew of N. Korea Nuke Deal'. Associated Press, 5 July 2008, available at http://www.heraldnet.com/news/scientist-pakistan-knew-of-north-korea-nuke-deal/.

Ahmad, Shamshad. 'The Nuclear Subcontinent: Bringing Stability Back to South Asia'. *Foreign Affairs* 78, 4 (July–August 1999): 123–5.

BIBLIOGRAPHY

Ahmad, T. 'Water Disputes Between India and Pakistan: A Potential Casus Belli'. Henry Jackson Society, Project for Democratic Geopolitics, 31 July 2009, http://www.henryjacksonsociety.org/stories.asp?id=1230.

Ahmed, Khaled. 'The Death of Zia'. *Criterion Quarterly* 2, 2 (May 2007), http://www.criterion-quarterly.com/the-death-of-zia-ul-haq/.

————. 'Islamic Extremism in Pakistan'. *South Asian Journal* 1, 2 (October–December 2003): 33–44.

————. 'Second Opinion: Decline of the Army Chief in Pakistan—Khaled Ahmed's Review of the Urdu Press'. *Daily Times*, 9 June 2006.

Ahmed, Mansoor. 'Pakistan's Nuclear Odyssey: An Organizational and Bureaucratic-Politics Perspective'. In Karthika Sasikumar (ed.), *Organizational Cultures and the Management of Nuclear Technology: Political and Military Sociology—An Annual Review*, vol. 39. New Brunswick, NJ: Transaction Publishers, 2012, 61–83.

————. 'Pakistan's Nuclear Programme: Security, Politics and Technology'. Ph.D. thesis, Quaid-i-Azam University, Islamabad, 2012.

————. 'Understanding Pakistan's Plutonium Option'. *Weekly Pulse*, 3 June 2011, http://www.weeklypulse.org/ details.aspx?contentID=706&storylist=2.

Ahmed, Munir. *How We Got It! A True Story of Pakistan's Nuclear Programme*. Lahore: Shaam-Kay Baad, 1998.

Ahmed, Nazeer. 'The Atomic Energy Commission'. *Pakistan Quarterly* 7, 3 (Autumn 1957): 14–16.

Ahmed, Samina. 'Franco-Pakistan Relations-II: The Issue of the Nuclear Reprocessing Plant'. *Pakistan Horizon* 31, 1 (First Quarter, 1978): 35–70.

————. 'Pakistan's Nuclear Weapons Program: Moving Forward or Tactical Retreat'. Kroc Institute Occasional Paper no. 18:OP:2, Notre Dame, IN: Kroc Institute, February 2000.

————. 'Pakistan's Nuclear Weapons Program: Turning Points and Nuclear Choices'. *International Security* 23, 4 (Spring 1999): 178–204.

Ahmed, Samina and David Cortright (eds.). *Pakistan and the Bomb: Public Opinion and Nuclear Options*. South Bend, IN: University of Notre Dame Press, 1998.

Ahsan, Aitzaz. 'In Memoriam: Benazir Bhutto'. *Daily Times*, 29 January 2008.

Akbar, Zahid Ali. 'Bhutto's Footprints on Nuclear Pakistan'. *The News*, 4 April 2006.

————. 'Bhutto's Vision: Dr Khan's Genius'. *The Nation*, 18 September 2006.

————. 'Munir Ahmad Khan: A Splendid Contribution'. *The Nation*, 24 April 1999.

Alam, Ghulam Dastagir. 'Dr. Qadeer was Ready to Sell Nuclear Technology Secretly'. *Assas and Lashkar* (Urdu), 12 June 1998.

BIBLIOGRAPHY

Alam, Muzaffar, Françoise Nalini Delvoye, and Marc Gaborieau (eds.). *The Making of Indo-Persian Culture*. New Delhi: Manohar, 2000.

Alam, Shah. 'Iran–Pakistan Relations: Political and Strategic Dimensions'. *Strategic Analysis* 28, 4 (October–December 2004): 526–45, http://www.idsa.in/system/files/strategicanalysis_salam_1204.pdf.

Albright, David. 'The A. Q. Khan Illicit Nuclear Trade Network and Implications for Nonproliferation Efforts'. *Strategic Insights* 5, 6 (July 2006); repr. in James A. Russell and James J. Wirtz (eds.), *Globalization and WMD Proliferation: Terrorism, Translational Network and International Security*. New York: Routledge, 2008, 49–62.

———. 'International Smuggling Networks: Weapons of Mass Destruction Counterproliferation Initiatives'. Statement to the Senate Committee on Government Affairs, 23 June 23 2004, http://hsgac.senate.gov/index.cfm?Fuseaction=Hearings.Testimony&HearingID=185&WitnessID=673&suppresslayouts=true.

———. 'An Iranian Bomb'. *Bulletin of the Atomic Scientists* 51, 4 (July/August1995): 20–6.

———. 'Nuclear Black Markets: Pakistan, A. Q. Khan and the Rise of Proliferation Networks'. Testimony before the House Committee on Foreign Affairs' Subcommittee on the Middle East and South Asia and the Subcommittee on Terrorism, Nonproliferation, and Trade, 27 June 2007.

———. 'Pakistan: The Other Shoe Drops'. *Bulletin of the Atomic Scientists* 54, 4 (July–August 1998): 24–5.

———. *Peddling Peril: How the Secret Nuclear Trade Arms America's Enemies*. New York: Free Press, 2010.

———. 'North Korea's Current and Future Plutonium and Nuclear Weapon Stocks'. *ISIS Issue Brief*, 15 January 2003, http://www.isisonline.org/publications/dprk/currentandfutureweaponsstocks.html.

Albright, David and Robert Avagyan. 'Construction Progressing Rapidly on the Fourth Heavy Water Reactor at the Khushab Nuclear Site'. Institute for Science and International Security, 21 May 2012, http://isis-online.org.

Albright, David and Mark Hibbs. 'Pakistan Bomb: Out of the Closet'. *Bulletin of the Atomic Scientists* 48, 6 (July–August 1992): 38–43.

———. 'Spotlight Shifts to Iran'. *Bulletin of the Atomic Scientists* 48, 2 (March 1992): 9–11.

Albright, David and Holly Higgins. 'A Bomb for the Ummah'. *Bulletin of the Atomic Scientists* 59, 2 (March–April 2003): 49–55.

———. 'Pakistani Scientists: How Much Nuclear Assistance to Al Qaeda?' Institute for Science and International Security, 30 August 12 2002, http://www.exportcontrols.org/pakscientists.html.

Albright, David and Corey Hinderstein. 'The Centrifuge Connection'. *Bulletin of the Atomic Scientists* 60, 2 (March/April 2004): 61–6.

————. 'Iran: Countdown to Showdown'. *Bulletin of the Atomic Scientists* 60, 6 (November–December 2004): 67–72.

————. 'Libya's Gas Centrifuge Procurement: Much Remains Undiscovered'. *ISIS Issue Brief*, 1 March 2004, http://www.isisonline.org/publications/libya/cent_procure.html.

————. 'Uncovering the Nuclear Black Market: Working Toward Closing Gaps in the International Nonproliferation Regime'. Institute for Science and International Security, 2 July 2004, http://www.isis-online.org/publications/southasia/nuclear_black_market.html.

————. 'Unraveling the A. Q. Khan and Future Proliferation Networks'. *Washington Quarterly* 28, 2 (2005): 111–28.

Albright, David and Serena Kelleher-Vergantini. 'Pakistan's Fourth Reactor at Khushab Now Appears Operational'. Institute for Science and International Security, 16 January 2015, http://isis-online.org.

Ali, Javed. 'Chemical Weapons and the Iraq–Iran War: A Case Study in Noncompliance'. *The Nonproliferation Review* 8, 1 (Spring 2001): 43–58.

Ali, Rafaqat. 'Dr Khan Seeks Pardon; Cabinet Decision Today; Meets Musharraf; Admits Error of Judgment'. *Dawn*, 5 February 2004.

Allison, Graham. 'Deterring Kim Jong Il'. *Washington Post*, 27 October 2006.

————. *Essence of Decision*. New York: Scott, Foresman & Co., 1971.

————. 'Nuclear Disorder: Surveying Atomic Threats'. *Foreign Affairs* (January/February 2010): 74–85, http://belfercenter.ksg.harvard.edu/publication/19819/nuclear_disorder.html.

————. *Nuclear Terrorism: The Ultimate Preventable Catastrophe*. New York: Times Books, 2005.

Allison, Graham and Philip Zelikow. *Essence of Decision*, 2nd edn. New York: Longman, 1999.

'Ambassador William B. Milam: Interviewed by Charles Stuart Kennedy'. Association for Diplomatic Studies and Training Foreign Affairs Oral History Project, 29 January 2004, http://adst.org/wp-content/uploads/2013/12/MIlam-William-B.pdf.

Amnesty International. 'Pakistan: Open Letter to President Pervez Musharraf'. 3 February 2004, http://www.amnesty.org/ar/library/asset/ASA33/003/2004/en/tVEIgb1kvUAJ.

Ansari, Massoud. 'Nuclear Scientists from Pakistan Admit Helping Iran with Bomb-Making'. *The Telegraph*, 25 January 2004.

Arif, Khalid Mahmud. *Estranged Neighbours: India Pakistan, 1947–2010*. Islamabad: Dost Publications, 2010.

Armstrong, David. 'Khan Man'. *The New Republic*, 9 November 2004.

Armstrong, David and Joseph Trento. *America and the Islamic Bomb: The Deadly Compromise*. Hanover, NH: Steerforth Press, 2007.

Aslam, Muhammad. *Dr. A. Q. Khan and Pakistan's Nuclear Programme*. Rawalpindi: Diplomat Publications, 1989.

BIBLIOGRAPHY

Aslam Lodhi, Muhammad. 'Dr. Samar Mubarakmand'. In *Qaumi Heroes*. Lahore: Ilm-o-Irfan Publishers, 2005.

Azam, Rai Muhammad Saleh. 'When Mountains Move: The Story of Chagai'. *Defence Journal* (June 2000), http://www.defencejournal.com/2000/june/chagai.htm.

Babar, Farhatullah. 'Advocate of Nuclear Responsibility'. *The Nation*, 30 April 2006.

————. 'Apportioning Credit for the Bomb'. *The News*, 21 June 1998.

————. 'Bhutto's Footprints on Nuclear Pakistan'. *The News*, 4 April 2006.

————. 'The Nuclear Sage of Pakistan'. *The News*, 22 April 2005.

————. 'Washing Nuclear Linen in Public'. *The Muslim*, 27 September 1990.

Bakier, Abdul Hameed. 'Jihadis Discuss Plans to Seize Pakistan's Nuclear Arsenal'. *Terrorism Monitor* 7, 14 (2009): 4–5, www.jamestown.org.

Banuri, Khalid and Adil Sultan. 'Managing and Securing the Bomb'. *Daily Times*, 30 May 2008, www.dailytimes.com.pk.

Barbash, Fred. 'Iran Says It Would Transfer Nuclear Technology'. *Washington Post*, 26 April 2006, A19.

Barnaby, Frank. *The Invisible Bomb: The Nuclear Arms Race in the Middle East*. London: I. B. Tauris, 1993.

Barzashka, Ivanka and Ivan Oelrich. 'Figuring out Fordow'. *Nuclear Engineering International*, 20 May 2010, http://www.neimagazine.com/story.asp?sc=2056428.

Bazoft, Farzad. 'Iran Signs Secret Atom Deal'. *The Observer*, 12 June 1988.

Beg, Mirza Aslam. 'Indo-US Defence Pact: Challenge and Response', available at http://www.friends.org.pk/Beg/Indo%20US%20Defence%20Pact%20Challenge%20and%20Response.htm.

Beg, Mirza Aslam. 'Outside View: Nuke Proliferators can't be Stopped'. United Press International, 7 March 2005, http://www.upi.com/Outside-View-Nuke-proliferators-cant-be-stopped/65941110230694/?spt=su.

————. 'South Asian Nuclear Security Regime'. *Dawn*, 7 March 2005.

'Beg's Advice to Iran: Scare the Enemy'. *The News*, 14 May 2006.

Bell, Mark. 'Examining Explanations for Nuclear Proliferation'. *International Studies Quarterly* 60, 3 (2016): 520–9.

Bennett Jones, Owen. *Pakistan: Eye of the Storm*. New Haven: Yale University Press, 2002.

Bernstein, Jeremy. *Nuclear Weapons: What you Need to Know*. New York: Cambridge University Press, 2008.

Bhargava, G. S. 'The Bomb for Pakistan: Ambitions and Constraints'. *The Statesman*, 13 March 1982.

Bhatia, Shyam. *Nuclear Rivals in the Middle East*. London: Routledge, 1988.

Bhutto, Zulfikar Ali. *Awakening the People: Speeches of Zulfikar Ali Bhutto, 1966–*

1969, comp. Hamid Jalal and Khalid Hasan. Rawalpindi: Pakistan Publications, 1970.

————. *If I am Assassinated*. New Delhi: Vikas, 1979.

————. *The Myth of Independence*. Karachi: Oxford University Press, 1969.

'Bhutto Death Threatens Democracy, Security'. CBS, 27 December 2007, http://www.cbsnews.com/stories/2007/12/27/eveningnews/main3651630.shtml.

Bidwai, Praful and Achin Vanaik. *South Asia on a Short Fuse: Nuclear Politics and the Future of Global Disarmament*. New Delhi: Oxford University Press, 1999.

Bielefeld, Tom and Hassan Abbas. 'The Khan Job'. *Bulletin of the Atomic Scientists*, 63, 4 (July/August 2007): 72–3.

'Bin Laden Had Visited Mansoora: Qazi Hussain'. *The Nation*, 18 March 2006.

Boer, Joop et al. *A. Q. Khan, Urenco, and the Proliferation of Nuclear Weapons Technology*. New York: Greenpeace International, 2004.

Bokhari, Farhan and James Lamont. 'Obama Says Pakistan Nukes in Safe Hands'. *Financial Times*, 29 April 2009, www.ft.com.

Bokhari, Farhan et al. 'Pakistan's "Rogue Nuclear Scientist": What Did Khan's Government Know about his Deals?' *Financial Times*, 6 April 2004.

Bolton, John. 'Statement to the House Committee on International Relations Subcommittee on the Middle East and Central Asia on Iranian Proliferation'. Undersecretary of State for Arms Control and International Security. 24 June 2004, https://2001–2009.state.gov/t/us/rm/33909.htm.

Boone, Jon. 'Former Pakistan Army Chief Raheel Sharif to Lead "Muslim Nato"'. *The Guardian*, 8 January 2017, https://www.theguardian.com/world/2017/jan/08/former-pakistan-army-chief-raheel-sharif-lead-muslim-nato.

Bose, Sugata and Ayesha Jalal. *Modern South Asia: History, Culture, Political Economy*. London and New York: Routledge, 1998.

Bowen, Wyn Q. *Libya and Nuclear Proliferation: Stepping Back from the Brink*, Adelphi Papers 380. New York and Abingdon: Taylor & Francis/Routledge for the International Institute of Strategic Studies, 2006.

Branigin, William. 'Iran Set to Scrap $34 Billion Worth of Civilian Projects'. *Washington Post*, 30 May 1979.

Brannan, Paul. 'Steam Emitted From Second Khushab Reactor Cooling Towers; Pakistan May Be Operating Second Reactor'. Institute for Science and International Security Report, 24 March 2010, http://isis-online.org/isis-reports/detail/steam-emitted-from-second-khushab-reactor-cooling-towers-pakistan-may-be-op/12.

Braun, Chaim and Christopher Cyba. 'Proliferation Rings: New Challenges to the Nuclear Nonproliferation Regime'. *International Security* 29, 2 (Fall 2004): 5–49.

BIBLIOGRAPHY

Broad, William J. and David E. Sanger. 'Iran Claims Nuclear Steps in New Worry'. *New York Times*, 17 April 2006.

Broad, William, David E. Sanger, and Raymond Bonner. 'A Tale of Nuclear Proliferation: How Pakistani Built his Network'. *New York Times*, 12 February 2004.

Brodie, Bernard (ed.). *The Absolute Weapon: Atomic Power and World Order*. New York and Manchester, NH: Harcourt, Brace & Co./Ayer, 1946.

Bunn, Matthew. 'Placing Iran's Enrichment Activities in Standby'. Cambridge, MA: Project on Managing the Atom, Belfer Center for Science and International Affairs, June 2006, http://belfercenter.ksg.harvard.edu/files/bunn_2006_iran_standby.pdf.

————. 'Realist, Idealist, and Integrative Approaches to Proliferation Policy'. Unpublished paper, 2003.

Bunn, Matthew, Martin Malin, Nicholas Roth, and William Tobey. *Preventing Nuclear Terrorism: Continuous Improvement or Dangerous Decline?* Cambridge, MA: Project on Managing the Atom, Harvard Kennedy School, March 2016, Executive Summary, i–ix, 96–132, http://belfercenter.ksg.harvard.edu/files/PreventingNuclearTerrorism-Web.pdf.

Burns, John F. 'Nuclear Anxiety: The Overview; Pakistan Answering India, Carries out Nuclear Tests; Clinton's Appeal Rejected', *New York Times*, 29 May 1998.

————. 'Pakistan, Answering India, Carries out Nuclear Tests; Clinton's Appeal Rejected'. *New York Times*, 29 May 1998.

Burr, William (ed.). *China, Pakistan and the Bomb: The Declassified File on U.S. Policy, 1977–1997*. National Security Archive Electronic Briefing Book No. 114, Document No. 15, 5 March 2004, http://nsarchive.gwu.edu/NSAEBB/NSAEBB114/index.htm.

————. 'Stopping Korea from Going Nuclear'. National Security Archive, George Washington University, 22 March 2017, http://nsarchive.gwu.edu/nukevault/ebb582-The-U.S.-and-the-South-Korean-Nuclear-Program,-1974-1976,-Part-1/.

————. 'The United States and the Pakistani Bomb, 1984–1985: President Reagan, General Zia, Nazir Ahmed Vaid, and Seymour Hersh'. National Security Archive Electronic Briefing Book No. 531, 14 October 2015, National Command Authority Press Release No. PR166/2011-ISPR, 2011, http://nsarchive.gwu.edu/nukevault/ebb531-U.S.-Pakistan-Nuclear-Relations,-1984-1985/.

————. 'US–Iran Nuclear Negotiations in 1970s Featured Shah's Nationalism and US Weapons Worries'. National Security Archive, George Washington University, 13 January 2009, http://nsarchive.gwu.edu/nukevault/ebb268/.

Bush, George W. 'President Announces New Measures to Counter the Threat of WMD'. 11 February 2004, https://2001–2009.state.gov/t/isn/rls/rm/29290.htm.

Lord Butler. *Review of Intelligence on Weapons of Mass Destruction*, Report of a Committee of Privy Counselors. London: The Stationery Office, 2004, https://www.loc.gov/item/2005363339/.

Butler, Kenley, Sammy Salama, and Leonard S. Spector. 'Where is the Justice?' *Bulletin of Atomic Scientists* 62, 6 (November/December 2006): 25–34.

Butt, Tariq. 'Iran, Libya Role Disappoints Islamabad'. *The News*, 7 February 2004.

Buzan, Barry. *People, States, and Fear: The National Security Problem in International Relations*, 2nd edn. Boulder: Lynne Rienner, 1991.

Carranza, Mario Esteban. *India–Pakistan Nuclear Diplomacy: Constructivism and the Prospects for Nuclear Arms Control and Disarmament in South Asia*. Lanham, MD: Rowman & Littlefield, 2016.

Central Intelligence Agency. 'Bhutto Seeks Nuclear Policy Assurances'. *National Intelligence Daily*, 24 May 1974, https://www.cia.gov/library/readingroom/docs/DOC_0000845825.pdf.

————. 'Pakistan Nuclear Weapons Programme: Personnel and Organizations'. Research Paper, Directorate of Intelligence, 1 November 1985, http://nsarchive.gwu.edu/nukevault/ebb423/docs/8.%20pakistan%201985.pdf.

————. 'Pakistan Nuclear Study'. CIA Electronic Reading Room, 26 April 1978, https://www.cia.gov/library/readingroom/docs/DOC_0000252641.pdf.

————. 'Pakistan: A Safeguards Exemption as a Backdoor to Reprocessing'. 20 May 1983, https://www.cia.gov/library/readingroom/docs/DOC_0000252643.pdf.

————. 'Pakistan: Nuclear Decision Makers—Unanimous Opinion'. Research paper, January 1999 (declassified September), https://www.cia.gov/library/readingroom/docs/DOC_0000252645.pdf.

————. 'PAKISTAN/USSR: The Soviet Campaign against Pakistan's Nuclear Program'. Declassified 7 August 1987, https://www.cia.gov/library/readingroom/docs/CIA-RDP90T00114R000700470001–0.pdf.

————. 'The President's Daily Brief 10 December 1965'. http://www.foia.cia.gov/sites/default/files/document_conversions/1827265/DOC_0005968042.pdf.

————. '"Significant" Chinese Aid on Nuclear Design'. 4 June 1982, https://www.documentcloud.org/documents/347024-doc-11-6-4-82.html.

————. Unclassified Report to Congress on the Acquisition of Technology Relating to Weapons of Mass Destruction and Advanced Conventional

Munitions, July 1 through December 31, 2001, http://www.cia.gov/cia/publications/bian/bian_jan_2003.htm#5.

———. 'US–Pakistan: Implications of an Aid Cutoff'. 15 July 1985 (declassified 30 October 2009), https://www.cia.gov/library/readingroom/docs/CIA-RDP85T01058R000506640001–5.pdf.

Chakma, Bhumitra. 'Road to Chagai: Pakistan's Nuclear Programme, Its Sources and Motivations'. *Modern Asian Studies* 36, 4 (2002): 871–912.

Charbonneau, Louis. 'Pakistan Offers Global Nuclear Fuel Services Again'. Reuters, 13 April 2010, http://www.reuters.com/article/idUSN1324 3044.

Chari, P. 'Declaratory Statements and Confidence Building Measures in South Asia'. In Michael Krepon, Jenny S. Drezin, and Michael Newbill (eds.), *Declaratory Diplomacy: Rhetorical Initiatives and Confidence Building*, 89–134. Henry L. Stimson Center, Report No. 27, April 1999, https://www.stimson.org/sites/default/files/file-attachments/declaratory-diplomacy-rhetorical-initiatives-confidence-building.pdf.

Chaudhri, M. A. 'Pakistan's Nuclear History: Separating Myth from Reality'. *Defence Journal* 9, 10 (2006): 14–50.

———. 'The Unsung Nuclear Hero'. *The Nation*, 22 April 2006.

———. *Emergence of Pakistan*. New York: Columbia University Press, 1967.

Chaudhry, Imran Husain. *Mohsin-e-Pakistan Dr. Abdul Qadeer Khan: Islami bomb kay Khaliq aur Ghaui Mizzile kay Mojid Ki Walwala Khez Dastaan-e-Hayat*. Lahore: Ilm-o-Irfan Publishers, 2003.

Chaudhry, Shahid Nazir. *Dr Abdul Qadeer Khan Aur Aitami Pakistan*. Lahore: Data Publications, 2004.

Cheema, Pervaiz Iqbal and Imtiaz H. Bokhari (eds.). *Arms Race and Nuclear Developments in South Asia*. Islamabad: Islamabad Policy Research Institute, 2004.

Cheema, Zafar Iqbal. *The Domestic Governance of Nuclear Weapons: The Case of Pakistan*. Case Report. Geneva: Geneva Centre for the Democratic Control of Armed Forces (DCAF), February 2008.

Chengappa, Bidanda M. 'The ISI Role in Pakistan's Politics'. *Strategic Analysis* (New Dehli) 23, 11 (2000): 1857–78.

Chengappa, Raj. *Weapons of Peace*. Delhi: HarperCollins, 2000.

Cirincione, Joseph. *Bomb Scare: The History and Future of Nuclear Weapons*. New York: Columbia University Press, 2007.

Cirincione, Joseph, with Jon B. Wolfsthal and Miriam Rajkumar. *Deadly Arsenals: Tracking Weapons of Mass Destruction*. Washington, DC: Carnegie Endowment for International Peace, 2002.

Clarity, James F. 'Iran Negotiates for Nuclear Energy Aid'. *New York Times*, 27 May 1974.

Clary, Christopher Oren. 'The A. Q. Khan Network: Causes and Implica-

BIBLIOGRAPHY

tions'. Master's thesis, Naval Postgraduate School, Monterey, December 2005, http://www.fas.org/irp/eprint/clary.pdf.

———. 'Command and Control Trends and Choices for the Next Decade in South Asia'. In Feroz Hassan Khan, Ryan Jacobs, and Emily Burke (eds.), *Nuclear Learning in South Asia: The Next Decade* (Monterey, CA: Naval Postgraduate School, June 2014), 95–101, https://my.nps.edu/documents/104111744/106151936/Nuclear+Learning+in+South+Asia_June2014.pdf/db169d3c-6c10-4289-b65d-a348ffc9480f.

———. 'Dr. Khan's Nuclear Walmart'. *Disarmament Diplomacy* 76 (March–April 2004): 31–6.

Cloughley, Brian. *A History of the Pakistan Army: Wars and Insurrections*. New York: Oxford University Press, 1999.

Cohen, Stephen P. *The Idea of Pakistan*. Washington, DC: Brookings Institution, 2004.

———. *India: Emerging Power*. Washington, DC: Brookings Institution, 2001.

———. 'The Jihadist Threat to Pakistan'. *Washington Quarterly* 26, 3 (Summer 2003): 7–25.

———. 'Nuclear Weapons and Conflict in South Asia'. Brookings Institution, 23 November 1998, https://www.brookings.edu/articles/nuclear-weapons-and-conflict-in-south-asia/.

———. *The Pakistan Army: 1998 Edition with a new Foreword and Epilogue*. Karachi: Oxford University Press, 1998.

Cohen, Stephen P., P. R. Chari, and Pervaiz Iqbal Cheema. *The Compound Crisis of 1990: Perception, Politics and Insecurity*. Champaign: University of Illinois at Urbana-Champaign, 2000.

Coll, Steve. *Ghost Wars: The Secret History of the CIA, Afghanistan, and Bin Laden, from the Soviet Invasion to September 10, 2001*. New York: Penguin, 2004.

Colley, Jan. 'Libel Damages for Engineer'. Press Association, 3 May 2005.

Collins, Catherine and Douglas Frantz. *Fallout: The True Story of the CIA's Secret War on Nuclear Trafficking*. New York: Free Press, 2011.

Commission on the Intelligence Capabilities of the United States Regarding Weapons of Mass Destruction. *Report to the President of the United States*. Washington, DC: GPO, 2005.

Cooley, John K. 'More Fingers on Nuclear Trigger?' *Christian Science Monitor*, 25 June 1974.

Cordesman, Anthony H. *Lessons of Modern War: The Iran Iraq War*. London: Mansell Publishing, 1990.

———. 'Weapons of Mass Destruction in the Middle East'. Center for Strategic and International Studies report, 1 January 2000, https://www.csis.org/analysis/weapons-mass-destruction-middle-east-0.

Cordesman, Anthony H. and Khalid R. Al-Rodhan. *Iranian Nuclear Weapons? The Uncertain Nature of Iran's Nuclear Programs*. Washington, DC: Center for Strategic and International Studies, 2006.

BIBLIOGRAPHY

Corera, Gordon. *Shopping for Bombs: Nuclear Proliferation, Global Insecurity, and the Rise and Fall of the A. Q. Khan Network*. Oxford: Oxford University Press, 2006.

Cowasjee, Ardesher. 'We Never Learn from History'. *Dawn*, 21 July 2002.

Crile, George. *Charlie Wilson's War: The Extraordinary Story of the Largest Covert Operation in History*. New York: Atlantic Monthly Press, 2003.

Cronin, Richard P., Alan Kronstadt, and Sharon Squassoni. 'Pakistan's Nuclear Proliferation Activities and the Recommendations of the 9/11 Commission: US Policy Constraints and Options'. Congressional Research Service Report RL32745, 25 January 2005, https://fas.org/sgp/crs/nuke/RL32745.pdf.

Dahlkamp, Jürgen, Georg Mascolo, and Holger Stark. 'Network of Death on Trial'. *Der Spiegel*, 13 March 2006.

Dalton, Toby and Michael Krepon. 'A Normal Nuclear Pakistan'. Stimson and Carnegie Endowment for International Peace, 2015, https://www.stimson.org/content/normal-nuclear-pakistan-0.

Daragahi, Borzou. '1987 Chemical Strike Still Haunts Iran'. *Los Angeles Times*, 19 March 2007.

Daskavi, Shahid Javed. 'If Nuclear Program Were under Supervision of Political Governments, God Knows What Would Have Happened: Samar Mubarakmand'. *Jehan Pakistan*, 5 February 2016.

Davis, Zachary S. 'The Realist Nuclear Regime'. *Security Studies* 2, 3–4 (1993): 79–99.

Davis, Zachary S., and Benjamin Frankel (eds.). *The Proliferation Puzzle: Why Nuclear Weapons Spread (and What Results)*. London: Frank Cass, 1993.

de Mesquita, Bruce, and William H. Riker. 'An Assessment of the Merits of Selective Nuclear Proliferation'. *Journal of Conflict Resolution*, 26, 2 (June 1982): 283–306.

Ditmer, Lowell. 'South Asia's Security Dilemma'. *Asian Survey* 41, 6 (November–December 2001): 897–906.

'Documents: Government of Pakistan Statements and Interviews'. *Pakistan Horizon* 27, 2 (1974): 115–64.

Done, Kevin. 'German Group Nears Deal in Iranian Power Station Dispute'. *Financial Times*, 31 March 1982.

Dorsey, James M. 'Saudi–Iran Rivalry Fuels Potential Nuclear Race', 5 April 2017, available at http://mideastsoccer.blogspot.com/2017/04/saudi-iranian-rivalry-fuels-potential.html.

Dougherty, James E. 'Proliferation in Asia'. *Orbis* (Fall 1975): 925–57.

'Dr Khan Says He Confessed to Save Pakistan'. *Dawn*, 8 April 2008.

Dunn, Lewis. 'Can Al Qaeda Be Deterred from Using Nuclear Weapons?' Center for the Study of Weapons of Mass Destruction, Occasional Paper no. 3. Washington, DC: National Defense University Press, 2005.

BIBLIOGRAPHY

Dupree, L. 'A Suggested Pakistan–Afghanistan–Iran Federation'. *Middle East Journal* 17 (1963): 383–99.

Dutch Ministry of Foreign Affairs. *Report of the Inter-Ministerial Working Party Responsible for Investigating the 'Khan Affair'*. The Hague: Dutch Foreign Ministry, October 1979.

Editorial Board. 'Can Israel and the Arab States be Friends?' *New York Times*, 27 August 2016, https://www.nytimes.com/2016/08/28/opinion/sunday/can-israel-and-the-arab-states-be-friends.html?_r=0.

'An Engaging Dictator Who Wants to Stay that Way'. *The Economist*, 12 December 1981, 48.

Epstein, William. 'Why States Go—and Don't Go—Nuclear'. *Annals of the American Academy of Political and Social Science* 430 (March 1977): 16–28.

'Ex-ISI Chief Reveals Secret Missile Shipments to Bosnia Defying UN Embargo'. *South Asia Tribune* 22, 23–29 December 2002.

Fair, Christine. 'Pakistan's Nuclear Program: Laying the Groundwork for Impunity'. 21 November 2016, SSRN, https://ssrn.com/abstract=2946 051.

Farnsworth, Clyde H. 'France Gives Iran Stake in Uranium'. *New York Times*, 4 January 1975.

Faruqui, Ahmad. *Rethinking the National Security of Pakistan: The Price of Strategic Myopia*. Farnham: Ashgate, 2003.

Feaver, Peter Douglas. *Guarding the Guardians: Civilian Control of Nuclear Weapons in the United States*. Ithaca: Cornell University Press, 1993.

'The First 10 General Elections of Pakistan'. PILDAT, May 2013, http://www.pildat.org/publications/publication/elections/First10General ElectionsofPakistan.pdf.

Fitzpatrick, Mark. *Nuclear Black Markets: Pakistan, A.Q. Khan and the Rise of Proliferation Networks*. IISS Strategic Dossier, 2007.

Foradori, Paolo and Martin B. Malin (eds.). *A WMD Free Zone in the Middle East: Regional Perspectives*. Cambridge, MA: Project on Managing the Atom, Harvard University, November 2013, http://belfercenter.ksg.harvard.edu/files/dp_2013–09.pdf.

Frankel, Benjamin. 'The Brooding Shadow: Systemic Incentives and Nuclear Weapons Proliferation'. In Zachary S. Davis and Benjamin Frankel (eds.), *The Proliferation Puzzle: Why Nuclear Weapons Spread and What Results*. London: Frank Cass, 1993, 37–78.

Frantz, Douglas. 'From Patriot to Proliferator'. *Los Angeles Times*, 23 September 2005.

Frantz, Douglas and Catherine Collins. *The Nuclear Jihadist: The True Story of the Man who Sold the World's Most Dangerous Secrets—And How we Could Have Stopped him*. New York: Twelve, 2007.

———. 'A Tale of Two Bhuttos'. *Foreign Policy*, November 2007.

BIBLIOGRAPHY

Fuhrman, Matthew. *Atomic Assistance: The Causes and Consequences of Peaceful Nuclear Cooperation*. New York: Cornell University Press, 2012.

—————. 'Spreading Temptation: Proliferation and Peaceful Nuclear Cooperation Agreements'. *International Security* 34, 1 (Summer 2009): 7–41.

'Full Text of Iran–India Joint Communiqué'. *Iran Almanac*, Tehran: The Echo of Iran, 1974, 176–7.

Ganguly, Sumit. 'India's Pathway to Pokhran II: The Prospects and Sources of New Delhi's Nuclear Weapons Program'. *International Security* 23, 4 (Spring 1999): 148–77.

Ganguly, Sumit and Devin T. Hagerty. *Fearful Symmetry: India–Pakistan Crisis in the Shadows of Nuclear Weapons*. Seattle: University of Washington Press, 2005.

Gannon, Kathy. 'Explosive Secrets from Pakistan'. *Los Angeles Times*, 30 January 2004.

—————. 'Iran Sought Advice in Pakistan on Attack'. *Washington Post*, 12 May 2006.

Gardels, Nathan. 'Musharraf Knew about A. Q. Khan's "Private" Proliferation'. *New Perspectives Quarterly* 21, 2 (Spring 2004): 39–43, http://www.digitalnpq.org/archive/2004_spring/bhutto.html.

Gauhar, Altaf. *Ayub Khan: Pakistan's First Military Ruler*. New York: Oxford University Press, 1996.

Gehriger, Urs. 'Interview with Abdul Qadeer Khan'. *Die Weltwoche*, 21 January 2009.

Gelb, Leslie H. 'US Nuclear Deal with Iran Delayed'. *New York Times*, 8 March 1975.

Gellner, Ernest. *Nations and Nationalism*. Ithaca: Cornell University Press, 1983.

'Gen. Asif Nawaz of Pakistan, 56, a Champion of Democracy, Dies'. *New York Times*, 9 January 1993.

Gharehbaghian, Morteza. 'Oil Revenue and the Militarisation of Iran: 1960–1978'. *Social Scientist* 15, 4/5 (April–May 1987): 87–100.

Ghori, Karamatullah K. 'Did Libya Stab Pakistan in the Back?' *Chowk*, 21 February 2004.

Gilbert, Paul. *The Philosophy of Nationalism*. Boulder, CO: Westview Press, 1998.

Gishkori, Zahid. 'A. Q. Khan Set to Launch Own Political Party'. *Express Tribune*, 27 August 2012.

Goldschmidt, Pierre. 'Statement to the Board of Governors'. 1 March 2005, http://www.iaea.org/NewsCenter/Statements/DDGs/2005/goldschmidt01032005.html.

Goswami, Namrata. 'The Essence of the South Asian Nuclear Debate'. *Strategic Analysis* 30, 3 (July–September 2006): 662–74.

Hagerty, D. T. *The Consequences of Nuclear Proliferation: Lessons from South Asia*. Cambridge, MA: MIT Press, 1998.

Haqqani, Husain. *Pakistan: Between Mosque and Military*. Washington, DC: Carnegie Endowment for International Peace, 2005.

Harrison, Selig S. 'What A. Q. Khan Knows: How Pakistan's Proliferator Could Help in Pyongyang'. *Washington Post*, 31 January 2008.

Hasan, Khalid. '*Washington Post* Names Dr Khan and Farooq as Those Who Sold N-Technology'. *Daily Times*, 29 January 2004.

Hasnain, S. A. 'Dr. I. H. Usmani and the Early Days of the PAEC'. *The Nucleus* 42, 1–2 (2005): 13–20.

Hauss, Charles. 'Nationalism'. Beyond Intractability, University of Colorado, Conflict Research Consortium, September 2003, http://www.beyondin-tractability.org/essay/nationalism.

Hearst, David. 'EXCLUSIVE: Pakistan Sends Combat Troops to Southern Saudi Border'. *Middle East Eye*, 17 March 2017, http://www.middleeast-eye.net/news/exclusive-pakistan-sends-combat-troops-saudi-southern-border-248886071.

Hechter, Michael. *Containing Nationalism*. Oxford and New York: Oxford University Press, 2000.

Hersh, Seymour. 'The Deal: Why is Washington Going Easy on Pakistan's Nuclear Black Marketers?' *New Yorker*, 8 March 2004, http://www.newy-orker.com/fact/content/?040308fa_fact.

———. 'On the Nuclear Edge'. *New Yorker*, 29 March 1993.

Herz, John H. *International Politics in the Atomic Age*. New York: Columbia University Press, 1959.

Hibbs, Mark. 'Agencies Trace Some Iraqi Urenco Know-How to Pakistan Re-Export'. *Nucleonics Week*, 28 November 1991.

———. 'Bushehr Construction Now Remote after Three Iraqi Air Strikes'. *Nucleonics Week*, 26 November 1987, 5–6.

———. 'Hot Laboratories'. *Der Spiegel*, 27 February 1989.

———. 'Pakistan Deal Signals China's Growing Nuclear Assertiveness'. Nuclear Energy Brief, 27 April 2010. Carnegie Endowment for International Peace, http://carnegieendowment.org/2010/04/27/pakistan-deal-signals-china-s-growing-nuclear-assertiveness-pub-40685.

———. 'Pakistan Developed More Powerful Centrifuges'. *Nuclear Fuel* 1 (29 January 2007): 15–16.

———. 'Pakistan Told the Netherlands it had Italian Centrifuge Design'. *Nucleonics Week*, 22 September 2005.

———. 'Zia Orders Pakistan AEC to Design Indigenous Nuclear Reactor'. *Nucleonics Week*, 13 November 1986.

Hibbs, Mark and Neel Patri. 'US to Ask New Delhi to Back Off on Research Reactor Offer to Iran'. *Nucleonics Week*, 21 November 1991.

BIBLIOGRAPHY

'History of PAEC'. Pakistan Atomic Energy Commission, 13 December 2011, www.paec.gov.pk/paec-hist.htm [link no longer available].

Hobsbawm, Eric J. *Nations and Nationalism Since 1780: Programme, Myth, Reality*, 2nd edn. Cambridge: Cambridge University Press, 1992.

Hoodbhoy, Pervez. 'The Bomb: Iran, Saudi Arabia and Pakistan'. *Express Tribune*, 22 January 2012.

———. 'The Flight to Nowhere: Pakistan's Nuclear Trajectory', Heinrich-Böll-Stiftung, November 2009, http://in.boell.org/sites/default/files/downloads/The_Flight_To_Nowhere_by_Pervez_Hoodbhoy_GE.pdf.

———. 'For God and Profit'. *Newsline*, February 2004, http://newslinemagazine.com/magazine/for-god-and-profit/.

———. 'The Man Who Designed Pakistan's Bomb'. *Newsweek*, Pakistan, 30 November 2013, http://newsweekpakistan.com/the-man-who-designed-pakistans-bomb/.

———. 'The Nuclear Noose around Pakistan's Neck'. *Washington Post*, 1 February 2004.

———. 'Pakistan: Inside the Nuclear Closet'. Opendemocracy.com, 3 March 2004, http://www.opendemocracy.net/conflict-iraqwarafter/article_1767.jsp.

———. 'Pakistan's Nuclear Future'. In Samina Ahmed and David Cortright (eds.), *Pakistan and the Bomb: Public Opinion and Nuclear Options*. South Bend, IN: University of Notre Dame Press, 1998, 70–4.

Huntington, Samuel P. 'The Clash of Civilizations?' *Foreign Affairs* 72, 3 (1993): 22–49.

———. *The Clash of Civilizations and the Remaking of World Order*. New York: Simon & Schuster, 1998 [1996].

———. 'Try Again: A Reply to Russett, Oneal & Cox'. *Journal of Peace Research* 37, 5 (2000): 609–10.

Hussain, Mushahid. 'Media off Target with Pakistan Nuclear Scare'. *Asia Times*, 7 November 2001, http://www.atimes.com/ind-pak/CK07Df01.html.

———. 'Pakistan–Iran Relations in the Changing World Scenario: Challenges and Response'. In Tarik Jan et al. (eds.), *Foreign Policy Debate: The Years Ahead*. Islamabad: Institute of Policy Studies, 1993, 211–22.

Hussain, Mushahid and Akmal Hussain. *Pakistan: Problems of Governance*. Lahore: Vanguard Books, 1986.

Hussain, S. R. 'Analyzing Strategic Stability in South Asia with Pathways and Prescriptions for Avoiding Nuclear War'. *Contemporary South Asia* 14, 2 (2005): 141–53.

Hussain, S. Shabbir and Mujahid Kamran (eds.). *Dr. A. Q. Khan on Science and Education*. Lahore: Sang-e-Meel, 1997.

Hussain, Tom. 'Pakistani Nuclear Scientist Khan Accused of Graft'. *The National*, 9 July 2011.

BIBLIOGRAPHY

Hussain, Zahid. *Frontline Pakistan: The Struggle with Militant Islam*. New York: Oxford University Press, 2007.

————. 'Nuked!' *Newsline*, January 2004, http://newslinemagazine.com/magazine/nuked/.

————. 'Pakistan Targets Nuclear Scientists for Selling Nuclear Secrets'. *Wall Street Journal*, 26 January 2004.

————. 'There is a Conspiracy against me by the Jewish Lobby: General Aslam Beg'. *Newsline*, Karachi, February 2004, http://www.newsline.com.pk/Newsfeb2004/cover3feb2004.htm.

Hymans, Jacques E. C. *The Psychology of Nuclear Proliferation: Identity, Emotions and Foreign Policy*. Cambridge: Cambridge University Press, 2006.

Iklé, Fred Charles. 'Nth Countries and Disarmament'. *Bulletin of the Atomic Scientists* 16, 10 (December 1960): 391–4.

Ikramullah. 'Shrinking Stature of Parliament and Prime Minister'. *The Nation*, 8 August 1991.

'In Memoriam: Munir Ahmad Khan'. *International Atomic Energy Agency Bulletin* 41, 2 (1999): 46, http://www.iaea.org/Publications/Magazines/Bulletin/Bull412/article11.pdf.

'In Musharraf's Words: "A Day of Reckoning"'. *New York Times*, 12 January 2002, http://www.nytimes.com/2002/01/12/international/in-musharrafs-words-a-day-of-reckoning.html.

'India's Embarrassing North Korea Connection'. al-Jazeera, 21 June 2016, http://www.aljazeera.com/indepth/features/2016/06/india-embarrassing-north-korean-connection-160620195559208.html.

'India and Pakistan Nuclear Tests'. *Disarmament Diplomacy* 26 (May 1998): 2–21.

International Atomic Energy Agency. 'Communication of October 17, 2011 from the Permanent Mission of Pakistan to the Agency Concerning the Export Control Policies of the Government of Pakistan and a Statutory Regulatory Order'. INFCIRC/832. 30 November 2011, www.iaea.org.

————. 'Implementation of the NPT Safeguards Agreement in the Islamic Republic of Iran'. Report by the director-general to the Board of Governors, GOV/2003/75, 10 November 2003.

————. 'Implementation of the NPT Safeguards Agreement in the Islamic Republic of Iran'. Report by the director-general to the Board of Governors, GOV/2004/83, 29 November 2004.

————. 'Implementation of the NPT Safeguards Agreement in the Islamic Republic of Iran'. Report by the director-general to the Board of Governors, GOV/2005/67, 2 September 2005.

————. 'Implementation of the NPT Safeguards Agreement in the Islamic Republic of Iran'. Report by the director-general to the Board of Governors, GOV/2006/15, 27 February 2006.

————. 'Implementation of the NPT Safeguards Agreement of the Socialist People's Libyan Arab Jamahiriya'. Report by the director-general to the Board of Governors, GOV/2004/12. 20 February 2004.

————. 'Implementation of the NPT Safeguards Agreement of the Socialist People's Libyan Arab Jamahiriya'. Report by the director-general to the Board of Governors, GOV/2004/33, 28 May 2004.

International Panel on Fissile Materials. 'Country Perspectives on the Challenges to Nuclear Disarmament'. 2010, http://fissilematerials.org/library/2010/05/country_perspectives_on_the_c.html.

————. 'Global Fissile Material Report 2014'. http://fissilematerials.org.

————. 'Global Fissile Material Report 2015'. http://fissilematerials.org/library/gfmr15.pdf.

'Interview with Abdul Qadeer Khan'. *The News*, 30 May 1998, available at http://nuclearweaponarchive.org/Pakistan/KhanInterview.html.

'An Interview with Gaddafi'. *Time*, 8 June 1981, http://content.time.com/time/magazine/article/0,9171,922551-1,00.html.

'Iran Profile: Nuclear Chronology 1957–1979'. NTI, http://www.nti.org/media/pdfs/iran_nuclear.pdf?_=1316542527.

'Iran's Nuclear Capabilities: Fast Facts'. CNN Library, updated 27 March 2017, http://www.cnn.com/2013/11/07/world/meast/irans-nuclear-capabilities-fast-facts/.

Irfani, Suroosh. 'Pakistan's Sectarian Violence: Between the "Arabist Shift" and the Indo-Persian Culture'. In Satu P. Limaye, Mohan Malik, and Robert Wirsing (eds.), *Religious Radicalism and Security in South Asia*. Honolulu: Asia-Pacific Center for Security Studies, 2004, 147–71.

————. *Revolutionary Islam in Iran: Popular Liberation or Religious Dictatorship?* London: Zed Books, 1983.

Islam, Nurul. 'Regional Co-operation for Development: Pakistan, Iran and Turkey'. *Journal of Common Market Studies* 5, 3 (March 1967): 283–301.

Jah, Syed Asif. *Muhsin-i-Pakistan Dr. Abdul Qadeer Khan*, 3rd edn. Multan: Sohni Dharti Publishers, 2000.

Jalal, Ayesha. *The Sole Spokesman: Jinnah, the Muslim League and the Demand for Pakistan*. Cambridge: Cambridge University Press, 1994.

Jeffrey, R. 'US Complains to China about Libyan Arms Shipment'. *Washington Post*, 28 April 1992.

Jentleson, Bruce W. and Christopher A. Whytock. 'Who Won Libya? The Force–Diplomacy Debate and its Implications for Theory and Policy'. *International Security* 30, 3 (Winter 2006): 47–86.

Jervis, Robert. *The Meaning of the Nuclear Revolution: Statecraft and the Prospect for Armageddon*. Ithaca: Cornell University Press, 1989.

————. 'Rational Deterrence: Theory and Evidence'. *World Politics* 41, 2 (January 1989): 183–207.

BIBLIOGRAPHY

Jha, Prem Shankar. *Kashmir 1947: Rival Versions of History*. Dehli: Oxford University Press, 1996.

Joshi, Shashank. 'Pakistan's Tactical Nuclear Nightmare: Déjà Vu?' *Washington Quarterly* 36, 3 (Summer 2013): 159–172, http://csis.org/files/publication/TWQ_13Summer_Joshi.pdf.

Kampani, Guarav. 'Proliferation Unbound: Nuclear Tales from Pakistan'. Monterey, CA: Center for Nonproliferation Studies, Monterey Institute of International Studies, 23 February 2004, http://cns.miis.edu/pubs/week/040223.htm.

———. 'Second Tier Proliferation: The Case of Pakistan and North Korea'. *Nonproliferation Review* 9, 3 (Fall–Winter 2002): 107–16.

Kamran, Mohammad. 'MMA Vows to Wage Jihad for Kashmir and N-Defence'. *Daily Times*, 6 February 2004.

Kapur, Ashok. *Pakistan's Nuclear Development*. New York: Croom Helm, 1987.

Kapur, S. Paul. 'India and Pakistan's Unstable Peace: Why Nuclear South Asia is Not Like Cold War Europe'. *International Security* 30, 2 (Fall 2005): 127–52.

Katz, Lee Michael. 'Nuclear Threat Different, Not Gone, Panel Warned'. *USA Today*, 23 January 1992.

Kelley, Jack. 'Russian Nuke Experts Wooed'. *USA Today*, 8 January 1992.

Kelley, Matt. 'Pakistan Threatened to Give Nukes to Iran'. *Washington Post*, 27 February 2004.

Kerr, Paul K. and Mary Beth Nikitin. 'Pakistan's Nuclear Weapons'. Congressional Research Service, Report RL34248, 1 August 2016, 6, https://fas.org/sgp/crs/nuke/RL34248.pdf.

Kerry, John and Hank Brown. *The BCCI Affair: A Report to the Committee on Foreign Relations* United States Senate (December 1992), http://www.fas.org/irp/congress/1992_rpt/bcci/05foreign.htm.

Khan, Abdul Qadeer. 'An Analysis of Propaganda against Pakistan's Peaceful Nuclear Programme'. *The Muslim* (Islamabad), 16 March 1984.

———. *Dr. A.Q. Khan on Pakistan Bomb*, ed. Sreedhar. New Delhi; ABC Publishing House, 1987.

———. 'Bhutto, GIK and Kahuta'. *The News*, 29 July 2009.

———. 'Capabilities and Potentials of the Kahuta Project'. *The Frontier Post*, 10 September 1990.

———. 'An Indomitable Man'. *The News*, 2 February 2015, https://www.thenews.com.pk/print/21756-an-indomitable-man.

———. 'Unsung Heroes'. *The News*, 12 January 2015, https://www.thenews.com.pk/print/17884-unsung-heroes.

Khan, Feroz Hassan. 'Comparative Strategic Culture: The Case of Pakistan'. *Strategic Insights* 4, 10 (October 2005), available at http://calhoun.nps.edu/bitstream/handle/10945/11241/khan2Oct05.pdf?sequence=1.

BIBLIOGRAPHY

————. *Eating Grass: The Making of the Pakistani Bomb*. Stanford: Stanford University Press, 2012.

————. 'Nuclear Proliferation Motivations: Lessons from Pakistan'. *Nonproliferation Review* 13, 3 (November 2006): 501–17.

————. 'Political Transitions and Nuclear Management in Pakistan'. http://www.npolicy.org/books/Security_Crises/Ch5_Khan.pdf.

Khan, Haris N. 'Pakistan's Nuclear Program: Setting the Record Straight'. *Defence Journal* 14, 1 (2010): 27–40.

Khan, Kamran. 'Business in Timbuktu: Conflict Views about Army's Awareness of Qadeer's Engagements'. *The News*, 1 February 2004.

————. 'Dr Qadeer's Fate Hangs in the Balance'. *The News*, 24 January 2004.

————. 'Foreign Accounts Having Proceeds from N-Technology Transfer Found'. *The News*, 25 January 2004.

Khan, Mohammad Ilyas. 'Why Pakistan is Opening Up over Its Nuclear Programme'. BBC, 21 October 2015, http://www.bbc.com/news/world-asia-34588009.

Khan, Munir Ahmed. 'Bhutto and the Nuclear Program of Pakistan'. *The Muslim* (Islamabad), 4 March 1995.

————. 'Development and Significance of Pakistan's Nuclear Capability'. In Hafeez Malik (ed.), *Pakistan: Founders' Aspirations and Today's Realities*. Karachi: Oxford University Press, 2001 (chapter 4).

————. 'How Pakistan Made Nuclear Fuel'. *The Nation* (Islamabad), 7 February 1998.

————. 'No Loose Nuclear Talk'. *The News* (Islamabad), 14 June 1994.

————. 'Nuclearisation of South Asia and Its Regional and Global Implications'. *Focus on Regional Issues* 16, 4 (Islamabad: Institute of Regional Studies, 1998): 11–43.

————. 'Significance of Chashma Plant'. *Dawn*, 8 August 1993.

————. Speech presented at the Chagai Medal Award Ceremony, Pakistan Nuclear Society, PINSTECH Auditorium, Islamabad, 20 March 1999, http://www.nuclearfiles.org/menu/key-issues/nuclear-weapons/issues/policy/pakistani-nuclear-policy/munir%20ahmad%20khan%27s%20speech.html.

Khan, Zafar. *Pakistan's Nuclear Policy: A Minimum Credible Deterrence*. Abingdon: Routledge, 2015, available at http://public.eblib.com/choice/publicfullrecord.aspx?p=1744191.

Khokhar, K. 'De-militarising the Siachen Glacier'. *The News*, 26 April 2012.

Kibaroglu, Mustafa. 'Iran's Nuclear Ambitions from a Historical Perspective and the Attitude of the West'. *Middle Eastern Studies* 43, 2 (March 2007), 223–45, available at http://mustafakibaroglu.com/sitebuildercontent/sitebuilderfiles/Kibaroglu-MES-March2007-IranNuclear.pdf.

Kinzer, Stephen. *All the Shah's Men: An American Coup and the Roots of Middle East Terror*. New York: John Wiley & Sons, 2003.

Klasra, Rauf. 'A. Q. Khan's Family Threatens Direct Action'. *The News*, 12 March 2008.

———. 'Nuclear Scientist Blasts HEC's Outgoing Chairman'. *The News*, 17 October 2008.

Koch, Andrew. 'Pakistan Persists with Nuclear Procurement'. *Jane's Intelligence Review* 9, 3 (March 1997): 131–4.

Koch, Egmont. *Der Physikar der Mullahs*, https://www.youtube.com/watch?v=G0uTiRSuKcQ [film].

Krepon, Michael. 'A. Q. Khan and Samar Mubarakmand'. Arms Control Wonk, 2 July 2009, http://www.armscontrolwonk.com/archive/402371/aq-khan-and-samar-mubarakmand/.

———. 'Nuclear Optimism'. Arms Control Wonk, 17 August 2010, http://krepon.armscontrolwonk.com/archive/2836/nuclear-optimism.

Kristensen, Hans M. and Robert S. Norris. 'Pakistan's Nuclear Forces, 2011'. *Bulletin of the Atomic Scientists* 67, 4 (2011): 91–9, available at http://journals.sagepub.com/doi/abs/10.1177/0096340211413360.

———. 'Pakistani Nuclear Forces, 2016', *Bulletin of the Atomic Scientists* 72, 6 (2016): 368–76.

Kroenig, Matthew. 'The History of Proliferation Optimism: Does it Have a Future?' *Journal of Strategic Studies* 38, 1–2 (January 2015): 98–125.

Kronstadt, K. Alan. 'Pakistan's Scheduled 2008 Election: Background'. Congressional Research Service Report RL34335, 24 January 2008, https://fas.org/sgp/crs/row/RL34335.pdf.

Kux, Dennis. 'The Pakistani Pivot'. *National Interest* 65 (2001): 49–65.

———. *The United States and Pakistan, 1947–2000: Disenchanted Allies*. Washington, DC: Woodrow Wilson Centre Press, 2001.

Lakshman, Narayan. 'Top US Official Says Pakistan Holding up FMCT Negotiations'. *The Hindu*, 1 February 2011.

Lamb, A. *Kashmir: A Disputed Legacy 1846–1990*. Hertingfordbury and Karachi: Roxford Books/Oxford University Press, 1991.

Lancaster, John and Kamran Khan. 'Musharraf Named in Nuclear Probe'. *Washington Post*, 3 February 2004.

———. 'Pakistanis Say Nuclear Scientists Aided Iran'. *Washington Post*, 24 January 2004.

Langewiesche, William. 'The Wrath of Khan'. *Atlantic Monthly* 296, 4 (November 2005): 62–85.

———. 'The Point of No Return'. *Atlantic Monthly* 297, 1 (January/February 2006): 96–7.

———. *The Atomic Bazaar: The Rise of the Nuclear Poor*. New York: Farrar, Straus & Giroux, 2007.

Latif, Asmir. 'Two Pakistani Atomic Scientists Arrested'. IslamOnline, 24 October 2001, www.islam-online.net/English/News/2001–10/25/article3.shtml.

Latif Khan, Major-General M. A. 'The Staff College as I Saw it'. In *Command and Staff College Quetta 1905–1980*, ed. and comp. Command and Staff College, Quetta. Quetta: Command and Staff College, 1982, 139–40.

Laufer, Michael. 'A. Q. Khan Nuclear Chronology'. Carnegie Endowment for International Peace, 7 September 2005, http://carnegieendowment.org/2005/09/07/a.-q.-khan-nuclear-chronology.

Lavoy, P. R. (ed.). *Assymetric Warfare in South Asia: The Causes and Consequences of the Kargil Conflict*. Cambridge: Cambridge University Press, 2009.

Lavoy, Peter. 'Civil–Military Relations, Strategic Conduct, and the Stability of Nuclear Deterrence in South Asia'. In Scott D. Sagan (ed.), *Civil–Military Relations and Nuclear Weapons*. Stanford: Stanford Centre for International Security and Arms Control, June 1994, 79–109.

———. 'Islamabad's Nuclear Posture: Its Premises and Implementation'. In Henry D. Sokolski (ed.), *Pakistan's Nuclear Future: Worries beyond War*. Carlisle and Washington, DC: Strategic Studies Institute, 2008.

———. 'Nuclear Myths and the Causes of Nuclear Proliferation'. In Z. S. Davis and B. Frankel (eds.), *The Proliferation Puzzle: Why Nuclear Weapons Spread (And What Results)*. London: Frank Cass, 1993, 192–212.

———. 'Nuclear Proliferation over the Next Decade: Causes, Warning Signs, and Policy Responses'. *Nonproliferation Review* 13, 3 (November 2006): 434–54.

———. 'Pakistan's Strategic Culture: A Theoretical Excursion'. *Strategic Insights* 6, 10 (2005), available at http://calhoun.nps.edu/bitstream/handle/10945/11264/lavoyOct05.pdf?sequence=1.

———. 'The Enduring Effects of Atoms for Peace'. *Arms Control Today* (December 2003), http://www.armscontrol.org/act/2003_12/Lavoy.

———. and Feroz Hassan Khan. 'Rogue or Responsible Nuclear Power? Making Sense of Pakistan's Nuclear Practices'. *Strategic Insights* 3, 2 (2004), available at http://calhoun.nps.edu/bitstream/handle/10945/13765/Rogue_or_Responsible_Nuclear_Power.pdf?sequence=1.

———. and Robin Walker. 'Conference Report: Nuclear Weapons Proliferation: 2016'. Center on Contemporary Conflict, Naval Postgraduate School, Monterey, California, 28–29 July 2006, http://calhoun.nps.edu/bitstream/handle/10945/30509/2006–07_Nuclear_Weapons_Proliferation_2016.pdf?sequence=1.

Leslie, Stuart W. 'Pakistan's Nuclear Taj Mahal'. *Physics Today* 68, 2 (February 2015): 40–6.

Levy, Adrian and Catherine Scott-Clark. *Deception: Pakistan, the United States, and the Secret Trade in Nuclear Weapons*. New York: Walker & Co., 2007.

BIBLIOGRAPHY

Lewis, Bernard. 'The Roots of Muslim Rage'. *Atlantic Monthly* 266, 3 (September 1990): 47–60.

Lewis, Jeffrey. 'Minimum Deterrence'. *Bulletin of the Atomic Scientists* 64, 3 (July/August 2008): 38–41.

————. 'P3 and P4 Centrifuge Data'. Arms Control Wonk, 15 February 2007, http://www.armscontrolwonk.com/archive/201399/p3-and-p4-centrifuge-data/.

Lewis, John Wilson and Xue Litai. *China Builds the Bomb*. Stanford: Stanford University Press, 1988.

'Libya's Nuclear Update—2004'. *Wisconsin Project on Nuclear Arms Control* 10, 2 (March–April 2004) [electronic journal; no longer available].

'Libya Profile: Nuclear Overview'. NTI, http://www.nti.org/e_research/profiles/Libya/3939.html.

Linzer, Dafna. 'Iran was Offered Nuclear Parts: Secret Meeting in 1987 May Have Begun Program'. *Washington Post*, 27 February 2005.

Lodhi, Maleeha and Zahid Hussain. 'The Night of the Jackals'. *Newsline*, October 1992, 32–3.

Lodi, Sardar F. S. 'Pakistan's Missile Technology'. *Pakistan Defence Journal* (May 1998), http://defencejournal.com/may98/pakmissiletech.htm.

MacLachlan, Ann. 'Eurodif's Balance Sheet Threatened by Iranian Problem'. *Nuclear Fuel* 16, 12 (10 June 1991): 4–5.

Mahmood, Sultan and Muhammad Nasim. 'CTBT: A Technical Assessment'. 7 January 2000, http://www.Pakistanlink.com/Opinion/2000/Jan/07/02.htm.

Malik, Iftikhar H. 'Pakistan's National Security and Regional Issues: Politics of Mutualities with the Muslim World'. *Asian Survey* 34, 12 (December 1994): 1077–92.

Malik, Zahid. *Dr. A. Q. Khan and the Islamic Bomb*. Islamabad: Hurmat, 1992.

Matinuddin, Kamal. *Nuclearization of South Asia*. Karachi: Oxford University Press, 2002.

————. *The Taliban Phenomenon: Afghanistan, 1994–1997*. Karachi: Oxford University Press, 1999.

McGirk, Tim. 'General Speaks Out'. *Time*, 19 October 1998, http://content.time.com/time/world/article/0,8599,2054276,00.html.

Mearsheimer, John J. 'Back to the Future: Instability in Europe after the Cold War'. *International Security* 15, 1 (Summer 1990): 5–56.

————. 'The Case for the Ukrainian Nuclear Deterrent'. *Foreign Affairs* 72, 3 (Summer 1993): 50–66.

Mehmud, Salim. 2007. Speech presented at the Munir Ahmad Khan Memorial Reference, Pakistan Agricultural Research Council Auditorium, Islamabad, 28 April 2007, http://www.pakdef.info/nuclear&missile/memorial_munirahmed.html.

Melman, Yossi. 'In Face of Iran Threat, Saudi Arabia Mulls Nuclear Cooperation with Pakistan'. *Haaretz*, 8 September 2011, http://www.haaretz.com/blogs/the-arms-race/in-face-of-iran-threat-saudi-arabia-mulls-nuclear-cooperation-with-pakistan-1.383153.

Meyer, Stephen M. *The Dynamics of Nuclear Proliferation*. Chicago: University of Chicago Press, 1984.

Mian, Zia. 'Fevered with Dreams of the Future: The Coming of the Atomic Age to Pakistan'. https://www.princeton.edu/sgs/faculty-staff/zia-mian/Fevered-with-Dreams-of.pdf.

————. *Nuclear Passions and Interests: The Founding of Atomic Pakistan*. Washington, DC and Amsterdam: Social Science Research Council/International Institute of Social History, 2005.

————. 'Out of the Nuclear Shadow: Scientists and the Struggle against the Bomb'. *Bulletin of the Atomic Scientists* 71, 1 (2015): 59–69.

————. *Pakistan's Atomic Bomb and the Search for Security*. Lahore: Gautam Publishers, 1995.

Mian, Zia and Alexander Glaser. 'A Frightening Nuclear Legacy'. *Bulletin of the Atomic Scientists* 64, 4 (2008): 42–7.

Miller, Steven E. 'Nuclear Collisions: Discord, Reform and the Nuclear Nonproliferation Regime'. American Academy of Arts and Sciences, 2012, http://www.amacad.org/pdfs/nonproliferation.pdf.

Ministry of Foreign Affairs, Government of Pakistan. 'Pakistan Deposits Instrument of Ratification of Amendment to Convention on Physical Protection of Nuclear Material in Vienna'. 24 March 2016, available at http://www.mofa.gov.pk/qatar/pr-details.php?prID=3579.

Mishra, B. 'Pak War Threat Led to Nuclear Tests: Mishra'. 10 November 2000, available at http://www.rediff.com/news/2000/nov/10nuke.htm.

Mishra, Rajesh Kumar. 'Pakistan as a Proliferator State: Blame it on Dr. A. Q. Khan'. South Asia Analysis Group, paper no. 567, 20 December 2002, http://www.southasiaanalysis.org/paper567.

'Missile Overview: India Profile'. NTI, http://www.nti.org/e_research/profiles/India/Missile/index.html.

Mohammadi, Mehdi. 'God's Hand Was at Work'. Interview with Dr Mohammad Sa'idi, Atomic Energy Organization of Iran deputy for planning and international affairs, *Kayhan*, 27 April 2005.

Montezeran, Ahmed and Kashif Mumtaz. 'Iran–Pakistan: Cooperation for Regional Stability and Peace'. *Strategic Studies*, 24, 1 (Spring 2004): 1–11.

Morgan, Patrick M. *Deterrence Now*. Cambridge: Cambridge University Press, 2003.

Morgenthau, Hans J. *Politics among Nations*. New York: Knopf, 1948; 7th edn, rev. Kenneth W. Thompson and W. David Clinton, New York: McGraw-Hill, 2006.

BIBLIOGRAPHY

Morley, Jefferson. 'UK Downsizes its Nuclear Arsenal'. Arms Control Association, March 2015, https://www.armscontrol.org/ACT/2015_03/News-Brief/UK-Downsizes-Its-Nuclear-Arsenal.

Moshaver, Ziba. *Nuclear Weapons Proliferation in the Indian Subcontinent.* London: Macmillan, 1991.

Lord Mountbatten. 'Reply from Lord Mountbatten to Maharaja Hari Singh'. 27 October 1947, available at http://www.kashmir-information.com/LegalDocs/Maharaja_letter.html.

Mowatt-Larssen, Rolf. 'Islam and the Bomb: Religious Justification for and against Nuclear Weapons'. Belfer Center for Science and International Affairs, Harvard Kennedy School, January 2011, http://www.belfer-center.org/sites/default/files/legacy/files/uploads/Islam_and_the_Bomb-Final.pdf.

Mubarakmand, Samar. 'A Science Odyssey: Pakistan's Nuclear Emergence'. Speech presented at the Khwarzimic Science Society, Centre of Excellence in Solid State Physics, Punjab University, Lahore, 28 November 1998, available at http://www.pakdef.info/nuclear&missile/science_odyssey.html.

Mufson, Steven. 'US Worries about Pakistan Nuclear Arms'. *Washington Post,* 4 November 2001.

Mukashaf, Mohammad. 'Pakistan Declines Saudi Call for Armed Support in Yemen Fight'. Reuters, 10 April 2015, http://www.reuters.com/article/us-yemen-security-idUSKBN0N10LO20150410.

Musharraf, P. *In The Line of Fire: A Memoir.* London and New York: Simon & Schuster/Free Press, 2006.

Myers, Steven Lee and Choe Sang-hun. 'North Koreans Agree to Freeze Nuclear Work; US to Give Aid'. *New York Times,* 29 February 2012.

Namboodiri, Udayan. 'Dr Khan's Story: Thy Hand, Great Gen!' *Pioneer,* 6 February 2004.

Narang, Vipin. 'Posturing for Peace? Pakistan's Nuclear Postures and South Asian Stability' *International Security* 34, 3 (Winter 2009/10): 38–78.

Nasr, Vali. *The Shia Revival: How Conflicts within Islam Will Shape the Future.* New York: W. W. Norton, 2006.

———. *The Vanguard of the Islamic Revolution: The Jama'at-i Islami of Pakistan.* Berkeley: University of California Press, 1994.

Nawaz, Shuja. *Crossed Swords: Pakistan, its Army and the Wars Within.* Karachi: Oxford University Press, 2008.

Nayyar, Kuldip. 'We Have the A-Bomb, Says Pakistan's Dr Strangelove'. *The Observer,* 1 March 1987.

Neuffer, Elizabeth. 'A US Concern: Pakistan's Arsenal: Anti-American Mood Poses a Security Risk'. *Boston Globe,* 16 August 2002.

'New Documents Spotlight Reagan-era Tensions over Pakistani Nuclear

Program'. National Security Archive, George Washington University, 27 April 2012, http://nsarchive.gwu.edu/nukevault/ebb377/.

Niksch, Larry A. 'North Korea's Nuclear Weapons Program'. Congressional Research Service Report, Washington, DC: Library of Congress, 5 October 2006, available at https://fas.org/sgp/crs/nuke/IB91141.pdf.

Norris, Robert S., Hans M. Kristensen, and Joshua Handler. 'North Korea's Nuclear Program'. *Bulletin of the Atomic Scientists* 59, 2 (March/April 2003): 74–7.

'North Korea's Nuclear Programme: How Advanced is it?' BBC, 6 January 2017, http://www.bbc.com/news/world-asia-pacific-11813699.

'Nuclear Plant Study Started'. *Kayhan International*, 19 December 1972.

'Nuclear Power in Saudi Arabia'. World Nuclear Association, updated on 27 March 2017, http://www.world-nuclear.org/information-library/country-profiles/countries-o-s/saudi-arabia.aspx.

Nuclear Suppliers Group Guidelines for Nuclear Transfers. London: International Institute for Strategic Studies, http://www.nuclearsuppliers-group.org/en/guidelines.

'Nuclear Technology at All Costs: Munir'. *Dawn* (Karachi), 20 February 1991.

Nuclear Threat Initiative. 'North Korea Profile'. Updated February 2017, http://www.nti.org/learn/countries/north-korea/.

————. 'Saudi Arabia: Nuclear'. Updated July 2016, http://www.nti.org/learn/countries/saudi-arabia/nuclear/.

'Nuclear Weapons Program—North Korea'. Federation of American Scientists, http://www.fas.org/nuke/guide/dprk/nuke/index.html.

Ogilvie-White, Tanya. 'Is There a Theory of Nuclear Proliferation? An Analysis of the Contemporary Debate'. *Nonproliferation Review* 4, 1 (Fall 1996): 43–60.

'Osama–Nawaz ties to haunt PML-N'. *The News*, 11 May 2011, https://www.thenews.com.pk/archive/amp/613747-osama-nawaz-ties-to-haunt-pml-.

Overbye, Dennis and James Glanz. 'A Nation Challenged: Nuclear Fears; Pakistani Atomic Expert, Arrested Last Week, Had Strong Pro-Taliban Views'. *New York Times*, 2 November 2001.

Pahlavi, Reza Shah, *Mission for My Country*. London: Hutchinson, 1961.

Pais, Arthur J. 'Bangladesh War: "Nixon, Kissinger Let Personal Judgements Cloud Their Thinking"'. *Rediff News*, 13 December 2013, available at https://defence.pk/pdf/threads/bangladesh-war-nixon-kissinger-let-personal-judgments-cloud-their-thinking.291475/.

'Pakistan Air Force: The Canadair Sabre Goes to War', http://www.pakdef.info/pakmilitary/airforce/ac/sabre.html.

Pakistan Atomic Energy Commission. '25 Years of PINSTECH: Silver Jubilee Technical Report, 1965–1990'. Scientific Information Division, PAEC, PINSTECH. Nilore, Islamabad, 1992.

BIBLIOGRAPHY

'Pakistan Became Nuclear State in 1983: Dr. Samar'. *The Nation* (Islamabad), 2 May 2003.

'Pakistan Blocks Agenda at UN Disarmament Conference'. *Daily Times*, 20 January 2010.

'Pakistan Can Make Hydrogen Bomb'. *STAR*, 30 September 1984.

'Pakistan and North Korea: Dangerous Counter-Trades'. *International Institute for Strategic Studies Strategic Comments* 8, 9 (November 2002): 1–2.

'Pakistan's Nuclear Bombshell'. *India Today*, 31 March 1987.

'Pakistan Nuclear Staff Go Missing'. BBC News, 12 February 2008, http://news.bbc.co.uk/2/hi/south_asia/7240414.stm.

'Pakistan PM: Remarks at First Plenary Session on Mar 24, 2014'. Nuclear Security Summit, 24 March 2014, available at www.nss2014.com.

'Pakistan Rejects Atom Bomb Material Cut-Off Talks, Cites Danger from India'. Reuters, 25 January 2010. www.reuters.com.

'Pakistan Said to Know of Nuclear Transfer'. *New York Times*, 3 February 2004.

'Pakistan Seeks Equal Access to Civil Nuclear Technology'. 2010. *Dawn*, 12 April 2010.

'Pakistan Tightens Security at N-Facilities'. *The News*, 27 January 2008.

'Pakistan Warns against India Nuclear Support'. *Dawn*, 25 January 2011.

Parviz, Irfan. 'Regional Atom Chiefs in Talks on Three-Country Organization'. *Tehran Journal*, 27 January 1975.

Patton, Tamara. 'Combining Satellite Imagery and 3D Drawing Tools for Nonproliferation Analysis: A Case Study of Pakistan's Khushab Plutonium Production Reactors'. *Science & Global Security* 20, 2–3 (October 2012): 117–40.

Paul, T. V. 'Chinese–Pakistani Nuclear/Missile Ties and the Balance of Power'. *Nonproliferation Review* 10, 2 (Summer 2003): 21–9.

Perkovich, George. 'Could Anything Be Done to Stop Them? Lessons from Pakistan'. Nonproliferation Policy Education Center, 26 July 2006, www.npec-web.org/Essays/20060726-Perkovich CouldAnythingBeDone.pdf.

————. 'Could Anything Be Done to Stop Them? Lessons from Pakistan's Proliferating Past'. In Henry D. Sokolski (ed.), *Pakistan Nuclear Future: Worries Beyond War*. Carlisle and Washington, DC: Strategic Studies Institute, 2008, 59–84.

————. *India's Nuclear Bomb: The Impact on Global Proliferation*. Berkeley: University of California Press, 2001.

Perry, William J. 'My Personal Journey at the Nuclear Brink'. European Leadership Network, 17 June 2013, http://www.europeanleadershipnetwork.org/my-personal-journey-at-the-nuclearbrink-by-bill-perry_633.html.

Peterson, Kara J. 'Abdul Qadeer Khan Brings Nuclear Bomb to Pakistan'. *World Press Review*, 1 September 1998.

BIBLIOGRAPHY

Pinkston, Daniel A. 'North Korean Motivations for Developing Nuclear Weapons'. Center for Nonproliferation Studies 30, October 2002, http://cns.miis.edu/research/korea/dprkmotv.pdf.

————. 'When Did WMD Deals between Pyongyang and Islamabad Begin?' Research Story of the Week, 21 October 2002. Monterey, CA: Center for Nonproliferation Studies, Monterey Institute for International Studies. http://cns.miis.edu/pubs/week/021028.htm.

Piracha, Shaukat. 'Beg asked Nawaz to Give Nuclear Technology to a "Friend", says Ishaq Dar'. Daily Times, 25 December 2003.

Poneman, Daniel. Nuclear Power in the Developing World. London: George Allen & Unwin, 1982.

Posen, Barry R. 'We Can Live with a Nuclear Iran'. New York Times, 27 February 2006.

Powell, Bill and Tim McGirk. 'The Man Who Sold the Bomb'. Time, 6 February 2005.

Powell, Colin. Remarks en Route to Kuwait, 18 March 2004, https://2001–2009.state.gov/secretary/former/powell/remarks/30562.htm.

Powell, Robert. 'Nuclear Deterrence Theory, Nuclear Proliferation, and National Missile Defense'. International Security 27, 4 (Spring 2003): 86–118.

Price, Matthew. 'Re-clash of Civilizations'. Boston Globe, 15 February 2004.

'Profile Abdul Qadeer Khan', BBC, 20 February 2004, http://news.bbc.co.uk/2/hi/south_asia/3343621.stm.

'Proposed Agreement for Cooperation between the US Government and the Government of Iran Concerning the Civil Uses of Atomic Energy'. Memorandum, 13 March 1969, Digital National Security Archive, http://nsarchive.chadwyck.com.

Rahman, Mir Jamil. 'Issues that Haunt'. The News, 10 July 2006, http://www.thenews.com.pk/print1.asp?id=27346.

Rahman, Mustaqur. Divided Kashmir: Old Problems, New Opportunities for India, Pakistan and the Kashmiri People. London: Lynne Rienner Publishers, 1996.

Rais, Rasul B. 'Pakistan's Nuclear Program: Prospects for Proliferation', Asian Survey 25, 4 (April 1985): 458–72.

Rajagopalan, Rajesh. Second Strike Arguments about Nuclear War in South Asia. New Dehli: Viking Penguin Books India, 2005.

Rana, Amir. A to Z of Jihadi Organizations in Pakistan. Lahore: Mashal Books, 2004.

Rascouet, Angelina and Wael Mahdi. 'Saudi Arabia to Select Nuclear Power-Plant Site "Very Soon"'. Bloomberg, 20 October 2016, https://www.bloomberg.com/news/articles/2016–10–20/saudi-arabia-to-select-nuclear-power-plant-site-very-soon.

Rashid, Ahmed. 'Bare All and Be Damned: Ex-Army Chief Reveals Nuclear Secrets'. Far Eastern Economic Review, 5 May 1994.

BIBLIOGRAPHY

―――. 'Bhutto Warns India against Testing Nuclear Device'. *Daily Telegraph*, 6 January 1996.

―――. *Taliban: Militant Islam, Oil and Fundamentalism in Central Asia*. New Haven: Yale University Press, 2001.

Rehman, Shahid. *Long Road to Chagai*. Islamabad: Print Wise Publications, 1999.

Remarks by the President to the National Defense University. Washington, DC, 11 February 2004, http://www.whitehouse.gov/news/releases/2004/02/20040211–4.html.

Richelson, Jeffrey T. *Spying on the Bomb: American Nuclear Intelligence from Nazi Germany to Iran and North Korea*. New York: W. W. Norton & Company, 2006.

Rizvi, Hasan Askari. 'Civil–Military Relations under General Beg'. *Defence Journal* 7, 6 and 7 (August 1991): 17–21.

―――. *The Military and Politics in Pakistan 1947–86*. Lahore: Progressive Publishers, 1987.

―――. 'Pakistan's Nuclear Testing'. *Asian Survey* 41, 6 (November/December 2001): 943–55.

al-Rodhan, Nayef. 'Strategic Culture and Pragmatic National Interest'. Geneva Centre for Security Policy, July 2015, http://www.gcsp.ch/News-Knowledge/Publications/Strategic-Culture-and-Pragmatic-National-Interest.

Rohde, David. 'Nuclear Inquiry Skips Pakistani Army'. *New York Times*, 30 January 2004.

―――. 'Pakistanis Question Official Ignorance of Atom Transfers'. *New York Times*, 3 February 2004.

Rohde, David and David E. Sanger. 'Key Pakistani is Said to Admit Atom Transfers'. *New York Times*, 2 February 2004.

Royal Malaysian Police. 'Press Release by Inspector-General of Police in Relation to Investigation of Alleged Production of Components for Libya's Uranium Enrichment Programme'. 20 February 2004, http://www.rmp.gov.my/rmp03/040220scomi_eng.htm.

Sagan, Scott D. 'The Causes of Nuclear Proliferation', *Current History* 96, 609 (April 1997): 151–6.

―――. 'The Evolution of Pakistani and Indian Nuclear Doctrine'. In Scott D. Sagan (ed.), *Inside Nuclear South Asia*, Stanford: Stanford University Press, 2009, 219–20.

―――. 'Keeping the Bomb Away from Tehran'. *Foreign Affairs* 85, 5 (September/October 2006): 45–59.

―――. *The Limits of Safety: Organizations, Accidents, and Nuclear Weapons*. Princeton: Princeton University Press, 1993.

―――. *Moving Targets: Nuclear Strategy and National Security*. Princeton: Princeton University Press, 1989.

————. 'Why Do States Build Nuclear Weapons? Three Models in Search of a Bomb'. *International Security* 21, 3 (Winter 1996–7): 54–86.

————. and Kenneth Waltz. *The Spread of Nuclear Weapons: A Debate*. New York: W. W. Norton & Company, 1995.

Sahimi, Mohammad. 'Iran's Nuclear Program. Part I: Its History'. *Payvand*, 2 October 2003.

Salam, Abdus, Azim Kidwai, and C. H. Lai (eds.). *Ideals and Realities: Selected Essays of Abdus Salam*. Singapore: World Scientific Publishing Co., 1984.

Salik, Naeem. *The Genesis of South Asian Nuclear Deterrence: Pakistan's Perspective*. Karachi: Oxford University Press, 2009.

————. 'Minimum Deterrence and India Pakistan Nuclear Dialogue: Case Study on Pakistan'. Landau Network–Centro Volta South Asia Security Project Case Study, January 2006, http://www.centrovolta.it/landau/South%20Asia%20Security%20Program_file%5CDocumenti%5CCase%20Studies%5CSalik%20-%20S.A.%20Case%20Study%202006.pdf.

————. 'Missile Issues in South Asia'. *Nonproliferation Review* 9, 2 (Summer 2002): 47–55.

Samore, Gary (lead author and ed.). *The Iran Nuclear Deal: A Definitive Guide*. Cambridge, MA: Belfer Center for Science and International Affairs, Harvard Kennedy School, August 2015.

Samore, Gary (ed.). *North Korea's Weapons Programmes: A Net Assessment*. London: International Institute for Strategic Studies, January 2004.

Sanger, David. *The Inheritance: The World Obama Confronts and the Challenges to American Power*, New York: Harmony, 2009.

————. 'The Khan Network'. Paper presented at the Conference on South Asia and the Nuclear Future held at Stanford University on 4–5 June 2004, http://fsi.stanford.edu/sites/default/files/evnts/media//Khan_network-paper.pdf.

————. 'Threats and Responses: Alliances; in North Korea and Pakistan, Deep Roots of Nuclear Barter'. *New York Times*, 24 November 2002.

————. 'So What about Those Nukes?' *New York Times*, 11 November 2007.

Sanger, David, Douglas Frantz, and James Risen. 'Nuclear Experts in Pakistan May Have Links to Al Qaeda'. *New York Times*, 9 December 2001.

Sattar, Abdul. *Pakistan's Foreign Policy: 1947–2005*. Karachi: Oxford University Press, 2007.

Schelling, Thomas. *Arms and Influence*. New Haven: Yale University Press, 1966.

Schofield, Victoria. *Kashmir in Conflict*. London: I. B. Tauris, 2000.

Schwartz, Stephen. *The Two Faces of Islam: The House of Saud from Tradition to Terror*. New York: Doubleday, 2002.

Sciolino, Elaine. 'US Sees Troubling Tilt by Pakistan to Iran'. *New York Times*,

BIBLIOGRAPHY

1 November 1987, http://www.nytimes.com/1987/11/01/world/us-sees-troubling-tilt-by-pakistan-to-iran.html.

Scomi Group Berhad. 'SCOPE's Press Statement on Its Contract in Dubai'. News release, 4 February 2004, http://www.scomigroup.com.my/publish/04news008.shtml.

Sechser, Todd S. (ed.). 'South Asia and the Nuclear Future: Rethinking the Causes and Consequences of Nuclear Proliferation'. Conference Brief, Center for International Security and Cooperation, Stanford University, http://www.strategicstudiesinstitute.army.mil/pdffiles/pub688.pdf.

Seervai, H. M. *Partition of India: Legend and Reality*, Bombay: Emmenem Publications, 1990.

Sethi, Najam. 'Nuclear Shenanigans: Najam Sethi's Editorial'. *Friday Times*, 15, 49, 30 January–5 February 2004.

Sevastopulo, Demetri. 'Bush Removes North Korea from Terror List'. *Financial Times*, 11 October 2008.

Shafqat, Saeed. 'From Official Islam to Islamism: The Rise of Dawat-ul-Irshad and Lashkar-e-Taiba'. In Christophe Jaffrelot (ed.), *Pakistan: Nationalism Without a Nation?* London: Zed Books, 2002, 131–47.

'The Shah Meets the Press'. *Kayhan International*, 5 October 1974.

Shamim, Anwar. *Cutting Edge PAF: A Former Air Chief's Reminiscences of a Developing Air Force*, Islamabad: Vanguard Books, 2010.

Siddiqa, Ayesha. *Military Inc.: Inside Pakistan's Military Economy*. London: Pluto Press, 2007.

Siddiqa-Agha, Ayesha. *Pakistan's Arms Procurement and Military Buildup, 1979–99: In Search of a Policy*. New York: Palgrave, 2001.

Siddiqui, Salimuzzaman. 'The Pakistan Council of Scientific and Industrial Research: A Review of its Activities'. *Pakistan Quarterly* 7, 4 (Winter 1957): 42–5.

Sinai, Joshua. 'Libya's Pursuit of Weapons of Mass Destruction'. *Nonproliferation Review* 4 (Spring–Summer 1997): 92–100.

Singh, Dalip. 'Delhi Dossier on Pak Bomb Daddy'. *The Telegraph* (India), 8 February 2004.

Singh, Jaswant. 'Against Nuclear Apartheid'. *Foreign Affairs* (September–October 1998): 41–52.

Slevin, Peter. 'Libya Made Plutonium, Nuclear Watchdog Says'. *Washington Post*, 21 February 2004.

Smith, R. Jeffrey and Joby Warrick. 'A Nuclear Power's Act of Proliferation'. *Washington Post*, 13 November 2009.

Spector, Leonard S., with Jacqueline R. Smith. *Nuclear Ambitions: The Spread of Nuclear Weapons 1989–1990*. Boulder: Westview Press, 1990.

Squassoni, Sharon. 'Closing Pandora's Box: Pakistan's Role in Nuclear Proliferation'. *Arms Control Today* 34, 3, Washington: Arms Control Association, April 2004: 8–13.

BIBLIOGRAPHY

————. 'Weapons of Mass Destruction: Trade between North Korea and Pakistan'. Congressional Research Service Report RL31900, 28 November 2006, https://fas.org/sgp/crs/nuke/RL31900.pdf.

Sreedhar (ed.). *Pakistan's Bomb: A Documentary Study*, 2nd edn. New Delhi: ABC Publishing, 1987.

'Statement of the Prime Minister of Pakistan Regarding the Indian Nuclear Explosion'. *Pakistan Horizon* 27, 2, 19 May 1974.

Stern, Jessica. 'Pakistan's Jihad Culture'. *Foreign Affairs* 79, 6 (November/December 2000): 115–26.

Stern, Jessica and Geoffrey Koblentz. 'Preventing Unauthorized Access to and Use of Nuclear Materials and Weapons: Lessons from the United States and Former Soviet Union'. Paper presented to the CISAC Workshop on Preventing Nuclear War in South Asia, Bangkok, 4–7 August 2001.

Stimson Center. 'Confidence-Building Measures in South Asia'. Washington, DC: Henry L. Stimson Center, 17 September 2010, http://www.stimson.org/research-pages/confidencebuilding-measures-in-south-asia-/.

Stockholm International Peace Research Institute. *SIPRI Yearbook 2015*. Stockholm: Stockholm International Peace Research Institute, 2015.

Subrahmanyam, K. 'India and the International Nuclear Order'. In D. R. SarDesai and Raju Thomas (eds.), *Nuclear India in the Twenty-First Century*, New York: Palgrave, 2002, 63–84.

Subramanian, Nirupama. 'A. Q. Khan's "Secret Agreement"'. *The Hindu*, 25 May 2011.

'Tactical N-Arms to Ward off War Threat, Says FO'. *Dawn*, 20 October 2015.

Tahir-Kheli, Shirin. 'Iran and Pakistan: Cooperation in an Area of Conflict'. *Asian Survey* 17, 5 (May 1977): 474–90.

Talbott, Strobe. *Engaging India: Diplomacy, Democracy, and the Bomb*. Washington, DC: Brookings Institution Press, 2004.

————. 'Dealing with the Bomb in South Asia'. *Foreign Affairs* 78, 2 (March–April 1999): 110–22.

Tellis, Ashley J. *India's Emerging Nuclear Posture*. Santa Monica: RAND, 2001.

————. *Stability in South Asia*. Santa Monica: RAND Corporation, 1997.

————. Christine Fair, and Jamison Jo Medby. *Limited Conflicts under the Nuclear Umbrella: Indian and Pakistani Lessons from the Kargil Crisis*. RAND Monograph Report, Santa Monica: RAND Corporation, 2002, http://www.rand.org/pubs/monograph_reports/MR1450/.

Tertrais, Bruno. 'Not a "Wal-Mart", but an "Imports–Exports Enterprise": Understanding the Nature of the A. Q. Khan Network'. *Strategic Insights* 6, 5 (August 2007): 23–31.

————. 'Pakistan's Nuclear Exports: Was there a State Strategy?' In Henry D. Sokolski (ed.), *Pakistan Nuclear Future: Worries Beyond War*, Washington, DC and Carlisle Barracks, PA: Strategic Studies Institute Publications Office/United States Army War College, 2008, 13–57.

BIBLIOGRAPHY

'Text of Dr Abdul Qadeer Khan's Statement Seeking Public Apology'. Transcribed text from Pakistan TV (Islamabad), 4 February 2004.

'Text of Musharraf's TV News Conference'. Translated text from PTV World (Islamabad), 5 February 2004.

'Text of Prime Minister Muhammad Nawaz Sharif Statement at a Press Conference on Pakistan Nuclear Tests'. Islamabad, 29 May 1998, http://nuclearweaponarchive.org.

Thompson, Mark. 'Does Pakistan's Taliban Surge Raise a Nuclear Threat?' *Time*, 24 April 2009.

Tisdall, Simon. 'Pakistan Nuclear Projects Raise US Fears'. *The Guardian*, 3 May 2009.

Tobey, William. 'A Message from Tripoli: How Libya Gave up its WMD'. *Bulletin of the Atomic Scientists* (December 2014), available at http://thebulletin.org/message-tripoli-how-libya-gave-its-wmd7834.

'Transcript: A Conversation with Gen. Khalid Kidwai'. Carnegie International Nuclear Policy Conference 2015, 23 March 2015, http://carnegieendowment.org/2015/03/23/conversation-with-gen.-khalid-kidwai-pub-58885.

Treaty on the Nonproliferation of Nuclear Weapons. 1968, http://www.fas.org/nuke/control/npt/text/npt2.htm.

Urban, Mark. 'Saudi Nuclear Weapons "On Order" from Pakistan'. BBC, 6 November 2013, http://www.bbc.com/news/world-middle-east-248 23846.

US Department of State. *Documents on Disarmament, 1945–1959*. Washington, DC: Department of State Publication, 1960.

————. 'Proliferation Security Initiative'. Washington, DC: Department of State, 5 July 2012, http://www.state.gov/t/isn/c10390.htm.

'US–Indo Ties Not a Matter of Concern for Pak: Sartaj Aziz'. Asian News International (ANI), 3 July 2016, available at http://indianexpress.com/article/india/india-news-india/indo-us-ties-not-a-matter-of-concern-for-pakistan-sartaj-aziz-2890921/.

'US Supplied Nuclear Material to Iran'. Digital National Security Archive, 29 January 1980, http://nsarchive.chadwyck.com.

Van Hollen, Eliza. 'Pakistan in 1986: Trials of Transition'. *Asian Survey* 27, 2 (February 1987): 143–54.

Vij, Shivam. 'Congratulations Pakistan'. *Express Tribune*, 24 May 2014.

Walker, William. 'International Nuclear Relations after the Indian and Pakistani Test Explosions'. *International Affairs* 74, 3 (1998): 505–28.

Walsh, Declan. 'Disgraced Atomic Scientist Disowns Confession'. *The Guardian*, 29 May 2008.

————. 'Militants Attack Pakistani Air Force Base'. *New York Times*, 16 August 2012.

Walsh, Jim. 'Bombs Unbuilt: Power, Ideas, and Institutions in International Politics'. Ph.D. thesis, Massachusetts Institute of Technology, 2001.

Walt, Stephen M. 'Alliance Formation and the Balance of Power'. *International Security* 9, 4 (Spring 1985): 3–43.

————. *The Origins of Alliances*. Ithaca: Cornell University Press, 1990.

Waltz, Kenneth. 'More May Be Better'. In Scott D. Sagan and Kenneth N. Waltz (eds.), *The Spread of Nuclear Weapons: A Debate*, New York and London: W.W. Norton & Company, 1995, 3–45.

————. 'Nuclear Myths and Political Realities'. *American Political Science Review* 84, 3 (September 1990): 731–45.

————. *Theory of International Politics*. New York: McGraw-Hill, 1979.

————. and Scott D. Sagan (eds.). *The Spread of Nuclear Weapons: A Debate Renewed*, New York: W. W. Norton, 2003.

Walzer, Michael. *Just and Unjust Wars: A Moral Argument with Historical Illustrations*. New York: Basic Books, 1992.

Warrick, Joby. 'Nuclear Scientist A. Q. Khan is Freed from House Arrest'. *Washington Post*, 7 February 2009.

Warrick, Joby and Peter Slevin. 'Libyan Arms Designs Traced back to China: Pakistanis Resold Chinese Provided Plans'. *Washington Post*, 15 February 2004.

Weeks, Joan. 'Aspects of Persian Culture: Professor Discusses 8,000-Year Legacy'. *Library of Congress Information Bulletin* 54, 16 (4 September 1995), http://www.loc.gov/loc/lcib/9516/persia.html.

Weinbaum, Marvin and Gautam Sen. 'Pakistan Enters the Middle East'. *Orbis* 22, 3 (Fall 1978): 595–612.

Weiss, Leonard. 'Pakistan: It's Déjà Vu All Over Again'. *Bulletin of the Atomic Scientists* 60, 3 (May–June 2004): 52–9.

Weissman, Steve, and Herbert Krosney. *The Islamic Bomb: The Nuclear Threat to Israel and the Middle East*. New York: Times Books, 1981.

'What is India's "Cold Start" Military Doctrine?' *The Economist*, 31 January 2017, http://www.economist.com/blogs/economist-explains/2017/02/economist-explains.

Wills, David K. 'Pakistan: Crash Program, Secret Bids for Nuclear Technology'. *Christian Science Monitor*, 30 November 1981.

Wilson, John. 'Iran, Pakistan and Nukes'. Observer Research Foundation, 2005, available at http://www.washingtontimes.com/news/2004/oct/4/20041004–015707–2087r/.

Wirsing, Robert. *Kashmir in the Shadows of War: Regional Rivalries in a Nuclear Age*. New York: M. E. Sharpe, 2003.

Wolpert, Stanley. *Jinnah of Pakistan*. New York: Oxford University Press, 1984.

Yasmeen, Samina. 'Is Pakistan's Nuclear Bomb an Islamic Bomb?' *Asian Studies Review* 25, 2 (June 2001): 201–15.

BIBLIOGRAPHY

Yusuf, Suhail. 'Dr I. H. Usmani'. *Dawn*, 16 June 2011.

Zaafir, Muhammad Saleh. 'Gen. Asif had Refused Nuclear Assistance to Iran, Says Javed'. *The News*, 14 February 2004.

Zaidi, Mubashir. 'Scientist Claimed Nuclear Equipment Was Old, Official Says'. *Los Angeles Times*, 10 February 2004.

CHRONOLOGY

1956

March: The Pakistan Atomic Energy Commission (PAEC) is established to participate in the Atoms for Peace programme announced by US president Dwight D. Eisenhower.

1958

October: Pakistan's nuclear programme begins when Zulfikar Ali Bhutto becomes the federal minister for fuel, power and natural resources.

1960

Pakistan signs contracts with both British Nuclear Fuels Limited (BNFL) and Belgonucleaire to prepare studies and designs for pilot plutonium separation facilities in the early 1960s.

The USA gives Pakistan a $350,000 grant to help build its first research reactor.

1962

The USA supplies a 5 MW light-water research reactor known as the Pakistan Atomic Research Reactor (PARR-1).

1965

The PARR-l begins operating at the Pakistan Institute of Nuclear Science and Technology (PINSTECH).

CHRONOLOGY

President Ayub Khan and his foreign minister, Zulfikar Ali Bhutto, meet Chinese prime minister Chou En-lai to seek Chinese support for Pakistan's nuclear programme.

1967

Pakistan produces the first batch of radioisotopes at PINSTECH.

1968

Pakistan refuses to sign the Nuclear Non-Proliferation Treaty (NPT).

1969

Bhutto, in his book *The Myth of Independence*, argues the necessity for Pakistan to acquire nuclear weapons to be able to stand against the industrialized states, especially a nuclear-armed India.

1970

Pakistan builds a pilot-scale plant at Dera Ghazi Khan for the concentration of uranium ores. The plant has a capacity of 10,000 pounds a day.

1971

The Canadian General Electric Company completes a 137 MW (electrical) CANDU power reactor for the Karachi Nuclear Power Plant (KANUPP).

Plans for setting up plutonium separating facilities, designed by BNFL, capable of separating up to 360 g of fuel a year, are finalized.

1972

A pilot reprocessing facility called the New Labs at PINSTECH is built.

20 January: Prime Minister Zulfikar Ali Bhutto initiates the nuclear programme after the 1971 war with India. Bhutto also appoints Munir Ahmed Khan to head the PAEC.

1973

A contract is signed with the Belgian firm Belgonucleaire to build a heavy water plant in Multan.

March: A contract is signed with French company Saint-Gobain Techniques Nouvelles (SGN) to prepare the basic design for a large-scale reprocessing plant (at Chashma), with a capacity of 100 tonnes of fuel per year.

27 December: Munir Ahmed Khan announces an ambitious plan to construct fifteen new nuclear reactors in the next twenty-five years to meet two-thirds of Pakistan's power requirements.

1974

Munir Ahmed Khan plans to develop the design of a weapon implosion system under the 'Wah project'. The project is expanded to include chemical, mechanical, and precision engineering of the system and the triggering mechanisms.

Western suppliers embargo nuclear exports to Pakistan.

Pakistan and Libya sign a ten-year cooperation agreement for a Libyan-financed Pakistani weapons programme.

18 May: India conducts nuclear tests.

21 November: The United Nations General Assembly approves a Pakistani proposal for the establishment of a nuclear-weapons-free zone in South Asia.

1975

July: Pakistani nuclear scientist S. A. Butt becomes the centre of the purchasing programme for the centrifuge project. Purchasing of components and know-how for the Kahuta uranium-enrichment centrifuge facility begins in August.

1976

Pakistan proposes to India a joint Indo-Pakistan declaration renouncing the acquisition and manufacture of nuclear weapons.

Pakistan discovers uranium deposits in western Punjab and begins to exploit them.

The first preparations for eventual nuclear tests begin.

18 March: France and Pakistan sign a safeguard agreement for the Chashma plant.

June: Bhutto develops an understanding with China to collaborate on nuclear weapons technology.

17 July: Bhutto gives A. Q. Khan autonomous control of the uranium enrichment project.

8 August: Henry Kissinger arrives in Islamabad to persuade Pakistan to drop the purchase of a reprocessing plant from France. Bhutto signs the Nuclear Reprocessing Plant Agreement with France.

23 December: Canada decides to break off its nuclear relationship with Pakistan because it had refused to submit to Canadian demands to sign the NPT and accept IAEA safeguards on its entire nuclear programme.

1977

The USA halts economic and military aid over Pakistan's nuclear-weapons programme.

France proposes that Pakistan alter the design of the plant to enable it to produce a mixture of uranium and plutonium rather than pure plutonium. Pakistan refuses.

1978

A declassified 1978 CIA report shows Pakistan's success in obtaining at least one of almost every component needed to build a centrifuge enrichment plant.

4 April: According to A. Q. Khan in a 1998 interview, the first enrichment is done at Kahuta. The plant is made operational in 1979, and by 1981 is producing substantial quantities of uranium.

15 June: The Council on Foreign Nuclear Policy formally decides to abrogate the contract, preventing SGN from completing the Chashma plant.

1979

The USA imposes economic sanctions under the Symington Amendment (Section 669 of the Foreign Assistance Act [FAA] of 1961) after Pakistan is caught importing equipment for its uranium enrichment plant at Kahuta.

Pakistan proposes to India mutual inspections by India and Pakistan of nuclear facilities.

Early 1980s

There are reports of Pakistan obtaining a pre-tested atomic bomb design and bomb-grade enriched uranium from China.

1980

12 January: The USA offers $400 million over the next two years in economic and military assistance to Pakistan in response to the threat posed by Soviet aggression in Afghanistan.

15 January: President Zia-ul-Haq indicates that the USA has not attached any preconditions for the aid offer. General Haq claims that the USA did not seek an end to Pakistan's alleged clandestine nuclear weapons programme or to the army's rule in Pakistan.

28 February: US State Department officials state that, despite US reservations, Pakistan is continuing to build its uranium enrichment facility. The US government has warned that continuation of the plant's construction will halt further US military support.

8 March: The proposed US aid programme to Pakistan is reported to be 'dead' after statements from both sides reveal differences over the issue. The US State Department spokesperson Hodding Carter says that 'the Pakistani government has indicated that it is not interested in the assistance we proposed'. Pakistani sources, on the other hand, indicate that the aid amount is very little, and too conspicuous.

2 July: The economic coordination committee of Pakistan's cabinet decides to increase the nuclear power generation capacity to 600 MW by 1988 in order to meet the growing demand for energy. The committee reviews other available sources of energy and concludes that nuclear energy provides the best alternative for Pakistan.

July–August: Pakistan buys parts for high-speed inverters from American firms such as General Electric, Westinghouse, RCA, and Motorola. The purchases are made by two small electrical equipment stores in Montreal. The parts are repackaged and shipped to the Middle East, and eventually to Pakistan.

3 August: A Pakistani foreign ministry spokesperson states that Pakistan's nuclear research programme is aimed at peaceful uses of nuclear energy and says that Pakistan does not wish to develop nuclear energy for military use.

5 August: India rejects Pakistan's proposal to create a nuclear-weapons-free zone in South Asia. According to a foreign ministry spokesperson, such a zone cannot be created without consulting all the countries in the region, and that any such zone must include China.

31 August: The chairman of the PAEC, Munir Ahmed Khan, announces that Pakistan has achieved self-reliance in the manufacture of nuclear fuel from uranium, and that a nuclear fuel manufacturing plant has been built at Chashma by Pakistani scientists.

September: Pakistani scientists are reportedly working on a clandestine plutonium reprocessing facility near Rawalpindi. The completion of the reprocessing facility will advance Pakistan's ability to test a nuclear device by about two years.

September–December:

Following Pakistan's declaration of its ability to manufacture its own nuclear fuel, the IAEA requests Pakistan to allow it to increase its surveillance capability at the KANUPP facility.

1981

The PAEC continues uranium exploration activities. It conducts geological mapping, radiometric measurements, drilling, and sub-surface excavations in the Potwar region.

February: Pakistan begins to load its KANUPP reactor with indigenously produced fuel bundles.

23 March: US officials indicate that the Reagan administration has tentatively decided to offer $500 million in aid to Pakistan. The US State Department indicates that the proposed aid to Pakistan will be provided only if it refrains from testing a nuclear device.

April: The IAEA informs Pakistan that the safeguards at the KANUPP reactor would have to be upgraded since Pakistan has started to produce its own fuel for the reactor. The IAEA and Pakistan begin talks over increasing the safeguards mechanism at the reactor.

2 July: Pakistan is planning to spend $56 million on a number of projects for the PAEC for the fiscal year beginning on 1 July. According to the Public Sector Development Plan, the funds are allocated mainly for a reprocessing plant, a nuclear power plant, detailed exploration for uranium, and for phase two of a radioactive minerals survey.

6 September: Western sources indicate that Pakistan's uranium enrichment plant, located 30 miles south-east of Islamabad at Kahuta, is expected to start operating by the end of the year.

1982

March–December: The USA believes that Pakistan is attempting to acquire components that could be used to produce several nuclear bombs. The components sought by Pakistan are identified as finely machined hollow steel spheres measuring approximately thirteen inches in diameter, and concave metal plates.

13 April: The Executive Committee of the National Economic Council of Pakistan approves the construction of a nuclear power plant at Chashma.

24 June: Pakistan allocates $72 million for the PAEC in its national budget for 1982–3. A major portion of the allocated amount is for the proposed 850–900 MW light-water reactor (LWR) at Chashma in Mianwali district in Punjab.

20 September: The USA bans American companies from selling reactor equipment to Pakistan.

1–9 December: Pakistan invites bids for the proposed MW nuclear power plant and issues tenders to 'over a dozen qualified suppliers'.

December: President Zia-ul-Haq is expected to seek resumption of Canada's nuclear fuel shipments for the KANUPP reactor.

1983

Pakistan is believed to have swapped its centrifuge technology with Beijing for a design of a nuclear weapon and enough highly enriched uranium for two bombs. China allegedly supplies Pakistan with a complete design of a 25kt nuclear bomb.

Early 1983: Pakistan conducts a uranium survey of over 60,000 km and discovers significant quantities of uranium ore in the Tharparkar desert in Sind Province and between Mansehra and Thakot in the

North-West Frontier Province (NWFP). The sampling of the uranium ore in the NWFP indicates ore with 0.2 per cent uranium.

The PAEC invites bids for the architectural–engineering component of the Chashma Nuclear Power Plant (CHASHNUPP).

11 March: The first 'cold test' of a weapon takes place under the leadership of Dr Ishfaq Ahmad of the PAEC.

29 March: The French foreign minister, Claude Cheysson, indicates that France is discussing the possibility of supplying a $1 billion 900 MW pressurized water reactor of Westinghouse design for the CHASHNUPP. Pakistan conducts negotiations with the IAEA over the plant's safeguards.

16 June: Pakistan's budget for 1983–4 allocates $30 million for the Chashma nuclear power project. The project is estimated to cost $1.3 billion.

24 November: West Germany's ambassador to Pakistan, Klaus Terfloth, states that West Germany will supply nuclear power plants to Pakistan on the condition that Pakistan provides assurances over their peaceful application.

December: Pakistan's finance minister, Ghulam Ishaq Khan, signs an agreement with the Soviet Union for the supply of a conventional power plant. Mr Khan also requests Soviet assistance in the construction of the CHASHNUPP.

1984

9 February: Dr Abdul Qadeer Khan, in an interview with the Pakistani newspaper *Nawa-i-Waqt*, states that Pakistan has attained the capacity to enrich uranium. Dr Khan states that 'Pakistan has broken the Western countries' monopoly on the enrichment of uranium ... Pakistan is now among the few countries in the world that can efficiently enrich uranium.'

11 April: Pakistan's production minister, Lieutenant-General Saeed Qadir, indicates that the government is seeking Soviet assistance for the nuclear power plant project at Chashma. The move is made following the failure of Western suppliers to submit bids for the project.

CHRONOLOGY

28 June: US sources indicate that Pakistan and China might be cooperating in developing each other's nuclear weapons programmes. According to sources, China is assisting Pakistan in resolving engineering problems in building centrifuges for uranium enrichment. In return, Pakistan might be providing advanced centrifuge designs for uranium enrichment. China uses gaseous diffusion process for enriching uranium.

2 August: According to a Pakistani news agency, Pakistan succeeds in enriching graphite to over 99 per cent, enabling its use in a nuclear reactor. The graphite is mined in the Neelam valley of Pakistan. Pakistani officials also believe that a graphite-processing plant might be built in the Pakistan-controlled part of Kashmir where half a million tonnes of good-quality graphite is available.

12 September: US president Ronald Reagan sends a personal letter to Pakistan's president, Zia-ul-Haq, warning that Pakistan might lose American military aid if it persists in pursuing its nuclear weapons programme. The letter warns President Zia not to enrich uranium beyond 5 per cent at the Kahuta enrichment facility.

5 October: A news report in the Pakistani daily *Nawa-i-Waqt* states that US president Ronald Reagan, in a letter to President Zia-ul-Haq, offered to place Pakistan under the US nuclear umbrella if Pakistan renounces its nuclear weapons programme.

17 October: President Zia-ul-Haq says that West Germany has provided training for Pakistan's nuclear reactor workers and has agreed to consider providing financial aid for the construction of the CHASHNUPP.

25 October: US State Department officials state that Pakistan is continuing its uranium enrichment effort and other efforts to purchase nuclear equipment despite recent warnings delivered by US assistant secretary of state Richard Murphy.

November: Nazir Ahmed Vaid, a Pakistani, pleads guilty to charges of attempting to smuggle fifty krytrons (high-speed switches) from the USA to Pakistan. US intelligence sources indicate that Pakistan also attempted to acquire precision-based explosives that are part of the triggering mechanism in a nuclear weapon.

1985

The US Congress passes the Pressler Amendment (section 620E(e) of the FAA), requiring economic sanctions unless the White House certifies that Pakistan is not engaged in a nuclear weapons programme.

25 March: The journal of the PAEC claims that Pakistan has joined the small group of countries that explore and mine their own uranium, as well as refine and upgrade it to the required specifications, fabricate it as fuel, and finally burn it in a commercial power reactor to produce electricity. Pakistan's top nuclear scientist, A. Q. Khan, states that 'Pakistan will supply its own fuel to its next nuclear power plant planned at Chashma'.

2 May: The US ambassador to Pakistan, Deane R. Hinton, categorically rules out the possibility of cooperation between the USA and Pakistan unless Pakistan signs the NPT or accepts full-scope safeguards on all of its nuclear facilities.

20 June: The IAEA Board of Governors approves the continuation of a programme to help Pakistan modernize the control and instrumentation systems of its 137 MW pressurized heavy-water reactor (PHWR) located at the KANUPP.

July: US media reports that Pakistan has tested US-made krytron electric triggers in conventional explosions. Krytron triggers can be used in the detonation of nuclear devices.

August: At the United Nations General Assembly meeting in New York, Pakistan's President Zia calls for India and Pakistan simultaneously to sign the NPT, accept mutual full-scope safeguards and inspections, and renounce the acquisition of nuclear weapons. This proposal is duly endorsed by US President Reagan but not by Indian prime minister Gandhi.

13 September: The Reagan administration expresses its concern about the 'possible development of a nuclear weapon by Pakistan and about overall tensions in the region'. Administration officials say that the 'underlying concern' in the region is 'the danger of Indian retaliation against any nuclear developments in Pakistan'.

18 December: Indian prime minister Rajiv Gandhi and Pakistani president Mohammad Zia-ul-Haq pledge not to attack each other's nuclear installations and to proceed with major new efforts to resolve disagreements that have increased tensions between the two nations.

1986

Pakistan embarks on a parallel plutonium programme.

A heavy-water reactor at Khushab is built with Chinese assistance and is the central element of Pakistan's programme for the production of plutonium and tritium for advanced compact warheads.

Khushab, with a capacity variously reported at between 40 and 70 MWt, is completed in the mid-1990s, with the start of construction dating to the mid-1980s.

26 April: Prime Minister Mohammad Junejo asks the USA and China to help Pakistan's peaceful nuclear programme in order to alleviate power shortages in the country. US ambassador Deane R. Hinton says the USA is willing to help Pakistan in nuclear technology, provided its peaceful uses are verified by international inspections.

1 June: The IAEA agrees to provide the PAEC with technical assistance worth $450,000.

26 June: Dr A. Q. Khan announces that Pakistan has a programme to manufacture an indigenous nuclear reactor. He also declares the programme is not weapons-oriented since President Zia-ul-Haq has given a commitment not to allow uranium enrichment of more than 5 per cent. Pakistan's efforts to set up a 900 MW nuclear power plant at Chashma in Mianwali have not been very successful due to an embargo set up by the suppliers of nuclear technology on the grounds that Pakistan has not signed the NPT or accepted full-scope safeguards.

July: US secretary of state George Shultz and Pakistan's foreign minister Yaqub Khan sign an agreement to transfer advanced US technology, including mainframe computers and communications equipment, with the condition that Pakistan cannot transfer the equipment to a third country and may not use it in any nuclear weapons programme.

September: Pakistan conducts 'cold tests' of a nuclear implosion device at Chagai.

15 September: Pakistan and China sign an agreement on the peaceful use of nuclear energy. The agreement includes the design, construction, and operation of nuclear power reactors.

16 October: The PAEC develops a noise-analysis surveillance system for its nuclear reactors. 'The surveillance system can detect malfunctioning of reactor components such as control rod, fuel element, or grid plate vibrations at a very early stage.'

30 October: The PAEC is pleased with the recent performance of the KANUPP. The plant 'has achieved near-record production during the first eight months of 1986'. Furthermore, it has 'generated 338,000 MW-hours, slightly over 42% nominal gross capacity, but PAEC sources said that plant availability has been at 84% and it has set a record of continuous operation of 104 days'.

November: Officials from the PAEC claim that they have commissioned a uranium mill at Dera Ghazi Khan entirely through indigenous efforts.

7 November: The United States warns Pakistan that it will cut off aid if Islamabad continues its efforts to make a nuclear bomb. The *Washington Post* reports that Pakistan conducted heavy explosives tests in September, in order to develop an implosion trigger device.

1987

Pakistan acquires a tritium purification and production facility from West Germany. The plant can produce up to 10 g of tritium daily.

Pakistani agents smuggle 0.8 g of pure tritium gas they had obtained from German parties who were convicted of illegally exporting tritium in 1990.

Pakistan proposes to India an agreement on a bilateral or regional nuclear test-ban treaty.

In violation of US nuclear export control laws, Pakistan acquires oscilloscopes and computer equipment (useful in nuclear weapons R&D) from California.

6 February: Pakistani nuclear scientist A. Q. Khan says that 'Pakistan's success in uranium enrichment is of tremendous economic significance as well as being for defence purposes'. He also comments that President Zia 'repeatedly made it clear that achievements in the nuclear sphere were for peaceful purposes'.

19 February: The solid state nuclear track detection laboratory at PINSTECH fabricates Chromium kF39, which is used in uranium exploration. This work has been done in collaboration with the IAEA.

1 March: The PAEC plans to develop the country's nuclear capabilities, including the construction of a 600 MW reactor using enriched uranium and plutonium fuel.

15 July: A Pakistani–Canadian businessman, Arshad Z. Pervaiz, is arrested in Philadelphia on suspicion of trying to export material to Pakistan that could be used in making nuclear weapons. Pervaiz allegedly sought to buy and send 25 tonnes of a special steel alloy to Pakistan.

18 July: US attorney David F. Levi announces the indictments of two Americans and one Hong Kong businessman for illegally exporting 'sophisticated instruments and advanced computer equipment' (which can be used to make nuclear bombs) to Pakistan.

22 September: US president Ronald Reagan meets Pakistan's prime minister Mohammad Khan Junejo at the United Nations and presses his Pakistani counterpart to open his country's nuclear installations to international inspection.

1988

President Reagan waives an aid cutoff for Pakistan due to an export-control violation.

A *New York Times* article quotes US government sources as saying that Pakistan has produced enough highly enriched uranium for between four and six bombs.

7 April: The PAEC begins to work on its pool-type research reactor located at PINSTECH. The work entails changing the reactor from 5 MW to 10 MW and converting its core from 90 per cent enriched uranium to 20 per cent enrichment. The reactor is being modified to keep pace with new requirements and also because the USA refuses to provide fuel of such high enrichment.

June: The PAEC announces that it plans to build up to five 900 MW light-water reactors by 2000. The Pakistanis deny a report that a second uranium enrichment plant was being built at Golra Sharif.

July: President Zia tells a Carnegie Endowment delegation that Pakistan has attained a nuclear capability 'that is good enough to create an impression of deterrence'.

9 August: Pakistan draws up a comprehensive plan of action for indigenization of its nuclear programme to achieve self-reliance in order to meet its needs for nuclear energy.

17 August: Pakistan acquires the essential technology for the exploration of uranium resources and other materials, production of uranium concentrate and oxide, and manufacture of nuclear fuel elements ready to be used in power reactors.

4 October: PINSTECH develops a new technique for exploring and mining uranium and thorium, which exist in large deposits in Pakistan.

1 November: A US government report states that Pakistan's Kahuta enrichment plant may be able to produce enough weapons-grade uranium to produce between one and three explosive devices annually.

31 December: Indian Prime Minister Rajiv Gandhi and Pakistani Prime Minister Benazir Bhutto sign an agreement not to attack each other's nuclear facilities.

1989

A 27 KW research reactor (PARR-2) is built at Rawalpindi with Chinese assistance.

Reports of Pakistan modifying US-supplied F-16 aircraft for nuclear delivery purposes; wind-tunnel tests cited in document reportedly from the West German intelligence service.

Test launch of Hatf II missile (payload: 500 kg; range: 300 km) capable of carrying nuclear weapons.

29 January: Pakistan announces that it is planning to hold consultations with the USA in order to convince the American government that its atomic programme is only for peaceful purposes and that its objective is to increase the production of electricity.

31 January: Pakistan proposes a 'nuclear pact', in which it would receive US-made nuclear reactors in exchange for guarantees that Pakistan's nuclear programme will be used only for peaceful purposes.

7 June: Pakistani prime minister Benazir Bhutto speaks to a joint session of the United States Congress and says that Pakistan is willing to throw open its nuclear installations to inspection if other countries in the region do the same. Furthermore, she also says that there is a need for a nuclear-free zone in South Asia and for Pakistan and its neighbours not to conduct nuclear tests.

August: Pakistan hopes to obtain three 300 MW nuclear power plants from China. Cooperation between the two countries was expected to extend to the supply and manufacture of research reactors.

24 August: KANUPP expects to return to operation in September after suffering a heavy-water leak in April. The PAEC assures the public that there is no radiation damage, and that no one sustained a radiation overdose.

15 November: Pakistan develops an understanding with China on the advancement of its nuclear programme. Under the agreement, China will help Pakistan build a 300 MW nuclear plant and will provide fuel and spares for the plant. A senior official of the PAEC states that the nuclear plant will be a pressurized water reactor guaranteed by the IAEA for safety and that the construction will commence in 1990 after the formal agreement between China and Pakistan is signed.

1990

Between 1983 and 1990 the Wah Group develops an air-deliverable bomb and conducts at least two dozen cold tests of nuclear devices with the help of mobile diagnostic equipment.

January–April: U.S. News cites 'western intelligence sources' claiming Pakistan recently 'cold-tested' a nuclear device and is now building a plutonium production reactor; the article says Pakistan is engaged in nuclear cooperation with Iran.

The *Sunday Times* in London cites growing US and Soviet concerns about the Pakistani nuclear programme; it claims that F-16 aircraft are being modified for nuclear delivery purposes, and that US spy satellites have observed 'heavily armed convoys' leaving the uranium enrichment complex at Kahuta and heading for military airfields.

May: The Pakistan military decides to activate its nuclear capability. It is believed that weapons-grade uranium production was resumed in May, and that 125 kg of highly enriched uranium hexafluoride (UF 6) that had been stored in casks until then was converted into metal, and fashioned into seven bomb cores.

August: A report prepared by the Indian intelligence organisation Research and Analysis Wing says that Pakistan has produced several nuclear weapons capable of hitting at least one target in India with nuclear weapons at the commencement of any war.

1991

Report emerge about a completely redesigned nuclear research reactor to be operational by July–August. The reactor, called Pakistan Atomic Research Reactor (PARR-1), reportedly had a capacity of 10 MW.

Pakistan puts a ceiling on the size of its weapons-grade uranium stock-pile; it ratifies an agreement with India, prohibiting the two states from attacking each other's nuclear installations.

Under US pressure, Prime Minister Nawaz Sharif temporarily stops enriching uranium to weapons-grade level.

A high-level Pakistani delegation led by PAEC Chairman Dr Ishfaq Ahmad visits Beijing to sign an agreement on acquiring a 300 MW nuclear power plant.

1992

June: The IAEA proposes the application of unprecedented stringent safeguards on 300 MW nuclear power reactors being acquired by Pakistan from China.

4 October: PAEC chairman Dr Ashfaq Ahmad says Pakistan would develop its own atomic reactor for the acquisition of self-sufficiency in energy generation.

1993

Pakistan proposes to India the creation of a missile-free zone in South Asia.

Islamabad tells Washington that it will freeze production of bomb-grade HEU indefinitely, and refrain from enriching uranium to a level above 20 per cent U-235.

25 August: The USA imposes 'Category Two' sanctions against certain Chinese and Pakistani entities that were involved in an M-ll missile-related transfer, which is prohibited under US law.

1994

Despite tremendous Western pressure, China promises to honour its commitment to Pakistan to supply the 300 MW nuclear power plant (CHASHNUPP—P-l) well within the stipulated time as per the agreement, according to Pakistani official sources.

Deputy Secretary of State Strobe Talbott visits Islamabad to propose a one-time sale of F-16 fighter aircraft to Pakistan. Delivery of the planes would be contingent on specific commitments from Pakistan regarding its nuclear programme, including a verifiable cap on the production of fissile materials.

The PAEC launches a project to make a breakthrough in nuclear power plant designing, engineering, and manufacturing.

Pakistan signs the Convention on Nuclear Safety at Vienna at the 38th IAEA General Conference.

1995

The NPT comes up for review and extension.

Pakistan purchases 5,000 custom-made ring magnets from China, a key component of the bearings that support high-speed rotation of centrifuges. The seller is a subsidiary of the China National Nuclear Corporation.

Pakistan begins work on Shaheen missile.

Pakistan decides to set up a third nuclear power plant, with a power-generation capacity of 300 MW, at Chashma, for which negotiations are in the final stages with the government of China.

April: Prime Minister Bhutto visits Washington; Pakistan's nuclear programme comes under discussion again with US officials.

1996

China hands over sensitive instruments and compressor vessels to Pakistan for use at the Chashma nuclear power plant, according to media sources.

CHRONOLOGY

January: India and Pakistan exchange lists of atomic installations which each side has pledged not to attack under the seven-year-old confidence-building agreement.

The Brown Amendment comes into effect, allowing nearly $370 million of previously embargoed arms and spare parts to be delivered to Pakistan.

March: Pakistan completes its un-safeguarded heavy-water reactor at Khushab. US officials believe that the reactor is being built with Chinese assistance.

October: Pakistani prime minister Benazir Bhutto calls for the convening of a South Asia security conference that would deal with, among other things, Kashmir and the nuclear arms issue.

1997

Dr A. Q. Khan says Pakistan is now working on smart bomb technology and has achieved a large measure of success.

4 July: Pakistan confirms test-firing of new indigenous nuclear-capable Hatf missile.

1998

April: Pakistan announces commissioning of an un-safeguarded 50 to 70 MW nuclear reactor.

May: The Institute for Science and International Security (ISIS) says that Pakistan has enough uranium for about ten weapons, which includes 210 kg of weapons-grade uranium that it has had since 1991 when it froze uranium production at the Kahuta research facility.

Prime Minister Nawaz Sharif reports that Pakistan has conducted five nuclear tests in response to Indian nuclear tests a few weeks earlier. Sharif says Pakistan would weaponize its intermediate-range Ghauri ballistic missile with nuclear warheads. Official sources in Islamabad suggest that the five tests carried out by Pakistan are fission devices. Three devices tested had yields in the sub-kilotonne (KT) range and the other two larger explosions had yields of 25 KT and 12 KT.

1999

PAEC chairman Ishfaq Ahmad says that Pakistan has acquired self-reliance in the production of heavy water, enriched uranium, and nuclear spare parts needed for domestic consumption.

August: prominent Pakistani nuclear scientist and PAEC chairman-designate, N. M. Butt, says on 18 August that Pakistan has the capacity and expertise to build a neutron bomb.

26 October: The 300 MW CHASNUPP is completed with the help of China.

24 November: CHASNUPP goes nuclear. PAEC chairman Ishfaq Ahmad presses the button to load the first fuel assembly of 121 assembly core required to produce 300 MW.

2000

February: Pakistan announces the creation of a new National Command Authority to control its missiles and nuclear programme.

15 June: CHASNUPP reaches another milestone when the plant, built in cooperation with China, is connected to the national power grid.

2001

Pakistan plans to establish another nuclear power plant with 100 per cent indigenous expertise and resources in six to seven years, said PAEC chairman Dr Ishfaq Ahmad.

Pakistan invites massive Chinese investment in nuclear power projects worth $ 3.9 billion to increase the country's nuclear power generation capacity by 2100 MW in the next fifteen years.

21 February: The Pakistan navy is thinking of equipping its submarines with nuclear missiles for defensive purposes, says the deputy chief of naval staff (operations), Rear Admiral Mohammad Afzal Tahir.

29 March: The $600 million 325 MW CHASNUPP is inaugurated.

25 June: The PAEC initiates a dialogue for the setting up of additional nuclear power generating units at Chashma and Karachi, PAEC chairman Pervez Butt says in Islamabad.

2002

The PAEC works on a plan to set up one unit each at its nuclear power plants at Karachi and Mianwali.

2003

KRL chairman Dr Javed Arshad Mirza says that the KRL is developing a missile defence system and laser technology.

March: China agrees to help set up another 300 MW nuclear power plant at Chashma.

26 March: Pakistan tests a nuclear-capable surface-to-surface Abdali missile, with a range of up to 125 miles.

31 March: The USA imposes sanctions on the KRL for selling nuclear equipment.

6 October: US national security adviser Christina Rocca and Richard Armitage meet Musharraf at the Army House and provide CIA documents on A. Q. Khan's links to Iran/Libya.

1 November: China agrees to help set up the next phase of CHASNUPP.

2004

31 January: A. Q. Khan dismissed. Three-member IAEA contingent reaches Pakistan.

1 February: Khan admits guilt. A senior military official says that he has made a statement confessing to supplying designs, hardware, and materials used to make enriched uranium for atomic bombs to Iran, Libya, and North Korea.

4 February: Khan appears on state television to make personal apology to the nation.

5 February: Musharraf pardons Khan.

11 February: President George W. Bush announces his Proliferation Security Initiative.

CIA team including chief George Tenet on a 'secret' visit to Islamabad via Chaklala base.

2005

April: Dr Ishfaq Ahmad, special adviser to the prime minister on the strategic programme, maintains that Pakistan is planning to build more nuclear power plants after the Chashma Nuclear Power Plant Unit-2 (CHASNUPP-2) to achieve its target of generating 8,800 MW by 2020.

August: Pakistan successfully test-fires its first cruise missile, the Babur, with a range of 310 miles and capable of carrying nuclear as well as conventional warheads.

2006

November: Pakistan successfully test-fires an advanced version of Hatf 5, its nuclear-capable medium-range missile (with a range of 800 miles).

December: Pakistan's Foreign Office maintains that Iran has the right to pursue nuclear technology for peaceful purposes, opposing UN sanctions against Iran for its refusal to halt uranium enrichment.

2007

November: Pakistan officially confirms reports of cooperation with the USA on securing Islamabad's nuclear weapons but clarifies that this cooperation involves training activities to help strengthen surveillance programmes.

December: Pakistan President Pervez Musharraf issues an ordinance providing a legal basis for the National Command Authority (NCA), the top decision-making body for the country's nuclear weapons programme.

2008

February: US Joint Chiefs of Staff chairman Admiral Mike Mullen during a visit to Islamabad states that Pakistan's nuclear weapons have adequate safeguards to prevent militants from gaining access to the devices.

May: Dr A. Q. Khan recants his confession that he illicitly provided North Korea, Iran, and Libya with nuclear technology and expertise.

November: Pakistani president Asif Ali Zardari, in an interview with Indian journalists, surprisingly says that he favours a no-first-use policy on nuclear weapons, but this is later claimed to be an 'off-the cuff' remark. The military leadership was not on board with this idea.

CHRONOLOGY

2009

April: According to media reports, Pakistan shares highly classified information on its nuclear weapons with the USA to reassure them on the security of its nuclear arsenal. Taliban violence is at its peak around this time.

May: The Pakistani government asserts that any US attempt to forcibly take over its nuclear weapons will fail. This is in response to some news reports that a US military unit has been trained for this specific purpose and is stationed in Afghanistan awaiting orders to deploy.

June: The Pakistan government increases the budgetary allocation for the atomic energy sector's research and development by 10 per cent.

2010

November: The Pakistan government confirms that China will supply Pakistan with a fifth nuclear reactor, in addition to those that it has already agreed to construct at the Chashma nuclear complex.

2011

January: Under a two-decade-old agreement (1991, under the bilateral Agreement on the Prohibition of Attack against Nuclear Installations), India and Pakistan exchange their lists of nuclear facilities.

May: American diplomatic cables released by Wikileaks covering the period 2005–2009 indicate that the USA attempted to persuade various countries, including Turkey, France, and China, to prevent industrial firms based in those countries from exporting any equipment to Pakistan that could assist its nuclear and missile programmes.

Pakistani Taliban spokesman Ehsanullah Ehsan says that the Taliban has no intention of attacking Pakistan's nuclear weapons arsenal, adding that 'Pakistan is the only Muslim nuclear-power state', and that the Taliban does not want to change this status.

Commercial satellite imagery analysed by *Newsweek* shows that Pakistan is speeding up construction of its fourth plutonium-production reactor at the Khushab nuclear complex.

2012–2014

Pakistan conducts around eight tests of various land-based ballistic or cruise missiles that it says are capable of delivering nuclear warheads. These include the Abdali (Hatf-2, range 180 km) on 15 February 2013, and the Shaheen-I on 10 April 2013, reportedly improving the missile's design and increasing range to 900 km.

2015

March: Pakistan successfully test launches the Shaheen-III surface-to-surface ballistic missile, capable of carrying nuclear and conventional warheads to a range of 2,750 km. In 2014 it had tested an advanced version of Shaheen-II, also capable of carrying nuclear and conventional warheads up to a range of 1,500 km.

October: Islamabad officially declares that it has developed tactical nuclear weapons (short-range missiles) named Nasr for battlefield operations in case of conflict with India. It reportedly tested this missile, with a range of 60 km, in April 2011.

2016

January: Pakistan flight-tests its air-launched cruise missile named Ra'ad (also known as Hatf VIII) with a range of 350 km. Its earlier version was tested in 2007.

2017

January: Pakistan successful tests a new medium-range ballistic missile called the Ababeel, with a range of 2,200 km, capable of delivering multiple warheads aimed at independent targets from a group of multiple targets (MIRV technology). Earlier in the month Pakistan also tested its first ever nuclear-capable Babur-3 submarine-launched cruise missile from a submerged platform off the Pakistani coast.

July: Pakistan successfully undertakes a series of flight tests of its battlefield nuclear-capable Nasr missile, enhancing its flight manoeuvrability and extending its range to 70 km.

August: According to a report from the Institute for Science and International Security, Pakistan has constructed a hardened, secure underground complex in Baluchistan province that could serve as a missile and nuclear warhead storage site.

INDEX

Iqbal, Dr Mohammad: 23, 90
Iran: 2–3, 5, 13, 18, 20, 81, 83–4,
86–9, 94, 111, 135, 151, 154,
164, 166, 172–3, 183, 199,
202–5, 207, 318–19; annual
income from oil, 88; Bushehr
nuclear power plant, 96–8;
Defence Ministry, 102; government of, 96, 177; importing
of North Korean missiles to,
125; Isfahan nuclear research
centre, 97; Islamic Revolution
(1979), 73, 89–90, 92, 96;
Islamic Revolutionary Guard
Corps (IRGC), 104, 107, 109;
Meharabad, 87; Ministry of
Intelligence and Security, 102;
Natanz nuclear enrichment
facility, 120; nuclear programme
of, 18, 81–2, 92–3, 95–8,
101–2, 114–16, 118, 120,
205–6; oil reserves of, 109; P-5
nuclear arrangement (2015),
208–9; Saghand, 97; Tehran,
7–8, 86, 89, 92, 102, 109;
Tricastin nuclear power plant,
96; US Embassy Hostage Crisis
(1979–81), 90; Yazd Province,
97; Zahedan, 87
Iran-Iraq War (1980–8): 91, 99,
108; targeting of Iranian nuclear
facilities during, 97; use of
chemical weapons during, 97
Iran-United States Agreement for
Cooperation Concerning Civil
Uses of Atomic Energy (1957):
extension of, 93
Iranian-Pakistani Treaty of
Friendship: 84
Iraq: 85, 159–60; 14 July
Revolution (1958), 87;
Baghdad, 92; Israeli Bombing

of nuclear reactor (1981), 74,
162; Operation Iraqi Freedom
(2003–11), 137
Islam: 14, 18, 25–6, 158–9, 162,
168–9, 186; sharia, 169; Shia,
25, 85–6, 89–91, 166; Sufi, 166;
Sunni, 89
Islamic Atomic Energy
Commission: proposals for, 160
Islamic Military Alliance to Fight
Terrorism (IMAFT): personnel
of, 209–10
Islamic Summit (1974): role in
development of Pakistan-Libyan
relations, 141
Israel: 46, 48, 51, 74, 119, 158,
161–2, 173, 206; Mossad, 163;
nuclear arsenal of, 140
Italy: Trieste, 65

Jalal, Prof Ayesha: 22
Jamaat-e-Islami (JI): 27, 89; founding of (1941), 169; influence
of, 171; majlis-i-shoora (central
consultative body), 171; member
of MMA, 170; members of, 89,
177; role in The Satanic Verses
fatwa (1989), 90
Jamaat-i-Ulema-e-Islam (JUI):
founding of (1945), 169; member of MMA, 170
Jamaat-i-Ulema-e-Islam Fazl group
(JUI-F)(Council of Islamic
Scholars): 169; coalition member in Benazir Bhutto administration (1993–6), 170
Jamaat-i-Ulema-e-Islam Sami
group (JUI-S): 169
Jammu and Kashmir: 15, 28, 32–3,
35–9, 86, 109, 128, 165–6, 168,
172, 192, 307; accession to India
(1947), 29; Azad Kashmir, 31;

resignation of (1969), 39, 61;
rise to power (1958), 86
Khan, General Yahya: 38–40, 61;
administration of, 127; resignation of (1971), 61
Khan, Ghulam Ishaq: 71, 157,
186–7, 193, 196; associates
of, 110; Pakistani Defence
Secretary, 68
Khan, Henny: family of, 203
Khan, Ishaq: 107, 111–12, 194;
Pakistani Finance Minister, 110;
visit to Tehran (1991), 112
Khan, Kamran: 7
Khan, Liaquat Ali: 85; assassination of (1951), 36, 85; Pakistani
Prime Minister, 84
Khan, Munir Ahmed: 59, 63–4,
70, 75, 79; background of,
58–9; Chairman of PAEC, 45,
63, 153, 162, 300, 304; role in
development of Pakistan nuclear
programme, 67–8, 300–1
Khan, Sir Zafrullah: Pakistani
Foreign Minister, 52
Khan, Tanvir Ahmed: Pakistani
Ambassador to Iran, 100
Khan Research Laboratories
(KRL): 5–6, 49, 74–6, 78,
118–19, 128, 145, 153, 162,
174, 184, 193–4, 196, 198–200,
202, 213; cold test of nuclear
device (1984), 75; facilities of,
77; formerly ERL, 72; General
Maintenance and Construction
Division, 199; North Korean
scientists hosted at (1999), 123;
personnel of, 5, 78, 81, 98, 103,
113, 154, 163, 176, 189, 197,
199–200, 318; role in development of North Korean bal-
listic missiles, 130–1; US State

Department sanctions against
(1998), 132
Khan, Yaqub: Pakistani Foreign
Minister, 309
Khokhar, Ijaz: 72, 113
Khokhar, Riaz: Pakistani
Ambassador to USA, 44
Khomeini, Ayatollah Ruhollah:
90, 97; fatwas issued by, 89–90;
opposition to nuclear weaponry,
96
Kidwai, Lieutenant-General
Khalid: 163, 212; head of SPD,
213
Kim Jong-Il: family of, 125
Kim Jong-un: family of, 125
Kim Il-Sung: 129; family of, 125
Kissinger, Henry: US Secretary
of State, 178; visit to Pakistan
(1976), 302
Koch, Egmont: 104
Korean War (1950–3): belligerents
of, 124
Kraftwerk Union of West
Germany: agreement with AEOI
(1976), 94–5
Krepon, Michael: 74, 216
Kumaratunga, Chandrika
Bandaranaike: Sri Lankan
President, 117
Kurchaov Institute: personnel of,
140
Kuwait: Iraqi Invasion of (1990),
112

bin Laden, Osama: 167, 176; visit
to JI HQ (1989), 171
Lamb, Alastair: 29
Langewiesche, William: 7–8
Lashkar-e-Taiba (Army of the
Pure): banning of (2002), 168;
Jamaat-ud-Dawa (Party of the

INDEX

INDEX

INDEX

(ORCD): as ECO, 91; Atomic Energy Commission, 94; founding of (1964), 86

organizational politics model: concept of, 12

Oxford University: 74

Pahlavi, Shah Mohammed Reza (Shah of Iran): 84, 88, 92–4; removed from power (1979), 98–9; state visit to Pakistan (1976), 89

Pakistan: 4, 10–11, 14, 16, 18–20, 22–4, 26–8, 41–6, 65, 77–8, 81–2, 84, 86–9, 91, 94, 108–9, 121–4, 127–8, 131, 135, 137, 147–8, 151–2, 158, 161, 169, 176–7, 181, 189, 207–8, 211–12, 215–16, 301, 307, 313, 316, 320–1; Bahawalpur, 51, 167; Baluchistan Province, 43, 73–4, 83–4, 86, 91, 170, 321; Bengal province, 39; borders of, 185; Constituent Assembly, 25; Dera Ghazi Khan, 300, 310; Federally Administered Tribal Areas (FATA), 29; foreign exchange reserves of, 132–3; Foreign Office, 8, 55, 303; Gilgit-Baltistan, 30; government of, 8, 27, 29–31, 57, 99, 147, 149, 152–3, 201, 320; importing of North Korean missiles to, 125; Independence of (1947), 21, 28, 33–4, 83–4; Inter-Services Intelligence (ISI), 107, 114, 133, 157, 167–8, 172, 186, 188, 197–8; Islamabad, 1–2, 73, 81, 112, 114, 117, 127, 152–3, 167, 202, 205, 302, 314, 316, 321; Islamabad High Court, 8, 152; Kahuta, 69, 72, 110, 198, 301–2, 312–13, 316; Karachi, 55, 57, 317; Khushab reactor, 175, 309, 316, 320–1; Khyber Pukhtunkhwa Province/ North-West Frontier Province (NWFP), 83, 111, 170, 189, 305–6; Lahore, 50, 74, 141, 171, 191; Lahore High Court, 199; *madrassa* in, 166–7, 170, 180; Mansoora, 171; Mianwali, 317; military of, 34–8, 111–12, 127–9, 168, 172, 196–7, 205–6, 209, 214–15, 314; Ministry of Defence, 66; Ministry of Finance, 64; Ministry of Fuel, Power and Natural Resources, 53; Ministry of Science, Technology and Production, 62–3; Muslim population of, 41; National Assembly, 115; National Command Authority (NCA), 194, 213–14, 319; navy of, 317; nuclear programme of, 2, 19, 21, 45, 47–52, 54–7, 59–63, 65–7, 71–2, 74, 79–80, 92, 100–1, 104, 106–7, 111, 143–4, 154, 162–3, 165, 177, 183–7, 193, 197, 204–7, 211–14, 299–300, 302–4, 309, 312–13, 319; nuclear tests (1998), 17, 43–4, 123, 181; Public Sector Development Plan, 304–5; Punjab Province, 83; Quetta, 52; Rahimyar Khan, 167; Rawalpindi, 57, 59, 187, 304, 312; Sargodha, 19, 75; Sargodha Attack (2007), 19; Senate, 113; Sind Province, 37–8, 187, 305; Strategic Planning Directive, 163; Strategic Plans Division (SPD), 194, 197, 213–15

Pakistan Atomic Energy

335

Commission (PAEC): 55, 57, 62, 66–7, 72–6, 78, 107, 123, 130, 175–6, 181, 184, 191, 193–4, 200, 213, 299, 304–6, 308–10, 313; aims of, 51–2; Aviation Development Workshop (ADW), 70; contract with UKAEA (1969), 60; creation of (1956), 51; development of nuclear weapons systems, 74–5; Directorate of Technical Development, 74; funding of, 304–5; personnel of, 19, 45, 51, 54, 59, 67, 69–70, 128, 153, 162–3, 174, 176, 197, 300–1, 304, 306, 314, 316–17; Project 706 (Directorate of Industrial Liaison), 70; reactor development projects, 56–8, 311–12; targeting of employees (2007), 19; Theoretical Physics Group, 65; uranium enrichment efforts of, 69; Wah Group, 65, 301, 313

Pakistan Atomic Research Reactor (PARR-1): 54, 299, 314

Pakistan Council for Scientific and Industrial Research (PCSIR): establishment of (1953), 51

Pakistan Institute of International Affairs: 53

Pakistan Institute of Nuclear Science and Technology (PINSTECH): 63–4, 299, 311–12; establishment of (1961), 53; New Labs, 300; Nuclear Materials Division, 176; personnel of, 142, 176; production of radio isotopes (1967), 57, 300; training of personnel, 99

Pakistan Nuclear Regulatory Authority (PNRA): 213; National Nuclear Safety and Security Action Plan (NSAP), 213

Pakistan People's Party (PPP): 105, 118, 186–7; activists, 106; electoral performance of (1970), 40, 61; formation of, 60; members of, 40

pan-Islamism: 6

Pashtun; Pathan (tribe): 30, 172

Pashtunistan: support for, 172

Patterson, Anne: US Ambassador to Pakistan, 153

Pelindaba Treaty: provisions of, 140; signatories of, 140

People's Democratic Republic of Yemen (South Yemen): 210

Perkovich, George: 64

Persian Gulf War (1990–1): 172–3; Iraqi Invasion of Kuwait (1990), 112

Pervaiz, Arshad: imprisonment of, 163, 311

Philippines: Manila, 85

Physical Dynamics Research Laboratory: 156

plutonium: 59–60, 64, 69, 72, 76, 93, 123, 141; extraction of, 125; weapons-grade, 60, 67

post-colonialism: 15

Punjab Boundary Commission: personnel of, 29

Punjab University: 50

Punjabis (ethnic community): 192

al-Qaddafi, Muammar: 89, 140–2, 147–8; dismantling of nuclear programme (2003), 137–8; meetings with Zulfikar Ali Bhutto (1972–4), 139; nuclear proliferation efforts of, 142; rise to power (1969), 139

Walsh, Jim: 3
Walt, Stephen: 22
Walters, General Vernon: meeting
 with General Zia-ul-Haq (1982),
 74
Waltz, Kenneth: 9, 11, 82; *Spread of
 Nuclear Weapons, The*, 10
War on Terror: 120, 168, 179
Warsaw Pact: 37
Washington Post: 7, 9, 310
Wasson, Brigadier-General
 Herbert: death of (1988), 180
Westinghouse: 303, 306
Wikileaks: 320
Wisser, Gerhard: 77, 145–6
Wolpert, Stanley: 22

Yadlin, Amos: 209
yellowcake: 142
Yemen: importing of North Korean
 missiles to, 125
Yom Kippur War (1973): oil
 embargo following, 88

Zardari, Asif Ali: 319
Zhou Enlai: meeting with Ayub
 Khan and Zulfikar Ali Bhutto
 (1965), 57
Zia-ul-Haq, General Mohammad:
 75–6, 79, 91, 99–100, 103,
 142, 148, 166, 170, 180, 186,
 303, 305, 309–10, 312; assassination of (1988), 106, 110,
 165, 180, 184, 194; foreign
 policy of, 73, 103–4, 185–6,
 308–9; imposition of martial law
 (1977), 89, 105, 164; meeting
 with General Vernon Walters
 (1982), 74; nuclear policy of,
 72–3, 309; Power Development
 Coordination Cell (PDCC), 193;
 regime of, 57, 68, 112, 184–5,
 194; rise to power (1977), 71,
 164; visit to Tehran (1977), 91;
Zakat Fun, 167
Zionism: 158–9
al-Zulfiqar Plan Hijacking (1981):
 106